THE ORDER HAS BEEN CARRIED OUT

HISTORY, MEMORY, AND MEANING OF A NAZI MASSACRE IN ROME

ALESSANDRO PORTELLI

palgrave
macmillan

THE ORDER HAS BEEN CARRIED OUT
Copyright © Alessandro Portelli, 2003.

First published in 2003 by PALGRAVE MACMILLAN™
175 Fifth Avenue, New York, N.Y. 10010 and
Houndmills, Basingstoke, Hampshire, England RG21 6XS.
Companies and representatives throughout the world.

PALGRAVE MACMILLAN is the global academic imprint of the Palgrave Macmillan
division of St. Martin's Press, LLC and of Palgrave Macmillan Ltd. Macmillan® is a registered trademark in the United States, United Kingdom and other countries. Palgrave is a
registered trademark in the European Union and other countries.

1–4039–6208–1 hardback

Library of Congress Cataloging-in-Publication Data
Portelli, Alessandro.
The order has been carried out : history, memory, and meaning of a Nazi massacre in
Rome / Alessandro Portelli
    p. cm.
  Includes bibligraphical references and index.
  ISBN 1–4039–6208–1
   1. Ardeatine Caves Massacre, Rome, Italy, 1944.   2. World War, 1939–1945—
Atrocities—Italy—Rome.   3. World War, 1939–1945—Prisoners and prisons,
German.   4. Rome (Italy)—History—20th century.   I. Title.

D804.G3P67   2003
940.53'45632—dc21   2003042995

A catalogue record for this book is available from the British Library.

Design by Letra Libre, Inc.

First Palgrave Macmillan edition: November 2003
10 9 8 7 6 5 4 3 2 1

Printed in the United States of America.

CONTENTS

Part III Memory

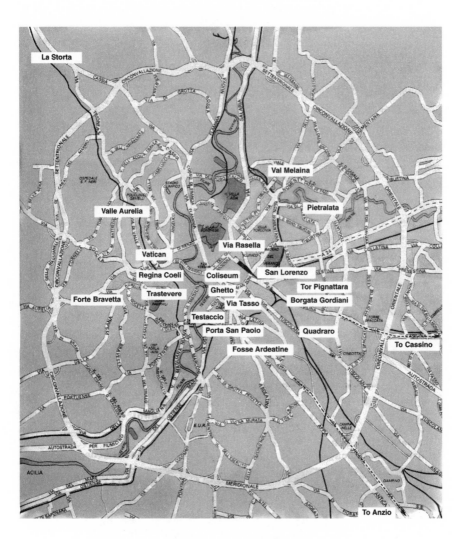

La Storta

Val Melaina

Pietralata

Valle Aurelia

Via Rasella

Vatican

Regina Coeli
Coliseum
San Lorenzo

Trastevere
Ghetto
Tor Pignattara

Forte Bravetta
Via Tasso
Borgata Gordiani

Testaccio

Porta San Paolo
Quadraro

Fosse Ardeatine
To Cassino

To Anzio

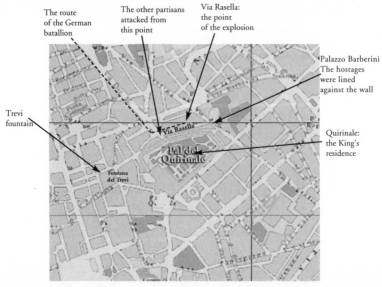

The route
of the German
batallion

The other partisans
attacked from
this point

Via Rasella:
the point
of the explosion

Palazzo Barberini
The hostages
were lined
against the wall

Trevi
fountain

Via Rasella

Quirinale:
the King's
residence

Pal del
Quirinale

Fontana
del Trevi

THE NARRATORS

This book is made of many voices. The narrators are its co-authors. This list includes the basic data about each of them, listed in the following order:

First name, last name (double last names are listed under the last), year of birth in parentheses (date of death is added if applicable), profession; political qualifications (if any); relationship to the events at the Fosse Ardeatine and the Resistance; and place and date of the interview(s). Unless otherwise indicated, all interviews were recorded by the author in Rome. Place names are included only if they refer to a historically relevant neighborhood in the city (e.g., Val Melaina) or if the interview was recorded in a place other than Rome, in which case the province is indicated in parentheses: e.g., Genzano (Rome).

Relatives of the men killed at the Fosse Ardeatine are italicized; former partisans are bolded.

All the original tapes and transcripts are kept in the "Franco Coggiola Archive" of the Circolo Gianni Bosio in Rome and can be consulted by request.

Elisabetta Agnini (1932), lawyer; niece of Ferdinando Agnini, killed at the Fosse Ardeatine; February 2, 1998.

Silvana Ajò Cagli (1927), Jewish bookstore owner; February 6, 1998.

Bruno Alfonsi (1942), carpenter; Giustiniana, July 10, 1998.

Roberto Bacchiocchi (1976), computer technician; Alleanza Nazionale local, piazza Bologna, February 13, 1998.

Alberto Baldazzi (1923), office worker; nephew of Cencio Baldazzi, founder of the Arditi del Popolo; partisan in the Partito d'Azione, friend and comrade of many partisans killed at the Fosse Ardeatine; Trionfale, May 5, 1998.

Pasquale Balsamo (1924), journalist, partisan in the central GAP, participant in the action at via Rasella; May 26, 1998.

Franco Bartolini (1920), varnisher; member of central GAP and Bandiera Rossa; former official of the National Crafts Council; Garbatella, May14 and 25, 1998.

Simone Benedetti (1975), vocational school graduate; conscientious objector; Torbellamonaca, May 5, 1998.

Rosario Bentivegna (1922), physician; partisan in the central GAP, participant in the action of via Rasella; February 6 and May 11, 1998.

Enrico Bertocci (1982), high school student; July 28, 1997.

Antonia Bianchi [pseudonym] (1976), English literature student; November13, 1997.

Leonardo Bocale (ca. 1930), wine farmer; Genzano (Rome), January 26, 1975.

Giuseppe Bolgia (1931), office worker; his mother was killed in the air raid of July 19, 1943; his father Michele Bolgia was killed at the Fosse Ardeatine; March 13, 1998.

Francesco Bonini (1976), sociology student; April 13, 1998.

Gaetano Bordoni (n.d.), barber; interviewed by Alfredo Martini, San Lorenzo, April 8, 1976.

Simone Bova (1982), high school student; September 12, 1997.

Antonello Branca (1936–2002), filmmaker; July 31, 1997.

Daniela Bruno (1982), high school student; February 17, 1998.

Lucio Bruscoli (1926), contractor; partisan; November 6, 1997.

Massimo C. [last name witheld on request] (1982), high school student; April 28, 1998.

Virginia Calanca (1925), confectioner; Trastevere, May 15, 1998.

Angelo Capecci (1922), city employee; brother of Mario and Alfredo Capecci, killed at Forte Bravetta and the Fosse Ardeatine; Isola Farnese, September 6, 1998.

Gianfranco Capozio (1938), professor of Economic History; nephew of Ottavio Capozio and Domenico Polli, killed at the Fosse Ardeatine; January 16, 1998.

Goffredo Cappelletti (1930), construction worker; nephew of Alberto Giacchini and Giovanni Senesi, killed at the Fosse Ardeatine; November 18.1997.

Stefano Cappelli (1981), high school student; April 6, 1998.

Carla Capponi, (1919–2000), Communist Party official, member of the central GAP, participant in the action of via Rasella; May 28, 1997 and August 14, 1998.

Lucan Carpette (1928), painter; Testaccio, March 18, 1998.

Carlo Castellani (1928), employee of the Ministry of the Interior; son of Luigi Castellani, killed at La Storta; March 6, 1998.

Rosa Castra (1967), physician; Torbellamonaca Center for Social Integration, May 5, 1998.

Luigi Catemario (1967), estate administrator; descendent of the Tittoni family, owners of Palazzo Tittoni in via Rasella; via Rasella, October 7, 1998.

Daniela Centi (1953), high school teacher; October 11, 1997.

Mauro Centi (1945), manager; October 11, 1997.

Nicola Centi (1978), engineering student; October 11, 1997.

Fabrizio Ceravolo (1982), high school student, February 17, 1998.

Luciano Chiolli (1949), railroad worker; nephew of Giuseppe and Francesco Cimelli, killed at the Fosse Ardeatine; Villa Gordiani, May 23, 1998.

Lina Ciavarella (1915), sister of Francesco Ciavarella, killed at the Fosse Ardeatine; Milan, January 9, 1999.

Marco Daniele Clarke (1951), politician in Alleanza Nazionale, president of the XX District; September 21, 1997.

Romina Cometti (1974), foreign language student; June of 1997.

Anna Cortini (1947), librarian; daughter of Laura Garroni and Giulio Cortini, partisans in the central GAP; November 19, 1997.

Emanuele D'Amore (1980), unemployed; Torbellamonaca, May 5, 1998.

Modesto De Angelis (1931), special-effects TV technician; son of Gerardo De Angelis, killed at the Fosse Ardeatine; December 11, 1998.

Paolo De Carolis (1938), civil service executive; son of Ugo De Carolis, killed at the Fosse Ardeatine; March and May of 1998.

Rina Del Pio (1923), seamstress; Trastevere, May 11, 1998.

Giovanni Di Ruscio (1974), university student; Alleanza Nazionale activist; February 13, 1998.

Sibilla Drisaldi (1967), musician, English student; December 12, 1997.

Tiberio Ducci (1899–1978), butcher, local Communist official; Genzano (Rome), April 29, 1975.

Duccio Ellero (1973), history student; Garbatella, December 20, 1997.

Bruno Eluisi (1918), office worker; brother of Aldo Eluisi, killed at the Fosse Ardeatine; Trastevere, May 7, 1998.

Tamara Eluisi (1947), niece of Aldo Eluisi, killed at the Fosse Ardeatine; Trastevere, May 7, 1998.

Don Giovanni Fagiolo (1913–2000), Salesian priest; among the first to enter the Fosse Ardeatine after the massacre; January 16, 1998.

Claudio Fano (1935), lawyer, former president of Rome's Jewish Community; son of Giorgio Fano, killed at the Fosse Ardeatine; December16, 1997.

Ester Fano (1936), professor of economic history; daughter of Giorgio Fano, killed at the Fosse Ardeatine; January 6, 1998.

Adolfo Fantini (1927), official in the cooperative movement; son of Riziero Fantini, executed in December of 1943 at Forte Bravetta; Genoa (Genoa), March 17, 1998.

Filadelfo Fetoni (1927), retired *carabiniere;* Giustiniana, July 30, 1997.

Anita Ferola (1940); seamstress; daughter of Enrico Ferola, killed at the Fosse Ardeatine; September 22, 1998.

Giuseppina Ferola (1932), hospital worker; daughter of Enrico Ferola, killed at the Fosse Ardeatine; November 22, 1998.

Raffaella Ferraro (1971), English student; May 3, 1998.

Gianfranco Fini (1952), secretary of the Alleanza Nazionale Party; December 1, 1997.

Mario Fiorentini (1918), professor of mathematics; member of the central GAP, participant in the organization of action of via Rasella; July 15, July 29, and November 1, 1997, January 5, March 2, and November 7, 1998.

Fiorino Fiorini (1910), construction worker; partisan; December 8, 1997.

Fabio Fortino (1978), electronics technician; Torbellamonaca, May 5, 1998.

Bruno Frasca (1942), post office worker; son of Celestino Frasca, killed at the Fosse Ardeatine; via Rasella, January 5, 1998.

Giovanni Frate, secretary of the San Lorenzo partisans' association; interviewed by Alfredo Martini, San Lorenzo, November 17, 1975.

Alberto Funaro (1953), rabbi, teacher; nephew of Alberto Funaro, killed at the Fosse Ardeatine; June 2, 1998.

Carla Gabrieli (1952), researcher in English literature; November 20, 1997.

Vittorio Gabrieli (1917), professor of English literature; partisan in the Partito d'Azione; February 17, 1998.

Vincenza Gatti (1935), concierge in palazzo Tittoni in via Rasella; October 14, 1998.

Chiara Gaudino (1979), high school student; March 25, 1998

Valentino Gerratana (1919–2000), professor of philosophy; member of the central GAP; July 19, 1997.

Federico Gherardini (1982), high school student; August 21, 1997.

Giovanni Gigliozzi (1919), journalist; president of ANFIM; cousin of Romolo Gigliozzi, killed at the Fosse Ardeatine; February 24, 1998.

Liana Gigliozzi (1941), daughter of Romolo Gigliozzi, killed at the Fosse Ardeatine; December 29, 1998.

Silvio Gigliozzi (1937), airport employee; son of Romolo Gigliozzi, killed at the Fosse Ardeatine; Ostia, January 2, 1998.

Siegmund Fago Golfarelli (1913), general director, National Tourist Agency; former captain in the grenadiers, awarded the gold medal for the defense of Rome; May 22, 1998.

Flavio Govoni (1964), physician; nephew of Aladino Govoni, killed at the Fosse Ardeatine; April 21, 1998.

Antonio Guidi (1982), high school student, April 6, 1998.

Roberto Guzzo (1915), writer; member of the leadership of the Movimento Comunista d'Italia (Bandiera Rossa); December 14, 1998.

Nicoletta Leoni (1962), secretary of ANFIM, granddaughter of Nicola Ugo Stame, killed at the Fosse Ardeatine; February 24, 1998.

Sara Leoni (1972), English student; September 12, 1997.

Silvano Leoni (1982), high school student, April 6, 1998.

Armandino Liberti (1924), porter; Communist Party activist, songwriter; Trionfale, November 21, 1973.

Daniele Limpido (1982), high school student, February 17, 1998.

Pino Lo Vetere (1967), cultural cooperative worker; Zagarolo, August 25, 1997.

Gemma Luzzi (1942), historian, high school teacher; November 23, 1998.

Marco Maceroni (1980), high school student, April 22, 1998.

Michele Manacorda (1971), law student; August 17, 1997.

Tommaso Manacorda (1976), anthropology student; August 21, 1997.

Riccardo Mancini, partisan in the Socialist Matteotti brigades; tortured at via Tasso; La Storta, June 4, 1998.

Iva Manieri (1907), mother of nine children; a political exile, with Antonio Gramsci, in Ustica in the 1920s; Val Melaina, January 24, 1998.

Maria Marcelli (1913), pottery artist; January 22, 1998.

Pierluigi Martino (1980), high school student; April 22, 1998.

Anna Menichetti (1940), daughter of Mario Menichetti, a political exile in the 1920s; Val Melaina, April 21, 1998.

Valtera Menichetti (1926), office worker; daughter of Mario Menichetti, a political exile in the 1920s; Val Melaina, April 15, 1998.

Maria Michetti (1922), professor of sociology; partisan, Communist member of Rome's city and province councils; September 4, 1997.

Miriam Mondati (1991), high school student; April 22, 1998.

Adriana Cordero Lanza di Montezemolo (1931), farmer; daughter of Giuseppe Cordero Lanza di Montezemolo, killed at the Fosse Ardeatine; April 17, 1998.

Adriano Mordenti (1946), journalist, photographer, musician; March 11, 1998.

Emanuele Moriconi (1982), high school student; February 27, 1998.

Orfeo Mucci (1911–1998), carpenter; political commissar of Bandiera Rossa— many activists of this movement, who were killed at the Fosse Ardeatine and at Forte Bravetta, were his friends and comrades; December 8, 1997.

Teresa Mussoni (1926); at seventeen, she was engaged to Alberto Cozzi, killed at the Fosse Ardeatine; Valle Aurelia, February 24, 1998.

Marisa Musu (1925–2002), journalist; partisan in the central GAP; July 24, 1997.

Aldo Natoli (1913), Communist Party leader; February 13, 1998 and (with Nicola Gallerano) February 17, 1987.

Antonio Neri (1980), high school student; July 18, 1997.

Antonio Nicolardi (1921), farmhand; Alessano (Lecce, Puglia), September 25, 1999.

Lucia Ottobrini (1924), partisan in the central GAP; July 15 and 27, 1997.

Antonio Pappagallo (1917), office worker; nephew of Don Pietro Pappagallo, killed at the Fosse Ardeatine; May 26, 1998.

Daniele Parrotta (1979); engineering student; October 11, 1997.

Vittorio Pavoncello (1954), merchant; May 16, 1998.

Vanda Perretta (1937), professor of German literature; February 4, 1999.

Puci De Vecchi Petroni (1920), wife of Guglielmo Petroni, writer, tortured at via Tasso; December 20, 1997.

Maria Grazia Petterini (1935), office worker; October15, 1997.

Fulvio Piasco (1931), brother of Renzo Piasco, killed at the Fosse Ardeatine; S. Angelo Romano, September 7, 1998.

Caterina Pierantoni (1915–2002), sister of Luigi Pierantoni, killed at the Fosse Ardeatine; May 29, 1998.

Daniele Pifano (ca. 1950), hospital worker; leader in Autonomia operaia; May 14, 1998.

Ada Pignotti (1920), retired office worker; her husband, Umberto Pignotti, her brother-in-law Angelo Pignotti, her husband's cousin Antonio Prosperi, and a brother-in-law once removed, Fulvio Mastrangeli, all were killed at the Fosse Ardeatine; February 23, 1998.

Angelo Pignotti (1949), office worker, nephew of Angelo and Umberto Pignotti, both killed at the Fosse Ardeatine; April 29, 1998.

Luciano Pizzoli (1937), city transit worker; July 4, 1997.

Gabriella Polli (1943), post office worker, daughter of Domenico Polli and niece of Ottavio Capozio, both killed at the Fosse Ardeatine; Alatri (Frosinone), May 18, 1998.

Stefano Portelli (1976), anthropology student; July 25, 1998.

Vanda Prosperi (1929), housewife; daughter of a Quadraro deportee; Quadraro, September 28, 1998.

Vanda Ravone (1933), fur maker; Giustiniana, June 4, 1998.

Maria Teresa Regard (1924–2000); journalist; partisan in the central GAP, prisoner in via Tasso; April 20, 1998.

Alfredo Ronconi (1927), restaurant owner; son of Ettore Ronconi, killed at the Fosse Ardeatine; Genzano (Rome), December 12, 1998.

Giovanna Rossi (n.d.), a pseudonym for a former partisan who does not wish to be identified here; September 4, 1997.

Maria Antonietta Saracino (1950), researcher in English literature; May 22, 1998.

Alessia Salvatori (1971), English student; December12, 1997.

Marzia Santilli (1981), high school student; February 17, 1998.

Marco Sbarrini (1974), engineer, son of Giulia Spizzichino; seven of his mother's relatives (the Di Consiglio family) were killed at the Fosse Ardeatine, nineteen in extermination camps; January 14, 1998.

Ugo Scattoni (1934), school janitor; son of Umberto Scattoni, killed at the Fosse Ardeatine; September 2, 1997.

Giulia Seller (1979), high school student, August 21, 1997.

Francesca Silighini (1983), high school student, October 14, 1997.

Vera Simoni (1922), daughter of Simone Simoni, killed at the Fosse Ardeatine; May 4, 1998.

Irene Sirchia (1982), high school student; Zagarolo (Rome), August 25, 1997.

Giulia Spizzichino (1926), merchant; seven of her relatives (the Di Consiglio family) were killed at the Fosse Ardeatine; nineteen in extermination camps; January 14, 1998.

Settimia Spizzichino (1919–2001), office worker; deported to Bergen-Belsen— her mother, two brothers, and three nephews and nieces died in extermination camps; Garbatella, November 22, 1997.

Valeria Spizzichino (1935), Hebrew teacher; seven of her relatives (the Di Consiglio family) were killed at the Fosse Ardeatine, nineteen in extermination camps; December 30, 1997.

Neelam Srivastava (1972), English student; September 25, 1997.

Rosetta Stame (1937), teacher; daughter of Nicola Ugo Stame, killed at the Fosse Ardeatine; February 28, 1998.

Achille Tartaro (1936), professor of Italian literature; November 6, 1998.

Paolo Emilio Taviani (1912–2001), Christian Democrat senator, former cabinet member; partisan; December 10, 1998.

Amedeo Tedesco (1943), salesman; son of Cesare Tedesco, killed at the Fosse Ardeatine; May 22, 1998.

Fortunata Tedesco (1912), wife of Cesare Tedesco, killed at the Fosse Ardeatine; eight of her relatives were deported and killed in extermination camps; Testaccio, June 3, 1998.

Ornella Tedesco (1939), daughter of Cesare Tedesco, killed at the Fosse Ardeatine; June 3, 1998.

Piero Terracina (1928), manager; deported to Auschwitz—his parents, a grandfather, two uncles, and four brothers and sisters died in the extermination camp; February 8, 1998.

Gabriele Tomassini (1981), high school student; May 5, 1978.

Peter Tompkins (Rome, 1919), journalist and writer; Allied agent in Rome in 1944; April 26, 1998.

Umberto Turco (1928), film-set designer and maker; partisan, former husband of a sister of Ornello Leonardi, killed at the Fosse Ardeatine; November 12, 1997.

Massimo Uffreduzzi (1925), journalist; militant in the Repubblica Sociale Italiana; May 15 and August 3, 1998.

Unidentified woman from Tivoli (ca. 1925); Fosse Ardeatine, November 8, 1997.

Unidentified speaker (name withheld by request), custodian at the Fosse Ardeatine monument; November 8, 1997.

Francesco Vincenti, concierge, folk poet; Bassiano (Rome), July 18, 1977.

Sergio Volponi (1934), office manager; son of Guido Volponi, killed at the Fosse Ardeatine; May 25, 1998.

Vera Yaria (n.d.), high school teacher; born and raised in via Rasella; April 6, 1998.

Matteo Zapparoli (1977), university student; September 6, 1997.

Maria Zevi (1917–1999), professor of architecture; partisan; November 19, 1997.

Giovanni Zuccheretti (1931), butcher; twin of Piero Zuccheretti, killed by the explosion of the bomb in via Rasella; December 15, 1997.

CHAPTER I

INTRODUCTION

Padre celeste Dio di tanto amore	Heavenly Father, ever loving God
Dona forza a mia Musa o gran sovrano	Give power to my Muse, almighty king.
Un fatto orrendo che mi strappa il cuore	An awful deed that tears my heart in two
E mentre scrivo me trema la mano.	And my hand shakes as I write.
Roma, giardino di rose e di fiori	Rome, garden of flowers and roses,
Sei dominata da un popolo strano	Is dominated by a strange people
Per dominar la nostra capitale	Who dominate our capital.
No' spera bene chi ci portò il male.	But evil mongers should expect no good.
	—Egidio Cristini, 1957[1]

1. There Was No Request

On March 25, 1944, the newspapers in Rome published a release from the state news agency. It was issued by the German Command of the city at 10:55 P.M. the night before:

> During the afternoon of March 23, 1944 criminal elements carried out an attack, by throwing bombs at a German Police column which was passing along the via Rasella. In consequence of this attack, 32 German policemen were killed and several wounded. This vile ambush was carried out by Badoglio-Communist elements. Investigation is still being carried out to clarify up to which point this criminal act is to be attributed to Anglo-American incitement.
>
> The German Command is firmly determined to put an end to the activity of these heartless bandits. No one shall sabotage unpunished the renewed Italo-German cooperation. The German Command, therefore, has given orders that for every German killed, ten Badoglio-Communist criminals will be shot. This order has already been carried out."[2]

Vanda Perretta. A flash. The three of us, very small, with my mother, facing a wall. And my mother reading aloud, half aloud, the posted bill that ended: "the order—has been—carried out." "The order has been carried out" is a phrase that has stayed in my mind, concerning the Fosse Ardeatine.[3]

On March 23, 1944, during the Nazi occupation of Rome, a unit of the Gruppi di Azione Patriottica (GAP), an underground Resistance group linked to the Communist Party, attacked a unit of German police, causing thirty-three German casualties. Less than twenty-four hours later, the Germans retaliated by killing three hundred thirty-five prisoners in an abandoned quarry on the via Ardeatina that came to be known as the Fosse Ardeatine. The next day, the official newspaper of the Vatican, the *Osservatore Romano,* carried the German press release, along with an editorial comment: "When facing such events, any honest soul is deeply pained in the name of humanity and of Christian sentiments. On one hand, thirty-two victims; on the other, three hundred and twenty persons sacrificed for the culprits who have escaped arrest [. . .] Standing apart from and above the contention [. . .] we invoke from these irresponsible parties the respect for human life, which they have no right ever to sacrifice; and the respect for innocence, which is fatally the victim; from those in positions of responsibility, we ask that they be conscious of their responsibility toward themselves, toward the lives they are to safeguard, and toward history and civilization."

These events and the struggle over their memory and meaning illuminate the history and identity of Rome, the contradictions and conflicts of Italian democracy, the ethics of armed resistance. This book deals with the events of those twenty-four hours by covering over a century of history and memory.

The fearful symmetry of action and reaction, attack and retaliation, crime and punishment was to dominate the memory of these events—as if the case had been opened and closed in the space of two paragraphs, as if nothing had happened before and nothing afterward, as if the sequence from the attack in via Rasella to the massacre at the Fosse Ardeatine was a self-contained and inevitable cycle. Once "the order has been carried out" and order has been restored, there is nothing left to say—we may as well bury the whole thing, as the Nazis buried the bodies under a pile of dark sand from the crumbling caves and a heap of garbage to disguise the smell.

Popular belief and political distortions of memory, perpetrated by the popular press, the media, the Church, and conservative political forces, have generated a widely believed narrative according to which the Germans asked the partisans to deliver themselves; and only after the partisans failed to do so did they proceed to retaliation. This belief has bred, in turn, a great deal of defamation of the partisans involved and of the anti-Fascist struggle as a whole. The above-quoted German press release, however, proclaims a simple truth, which the Nazi commanders would reluctantly confirm in their postwar trials: the retaliation was carried out less than twenty four hours after the attack and was announced only after it was already accomplished. There was no request made to the partisans to turn themselves in, there was no opportunity for them to do so—nor was there any real search for "the culprits."

All this has been a matter of public record in archives and publications for half a century. Yet these events have been obfuscated by popular beliefs and narratives drenched in ignorance and misinformation that turn responsibility around and do not so much accuse the Germans of perpetrating the massacre as accuse the partisans of causing it by an "irresponsible" act and by not turning themselves in to prevent the retaliation. This narrative is hard to resist, because it possesses the appeal of a nonconformist counternarrative, an alternative to the official story of the Resistance as the foundation of the republic, and yet it avails itself of the institutional power of agencies, parties, and media, which are far from marginal or subaltern in the nation's public life. All is welded together by the commonsense belief that one does not take revenge on three hundred thirty-five innocents before even trying to find the perpetrators.

The *Osservatore Romano* editorial is exemplary in this sense. It describes the partisan attack as a criminal act, with "victims" (the Germans) and "culprits" (the partisans), while the men killed in the Fosse Ardeatine are merely "sacrificed." Such a religiously loaded term can hardly be used by the newspaper of the Catholic Church in a neutral, incidental fashion. A "sacrifice," the act of making sacred, is a reparation for guilt, a necessary purification and atonement after a crime. Unwittingly perhaps, yet significantly, the Church's organ seems to suggest that what happened at the Fosse Ardeatine was some kind of liturgical event.

The *Osservatore Romano* editorial also gives the impression that the Germans tried to arrest the culprits before they resolved to commit the massacre. The Germans did not—but I'm not aware of any corrections or revisions from Church sources. This is the beginning of the shift of guilt from the Nazi executioners to the "cowardly" and "irresponsible" partisans. Along with the political Right, media and sources close to the Church and the Catholic world were to play a major part in perpetuating this version over the years, allowing it to seep into the veins of public imagination and thus contributing to poisoning the memory of the event, and along with it the memory of the Resistance and the identity and origins of the Republic. Herein lies the real, long-term success of the Nazi retaliation.

———•———

On the day I began to think of writing this book, I mentioned the Fosse Ardeatine to a friend: a very intelligent, highly educated woman with a lifetime of Left activism. She reacted: "Look, I'm asking you this *in camera caritatis* [confidentially] and would not say it elsewhere: why didn't they turn themselves in?" My friend did not know that the news of the attack and the retaliation was released only after the massacre had taken place and that therefore there was no request to surrender nor any opportunity to do so. She did not know that in a 1950s court case the partisans who participated in the attack were declared not responsible for the German retaliation (the Supreme Court rendered a similar verdict in the spring of 1999; so long has this accusation been kept in circulation).[4]

The fact is that I didn't really know it either—at least, not until the controversy flared up again after one of the Nazi executioners, the former SS captain Erich Priebke, was identified in Argentina, extradited to Italy in 1994, and sentenced to life imprisonment in 1998. I had never subscribed to the theory of the partisans' guilt, yet the origin of this book is due in part to my surprise at discovering to what extent I, too, had been subject to this false belief, so deeply rooted in commonsense.

One Saturday morning, November 1997, in the crypt in which the graves of the victims are laid at the Fosse Ardeatine, I overheard a conversation between a group of elderly ladies. They had been on a religious visit to the Divino Amore (the Shrine of Divine Love), a popular holy site nearby, and then came to the Fosse. They were deeply moved. Yet they were convinced that the Nazis were only "following orders," and were resentful of the partisans: "And then they awarded a gold medal to the one who planted the bomb in via Rasella, but he's the one I would have shot. Because if he was such a hero, he might have come out and said: 'Instead of killing all these people, here I am, I'm the one who did it.'"

In my office at the University of Rome, a student, Sara Leoni, told me a fantastic tale: "My grandmother took in, in her home, one of the people who threw the bomb in via Rasella—Carla Capponi. And they all kept telling her, you have to confess, or else they'll kill two hundred people. And she decided she wouldn't confess." It's a mythic tale—like many others whose function is to reinforce the narrators' personal involvement in an important event in history—and it's far from being the only wrong narrative about the actions of the partisans after via Rasella (incidentally, the bomb was not "thrown"). Later, Sara Leoni's aunt explained that the person who had stayed with her parents before and after via Rasella was actually Carla Capponi's mother. Yet she, too, thinks she remembers heated discussions on the need for the partisans to turn themselves in.

Gianfranco Fini, secretary of the post-Fascist Alleanza Nazionale (National Alliance) party, the initiator of a process of formal disentanglement of the Italian Right from its Fascist origins and identity, vice-prime minister in the Berlusconi government, explained: "The military action as such was considered—even by the old men who had fought in the Repubblica Sociale [Mussolini's Fascist Italian Social Republic of 1943–45, supported by the Nazis], who had remained Fascists to the end—it was considered legitimate. What was considered cowardly was the fact that they didn't turn themselves in, although everyone was aware of the consequences because everyone knew about the law of retaliation." Mario Fiorentini, a member of the underground partisan Gruppi di Azione Patriottica (GAP) and one of the organizers of the attack in via Rasella, commented: "In Rome, if you ask ten persons about via Rasella, maybe three uphold the point of view of the GAP, two don't know what to say, and five are against it." This state of public opinion is based on a few widespread assumptions: that the retaliation was automatic, and therefore that the partisans ought to have expected it; that all would have been avoided had the partisans turned themselves in; and that the executioners were not responsible for the massacre because they were merely carrying out orders. The German soldiers killed in via Rasella and the men killed at the Fosse Ardeatine thus all appear equally as victims of the partisans.

The story of via Rasella and the Fosse Ardeatine is perhaps the one ground on which the discourse of the most extreme Right has merged seamlessly with middle-of-the-road commonsense, a convergence that makes the prevalent and false narratives on the Fosse Ardeatine so deeply disturbing. I remember the shocked surprise of many historians and anthropologists at a 1994 conference on Nazi massacres in Europe when they discovered the "divided memory" of Civitella Val di Chiana and other communities.[5] If only they had read what conservative and moderate media had been writing for years, or listened to the conversations of common people in bars and barbershops and trains, they would have been better prepared. Unfortunately, these levels of discourse have apparently been considered below the dignity of politicians, historians, and anthropologists. The anti-partisan literature is, indeed, often professionally despicable; and the delusion of a general anti-Fascist consensus, fostered by politicians and intellectuals, led to the belief that Fascism was beyond the pale of credibility in democratic, Resistance-born Italy. For these reasons, the intellectual and political Left did not feel compelled to take notice of such narratives and popular beliefs—until it found itself suddenly staring them in the face, aggressive and arrogant, in the years of historical revisionism and negationism.

2. The Sense of History in Rome

Via Romagna, via Tasso principale	Via Romagna, via Tasso was the place;
ventitre marzo fu la ricorrenza	March 23 was the anniversary
di chi ci fe' passa' tempi brutali	Of those who made us live us such brutal times.[6]
Li tedeschi la presero avvertenza	The Germans were well upon their guard,
Misero gran pattuglia ogni viale	They placed patrols on every avenue.
Chi s'ha da vendica' no' ha più pazienza	The patience of the avengers has run out:
chi bomb'a mano chi co' rivoltella	Some with grenades, some with gun in hand,
tedeschi morti pe' la via Rasella	And Germans lie dead along the via Rasella.

—Egidio Cristini, 1957

It is no wonder that folk poets should sing of via Rasella, of the Fosse Ardeatine, of via Romagna, where the men and women of the Resistance were tortured by the Fascists, or of via Tasso, where they were held and tortured by the SS, under the command of Albert Kappler and his subaltern Erich Priebke. Because of the sheer numbers of the victims and of the endless controversies surrounding their memory, the Fosse Ardeatine has become an open wound in the memory and feelings of Rome. One has only to scratch the surface of memory and the stories gush out. Rome is filled with them; in one way or another, they touch all Romans. I hardly had to step out of my office to collect from students and colleagues any number of stories not unlike Sara Leoni's family myth. As for me, only when this book was all but finished did I find out that Pilo Albertelli, one of the most illustrious victims, had been my mother's philosophy teacher; that two other victims, Mario and Alfredo Capecci, as children used to run and play in the fields where my house was later built; that a student whose thesis I advised was the grandson of another victim; and that, according to my cousin, a friend of my father's was among those who were arrested and held briefly after via Rasella.

Many of the stories I heard from colleagues and students, and later in the city at large, are family narratives that combine the appropriation of the historical event ("I was there" or "My father was there") with classic tales of escape from danger: "In my family this narrative was always handed down: Dad talked about how that day he had passed by via Rasella just before or just after; he heard screams, he didn't know what was going on, he realized only later. A lot of people he knows kept replaying this movie: 'You see, that man was walking maybe twenty steps ahead of me and he was taken when they closed the street, it's a miracle I'm alive'" (Antonietta Saracino).

Other stories are about memory, names, places, rituals: "I, too, have a personal recollection. A girl in my class, a friend of mine, her grandfather died at the Fosse Ardeatine, and there's a square near where I live in which there's a plaque; it says that he died at the Fosse Ardeatine, and she used to tell me about it. So this was my first impact with this episode that I hardly knew anything about, so it was very direct. His name was Zicconi. But I don't know his first name" (Neelam Srivastava); "[My parents] were in the Partito d'Azione [the Party of Action, a democratic Left, anti-Fascist organization], and they used to tell me about those times, and about the Fosse Ardeatine in particular. They were close friends with two people killed at the Fosse Ardeatine—Pilo Albertelli, and another whose name was Pierantoni" (Carla Gabrieli).

Vanda Perretta—When they opened up the Fosse Ardeatine, my mother grabbed us three little girls by the hand and took us there, to the Fosse Ardeatine. Which weren't as they are today, and it has always stayed in my memory as something very soft, because the ground was soft, because of the sand, you walked on soft ground, as if on a big carpet. And there was this soft smell of the tuberoses, which since then I can no longer bear around me. Because I thought I recognized in the tuberoses the smell of death that was inside the Fosse Ardeatine.

Finally, other narratives described a relationship with the urban space: "One may not have a specific knowledge of what happened, but one knows anyway because living in Rome, living in that neighborhood, every year there are ceremonies or something, it is always commemorated, it's not a thing that sinks into oblivion. I live [nearby] at Eur, so one often goes by the Fosse, on the via Ardeatina. I also remember that, as a child, it was natural to ask what it was. I remember that I was taken there, I was rather small, and I was shaken, truly, by this frightening image of this expanse of, let's say, graves" (Alessia Salvatori).

Three hundred and thirty-five people mean three generations of as many families, both close and distant relations; for each person killed and each survivor

there are friends, coworkers, party and union comrades, schoolmates, church relations, and neighbors. The story of the Fosse Ardeatine is a sequence of con-
centric circles that widen until they cover the entire city. Only among young
people in the periphery whose families immigrated to Rome one generation
after the war did I find that this story was not known or was only a dim detail
out of history books in school. To speak of the Fosse Ardeatine and its memory,
in other words, is to speak of Rome.

Antonio Pappagallo, who came from the same small southern town as his
uncle Father Pietro Pappagallo and his friend and mentor Gioacchino Gesmundo, both killed at the Fosse Ardeatine, says:

> Many times they invited me to a school down in Terlizzi, which I don't like; I
> don't know how to speak in public. The principal says, "Speak, say something."
> He left me out there on the podium, and I had to, I made an effort, and said:
> "Children, let me give you one example and that's all. Take Gesmundo and Don
> Pietro, who are from your town, and imagine a funnel; and they are dropped in
> it, this mixture of two opposites—in theory: my uncle, Catholic, a priest; and
> Gesmundo, a free thinker—the Communist that he was. How is it that, after
> these two persons go through the funnel, you can no longer tell which is Don
> Pietro and which is Gesmundo, because their identities merge, and we couldn't
> say that one is more of a priest than the other or that the other is more of a Com-
> munist, if by Communist we mean altruism toward one's neighbor."

"At the Fosse Ardeatine, you'll find my father [an Air Force general], but you'll
also find a fourteen-year-old child, you'll find priests, you'll find workers, you'll
find clerks, the military, *carabinieri* [army police]—you were right perhaps when
you said a while ago that the Fosse Ardeatine is the symbol of Italy's tragedy as a
whole, because that's where everything is gathered, all are represented, it was but
the symbol of what was happening everywhere, in the streets of Rome" (Vera Simoni). The men killed in the Fosse Ardeatine were Catholics, Jews, atheists; some
had no politics, most came from the whole range of political ideals: Communists
of many stripes, Socialists, Liberals, members of the Partito d'Azione, Christian
Democrats, and monarchists. There are military men and civilians; aristocrats,
peddlers, manual workers, merchants, lawyers. Some were active participants in
the Resistance and had staked their lives on the struggle; others were just rounded
up at random, in the wrong place at the wrong time, still others were included to
fill a quota or for not renouncing their Jewish identity and faith. "When I think
of the Ardeatine," writes Vittorio Foa, one of the "founding fathers" of Italian
democracy, "inspirations are almost naturalistic: the unification, the convergence
of life lines . . . They killed Jews because they were Jews, not because of what they
thought or did; they killed anti-Fascists for what they thought or did; they killed
men that had nothing to do with the Resistance, only because they were numbers,

needed to fill a quota."[7] The men who died at the Fosse Ardeatine came from every neighborhood, suburb, slum (*quartiere, rione, borgata*) in Rome—Trastevere and Montesacro, Torpignattara and Trionfale, Portico d'Ottavia and Centocelle, Testaccio and La Storta. Many were born in the city; but Rome is a place to which people come from many places, and the Fosse Ardeatine saw the end of lives begun in other parts of Italy—in Abruzzi, in Puglie, in Turin, in the Roman hills—and in foreign countries—in Luxemburg, Hungary, Turkey, and Ukraine.

In Rome, history wears a capital H, and its burden seems to frustrate and annihilate the work of memory or to make it seem irrelevant. Too often, history is a faraway sphere, distant from the daily lives of its people or a crushing, annihilating weight upon them. This is why the relationship between Rome and the Fosse Ardeatine is so important. As I worked on this book, I relearned the streets and the buildings of "my hometown." I saw St. Peter's and the Coliseum, but I also discovered other sites of history, other monuments of my Rome: not so much the mausoleum of the Fosse Ardeatine as some of those huge popular housing projects, as big and teeming as cities and as beautiful: in Trionfale, where Cencio Baldazzi raised a generation of anti-Fascists into the Partito d'Azione; in Testaccio, where the tenants placed a stone in the middle of the courtyard in memory of their neighbors killed at the Fosse Ardeatine and at Auschwitz; in Val Melaina, a tenement building once called Stalingrad, and even today a bulwark of class consciousness, again with a plaque on the main gate to commemorate neighbors killed at the Fosse Ardeatine.

The Fosse Ardeatine was not the only, and by no means the worst, Nazi massacre in Italy or in Europe. But it was the only "metropolitan" massacre, the only cold-blooded mass execution perpetrated in the space of a big city, in which the variety of the victims synthesized the complex stratification of life stories in a metropolis. This is why it has such a powerful hold on memory and identity. The only thing the dead have in common is their gender: they are all men. But this fact underscores the role of women in surviving and remembering.

The Fosse Ardeatine is the symbolic maelstrom in which the space of the city and a century of its stories come together, so that to speak about it is to speak of the whole history of Rome in the twentieth century, the history of "this rebel city that was never tamed," as the old Communist song proclaims, a city so different from the clichés and stereotypes, a city that resisted the Nazis actively and passively, intensely and diffusely, and for this paid such a terrible price.

3. Context and Background

Rome is an ancient city but a relatively recent capital, just as Italy is an ancient country but a relatively young nation and an even younger democracy. Until

1870, Rome was the capital of the pope's temporal domain, which covered most of central Italy. The rest of the country was broken into small states and foreign possessions and became united and independent only in 1861 under the former king of Sardinia. Only in 1870 did the Italian army enter Rome. The Church did not recognize the new state of things until 1929, when it reached an agreement with Benito Mussolini's Fascist regime; since then, and especially after World War II, it has systematically interfered in Italian politics.

The growth of a modern and democratic Italy, in the midst of social conflict, colonial wars in Ethiopia and Libya, and the traumatic experience of World War I, took a dramatic detour with the rise of Fascism in 1922. While it continued and accelerated the modernization of certain aspects of Italian life, the Fascist regime jailed and exiled political opponents, abolished freedom of speech and of the press, destroyed working-class organizations, and made living and working conditions worse for the popular classes, at the same time that it sought and at times achieved consent with demagogic and paternalistic policies and by creating the illusion of Italy as a great power that revived the glories of the Roman Empire. Throughout this time, an anti-Fascist underground was active both in the country and in exile: Communists, Socialists, and Partito d'Azione (a radical-liberal group with Socialist influences) were the most organized opposition, but Liberals and some Catholics also kept dissent alive. Support for the regime peaked after the occupation of Ethiopia, but it began to ebb after the alliance with Hitler's Nazi Germany and the racist laws discriminating against Jewish citizens in 1938.

After Italy joined the war in 1940, defeats in North Africa, the Italian army's disastrous participation in the Russian campaign, the Allied landings in Sicily and Salerno, the impact of the war on living conditions, and the stepping up of repression dissolved popular faith in the regime. The air raid on Rome on July 19, 1943 brought the Fascist regime to an end. Mussolini was removed from power; General Pietro Badoglio's new government signed an armistice with the Allies on September 8, 1943 (Italy joined the war on the Allied side a few months later); on the same day, the Germans occupied Rome and began taking control over the central and northern parts of the country. Under German supervision, Mussolini established the so-called Repubblica Sociale Italiana (RSI).

Resistance to the German occupation and to Mussolini's puppet government began immediately upon the Germans' takeover. The battle fought by Roman military and civilians at the city gate of Porta San Paolo soon after September 8 was the beginning of a mass struggle that lasted, in the cities and the hills, until liberation was proclaimed on April 25, 1945. The Resistance was coordinated by a Comitato di Liberazione Nazionale (CLN), which included most of the anti-Fascist political parties: Communists, Socialists, Partito d'Azione, Christian

Democrats, Liberals, Labor Democrats, and other smaller groups. Military personnel loyal to the king and to Badoglio's government (therefore labeled as "badogliani") participated in the Resistance through the Fronte Militare Clandestino, the underground military front; dissenting Communists and Leftists created the Movimento Comunista d'Italia–Bandiera Rossa (Red Flag). While political leadership was shared in the CLN, the actual fighting was conducted predominately by units organized by the Communist Party and the Partito d'Azione (named, respectively, Brigate Garibaldi and Giustizia e Libertà). As the historian Claudio Pavone has shown, the Resistance was a combination of three wars, partly distinct and partly overlapping: a war of national liberation from German occupation; a class war against capitalism; and a "civil war" between anti-Fascists and Italian supporters of Hitler and Mussolini.[8]

The German occupation of Rome lasted nine months, from September 8, 1943 to July 4, 1944. It was a time of hunger, fear, Allied bombardments, repression, and mass deportations, which culminated in the deportation of the Jews (beginning on October 16, 1943) and the massacre at the Fosse Ardeatine. Throughout this time, the partisan movement struck the Germans at every opportunity, especially through the Gruppi di Azione Patriottica (GAP), a small underground unit organized by the Communist Party. The GAP's most successful action was the attack on a Nazi police unit at via Rasella, in the center of Rome, on March 23, 1944, resulting in thirty-three German casualties. The next day, the Germans retaliated at the Fosse Ardeatine.

After the war, Italy's government consisted of a coalition of the CLN parties that had led the Resistance. A 1946 referendum ended the monarchy and established a republic; in 1948, the new constitution was approved. It is one of the most democratically advanced constitutions in the West, based on a concept of participatory and egalitarian democracy founded on the experience of the Resistance. Meanwhile, however, U.S. influence had caused the ousting of the Communists and Socialists from the government coalition. After the Left's defeat in the 1948 elections, the Christian Democrat party stayed in power until 1992, when it dissolved after charges of corruption. The anti-Fascist foundations of the written constitution were largely overshadowed by the Cold War and by the influence of the Church: many of its provisions were never enforced.

Throughout the 1950s, it was the Left that kept the memory of Resistance alive, both because the Left subscribed to its democratic ethos and because the Resistance legitimized Communists and Socialists as co-founders of the democratic republic. The narrative of the Resistance as foundation of the state was retrieved by the Center-Left governments (a coalition of Christian Democrats and Socialists) after the 1960s. By then, however, the memory of the Resistance was too often a patriotic ritual emptied of its radical and participatory message. Indeed, the belief that Italian institutions were too democratic to allow for effective government became widespread also in progressive and Left opinion. When the Right-wing coalition headed by Silvio Berlusconi, including the neo-Fascists of the Movimento Sociale Italiano (later renamed Alleanza Nazionale), won the 1994 elections, the drive to change the constitution was supported by a historical revisionism that challenged the meaning of the Resistance as the foundation of the Italian state. In 2002, the Berlusconi government has announced a drive to purge history textbooks of anti-Fascist "bias."

This context accentuates the historical and political meaning of the Fosse Ardeatine. On the one hand, the massacre is remembered as the most dramatic war crime perpetrated in the country's capital, the most symbolically powerful event of the brutality of Nazi occupation. On the other hand, the mythic narrative that blamed the Resistance for bringing it about and not stopping it is a powerful element in the anti-partisan, anti-anti-Fascist discourse of today's dominant ideology.

4. Where Stories Begin and End

If you look up "Fosse Ardeatine" on the Internet, you will hit a tourist information site with a page in English on the monument and its history. It begins: "23 March 1944 a bomb exploded in Via Rasella killing thirty-two German troops. In retaliation the Germans decided to kill ten Italians for each man that was killed." [9]

Stories, says the anthropologist Bruce Jackson, generate their own boundaries of acceptable reality: nothing worth mentioning happens before the stories begin, and nothing happens after they end.[10] A narrative beginning disturbs the order, an ending restores it. While the bulk of historical literature on via Rasella and the Fosse Ardeatine treats them as a single, self-enclosed event, the purpose of this book is to question this approach. In the first place, I will try to demonstrate that the partisan action in via Rasella and the Nazi massacre at the Fosse Ardeatine are not *one* event but *two*, bound by a relationship that is undeniable but nevertheless problematic. In the second place, I will try to show that they are part of a sequence of events that did not begin with the explosion in via Rasella and did not end with the explosion triggered by the SS to close the caves over the bodies of the victims.

The story does not begin there, in the first place, because that is not where the stories of the victims begin, and because while via Rasella was indeed the most dramatic partisan action in Rome, contrary to popular belief it was not the first, and not even the first that resulted in German casualties. Yet none of the previous attacks triggered an automatic retaliation.

And it does not end there, either, because the Fosse Ardeatine was not the only—nor the last—Nazi massacre in Rome. It was preceded and followed by the execution of seventy-two political prisoners at Forte Bravetta, ten men at Pietralata on October 23, 1943, ten women guilty of taking bread from a bakery at Ostiense, fourteen prisoners murdered by retreating Germans on June 4, 1944, the day of Rome's liberation, at La Storta. In no case was there any partisan "provocation" to motivate or "justify" the crime. And we should not forget the mass deportations and the thousands of deaths they entailed: twelve hundred Jews arrested and deported on October 16, 1943, and eight hundred arrested and deported in the following months, only a handful surviving; hundreds of *carabinieri* deported; thousands of able-bodied men taken off the streets and pressed into forced labor in Germany and at the front; seven hundred men arrested and deported from the working-class neighborhood of Quadraro in April of 1944. And all the other faces of war: air raids, hunger, deserters and dodgers from the Fascist draft in hiding, refugees camping out, curfews.

The story does not end there, with order restored after the massacre, most of all because the Fosse Ardeatine is not only the place where so many stories lead but is also the place from which countless other stories emerge and branch out. There is the story of the public struggle over meaning and memory that is still being waged in the media and the courts, as well as over symbols, plaques, inscriptions, and ceremonies: over this "ugly story" trials and court cases go on more than half a century later, and people are still literally coming to blows. Much more painful, almost always silent and unheard, are the burdens and the tensions that pervade the lives and feelings of those who were left behind—parents, wives, children, grandchildren, sisters and brothers of the murdered. To write the history of public mourning over the massacre is to re-read the mutations of political climate over half a century, from the Cold War to the 1960s to the current age of revision and negation; to write the story of private mourning is to try to understand how it has been possible to carry on afterward. The history of the Fosse Ardeatine is truly, as in the title of Robert Katz's pioneering 1965 book, the history of *Death in Rome,* but in a broader sense, because it is the history of how the city—its institutions and its inhabitants—elaborated, sometimes in agreement, often in conflict or in mutual disregard, the sense of this mass death that yet was the absurd, violent, cruel death of individuals.

Ada Pignotti was twenty-three and had been married only a few months when her husband and three other relatives were killed at the Fosse Ardeatine. None of them was known to have been involved in the Resistance but they all happened to be near via Rasella on the day of the attack. She says:

In those days, after it happened, in 'forty-four—you didn't talk about it, there was no way you could talk about it. I worked for forty years, and even at the office, most of the time, whenever they asked me, I wouldn't say a thing—because they always reacted: oh well, blame it on the one who placed the bomb. I acted like I didn't hear them, because it was always the same reaction: oh, it wasn't the Germans' fault; the fault was of the one who set the bomb. They'd say, because if he had turned himself in, they wouldn't have killed them. But where does it say so, where is that written? When did they say so? When? They didn't say a word, they didn't post any bills—they did it later, after they had already killed the 335. Because we followed it day by day, the whole tragedy; and as I said, when we read it in the paper, my sister-in-law and I, I nearly fainted and she along with me. There was no way to talk about it, it was always the same: what, are you defending those who set the bomb? I'm not defending anyone, but this is the way things are, there's no way you can turn them around.

The alibi of the partisans' guilt exorcises the experience of these women who by their very presence disturb the peace of pacified consciences. For each of them, it was difficult and painful to come to terms with the reasons and the causes of what befell them, and not all of them reached the same conclusions. The same is true for the partisans who took part in the attack at via Rasella and in other actions in which they had to kill. "The act of giving death, of destroying, is something that destroys you in turn, it cuts off a piece of you each time," says Carla Capponi. For them, too, coming to terms with these events was a long and complex effort, with differing conclusions, leading some to an active struggle for memory and others to silence, some to a life of political activity and others to a turn away from politics and toward professional or intellectual work.

5. Oral Sources

The word for *revenge* is "report a crime" or "report to five families." The revenge is the story."
—Maxine Hong Kingston, *The Woman Warrior*[11]

One of the differences between oral and written sources is that the latter are documents while the former are always acts. Oral sources are not to be thought of in terms of nouns and objects but in terms of verbs and processes; not the memory and the tale but the remembering and the telling. Oral sources are never anonymous or impersonal, as written documents may often be. The tale and the memory may include materials shared with others, but the rememberer and the teller are always individual persons who take on the task of remembering and the responsibility of telling. Settimia Spizzichino, the only woman survivor among the Jews deported on October 16, 1944, said: "I made a promise when

I was in the camp, I made a solemn promise to my companions, who were being picked out [to be killed] or dying from disease and abuse. I rebelled, I didn't know whether to curse God or pray to Him, and repeated over and over, Lord save me, save me, because I must go back and tell."

However, to tell—as many extermination camp survivors were dramatically to discover—requires the presence of someone who will listen. One of the things that make oral sources different is that they are the achievement of a shared labor between the narrators and the researcher who seeks them out, listens, and interrogates.

I, too, felt a personal responsibility toward this story. I first felt the impulse to "report a crime" on a summer day in 1994, a few months after the Right-wing coalition headed by Silvio Berlusconi won the elections, when for the first time in postwar Europe a party harking openly back to Fascism (the Movimento Sociale Italiano, which later changed its name to Alleanza Nazionale) returned to state power. That day, I discovered a big black swastika painted over the stone, across the street from where I live, that commemorates the fourteen men murdered by the Nazis on June 4, 1944 at La Storta. As I watched the neighborhood artisans discuss the best mean to erase the outrage from the monument, I felt that it was my duty, as a citizen, to respond to this revival of Fascism with all the means at my disposal—that is, with the tools of my trade.

Yet, this story was calling me not only for reasons of civil morality but because it was a unique intellectual, methodological challenge and opportunity for the practice and theory of oral history. Oral history is basically the process of creating relationships: between narrators and narratees, between events in the past and dialogic narratives in the present. The historian must work on both the factual and the narrative planes, the referent and the signifier, the past and the present, and, most of all, on the space between all of them. But it was not only I as researcher and the narrators who spoke to me who thought of this work as something that had to be done. Many of those who helped me transcribe the interviews made a gift of their work; others, who could not afford to, accepted payment that was all but symbolic. They did this not for my sake but for the sake of the story that needed to be told.

Now, the Fosse Ardeatine is both an event that actually happened and one that is intensely remembered and conflictually narrated. It has generated such a large and heterogeneous bibliography that we might be tempted to say, in the words of Washington Irving, that it has been made unknowable by a surfeit of historians.[12] I do not intend to join their number, so this book contains no new factual revelations or discoveries. As far as the material sequence of events goes, I rely on the skepticism and conclusions of existing scholarship. Aside from a few personal documents made available by the interviewees, my documentary sources are books, essays, news items, and court records that were all previously published and available. I use them mainly to establish a problematic but plausible framework of events, against which the creative work of memory and narrative can be measured and tested.

Thus, I do not make "history with oral sources only," as the saying goes. Yet, oral sources are what interest me. In the first place, the personal and private feelings and stories they tell have operated below the level of attention of most historians, cultural institutions, and official media, overly concerned with a narrow definition of what constitutes "fact" and remaining all but unaware of the lives that came before and, most of all, after—until they rediscovered them, as if frozen in time, during the Priebke trial. Through these narratives, we fill this temporal gap and follow the transformations of the meaning of the Fosse Ardeatine for the persons involved and for the city of Rome. These stories function as the tool that allows us to reconstruct the struggle over memory, to explore the relation between material facts and personal subjectivity, and to perceive the multiple, mutable ways of elaborating on and facing death.

In the second place, I am specifically fascinated by the pervasiveness of erroneous tales, myths, legends, and silences, such as those that have been woven around these events. Though oral history is careful to distinguish between events and narratives, history and memory, it does so in order to treat narratives and memory as historical facts. When an incorrect reconstruction of history becomes popular belief, we are not called on only to rectify the facts but also to interrogate ourselves on how and why this commonsense took shape and on its meanings and uses. This is where the specific reliability of oral sources arises: even when they do not tell the events as they occurred, the discrepancies and the errors are themselves events, clues for the work of desire and pain over time, for the painful search for meaning.

This is all the more necessary at a time like this, when the struggle over memory not only concerns the debates among historians or factional recriminations over the past but becomes the ground on which the very identity of our Republic and our democracy, born out of those events, stands or falls.

6. Creation and Use of Sources

A few technical notes on the creation and treatment of the oral sources. This book is based on about two hundred interviews, of different length (a few, especially with young people, from ten to thirty minutes; one was over twelve hours long; most go from one and a half to three hours). Some of the narrators were interviewed more than once. In some cases, I recorded group interviews, ad hoc meetings in schools, public debates, ceremonies, and commemorations. All the interviews were taped by me between July 1997 and February 1999. I

also used some earlier recordings, made by myself or—in three or four cases—
by others but for projects in which I participated. I transcribed about 30 percent
of the interviews myself, and parceled out the others. I had verbal authorization
(usually on tape) from the narrators to use the interviews for this book; most of
them were shown the passages of the manuscript in which they were quoted and
suggested changes and clarifications.

The choice of interviewees was based on the following criteria:

- relatives of the persons killed at the Fosse Ardeatine were chosen in order
  to seek a balance between those who were noted for their participation in
  public struggle for memory, and others who had been less visible or more
  silent and sometimes had a more ambivalent attitude toward the events.
  The families' association (ANFIM) gave me all the help I asked for, but I
  also went outside the organized circle of relatives;
- partisans: the members of the GAP (Gruppi di Azione Patriottica), the underground unit that conducted the attack in via Rasella, as well as those
  who were members of other organizations or had been active in other parts
  of the city, were interviewed to provide a sense of the context in which the
  events in via Rasella took place;
- the areas in the city where those who were killed lived, and those in which
  the partisans had acted: Trastevere, Testaccio, Trionfale, Val Melaina, the
  Ghetto, Quadraro, Torpignattara, and others. In order to document these
  spaces, I also interviewed persons who were not directly involved but were
  helpful in recreating the context;
- bearers of Right-wing memory, especially young people, not just in the
  name of some abstract notion of pluralism, but because they have information and experiences that I could not have tapped otherwise, and because a battle over memory cannot be waged by pretending that the other
  side does not exist;
- people who were not directly involved, generationally and socially diverse,
  but who were important for their relationship to the city and its memory
  or who helped me to understand the impact of the events beyond the circle of those personally affected;
- many young people, ages fifteen to twenty five, friends of my sons, students
  in my department and in other schools, to find out what they knew and to
  investigate the generational change in the meaning and perception of the
  Fosse Ardeatine as an event and as a place.

I constructed the book as a multivoiced narrative, a montage of fragments of
varying lengths, because it was impossible to use all of the thousands of pages of

transcript and because oral history is not just the collection of stories but also their interpretation and representation. The interpretation begins with the selection of sources, continues in the researcher's active role in the interview, and culminates in the open comments of the authorial voice and the meanings implicit in editing and montage. The explicit and implicit interpretive dimension of this book is, of course, my responsibility, which is why it appears under my name.

The quotations are reported as verbatim as possible, because the meanings implicit in the narrators' linguistic choices and narrative strategies cannot be extracted without destroying them. Yet, for reasons of space and readability I have made frequent internal cuts, montage, and transpositions. I wanted the printed words to retain the same *quality* as the oral performance: I do not believe in the "objectivity" and "fidelity" of a literal transcription that reproduces a gripping oral discourse as a boring written text. My editorial interventions vary in proportion to the factuality of each quotation: there is more editing if the factual function prevails, less if I am attempting to draw attention to the quality of the speech. Also, I took into account the desired self-fashioning of the interviewees, some of whom preferred not to be quoted in the colloquial, often vernacular language that we used spontaneously in most interviews (a good deal of which is inevitably lost in translation). I have tried to retain the dialogic, conversational context in which the narratives took shape. Finally, the only objective criterion is that I do not attribute to my interviewees a single word that they did not actually say.

I kept all the interviews in mind in the course of my work, but I did not have the space to quote them in full. As I wove the narrators' voices into one another and into my own, I felt that I was running the risk of fragmenting the wholeness of each personal narrative. I made up for this limitation by opening each chapter with installments of one story, which is thus reported almost in its entirety; and by closing each chapter with longer excerpts from individual stories. I hope this will allow readers to know in depth at least one person and to obtain a fuller sense of the rhythm of the narratives. I did not have the time and the energy to conduct the many interviews I should have. I must therefore render both my apologies and thanks to the persons I interviewed and who are not mentioned in the book, or who are quoted only in fragments, and to the persons who are not in the book because I did not seek them out or find them, or because they no longer wished to speak about these things.

7. The Time of Names

Late October 2000. In a room of the former Nazi prison at via Tasso in Rome, now a museum, a young actor, Ascanio Celestini, performs a one-man monologue based on the first edition of this book. With all the tenderness it takes to tell a terrible story, he goes over the events and the feelings, weaving the stories in this book with his own personal and family narratives. The stories that Ada Pignotti and Gabriella Polli told me are now his, and through him they are returned to a community of listeners.

December 2002. Giovanna Marini, Italy's greatest musician, sits in my living room and sings for the first time the long ballad she has composed after reading this book. It has taken her three agonizing years to boil it down to ten minutes. She was a child at the time, and she remembered the discussions at home, the names of the killed. "This story needs to be told," she says.

The function of a book made of stories is to generate other stories, to feed the engine of remembering and telling. Thus, once the book was finished, I was unable to close it. It was constantly reopened by its readers' need and desire to tell, recall, and discuss. The story kept calling to me, even louder than at the beginning.

November 15, 2000, at the City Council Hall in Rome's Capitol: the launching of Carla Capponi's autobiography, *Con cuore di donna*—with a woman's heart. Carla is one of the protagonists of the Resistance and of this book. As I look over the room, I see many beautiful gray haired faces, a generation gathering around one of its living symbols. Of the speakers on the platform, I am the only one who is not from that generation, and I wonder why I have been included. Then Carla generously mentions my book, and I understand. So many times, in allusions, suggestions, and fragments, the members of the generation of the Resistance and the relatives of the killed at the Fosse Ardeatine have asked me: "Who will tell this story after we are gone?"

Much of my oral history work stems from the experience of reading William Faulkner's *Absalom, Absalom!* In that book, young Quentin Compson wonders why old Miss Rosa Caulfield is telling her life story to him, of all people. Then he understands: she is telling him the story because he already knows it, so that—weaving it with other stories and passions—he will be able to keep telling it. Carla Capponi and Ada Pignotti did not "choose" me the way Miss Rosa chose Quentin; it was I who sought them out. But because I listened to their stories and wrote them down, I am bound to keep telling them.

I knew then in practice what I had known in theory. A tradition is a process in which even mere repetition is a crucial, a necessary task; every silence an irreparable tear in the delicate lace of memory. It is not only in Africa that, as Jomo Kenyatta once said, each time an old person dies a library is burned. In our world, also, when an anti-Fascist is silent, a piece of liberty is burned. Carla Capponi died two weeks after her book was released. But she had told her story, and helped me tell mine.

Over the years, I have attended many ceremonies and rites in commemoration of the massacre of the Fosse Ardeatine. I would like this book to be, like all ceremonies, a narrative of history and memory, but also an active intervention in history (and today memory itself has become a crucial historical *fact*). Because, as Primo Levi said, "it happened, so it can happen again." The use of rituals, if they have one, is to stand against such returns.

Of all the rituals and ceremonies I have witnessed at the Fosse Ardeatine, the most moving moment for me is the simple, endless roll call of the names of the dead. Some of the relatives, who have been listening to it for half a century, are weary even of this: "always the same thing, the list of names, you stand there for three hours, listening to all the names. They ought to do a little more, say a little more, and all they do is they set up a nice wreath, call these names, and go out to lunch" (Gabriella Polli). Others are still moved: "Listen, each year, when they name them, when they read the list of all the people, all the names, one really feels the life of each of them, of these very different people" (Adriana Montezemolo). For me, to whom it was new, it was another demonstration of how "the three hundred and thirty-five" are both a symbolic collective entity and three hundred and thirty-five concrete, distinct individuals. And if it takes so long to call their names, it must have taken a very long time to kill them. How slow, how long was this death!

So let us begin: Ferdinando Agnini, Antonio Ajroldi, Teodato Albanese, Pilo Albertelli, Ivanoe Amoretti, Aldo Angelai, Virgilio Angeli, Paolo Angelini, Giovanni Angelucci, Bruno Annarummi, Lazzaro Anticoli . . .

PART I

ROME

CHAPTER 2

PLACES AND TIMES

. . . Vito Artale, Cesare Astrologo, Raffaele Aversa, Carlo Avolio, Manfredi Az-
zarita, Ugo Baglivo, Giovanni Ballina, Aldo Banzi, Silvio Barbieri, Nino Benati,
Donato Bendicenti, Lallo Berardi, Elio Bernabei, Secondo Bernardini, Tito
Bernardini, Aldo Berolsheimer, Giorgio Leone Blumstein, Michele Bolgia . . .

Ada Pignotti. *I, after we'd talked to the friars, at [the catacombs] of San Callisto, they told us,
they explained, said, see there? That's where they buried them. We rushed to see. And what did we
find? Nothing, a garbage dump. It was nothing but trash, stuff—imagine, we had, those heaps,
we had to make our way through them. And on one side there was the passage they went through,
and there, there they dragged them, they carried them inside. So we went in—flies, I can't tell
you what we found. A stench, such a stink that you couldn't breathe, human flesh decaying. And
we went in, only part of the way, because it was barred. It's barred on this side, it's barred on that
side, because [the Germans] set off two bombs and walled them in. You see, they dumped them in
a dungeon, all of them. So day after day people, like us, went to see, and we did see—in fact,
after a while they began to bring photographs of the missing, hoping, you know, that someone
might recognize them and say they had seen them somewhere else—I mean, it was a delusion,
life was nothing but a delusion. So it was.*

    *Later, though, when they began to exhume them, then we went every day. I remember that I
was there when they found my husband, who—my brother-in-law [Angelo] was found the day
before; the next day they found my . . . my husband. And my brother in law's wallet lay on his
legs. Therefore, my husband died first and after him died . . . after him they killed [my husband].
One on top of the other. So it was. But what was there for you to see? What was there to identify?
What? Nothing! They had heaped them inside one another, so all, all that was there, the ooze,
the thing, something, something that, that made you lose your . . . I don't know, that drove you
crazy, the things you saw. And his face—what was there to see, his face, it was all askew . . . And
then, the blackened skin, and nothing else. Horrible, just horrible.*

1. Beginnings

"What is, after all, a beginning?" asks the Israeli author Amos Oz: "Is there, after all, a truly appropriate *incipit* for a story? Or isn't there always—latent, but always there—a beginning before the beginning?"[1]

Where does this story begin? Does it begin with the explosion of the charge set by the partisans in via Rasella (April 23, 1944), with the collapse of the Italian state and the Nazi occupation of Rome (September 8, 1943), with the fall of Fascism (July 25, 1943), or much earlier than that? All the narrators move backward in time, searching for another beginning to give the story shape and meaning. A biography of General Sabato Martelli Castaldi, killed at the Fosse Ardeatine, begins with his birth in another century: "It is one p.m. of August 19, 1896, and Argia gives birth to her first child." Even the SS captain Erich Priebke, one of the perpetrators of the massacre of the Fosse Ardeatine, tries to explain himself by going back in time: "I, Erich Priebke, was born on July 29, 1913, in Berlin-Hennigsdorf . . ."[2] When I began to discuss this project, friends told me that I ought to begin with October 16, 1943, the date of the raid and deportation of the Roman Jews; others set the start further back, on the day the Fascist government issued the race laws discriminating against Italian Jews: "November 11, 1938—a day no one forgets."[3] Perhaps we should go further back still. The symbolic meaning of the Fosse Ardeatine is intimately connected to the urban space where it happened, to its meaning and identity. So this chapter is about the deep background of the massacre, about the city where this history began, and about the people who lived in it.

Adolfo Fantini. The story starts at the beginning of the century. My father came from an extremely poor family, he lived in a small village in the countryside in the Abruzzi, called Coppito. My grandfather was a brick maker; they used to pug clay by hand and when school was out my father would go along with my grandfather, make the rounds of those kilns, making bricks. They lived in the steepest, rockiest part of the village; in winter, water ran downhill mingled with the sludge from the animals, because the ground floors of the houses were stables. This was the kind of village from which my father left to go to America. When my mother tried to clean up and modernize those hovels, where my father was born, they dug out the floor where the stable used to be—she had turned it into a living room—and on the doorstep they found, carved in the concrete: "Viva il socialismo." I'm talking about a century ago . . .

"We, our village's name was Oricola [in the Abruzzi]. Dad was poor, he had nothing, he was a peasant. What we raised, we made two parts for those who work the land and one part for, how shall we call him, for the landlord. But when all was said and done, the landlord took everything. And then the strike happened" (Ada Pignotti). At the turn of the century, poverty, exploitation, political repression pushed the rural population to seek a better life elsewhere. Migration was both an alternative to and a form of class struggle. Millions emigrated to the Americas; tens of thousand, especially from the rural South, flocked to Rome, the capital of newly united Italy, where hands were needed for rebuilding and expansion.

Orfeo Mucci. I was born in Rome, in San Lorenzo, one hundred percent proletarian neighborhood. My father was a carpenter and he was the secretary of the woodworkers' league of the general union [Confederazione generale del lavoro, CGL]. An anarchist, an anarchist by faith. He was born in '84, my dad, but in 1908–10 he was already an activist. My grandfather, in Benevento, had taken part in the insurrection of the First International [1874]. They were defeated, of course, and were arrested by the *carabinieri,* always the *carabinieri,* and he had to leave Benevento and came to Rome, with his children. By the time he was two, my father was already in Rome.

Ada Pignotti's husband was killed at the Fosse Ardeatine; Adolfo Fantini's father was one of the first partisans executed, in December of 1943 at Forte Bravetta, in Rome; Orfeo Mucci was the political commissar of Bandiera Rossa, a Left splinter group that lost more than sixty members at the Fosse Ardeatine. Their memory contains all the space and all the time of social opposition movements in Italy: the First International and the insurrection led by the founder of anarchism, Mikhail Bakunin himself, in the Matese mountains near Benevento, in 1874; the rural poverty and the birth of socialist ideals; emigration, America; the struggles of Southern peasants for rights and for land . . . Orfeo Mucci died in 1998. The young people of the *centri sociali* (independent aggregations of alternative youth) erected a plaque, on a street of his native San Lorenzo, to this old man whose life and memory encompassed all the history of opposition in Italy.

Adolfo Fantini. So, my father in that village managed to go to school up to the third grade, because that's all there was. As a young boy, he had already joined the early socialist circles. He cried when he had to quit school; anyway, at sixteen, in 1910, he sails with a group of other emigrants to America. [In Boston] he worked as a digger, and he went to school at night, to the night school. There he joined the anarchist groups, and wrote for a newspaper, *La Scintilla* [*The Spark*]. He had been excited by reading Jack London, and would sign himself "Jack" in those articles he wrote. He was a friend of Sacco and Vanzetti; my brother still has a letter that Sacco and Vanzetti wrote to him from jail because he had come back to Italy in '22 to campaign to save Sacco and Vanzetti and spoke at a number of rallies, and they wrote to thank him . . . In 1920, '22, when it seemed that there might be an upheaval, a revolution—he was excited, and came back to Italy.

2. The Magnet

The first capital of independent Italy, in 1861, was Turin, in Piedmont, the seat of the royal Savoia family. The capital was moved to Florence in 1865, in preparation for the final move to Rome, which was accomplished in 1870, when the city was liberated from the pope's domain. Within twenty years, the population of the newly proclaimed capital rose from 240,000 to 460,000. About 90 percent of the increase was from immigration. First came the elite and the bureaucracy of the new national state, then a much larger contingent of rural migrants that became the new working classes: masons and laborers—hands for the gas works, the water works, the flour mills, the slaughterhouse, the market—drivers for the first streetcars.[4] From Umbria, Abruzzi, Puglia, Marche, and from the Roman countryside, rural workers and their families flocked to Rome in a flow that Fascism would later try to stem. Children and grandchildren of these first generations of new Romans are listed both among the partisans of via Rasella and among the men killed at the Fosse Ardeatine:

Bruno Frasca. My father was from Veroli [Southern Lazio]—actually, the countryside around Veroli, a hamlet called Santa Francesca. My grandparents were peasants. They might have owned a little parcel, but mostly they worked on shares: half the crop went to the landlord, and they kept the rest. They grew olives, grapes, wheat, those wheat fields were something to see . . . Now most of it is all gone to pasture . . . it's sad when you go out there and all you see is pasture. I went to school, there; fourth and fifth grade. I remember those old rough houses which if they came back today, young people would have a heart attack—the poverty of those times . . . In fact, the people from my father's village began to live a little better only in the '50s, when they came to Rome to work as laborers, construction workers, even if they didn't have resident's papers . . .

At the turn of the century, the Capecci family moved from estate to estate in the Roman Campagna, following the cattle routes. Angelo Capecci recalls: "Three months in one place, six months somewhere else, a year in another place. Because the cattle growers rented the land. My father was a farmhand, and he tended the cattle, and so on. They changed so many places, in the midst of malaria, lost two children to malaria. All kinds of trouble: we'd load our few possessions on a cart and leave, and perhaps from Sutri we'd wind up all the way to Castel Romano, thirty kilometers on the via Casilina . . . In '35, we came here [at Isola Farnese]." Angelo Capecci's brother, Mario, was executed at Forte Bravetta for his role in the resistance; his other brother, Alfredo, age nineteen, was killed at the Fosse Ardeatine.

"Out of 335 Italians slaughtered that day by the Germans, 13 came from Puglia."[5] The "heel" of Southern Italy, Puglia was a land of stark class oppression, with rich agriculture, poor farm workers, and impoverished middle classes. Among them were Teodato Albanese, lawyer; Umberto Bucci (b. 1892), who was killed together with his son Bruno; Gaetano La Vecchia (b. 1902), cabinet maker; Giuseppe Lotti (b. 1903), plasterer; Uccio Pisino (b. 1917), navy officer, military commander of Bandiera Rossa; Antonio Ayroldi (b. 1906), army general; Ugo Baglivo, lawyer; Nicola Stame, opera singer, a leader of Bandiera Rossa . . . From the same small town, Terlizzi, came a priest, Pietro Pappagallo (1888) and a Communist teacher of philosophy, Gioacchino Gesmundo (1908).

Antonio Pappagallo. My father had seven brothers; five were in the same trade, rope makers. In those days all agriculture was based on carts, there were no machines, so they made good money, they were well-to-do artisans for the times. I remember in Terlizzi, which now has been cut down almost to nothing, we used to go to the theater, to the beach, we'd rent a coach and go to Molfetta . . . My father and my mother gave birth to thirteen children, seven living; and one child is one thing, and seven is another. My mother, at fifty, was finished, nephritis and all, it's no shame to talk about these things. I was the youngest: you divide wealth and share poverty.

Time is long and geography is wide in these stories. They begin in all corners of Italy, go on for generations, and converge into the darkness of the caves on the via Ardeatina.

Bruno Frasca. My father had gone to Africa; the firm he worked for built all the sidewalks of Addis Ababa [in Ethiopia, then an Italian colony]. Then he came home and I guess he wanted to get married, and he went back to his hometown, and he was talking to a person who, ironically, happened to be my wife's grandmother, and he says, "Well, I'm back, now I'd like to find a good girl, and get married." And this lady said to him, "There's a good girl who is in Rome now, she's working in Rome"—because my grandmother, my grandfather, and my mother worked in Rome, in a hotel near via Sistina. And the moment they told him she was in Rome and was a good girl, they say he felt like a chill all over, and my mother says, "It was the shudder of death." In fact, they met, got married, he moved to Rome, and that's where he met his death.

3. Building Fever

Celestino Frasca settled in a street in the center of Rome called via Rasella. His wife ran a laundry and he worked as a mason. As historian Italo Insolera writes, "In the 1870s, peasants and farm workers from Lazio or Abruzzi, who had fallen into poverty in their villages used to stand around in piazza Montanara or piazza Farnese waiting to be hired for the sowing, harvesting, haymaking in the malaria-ridden campagna." They became the thousands of construction workers required by the "building fever" that accompanied Rome's population boom in the 1880s.[6] Among the builders of modern Rome who came at that time was the ancestor and namesake of the protagonist of the GAP action at via Rasella.

Rosario Bentivegna. My grandfather [also named Rosario Bentivegna] came to Rome soon after 1870. He was [an architect], he had quite a scientific and professional career; he's the one who built Mondello [the beach suburb] in Palermo. He was from Palermo, his family came from Corleone, and he had ancestors who had been executed by the Bourbons [kings of the Two Sicilies] for being *garibaldini* [followers of independence hero Giuseppe Garibaldi]. My grandfather's father, Vincenzo Bentivegna, was one of the three colonels who were with Garibaldi on the Aspromonte; my grandfather's uncle, Francesco Bentivegna [was] executed in 1856, a friend of [Risorgimento hero Carlo] Pisacane.[7] My grandfather Rosario was a Mason, he was a member of the radical party, and he was vice-mayor in the [progressive] Nathan administration in Rome [1907–1913]. He drafted the city plan of 1911, the building of the first working-class neighborhoods—Ostiense, Testaccio, all that area. Then he designed Valle Giulia, via Veneto.

The building fever needed building materials. "In the immediate Southern surroundings of Rome, outside the San Paolo and San Sebastiano gates [the departure points of the via Appia, from which the via Ardeatina branches off], lithoidal tuffs are found along or upon strata of loose granulated tuff, a sort of reddish-colored lapillus that makes up *pozzolana,* which, when mixed with lime, generates a mass that hardens to air or water. The best *pozzolana* is the brown-red type, and is quarried in many sites, both for building use in the city and for export."[8] Around the turn of the century, quarrying and brick-making establishments multiplied quickly; at the apex of the building fever, no fewer than one hundred and seventy quarries were scattered in the southern quadrant of the periphery.[9] The so-called Cave Ardeatine, Ardeatine "caves," or quarries, were among the sources from which the materials with which Rome was built were extracted. The name would be changed to *Fosse* Ardeatine, Ardeatine "graves" (or "ditches") after the massacre.

The new building trades mingled and merged with the old artisan crafts. Blacksmiths such as Enrico Ferola (b. 1901), or house painters and varnishers like Aldo Eluisi (b. in Venice, 1898), were among the protagonists of popular anti-Fascism who died at the Fosse Ardeatine. Many of the men killed at the Fosse Ardeatine came from the wood trades: they were cabinet makers, carpenters, joiners, house painters. Some were immigrants, like Antonio Gallarello

(b. 1884, Benevento, Campania), Otello Di Peppe (b. 1890, Chieti, Abruzzi), Antonio Margioni (b. 1900, Civitavecchia, Lazio), and Vincenzo Saccotelli (b. 1897, Andria, Puglie); others were native Romans, like Orazio Corsi (b. 1891), Fernando Norma (b. 1907), Umberto Scattoni (b. 1901), and Duilio Cibei, who was only fifteen.

Orfeo Mucci. Back then my father was a carpenter and he did window casings and frames for [public housing projects]. He got married in 1908 and rented an apartment; he was the union secretary, so he wouldn't accept a project apartment because, he'd say, "I don't want later on people to say that I was privileged because I was the secretary." So we were left homeless. Anyway, there were an older brother, born in 1909; myself, born in 1911; my brother, who died, born in 1913; and my sister, 1916. All this time we lived in San Lorenzo, where we had a small apartment: one room, kitchen, toilet, I mean, and a small room, and that's where we grew up.

The artisans, with their combination of self-employed individualism and class consciousness, of old traditions and modernity, were a key group in unions and radical movements in Rome.[10] Franco Bartolini, a former partisan and a skilled artisan, notes: "Artisans, skilled crafts workers, they're a category, a social order, that is seldom mentioned; but in those days [under Fascism] we made our living with crafts, because there were no factories in the center of Rome. Artisans were independent by nature, and some of them had some kind of [cultural] background. And out of them came cadres, comrades who fought along with me in the [Resistance]: Pietro Benedetti, [Guido] Rattoppatore [both executed at Forte Bravetta], [Umberto] Scattoni, Vittorio Buttaroni, [Antonio] Gallarello, and many more [all killed at the Fosse Ardeatine]."

4. The Heart of the State

After the capital was moved to Rome in 1870, "Immigration to Rome [. . .] was of two different stripes. From Turin, via Florence, came the government workers who had been transferred there from Turin, and the merchants and services that went with them. From the rural surroundings of Rome and from the South came a motley crowd of people hunting for fortune, or at least for status, for a little job to eke out a living. . . ."[11]

If we turn our attention from the popular classes to the middle classes, the geography of the Fosse Ardeatine becomes even broader. As Rome became the center of the state machine, many businesses moved their headquarters there, and the increase in the population generated jobs for clerks and managers, clients for lawyers and doctors, schools for teachers. The peasant immigration from Southern and

Central Italy mingled with the influx of a middle class that came also from other regions, including the North. The massacre at the Fosse Ardeatine, in other words, was not an exclusively Roman wound: by striking the capital, it struck the whole country, in a symbolic as well as in a literal, demographic sense.

On the walls of the Nazi detention and torture chambers in via Tasso, now a museum, the men killed at the Fosse Ardeatine are listed by profession. Clerks and office workers are the largest group—eighty seven. There are seventy-one merchants, forty-six members of the armed forces (as well as thirty-nine industrial workers and twenty-seven artisans). They are the protagonists and heirs of the middle-class expansion that characterizes the growth of the city. Many came from the nearby central regions or from the south; but others came from Emilia, Tuscany, Marche, Piedmont, Veneto. Among the eleven lawyers killed at the Fosse Ardeatine, some were from Rome and Lazio, others from the south (Puglie, Sardinia), still others from Tuscany or Piedmont.

The population increase and the change in social composition generated a growth in education that drew teachers and professors. Among them were Paolo Petrucci, from Trieste, who had been acquitted by a German military court and yet was killed at the Fosse Ardeatine; Salvatore Canalis, from Sardinia, a member of the Partito d'Azione; Pilo Albertelli, from Parma, a teacher of anti-Fascists and a protagonist of the Resistance; and Gioacchino Gesmundo from Terlizzi, near Bari. Pietro Ingrao, a former student of his and later a charismatic Communist leader, writes: "I met Gioacchino Gesmundo back in 1933, when he taught in my lyceum in Formia. In the climate of conformity and cowardice that engulfed Italian society at the time, we were stunned by professor Gesmundo's daring audacity—which would later contribute to his arrest. He openly challenged the Fascists, also in the choice of textbooks: he would make us read [liberal authors like Benedetto] Croce and [Gaetano] Salvemini, though he knew that the regime hated them."[12]

This reckless courage would lead Gioacchino Gesmundo to blow his cover, resulting in his arrest, torture, and death at the Fosse Ardeatine. "In practice, he was the first political commissar for the GAP," says Rosario Bentivegna, and he played a crucial part in the theoretical and moral formation of a generation of partisans, including the protagonists of the action at via Rasella. Carla Capponi, another member of the GAP who acted in via Rasella, recalls that "Gesmundo used to come to my house and lecture"; Rosario Bentivegna remembers that he explained why "German soldiers were enemies that we ought to strike":

"What about retaliations?" we would object.

"Retaliations, indeed," he would reply. "Look," Gesmundo would tell us: "our action is not the isolated act of a group of terrorists, that has no impact and echo among the masses. We are the vanguard of a struggle in which the great majority of the people take part. The enemy knows it, too: this is why they resort, in Italy and elsewhere, to retaliations."[13]

5. Soldiers

The leading force in the liberation and unification of Italy had been the kingdom of Piedmont; thus, after the government and the royal family moved to Rome from the Piedmontese capital of Turin, "many had the impression that Rome had fallen into the hands not of the Italians, but of the Piedmontese," who formed the backbone of the bureaucracy and the military.[14]

———— • ————

In the very conservative middle-class neighborhood of Monte Mario, a small square is named after Giuseppe Cordero Lanza di Montezemolo, staff lieutenant colonel, leader of the underground Front of Military Resistance, killed at the Fosse Ardeatine. There's a pub at the corner. I ask the young owner and a girl there whether they know who he was; they have no idea. Next to the street sign, a black graffito screams: "Honor and freedom for Priebke." I wonder if whoever wrote it was aware of the irony of honoring the killer in a space named for the killed. Another hand, in red, has attempted to correct it, changing *libero,* "free," into *boia,* "murderer," but to no avail. Nearby, another graffito says in red: "No to military expenses." Perhaps Colonel Montezemolo, military hero, would not have liked this one either.

Adriana Montezemolo. Our family comes from Piedmont, we have family stories that we know, going back for centuries. I guess the first one we hear about was a Cordero, from the time of the Crusades; he must have been, I think, of Spanish origins. He went to the Crusades, and on his way back he stopped in Piedmont and stayed. And then there were several branches of the Cordero family, among which was Cordero di Montezemolo. Later, my father added this other name, Lanza, because his grandmother was a Lanza, and she was the last of the name so he added it to our family name.

We are a military family by tradition: a number of navy officers, army officers and, yes, we are a big family, we have cousins everywhere. My father's father was the sixth of nine children; [my father] was one of three brothers: he was an army officer, a general staff officer, and his brothers were officers in the navy. Unfortunately, the last one, the youngest, died in the very first year of the war. He was commander of a submarine in the Aegean Sea, and did not come back, did not return to base, he was never found. The second instead, after many vicissitudes, also joined the military underground.

The family always remained in Piedmont, our place of origins actually is Mondovì, and there is a small town called Montezemolo, near Mondovì. We moved to Rome because during the [second world] war my father was ordered to the Supreme Command and we came to Rome to keep him company, and then we stayed, because that time is so vivid in history, so important, that we didn't have the heart to go back to Turin.

Twenty-seven members of the armed forces were killed at the Fosse Ardeatine. The armed forces drew personnel from all over Italy to the central headquarters in Rome. Among those who were killed at the Fosse Ardeatine were southerners such as Sabato Martelli Castaldi, Ugo De Carolis, Roberto Rendina, Romeo Rodriguez Pereira, all from Campania; northerners such as Giovanni Frignani, the officer who arrested Mussolini (Ravenna), Aladino Govoni, an active-service officer in the grenadiers and a military commander of Bandiera Rossa (Ferrara), Fiorenzo Semini, navy ensign (Genova), and Manfredi Azzarita, a cavalry captain (Venice).

Vera Simoni. [My father] had fought in the First World War, 1915–18, and he had four silver medals, two bronze ones, and a war cross. At Caporetto [where the Italian army suffered a humiliating defeat] he held his post and received a silver medal for this, I think I ought to tell you about it so you can understand how brave he was. It was a stronghold at Caporetto, and my father led a small group of soldiers, but the foreign bulletin, the German bulletin, later said: we are trying to take this stronghold, but it is invincible. He held it for three days, and the enemy thought it was held by quite a force. Then the post was taken, with the use of gas, my father was taken prisoner, and learned of the birth of his son when he was in the camp.

Orfeo Mucci's father also served in the war, in a different rank: "While the sons of the bourgeoisie were concerned with the honor of the homeland, the sons of the proletariat, including myself, were worried about the ruin in their families, because since 1911 with the invasion of Libya, then Albania, war was in their blood. In fact in 1914 the peasants, the poor Christs, went to war to put the crown on the head of the dwarf that called himself king of Italy. During the war, my dad was on the line of fire; my brother died, and they didn't let [my father] come home to see him. Then my sister was born, in 1916; they gave him home leave and he stayed home for nine months. He was a man who would never wear a cap on his head so he wouldn't have to take it off to salute his superiors. Very stern. And we, all of us children, sang verses against the government, against the king, and we were the rebels of the neighborhood."

Armando Bussi, a Republican, lost his left eye in World War I; he was a prisoner in Germany, escaped, fought for the revolution in Bohemia, and in the next war joined the military committee of the Partito d'Azione, held firm under torture by a Fascist gang, and died at the Fosse Ardeatine.[15] Two of Enrico Ferola's brothers were killed in that war: "They had volunteered, and they died. He had another brother, and the Fascists beat him so hard that his lungs busted and he died" (Giuseppina Ferola). Enrico, the only brother left, was killed at the Fosse Ardeatine.

Roberto Lordi, Sabato Martelli Castaldi (a silver medal, two bronze medals, two commendations), and Ugo De Carolis (two silver medals) were career officers in World War I; they were all killed in the next war, at the Fosse Ardeatine. Vincenzo "Cencio" Baldazzi was a volunteer: "Four brothers, all volunteered to the First World War, and all came back mutilated, invalid, and one died from the wounds. I think Cencio was sixteen when he joined the Arditi [army commando troops]; he was hit by a grenade in his thigh, and he wore a silver plate, he walked with a limp for the rest of his life"(Alberto Baldazzi). A veteran of the Arditi assault troops, soon after the war Cencio Baldazzi was the founder and soul of the Arditi del Popolo, the people's assault troops, who fought Fascism hand to hand until the end.

6. In the Shadow of St. Peter's

Carla Capponi. My ancestors on my father's side had four quarters of nobility—ruined aristocracy, pitiful, had lost everything. They were from Ascoli Piceno and had been master paper makers since the 1600s. So they had those very ancient books in the house, because it seems that they used to be suppliers of paper to Venice from Ancona . . . all those ancient papers were later lost and scattered, a tragic thing, because they sold their palace, went bankrupt. My great-grandmother is the one who translated [Henryk] Sienkiewicz['s *Quo Vadis?*]. She spoke German perfectly because her mother was German and Jewish, she was from Vienna and had married an Italian— I'm talking about the 1820s, the very beginning of the century. And they came to Rome often, my great-grandmother with my great-grandfather, because he was the supplier to the Vatican state for stamps and stamped paper, and he brought them to Rome on his coach. This wife of his, the marchioness Silvestri—the lottery had just been invented, and she was crazy about the lottery and wasted a fantastic amount of money on the lottery. I found a piece of paper she had written, in a very very thin handwriting, where she listed her bets—I mean, bets of a thousand lire, in those times! You know what a thousand lire meant—a girl's dowry. And [Bartolomeo] Pinelli painted her portrait.

Rome became the capital of the state in 1870, but it had always been the capital of the Church. This was the vernacular, picturesque, paternalistic, irreverent, and devout Rome depicted by painter Bartolomeo Pinelli and poet Gioacchino Belli, with its turbulent folk, petty aristocracy, omnipresent clergy, and rising country merchants: "I have a paper here, in which Prince Boncompagni writes a letter to my ancestor Antonio Tittoni, who was a big landowner, he owned a number of farms, and he was the only supplier to the pope and to the French garrison stationed in Rome to protect the pope, and he wanted a house in Rome; and the letter says, 'You're the only person to whom I can sell this house'—in via Rasella" (Antonio Catemario).

After Rome was reunited with Italy, these old Church-connected families were joined by new families with connections both to the Church and to the armed forces: a son of Giuseppe Montezemolo is a cardinal, and former Vatican ambassador to Israel; a brother of air force general Giuseppe Simoni was a cardinal, Vatican ambassador to the United States, a decorated military chaplain, confessor to Mother Francesca Cabrini and, according to his niece Vera Simoni, inventor of the phrase "Praise the Lord and pass the ammunition."

Rome, however, also drew humbler priests, such as Don Giuseppe Morosini, chaplain to the military underground, who was executed at Forte Bravetta (he is the source for the main character in Roberto Rossellini's *The Open City*). Don Ferdinando Giorgi was "a splendid example of [a] patriot priest," one who gathered arms and organized sabotage actions with the Partito d'Azione and the military underground; he was among the first to discover the bodies after the massacre in the Fosse Ardeatine.[16] Don Primo Vannutelli was a teacher of anti-Fascists; Don Pietro Pecoraro was among the demonstrators for peace in St. Peter's Square on April 13, 1944. And Don Pietro Pappagallo: "He came to Rome in '25, served at a number of churches as a young priest, a vice-parson, then at St. John's in the Lateran, the Sanctuary of Divine Love, and other churches. My uncle was a priestly priest, a priest to the nth power, in the sense of altruism: he truly felt his mission, whoever knocked at my uncle's door . . ." (Antonio Pappagallo).

Don Pietro Pappagallo was arrested for providing refugees and members of the underground with false documents. "He said: all that is needed is a photograph and a stamp—a mysterious Neapolitan stamp that gave legal refugee status to all those unhappy lost and wanted people, swept in the terrible whirlwind of persecution."[17] Together with the priest Don Pappagallo, in his apartment, the Fascists arrested Roberto Rendina, a colonel of the military underground. They died together at the Fosse Ardeatine, another type of alliance between the army and the Church. Don Pietro's nephew, Antonio, says: "He was a victim of his mission, I believe that for a priest to die this way means that he was a priestly priest, a priest for real."

Antonio Pappagallo. In 1927, I think, he was assigned to the Snia Viscosa. It was a [chemical] plant of three thousand workers, who worked round the clock, three shifts round the clock. So many people came to Rome to work, and there weren't enough houses, and many young workers came from Southern Italy, so the owners had set up a boarding house in the plant. It was a boarding house for young workers, so that instead of having to search all over for a place to live, they could get room and board there— they paid of course . . . And the boarding house was run by two priests, my uncle and Don [. . .], and by the nuns.

Some divisions of the Snia Viscosa were somewhat dangerous, poisonous, so that sometimes some of the workers wouldn't show up to work, and [the managers] would call the boarding house and ask for volunteers to do overtime. Which Don Pappagallo did not accept: it wasn't right that the worker who had already done his seven hours, out of greed or out of need [should do more]. These were dangerous places, you could only stay in them a certain amount of time. So there was a disagreement between him and the management and, to make a long story short, he left and finally landed at the Vatican.

Before 1870, the Vatican was the hub of an underworld of petty jobs, alms, errands, deals, crafts, and trades that virtually supported the whole population of Rome. The Italian state and the Fascist regime would curb but not abolish this role.

Giovanni Zuccheretti. The Zuccherettis have been around the Vatican for three generations and they still are, of course. My uncle worked in the commissary. When we were kids, my brother and I would go into the Vatican for breakfast: white bread, butter, milk. My uncle worked in the bakery: bakery, milk store, everything. And the Vatican guards, they saw us two little twins and let us through; we'd go over, white bread, butter, and everything . . .

Carla Capponi. We lived in a house and garden that belonged to a man who restored ancient armors for the Vatican Museum. Imagine us, little girls, with these armors hanging on the wall, that used to belong to those knights in silver armor. He polished them, and I guess, he also made some deals on the side. We lived in via di Porta Fabbrica, and lived there until 1930. It was called Porta Fabbrica [Works' Gate] because it was a neighborhood by Porta Cavalleggeri [old city gates] that had originated when construction began on Saint Peter's Church; that's why the street was called via delle Fornaci [Kiln Road], because they cooked tiles, bricks; and via di Porta Fabbrica because of the great *fabbrica,* the making of St. Peter's."

Behind St. Peter's Church, squeezed between Porta Cavalleggeri, the tunnel under the Gianicolo hill leading to the embankment on the Tiber, and the urban rail station, almost smothered by the monument they helped build, stood the hovels, alleys, and slums of an ancient, ever-shifting proletariat. In 1925, the city administration contracted private interests to tear down what Rome's governor

Filippo Cremonesi described as "this sort of Abyssinian village," and replace it with "a truly distinguished residential neighborhood"—of course, with a different population. Fifteen years later, however, at the beginning of World War II, the houses and the people were still the same.[18]

Carla Capponi. That's where the *popolino,* the small people, so called, lived. Actually, this was an expression that the Fascists used: *popolo, popolino, popolame*—lower people, populace—meaning "common people." They were the workers, but the kind of workers that construction workers are in Rome: with no permanent job and no fixed abode, they were living in shacks.

"It was a neighborhood of common people, in a way, because it was just outside the [Vatican] gate, beyond the tunnel. [During the war] the tunnel was always filled with refugees; they had set up partitions to separate the families that lived, ate, slept, did everything in there" (Giovanni Zuccheretti). In this Rome teeming with ruses and strategies for survival, Giovanni Zuccheretti grew up with his twin brother Piero, who was killed at age eleven from the explosion in via Rasella; in the same streets, in the shade of the same palaces and monuments, grew up Carla Capponi, a member of the GAP unit that led the attack and set the bomb that killed him.

Giovanni Zuccheretti. My [maternal] grandfather came to Rome when he was seventeen, ragged and hungry; then he went back for his children and took them up here. He did sleight of hand, card tricks; he came from Naples to Rome doing that. Then he joined the pawnshop gang, a mafia of sorts [that bought pawned jewelry cheaply, by scaring competition away]: "They won't let you buy the stuff, they'll threaten you, too." But my grandfather couldn't stay out of trouble, because he was afraid of nobody. Then by 1929 he managed to get a franchise for photographs on Saint Peter's Square, and he had a little photo shop in piazza Sforza Cavalli, across from St. Peter's Church, which was torn down [in the 1920s by Fascist urban renewal].

Carla Capponi. Imagine, I remember, I was a child: they still had the *borghi* [ancient narrow streets in the neighborhood of St. Peter's]. Along via Traspontina, there was this woman who sold vegetables, and she had a coal stove and a huge big pot; she used to cook chicory, she'd clean it herself, boil it, and sell it in big cooked balls, like that, you know, she had a basket and all these cooked balls, which my mother would buy. And do you know why she did it like this? She was paralyzed, and they kept her in a chair with a hole underneath and she wore a big apron up front. And she would push this thing around—she was huge . . . But I remember so many weird things . . .

7. Roman Hills

Don Giovanni Fagiolo. That morning, my mother's brother and cousin, they were delivering wine in via Rasella, via del Boccaccio; and, as it happened, the bomb went off, they tried to get away, but my mother's cousin didn't make it and was arrested. And he was killed then [at the Fosse Ardeatine]. Ronconi—Ettore. My mother's brother instead managed to get away, so he wasn't caught. The other, instead, was caught, taken to Regina Coeli [jail], and then . . . But he didn't know a thing about it. I mean, he was nothing special, he was a worker, I think he had communist ideas . . .

Ettore Ronconi, born in 1897 in Genzano, was an anti-Fascist. In the 1920s, like many opponents of Fascism, he had been exiled to Sardinia and Lucania for seven years. "He was a wine broker, he sold wine. He was in via Rasella, delivering wine to the little inn near via Rasella, and what happened happened. He was having lunch with the owners, and they were all arrested; the others were released, though, but they kept my father because they checked the record and found that he was an anti-Fascist. He never came back" (Alfredo Ronconi). Ettore Ronconi was one of four men from Genzano killed at the Fosse Ardeatine. The others were Ivano Scarioli (b. 1921, farmhand); Sebastiano Silvestri (b. 1915, farmer), and Vittorio Buttaroni (b. 1915, chauffeur; he had fought in the defense of Rome on September 8, 1943 and in the Resistance with the Partito d'Azione, Bandiera Rossa, and the Communist GAP).

Genzano was the red heart of the Castelli Romani, the hill towns that overlook Rome from the Alban hills: a crucible of rebel ideas and dramatic struggles, a crossways between the modernity of the city they look down on, the ancient rural poverty of small farmers and farm hands, and the persistence of feudal estates.

"Yes, it was in [18]98: the insurrection. Food prices were going up, and in Genzano there was a revolution, for real, a rebellion" (Leonardo Bocale). Those were the years when a flour tax brought working people to the edge of starvation. Protests broke out all over Italy; in Milan, General Bava Beccaris fired cannons on the workers' demonstration (the king gave him a medal). In Genzano, two men were killed.

Tiberio Ducci. I was born in [18]99, but I had the close, tangible mediation of living men who went through those times. On May 8, 1898, the town was seething, and those who actually started it were the young people—not the men, the women! They carried a jacket, it was called *pollacchera* then, a jacket on the tip of a cane, red; and they screamed that they wanted to eat, so to speak. They wanted scales, public scales, to check the weight of bread. Along the streets, out there, it started; then the conflict, the conflict broke out. I mean—the soldiers fired upon the crowd, that's it. There were two dead, two dead—it so happens one's name was Pace and the other's Tempesta: Peace and Tempest. After that, the repression came, arrests, and then jail.

Don Giovanni Fagiolo. After all, Communism in Genzano is understandable, because they were all poor. I was a boy, and, in the morning, when school was out, we'd go help my father in his vineyard. We would walk by a square, and see these groups of men, with hoe in hand, waiting to be called and hired. And they said, if one returned home, who hadn't been hired for the day, his wife wouldn't set the pot on the fire. They owned nothing, only their arms; if they weren't called to work, what could they do? This is why they accepted these doctrines that gave hope for something. They didn't study the Communist doctrine, they didn't have the time; but it gave them hope.

The peasants' and farm workers' league, outlawed after 1898, was reestablished in 1907. "And the battle came, and it was bloody," said Tiberio Ducci. Seventy years later, at first Ducci asked to have the tape recorder turned off when he talked about the "bloody" sabotage—the cutting of the vines, a tragic wound for this wine-centered culture: "I mean, even if someone hears, it's been so long . . . So many vines were cut. They had no other support, no other weapon and force, because they were on strike and had nothing to eat." After two years of struggle, "the owners gave the six hour day to the hands, and the possibility of negotiating wages through the organization." It was then that Dandolo Spinetti, about ten years old, learned the song about the Commandments of Socialism: " . . . six, my children like yours, they must all go to school; seven, if you don't have heart, stay away, when the big bang comes . . ."

Alfredo Ronconi. And so my father—I'll tell you right away. I had no father from thirteen on, because he was a political exile for seven years. I was thirteen, and when I saw him again I was twenty. He was exiled because the Fascists were going down the street with their pennant, and he did not give the Fascist salute. They got him, they beat him up, purged him, and I never saw him again, he was sent to the islands, that's all. He was an anarchist; in those days, we were just boys, and we were beginning to shout *viva il comunismo,* and women from the windows kept telling us to shut up, "If they catch you they'll put you in jail. . . ."

I remember a day in the 1970s, April 25, the anniversary of liberation from Fascism, in Genzano: six former partisans on a stage, there to tell the story of the Resistance. The "bobjacks," the four-pronged nails that rent the tires of German trucks on the via Appia, the blowing up of Nazi trains and convoys, the refugees hidden and protected by the population, the armed skirmishes[19] . . . Each narrator strove to outdo the others, tracing the origins deeper and deeper in the past: anti-Fascism in the 1920s and '30s, the Socialist electoral victory in the 1910s, the struggles at the turn of the century, the rebellion of 1898, and further back still, in an extraordinary reverse narrative in search of a beginning.

Leonardo Bocale. Back again to ancient things, Genzano was always in rebellion, even in the 1800s. In the 1800s, in the days of the pope's state, the *genzanesi* were always rioting. And I remember—the old timers told me, the old folks—that Cardinal Jacobini invited His Holiness to his house in Genzano. And so all the hungry *genzanesi* stood in front of the pope's coach (I don't know who was the pope in those days, I guess it was Pius IX, for sure); they all stood around, sort of overran this coach, and he from behind the curtains, the pope, said: "What's the matter with all these people? What do they want?" And the people then were so uncouth, and screamed, "Holiness, big loaves! Holiness, big loaves!" Because the price was always the same, a *baiocco* a loaf, but the loaf kept getting smaller and smaller. The bakers were making smaller loaves, and the pay was always the same. The ancients told me about it.

Salvatore Capogrossi, union organizer and former mayor of Genzano, writes in his memoirs: "The farm hands were paid a lira a day for work that started at dawn and ended at sunset, at the bells of the Ave Maria—which, by silent agreement with the landowners, the parsons of Genzano and Lanuvio always rang later than it was supposed to be."[20] The Castelli were "dominated for centuries directly by the Church's hierarchy or by the baronial families," which dotted the landscape with villas and palaces (including the pope's summer residence in Castelgandolfo);[21] still, the lot of the common people was a rural poverty hard enough to stir resentment but not so desperate as to forbid organization. Social ideas reached the Castelli through summer visitors and tourists coming up from Rome or wine dealers like Ettore Ronconi commuting to and fro. This relationship generated both a paternalistic sense of dependency and a rebellious republicanism, which inspired the *carbonari* underground and the *garibaldini* ranks in the Risorgimento (the struggle for Italy's independence and unification).

Umberto Turco. I had a grandfather, who was my mother's father, who was a railroad construction worker from Naples, and he wound up in this little town of Lanuvio, working on the Rome-Naples line. And this grandfather was, in a way, the elite of the working class, because he was a railroad worker and a railroad worker in those days was important. And he was a Socialist, who brought Socialism to this town of Anarchists and Republicans. My father tells me they had a ritual where they cut their finger, drew blood, and then they were supposed to stab some kind of puppet with knives, I mean, strange forms of Republican-type initiations.

This impatient and irreverent republicanism, so vivid in the Castelli as well as in the popular neighborhoods of the pope's city, is at the roots of Socialism and Communism in Rome; but it also flows through the fighting anti-Fascism of the Arditi del Popolo, into the popular soul of the apparently elitist radical-democrat Partito d'Azione and its partisan arm, Giustizia e Libertà. Vincenzo "Cencio" Baldazzi, founder of the Arditi del Popolo, a mythic figure in Rome's people's movements, was born in Genzano in the dramatic year of 1898: we will find him on the barricades that stopped the Fascists in San Lorenzo and Trionfale in 1921 and (after years of jail and exile) at the defense of Rome at Porta San Paolo on September 8, 1943.[22] In those years, the Castelli gave other members to the Partito d'Azione: Vittorio Buttaroni (from Genzano); Mario Intreccialagli (b. 1922, shoemaker, from Montecompatri); Edmondo Fondi (a disabled veteran); the brothers Italo and Spartaco Pula (a varnisher and a blacksmith from Velletri, whose very names testify to their family's beliefs). Pilo Albertelli wrote that Spartaco Pula was a man "who fears nobody and nothing," the author of daring sabotage actions at the military airport in Centocelle, "always the first to fire upon police patrols he happened to clash with."[23] They were all killed at the Fosse Ardeatine.

8. Portico d'Ottavia

It would be better to include Jews in the list, rather than Italians. . .
—SS Obersturmführer Herbert Kappler

. . . because the Jews held all the capital, they ran the economic destinies of Rome, didn't they? Besides, like all Protestants, they always tried to accumulate capital . . .
—Antonia Bianchi

Alberto Funaro. I was born in 1953, in Rome, in a family that has been in Rome for many years—according to what I have been able to reconstruct from the archives of the Jewish community, I think at least from 1700—who knows, perhaps, if we went even farther back . . . But unfortunately the documents were destroyed or taken away by the Nazis when they raided the community's library. My father was, I'd say, a working man, my mother was a housewife, my grandparents I think were merchants of some kind. My grandfather on my mother's side was deported to Auschwitz, with a daughter; and on my father's side, my father's brother, whose name I wear, Alberto Funaro, was executed at the Fosse Ardeatine. Generally, in Rome, Jews name their children after their father; my grandfather's name was Lazzaro, which he was probably the only Lazzaro Funaro in Rome. When I was born and my father brought him the news, my grandfather said, "Look, I don't want you to name him after me; give him the name of that poor son of mine who was executed at the Fosse Ardeatine."

"Oh, I'm a true Roman. Because us Jews, we're the real Romans of Rome" (Settimia Spizzichino). "I feel deeply Roman, in this Roman tradition, the Roman Jews are the only Romans who can trace back for generations, take it for granted like the air you breathe, this familiarity with the city" (Claudio Fano). There has always been a Jewish community in Rome, at least since the second century before Christ. Of course, Jewish culture also has a tradition of mobility: at the Fosse Ardeatine, it is witnessed by men like Salomone Drucker and Giorgio Leone Blumstein, born in L'vov (Lemberg, now in Ukraine). But if we go through the list of those killed at the Fosse Ardeatine, the correspondence between Jewish identity and Roman birth is striking: the Jews were less than half of one percent of the population of Rome, but they are 50 percent of the native Romans killed at the Fosse Ardeatine.

Adriano Mordenti. The culture of [Rome's Jewish ghetto] is deeply steeped into *romanitudine;* the Communist local of Ponte Regola Campitelli was a local deeply steeped in Jewish Romanness—with an additional trait that is not just resignation—it's more like exorcism, with a talent for sarcasm, for baroque humor, that makes it unique. With this firm belief: that one cannot help being a Jew given the proximity to the *cupolone* [St. Peter's dome]. And I have a theory: that the proximity to the Vatican has functioned somewhat like the Vesuvius in Naples, or the earthquake in California. The Vesuvius may erupt any moment, and Pompei is here to remind us, and this is why Neapolitans are crazy, a city of philosophers. In Rome, we had the Vatican, and so—I mean, there was this tradition that many really believed was true: my mother really believed that it was part of Rome's *hagaddah* [the story of the Jews' exodus out of Egypt] that Roman Jews were allowed to eat ham, the only ones in the world. Why? Because we have this pain in the ass of living right here, a hundred yards from the enemy.

Claudio Fano. My [paternal] great-grandfather had been a rabbi of sorts, because he had lived through the last years of the ghetto, when you couldn't get an education, so he was not entirely self-taught but had learned from those who had come before him and had been cut off from what we would call today the free world. And in fact in Rome they also told the story that after a couple of rabbis died who had a personality, a culture of their own, Rome was left with no rabbis at all because no one wanted to come to the last ghetto still open—still closed, rather—in Europe. So finally they got this rascal who came from Israel and later the community had to kick him out; and they set up a triad of rabbis who had a little knowledge, and my great-grandfather was one of them. This is a story of the 1850s, just about; the ghetto was opened in 1870.

The participation of many Jews in the struggle for Italian unity and independence, followed by the opening of Rome's ghetto by the Italian administration after 1870, generated a strong identification between the Jewish community and the Italian state that was to last until the end of the 1930s.

Piero Terracina. My grandfather was born in 1860. He remembered very clearly when the Italians, the *bersaglieri,* liberated Rome. The ghetto had already been opened during the Roman Republic, in 1848. After the Republic, they put the gates back up, but it was a lot milder. From what he remembered, as early as 1870, practically they still lived in the ghetto but they would go out regularly and came back in at night. As a boy, like most Roman Jews born in the ghetto, he had attended the ghetto school, where they taught the Torah, mainly. So he was very religious, he had a large library of books in Hebrew, he read Hebrew books all the time. We of the later generations perhaps were a little less observant; we would not observe the Sabbath properly. He wouldn't ride a bus, wouldn't do certain things. We did. So I'd say, we were believers, yes; but observant, much less.

Adriano Mordenti. I had [my Jewish heritage] also thanks to my grandfather, the family, the local—Grandpa Dino was the Jewish-est presence in the family, the one who was educated, who spoke Hebrew, and who retained an identity beyond the delusions of assimilationism. His father had known the closed ghetto, his grandfather spoke Hebrew and didn't speak Italian; and this came through, in spite of the euphoria for the liberation of Rome. Just look at the Temple: it smacks more of Mazzini than of Moses. It went to the Jews' head: just read the sonnets of Crescenzo Del Monte [the Jewish vernacular poet]. He has this very funny one about the knight crosses, when the Jews started being knighted and were getting these crosses from the state and didn't know whether to accept them or not; finally they take it but laugh about it. Mayor Nathan, all know but won't tell, was the son of a Jewish woman. I mean, they were all persuaded that it was all over, we're citizens like the rest—but it wasn't that way at all. And even if it were, it wouldn't be a good reason for giving up everything, would it?

"My [maternal] grandmother, Clara, had been born in Naples. Her father had been a volunteer with Garibaldi, or at least he had tried to be, because he left Naples to fight in the Third War of Independence [in 1866], but the king wanted to keep the *garibaldini* out of the war, so he never fought, he just waited, and came back" (Ester Fano). Ester and her brother Claudio, children of Giorgio Fano, who was killed at the Fosse Ardeatine, tell a representative story of the combination of intellectual and commercial pursuits in a middle-class Jewish family. On the one hand, the maternal side was steeped in the liberal, intellectual heritage of the relatively liberated Naples ("They spoke of progress and freedom, hardly ever of religion: being Jews meant that they had become attuned to progress earlier than the rest"). On the other hand, the paternal side resented the isolation and closure of the ghetto of Rome: "Rome was a sleepy hamlet," says Ester. "It didn't have a middle class, and there was this popish presence in all its forms, which were never modern. And the ghetto was a world aside, also linguistically. It had a thin bourgeois crust, and all the rest was sub-popular, less than lumpen." Yet her brother Claudio also tells of the initiative and enterprise of a rising merchant class:

Claudio Fano. My grandfather had a lace store, and in those times lace came from England. So he had the idea—in this ruin that was life in the ghetto—of sending his son to England by himself. So this son went to England, studied lace making, learned certain techniques, returned to Rome, and started making the rounds of the Castelli teaching the women how to make lace. He would give them thread, parcel out the work, and then he'd come around, and the lace they made would be sold as English lace.

"I come from a big family, six children. A petty bourgeois family, my father was a small, small merchant" (Settimia Spizzichino). There were no Rothschilds in Rome. When we read "merchant" by the names of Jews killed at the Fosse Ardeatine, we must envision less a prosperous mercantile and financial bourgeoisie (Giorgio Leone Blumstein, born in Lemberg in 1895, "banker") than the petty trade and service sector of Rome's vernacular economy (Jewish and non-Jewish), halfway between street life and lower–middle class, from the small traffic of street peddlers (like Pacifico Di Segni, Leone Fornaro, Settimio Funaro, and Cesare Mieli) to the small businesses of large families (Michele Di Veroli worked in his father's, Attilio's, store, and they were killed together), to the salesmen and brokers, up to larger enterprises whose origins were still rooted in this environment. "Most of the rag-and-bone peddlers in Rome were Jews. They had a role then, because in those times [it was important to] retrieve rags, papers, stuff. My mother'd set aside all her rags, now we throw it all away, but my mother used to set them aside because she would trade them for a couple of glasses or something, this was the economy of the city of Rome" (Umberto Turco). These were the tolerated, and therefore obligatory, activities for Jews in Rome until Fascism barred them even from this petty trade.

Even the more prosperous middle class suffered from the Fascist regime. The family firm of Ester and Claudio Fano's ancestors had become suppliers to the king and made their fortune on women's trousseaus and military supplies. Then the firm declined, partly because the younger generations were less interested in the trade, partly because of the restrictions caused by Fascism and the war.

Claudio Fano. During the war they couldn't get the material, after the war they were confiscated by the Allies for two years. Meanwhile, one of the partners had been deported [to the extermination camp], my grandfather had no sons who had gone into the business, mother's brother had escaped to the United States after the race laws, you may have heard of him, Paolo Milano [a major literary essayist and critic]: he was anything but a merchant. There was this family atmosphere whereby commerce is not as noble as intellectual pursuits . . .

9. Monuments: Testaccio, Trionfale . . .

Righetto Ferruggia. I am Righetto, from Testaccio, born in 1930, April 6. Son of a Republican—they were real [Republicans], not like the Republicans of today. They were *carbonari* for real, anti-Fascists by nature. He was a fisherman, he made a living out of the fish he fished out of the river, and then the guards would come to the house and pick him up, take him up to the police station, keep him a couple of nights because an ambassador or something was coming [and all subversives were rounded up]—and he was subjected to being picked up like that. All around here, it was nothing but countryside. Testaccio was dangerous, because of the outlaws, the bandits. Testaccio was known for knife fights, for the outlawry in it.

Testaccio was one of the neighborhoods that Rosario Bentivegna's grandfather helped plan and build, conceived as a model working-class neighborhood, intended for the "clamorous arts," the noisy trades of artisans and industrial workers. However, the firm that had contracted its construction from the city administration in 1872, under extremely favorable terms, left the project unfinished. In 1907, "the State found itself faced with the onerous, passive legacy of a pseudo-free enterprise that had proved itself economically rather inept, politically reactionary, socially class-biased." At that point Testaccio, unfinished, with hardly any services, "could very well be described as a throwaway neighborhood" whose population "was crowded, from 2.4 persons to each room at best up to 4.8 in the most crowded dwellings."[24]

In time population growth, the nearby slaughterhouse, and the inflow of Jewish families from the adjacent and even more crowded ghetto generated small businesses and enterprises. "Then, step by step, it got civilized, the buildings went up, the church was born, the slaughter house was born, so many houses were born, and here it is, nowadays . . . Testaccio is a warm-hearted neighborhood, a humane neighborhood—and the food is good in Testaccio. Anywhere you go, the food is good" (Righetto Ferruggia).

Valeria Spizzichino. All right: I was born in Testaccio, from a Jewish family; my father was a merchant, he sold house linen and carpets. My father was from a poor family, he had to leave school at age nine—I mean, he only had a second grade education, but he kidded us because though I had a diploma and all I wasn't as good as him with figures. He worked at all kinds of trades, he was a laborer, he sold door to door, paintings, he ran this store, and he was very well liked. I remember perfectly via Amerigo Vespucci, the Giolitti ice cream store near the corner, I grew up with their *cassata* and ice-cream cups . . .

The boundary between the popular plains of Testaccio and the elite Aventino hill, from the Tiber to Porta San Paolo (St. Paul's Gate), is a broad straight street: via Marmorata. Along this street, the battle for Rome was fought on September 8, 1943; Allied tanks paraded here on the day of liberation, June 4, 1944, and the workers of Rome fought horse-mounted police in July 1960.

Testaccio stands where the river harbor of ancient Rome used to be. It takes its name from the mound of piled up ancient pottery shards (*testae*) that overlooks the neighborhood. Today, this huge pile of scraps that "documents, at a distance of twenty centuries, the commerce of Rome" is dotted with small restaurants and trendy music clubs. The land where the housing projects stand today used to be occupied by the Roman warehouses and docks, *emporium* and *horrea*. At the center of the courtyard in one of the project buildings in via Marmorata, number 169, stands a square marble stone that carries on one side a Latin inscription—*ex horreis reis publicae*, "from the warehouses of the Republic"—and on the other a more recent one: "To restore justice and liberty to Italy / Adolfo Caviglia / Cesare Tedesco / fell at the Fosse Ardeatine / victims of Nazi inhumanity / Guglielmo Caviglia / Lazzaro Di Porto / Davide Moresco / Mario Milano / Mario Natili / died in concentration camps in Germany."

Fortunata Tedesco. First we lived near via del Mare, in via dei Fienili; we sublet from a family, they rented us two rooms and we moved in. Later, however, my sister found a place here in Testaccio, at via Marmorata, number 169. She had been married in April, too, she had a little girl, I had no children, so she rented this apartment where she still lives; I lived in it for twenty-two years. In fact, when they took my husband away I was living there. The people in the building were butchers, fish mongers, fruit sellers . . . tradespeople. Now it's changed, because so many people are from lower Italy, not that they're bad but they have different things. And in there, there is the stone for my husband, and for the other one who died at the Fosse Ardeatine, Caviglia, [who lived] one floor above us. In fact, when I escaped [from the Nazi raid of October 16, 1943] I moved to another [apartment] in the same building, because I was eight months pregnant. My son was born in this family's place, they're dead now, but he was born there.

All over Rome, these huge square blocks of project housing, ranged around the big middle courtyard, with dozens of stairs leading up on four sides, stand like places of memory. Trionfale is another popular neighborhood, on the opposite side of town: "Here in piazzale degli Eroi, number 8, where my uncle Cencio [Baldazzi] lived, where I lived, where I was born, this is where everything really began" (Alberto Baldazzi). Like via Marmorata 169, piazzale degli Eroi 8, built in the early 1920s, is as full of people and stories as a city and as tight as a fortress.

Alberto Baldazzi. Actually, our block has seven staircases; each staircase is five floors, one hundred and five apartments altogether. And they were all assigned to newlywed couples, all newlyweds, and their children were born there. Indeed, there must have been fifty of us kids, we grew up together. Yes, it was a fortress, we were very close, still are today; the ones who are still living, we get together once in a while, and all we talk about is those times, because they were the worst of times and thus the best today to remember. All my friends who were born inside that gate grew up anti-Fascist. I breathed anti-Fascism as a child, as a boy, and of course it is in my blood. They were all workers. Vincenzo Saccotelli, who lived on the second floor, was a cabinet maker, but I think he was retired, because he was in poor health, he was getting on in years. Fernando Norma, who lived down here in via Giulio Cesare, across from the Giulio Cesare movie theater—[was killed] at the Fosse Ardeatine. Saccotelli, also the same. At the Fosse Ardeatine, it must have been at least eighty who were our friends, all from this neighborhood, all from this area.

One of the families who lived at number 8 of piazzale degli Eroi, Baldazzi recalls, was that of Umberto Bucci. "He was a Fascist, he wore the uniform all the time, but he was a good person, I'd known him as a boy, I'd grown up with his son. And one day this man Bucci stops me and says, 'Look, I never had a chance to meet your uncle Cencio, but I'd like to talk to him. You understand, I was in Fascism but I would like to join Giustizia e Libertà.' My uncle says, 'No, I don't think it would do, but give him some papers anyway. Let him read them and then we'll talk.' And one evening I went to their place and brought these, these papers, and unfortunately they were the cause of their death, the father's and the son's." That very evening, alerted by a local informer, the notorious Fascist Koch gang raided Umberto Bucci's apartment, found a copy of *Italia libera* under his son Bruno's bed, and arrested them both. "And I can never forgive myself, for bringing those papers to them . . . They took them to Regina Coeli. When it was about six P.M., Bruno Bucci's sister came to my house crying, she said they had been arrested. They took them away and unfortunately they ended up at the Fosse Ardeatine, both of them."

10. Via della Pelliccia

On the gate of number 8 in via della Pelliccia, in the heart of Trastevere, the old popular neighborhood across the river, a plaque commemorates: "At the Fosse Ardeatine / Enrico Ferola / died / for an ideal of Justice and Liberty / The Partito d'Azione—in memory / Q.M.P." The owner of a tavern across the street saw me looking at it, came out, and commented: "I guess Q.M.P. means Qui Muori in Pace, Here Die in Peace. I'm not sure though, 'cause I'm not educated. All I know is that Enrico Ferola was a friend, a friend of our family, and they arrested him together with my brother-in-law," who returned from Auschwitz "with his mind gone. He's been dead two years. The Germans took his life and took his reason."

Trastevere—literally, "across the Tiber"—claims to be the home of "the true Romans" but also of the "true anti-Fascists" like the communist bricklayer Mario Menichetti, an exile with Antonio Gramsci in the island of Ustica, father of nine children. "Each time they picked him up, he'd come back from jail, and he wouldn't listen to reason, had only one thing on his mind, and I alone know how many nights I stayed awake to keep him away from me! But then after a while I'd fall asleep. So—we must be frank about these things—I did try once, I'll tell you the truth, to get [an abortion], but it nearly killed me—and I would have left all these other children . . ." (Iva Manieri Menichetti).

Valtera Menichetti. He came from a poor family, because my grandfather was a cart driver; and he was a *trasteverino,* my father was a true seventh-generation *trasteverino.* We lived around there, in Trastevere, in via della Pelliccia; and we lived next to this other man, who was a Republican, who was killed by the Germans. We lived next door. He, too, was an anti-Fascist, a true one, and I know he used to meet with my father, too, though he was a Republican [and my father a Communist]. In fact, when I'd go over to their place, because I was friends with his daughter as a little girl, on the wall near his bed he had a portrait of [Giuseppe] Mazzini [a hero of national independence and the Roman Republic of 1849].

The Republican next door was Enrico Ferola, blacksmith, a member of Giustizia e Libertà and the Partito d'Azione, in the Risorgimento tradition of Mazzini and Garibaldi: "[His] dad, my grandpa Giovanni, was in boarding school; and he ran away from the school to go and fight with Garibaldi. That's how far back it goes" (Giuseppina Ferola). Enrico Ferola was a maker of the most effective weapon of the Roman resistance: the three- or four-pronged nails similar to the "bobjacks" used in miners' strikes in the United States. Strewn along the roads from Rome to the Anzio and Cassino front, these nails stopped German convoys in their tracks, rending their tires to pieces. "The first three-prong nail that was made was buried in a flower pot. And [the police] came all the time, all the time, to search the house, but they never found them. And they printed certain papers, for the Partito d'Azione. These papers would be brought home, folded, and then at night—I too went, along with dad—we would go from door to door, quietly, and slide them under the thresholds" (Giuseppina Ferola).

Anita Ferola. I remember well where we used to live. Because . . . From when I was born till I was—eighteen and more, in Trastevere. And . . . in fact, I still miss . . . I mean now it's been redone all over and I wonder what they've made of it. You know, we left because it had become impossible, those old houses, lousy with bugs, roaches and all, I mean, we couldn't go on. Old time houses, with the toilet in the kitchen, the windows looking onto the courtyard . . .

Iva Manieri Menichetti. We lived in this cellar in Trastevere, lousy with roaches—there's no way I can explain the way we lived in that place. It was one big room, with a toilet bowl in a corner on one side. Mario had built a kind of closet around it, and we lived in this big room, with all these children . . . And the rats, the mice; we'd set a bowl of water on the floor at night and in the morning it was black with roaches . . . When we had it, we ate; when we didn't, we'd go without.

Valtera Menichetti. And yet it was a house that was always full of people, our house, because among the comrades who came, and many of them helped us, too, there was great solidarity. I remember, for instance, a butcher who always used to give us meat, all the time. You see, some of the people who lived there, in Trastevere, they, they were thieves. But it was almost like one big family. Some of them were our neighbors, I remember them well, who would go out and pick pockets, but they had heart—when there was a need, they would be the first to give money, for people like us, for those who were in jail.

Giuseppina Ferola. Via della Pelliccia—a narrow, narrow alley; in the summer, in the evening, the older ladies would come down to the street, carrying a chair or a stool, and sit and talk, and the children played in the street . . . Mostly working people. On the ground floor across the street from us, lived a man who used to go out with his cart, he was a fruit peddler. There were plumbers, working men, too; draymen—at the end of via della Pelliccia, in vicolo del Cedro, right below the Gianicolo hill, [lived] Agnese [Angelucci], her husband was executed at the Fosse Ardeatine, and she, too, had a very small little girl, and was pregnant with another one, who was born later. And it was all stables there. Up in vicolo del Cedro, below the Gianicolo—there were people who butchered horses, mainly horses, and pigs—and mother would carry

CHAPTER 3

TWENTY YEARS:
FASCISM AND ITS DISCONTENTS

. . . Ottavio Capozio, Ferruccio Caputo, Emanuele Caracciolo, Francesco Ca-
rioli, Federico Carola, Mario Carola, Andrea Casadei, Adolfo Caviglia,
Giuseppe Celani, Oreste Cerroni, Egidio Checchi, Romualdo Chiesa, Aldo
Francesco Chiricozzi, Francesco Ciavarella, Duilio Cibei, Gino Cibei, Francesco
Cinelli, Giuseppe Cinelli . . .

Ada Pignotti. *I can tell you what happened [to me]: as for all the rest, you already know it.
We lived in via Nomentana; that day, we went to see my brother-in-law, who lived [in via Quat-
tro Fontane, at the corner of via Rasella]. My husband—"Let's go, let's go, let's go"—it seemed
like he had an urge to get there. And so it happened, there, the whole thing. But I, that day when
I got there, March 23, we went out. He was supposed to get a haircut. So we walked—I said,
"Umberto"—I said—"Weren't you supposed to get a haircut?" He says, "Well, on our way back."
Just five minutes, it would have made a difference.*

*My brother-in-law had a store in via Quattro Fontane; he had the store there, and lived right
next to it. Next door: the store front, and where he lived. So my husband stayed in the store. And
I went to the house, to my sister in law's, I mean, his wife. Five minutes later, or less, I had hardly
just sat down, a big bang; then another—What can it be? What can it be? . . .*

*My brother-in-law and my husband, from the store, ran back to the house: "Don't worry, it's
nothing—he says—must be a bus tire that has, that has burst, and made all this noise." Perhaps
he wanted to calm us down, we were all upset—and so we stayed there. "What can it be, what
can it be, will the Germans come, will they not . . . ?" "If the Germans come . . .": my brother-in-
law, the last words he said; after that he never made a sound, he never spoke again—and neither
did my husband, nor the other two who were with us, because there were four of them, four men.
He says, "Don't you worry, we haven't done anything, we're honest people, they've known us a
long time—he says—so what can they do to us? After they find out who we are, they'll let us
go. I mean, even supposing they take us in." But fear, we were so full of fear.*

About half an hour after it happened, a knock on the door. With a rifle butt, imagine. My brother-in-law went to the door; he hardly managed to open it before they started hitting him with the rifle butt. He fell down twice; we tried to help him up, but nothing, they leveled their rifles at us—Italians, and Germans. Italians, mostly. I mean, the Germans weren't very nice either. They saw the men, that's all they needed to see. My husband's cousin, there, he had three children, the smallest girl was five. He was holding this little girl; one of them tore her from him and threw her to his wife, who was holding another. And they took him away. They took him— my brother-in-law; my husband, my brother-in-law's brother-in-law, the brother of my brother-in-law's wife; and this cousin of my husband's. To make a long story short, before they carried them away they beat them up almost to death.

1. Working-Class Worlds:
San Lorenzo and the Valley of Hell

In San Lorenzo, on the wall a building cut in half by the Allied air raid of July 19, 1943, a huge graffito remained visible for years: "Legacy of Fascism." In the 1990s, while the neighborhood's artisan shops were being replaced by fashionable small restaurants and clubs, it was painted over, perhaps with a mind to gentrify the place. It was a gesture of tangible revisionism, which literalized a number of worn-out metaphors: whitewashing history, erasing the past.

The Fosse Ardeatine was the crowning conclusion to twenty years of Fascist dictatorship. This chapter and the one that follows are about that time. We begin with the geography and history of Rome under Fascism: the old working-class neighborhoods and the new slums created by the regime, the persistence and growth of dissent, the formation of an anti-Fascist conscience in the new generations in the middle class and among the intellectuals as well as in the working class. And then, in the next chapter, we go on to the history of anti-Semitism, colonialism, racism, and wars—the wars that Italy fought beyond its borders, and those fought on Italian ground, including the regime's persecution of its own Jewish citizens. All of this paved the way for the Fosse Ardeatine.

Fascism in Rome began on November 9, 1921. On that day, the newly founded Fascist party called, for the first time, a national rally in Rome. The trains carrying the participants arrived at the station located in the midst of a working-class neighborhood, San Lorenzo. There were protests, and a railroad worker, Guglielmo Farsetti, was killed by a shot from the train. The people of San Lorenzo took to the streets and pushed the Fascists back. It would be another year before they were able to hold a mass meeting in Rome.

San Lorenzo is a tight-knit "urban village," created during the "building fever" of the late 1880s, wedged between the railroad, the cemetery, and later the university. In the early decades of the century, "its population was about 45,000, but each apartment was home to three, four families . . . We lived in the dreariest poverty. We struggled for bread, for a piece of bread . . ." (Giovanni Frate).

Its old inhabitants like to describe it as a "totally proletarian neighborhood" (Orfeo Mucci). Actually, it was a composite of the old substratum of craftsmen and artisans and the new working class employed in construction, railroads, and services.[1]

Its crowded and unsanitary conditions resulted in "dirt, immorality, and often crime,"[2] but also in a rebellious spirit, an "instinctive hatred," a "healthy class instinct" that has remained ingrained in the local identity. "Even the thieves, I mean, the roughs, the illiterates, poor people who lived in the extreme margin" rallied to keep the Fascists out of their streets.[3] It was the artisan component, however, more independent and individualistic and less subjected to Fascist discrimination, that was the backbone of San Lorenzo's "rebel spirit" (Giovanni Frate), republican and anarchistic before it was Socialist and Communist. San Lorenzo was home to one of the early units of the Arditi del Popolo, the proletarian self-defense anti-Fascist organization founded by Cencio Baldazzi.

On the day Guglielmo Farsetti was murdered, workers from all over Rome and neighboring towns joined in what became known as the first battle of San Lorenzo (there were two more, on May 24 and on October 30, 1922, and they merge in memory to form the neighborhood's narrative of identity). Artisans' shops were turned into forges to make weapons; brick makers from across town joined the battle, dock workers from Civitavecchia made bombs, steel workers from Terni brought ammunition. Women and children threw paving stones and all kinds of objects from windows and rooftops.[4]

Orfeo Mucci. [The Fascists] came—there was road work on, loose stones on the ground—so I, at the head of the neighborhood kids, began to make barricades with these *sampietrini* [heavy paving stones], we'd take the stones to the rooftops all around, and from up there we'd drop them on [the Fascists]. In other words, I was on my first barricade at age eleven. [A woman] in via dei Sardi stood behind her window and as she saw them go by, bang, she'd flatten them against the wall. They had to send armored cars to drive [her] out, I think you can still see the holes on that wall.[5]

The fighting spread from San Lorenzo to the rest of proletarian Rome. Along the Tiber, Aldo Eluisi, a house painter and varnisher and a veteran of World War I, led a charge on the police that protected the Fascists, thus allowing Baldazzi and his men "to storm the Fascists and beat them up."[6] We will meet Aldo Eluisi again: with Cencio Baldazzi in the battle of Porta San Paolo; in the Nazi jail at via Tasso with Pilo Albertelli; and at the Fosse Ardeatine, where he was killed. The battle lasted five days, leaving seven dead and two hundred wounded (including Baldazzi); and the Arditi del Popolo celebrated their victory in song: "*Ma Roma è sempre stata bolscevica / trionfa sempre sì / martello falce e spiga*" ("Rome was always Bolshevik—the hammer and sickle and corn-spike shall always triumph").[7] The Fascists never forgave San Lorenzo.

Among those who joined the fight to push the Fascists back in 1921 was Vittorio Mallozzi, who would go on to fight in the Spanish Civil War, spend years as a political prisoner, and be executed as a leader of the Resistance in 1944. He was a brick maker by trade, from the solid working-class cluster of Valle Aurelia. A smoky valley of kilns and brick works, Valle Aurelia was known as Valle dell'Inferno (Valley of Hell): "They said that a pope, I don't remember which one, looked out from Saint Peter's and said: What is this, is it the valley of hell? Because of the smokestacks . . . and this is how the story started, of the Valley of Hell" (Teresa Mussoni).

The name, however, also designates "the 'hell of a life' spent in the heat of the kilns, the dust, the sweat, the driving rhythms of piecework production."[8] "These brick makers of Valle Aurelia had a homogeneity, a class toughness, all their own. They were a group of highly skilled workers, with a great tradition in Rome. They were a clan, as it were, of families, of workers who worked at the kilns, and made bricks, because [the neighborhood] was near some big strata of clay. So there had grown this layer, this very homogeneous group of workers and some of there were very highly skilled"(Aldo Natoli).

Teresa Mussoni. The story of the Fascists' arrival in Rome, everyone was running down via Candia, along those streets—because at the beginning of via Candia there was a kiln, and my father was arrested in the stampede . . . He always said he had picked up a gun he'd just found on the ground, now I don't know if it's true or not: I believe my father. And for that, they arrested him, they loaded him on a truck with these other men, they beat them, and took them to Regina Coeli. And he spent six months there and then he got out, but my mother said—you know, back then dad used to give her presents, gold chains and so on—she always said, "We even had to pawn our mattress to pay the lawyer, we didn't have a thing left."

In San Lorenzo, the "Legacy of Fascism" inscription has disappeared; in Valle Aurelia, the whole neighborhood and its memory have been razed.[9] The kilns closed in the 1950s, and the rickety houses that the workers had built with their own hands have been replaced by huge projects. "If you'd like, I'll take you to

TWENTY YEARS / 55

the Casa del Popolo [the 'People's Home,' where all the working-class institutions used to be housed]. Now it's all forsaken, because out there ten years or so ago they tore down the whole place and built these big red projects" (Teresa Mussoni). In the weeds, behind a closed gate and a watch dog, I glimpse another plaque. It commemorates "the sacrifice of five martyrs of Valle Aurelia / who fell under the oppressor's gun / for our freedom." Their names are Andrea Fantini, Augusto Paroli, Vittorio Mallozzi, executed at Forte Bravetta; and Andrea Casadei and Alberto Cozzi, killed at the Fosse Ardeatine.

2. Historic Streets:
Ponte, Regola, Tor di Nona . . .

Ugo Scattoni. I have a sister who is mentally ill, and she lives a life of persecution, she does. Which because she was a little older than me—I was eleven, she was thirteen— she was always the one who brought dad's laundry to [the jail at] Regina Coeli, his change of clothes. And she had brought a bundle for dad, and this Fascist told her, "Take it back—they've all been taken to be killed, they've killed them all." She fainted, and they had to carry her home, my sister. She never recovered; in fact she's been certified mentally ill. She still lives the persecution, she's afraid of the Fascists, she can't watch the news on TV, when she hears "Fascists" she's terrified. She is a victim of my father's persecution . . . We lived in via dei Coronari, not far from Saint Peter's. And, well, the other night I went for a walk around piazza Navona, Ponte, Regola, Coronari. It's become nothing but a tourist thing, that's all. It used to be popular, people lived in the shops. Now it's all antique stores, it's all restaurants, ice cream bars, those sort of things.

If one walks the historic streets of central Rome looking for Baroque churches, fountains, and statues, one may find signs of another history. In via della Scrofa, on the gate of an old building, which is now the central office of the ex-Fascist Alleanza Nazionale, a plaque acknowledges Alberto Marchesi, killed at the Fosse Ardeatine. Nearby, in via della Stelletta, two stones commemorate Domenico Iaforte, Antonio Giustiniani, and Rosario Petrelli; a few blocks away, next to the Trevi Fountain, there is a memorial for Giuseppe Celani. Amid the artistic wonders of piazza Navona, the elegant stores in via del Tritone, and the scenic Spanish Steps, the walls of Rome talk to each other. On the front of the central post office in piazza San Silvestro a stone lists the postal workers killed at the Fosse Ardeatine, in prison camps, and in the Resistance. Between San Silvestro and the fashionable shopping streets of via Condotti and via Margutta a plaque honoring Uccio Pisino, the military organizer of Bandiera Rossa, faces one that commemorates a seventeenth-century visit by sculptor

Lorenzo Bernini. Nearby, a black graffito once again screams: "*Priebke libero*"— free Erich Priebke, one of the perpetrators of the massacre.

At the beginning of the century, "the Romans who already lived in the city before 1870, and who were the lower classes of the Pope's capital, still live[d] in the old city center, in the Renaissance quarter, in the Suburra." When Rome became Italy's capital, "their lives didn't change much, nor did their living conditions."[10] Later, the Fascist theatrics of imperial grandeur and monumental urban renewal brought along the gutting of the ancient neighborhoods and the removal of their population. Yet, at the end of World War II, one could still recognize in this part of Rome the traits of a deep-rooted vernacular identity and spirit. It was, among other things, a food culture: Alberto Marchesi, who was killed at the Fosse Ardeatine, owned a trattoria, where he often fed comrades a free meal; Guido Rattoppatore, a tramway worker and partisan who was executed at Forte Bravetta, once assembled "maybe forty comrades at [a] trattoria and held a political meeting among *pagnottelle* and *fojette*," hunks of bread and glasses of wine.[11]

Ugo Scattoni. I remember, I remember that Fascism was in power, that dad was persecuted, so much that he was for two years under police surveillance; he had to be home by eight P.M. each night. Every time the Duce made a speech, they came to pick him up ten days ahead of time. I, being a child, saw my father suffer, so that—I thought: What do these people want from my father? Always in jail, always behind bars . . . and that's where it began, I was a child and they were hurting my dad and I hated them.

As an anti-Fascist, Umberto Scattoni couldn't hold on to a job, and he eked out a living as a house painter and a car wrecker. "He had a whole library with Lenin, Marx, all his books, which after the liberation the Party requested all his books to set up the local's library" (Ugo Scattoni). He was "an Anarchist of sorts, a typical Roman worker, he had a wife and small children, he was always hungry because he gave his food to his children and kept little for himself . . . He had a passion: Greek philosophers. He was always quoting Protagoras, Socrates. . . ." Like his friend Rosario Bentivegna, Scattoni came from a Trotskyist background; like other GAP members of his neighborhood, he joined the Communist Party but was also sympathetic to the heretics of Bandiera Rossa.[12]

Ugo Scattoni. Mom was a leftist, a Communist, too. All of dad's persecutions, she suffered them, too. Mom was a woman who shared my father's ideas. She helped him in every respect, she never abandoned him. Another woman would have said, "What's the use of standing by a man who's persecuted this way?" But mom was always a Communist too, a comrade too. She stood in the breadlines, went to the bakeries to demonstrate [for bread] . . .

In these anti-Fascist streets, a natural environment for the GAP, significant fragments of the early Roman resistance to Fascism managed to survive throughout the duration of the regime: groups of "old comrades" who would later converge in Bandiera Rossa met in Rione Ponte; in Tor di Nona, Aldo Eluisi kept up throughout the 1920s and '30s the presence of the Partito d'Azione and the resistance he had begun in 1921 in the Arditi del Popolo.

Bruno Eluisi. Whenever those Fascist goons came around, he wouldn't stand for it, and one night [in 1922] they stabbed him, he was taken to the hospital . . . That's just the way he was. Sometimes he actually went out hunting for Fascists, looking for them, because of what they had done to him when they stabbed him. His friends [said]: "You can't even go to the movies with him! Because if they play *Giovinezza* [the Fascist anthem], everyone stands and he doesn't, and it ends up in a fight every time. . . ." No way, he just couldn't swallow the dictatorship, that's all.

In these streets, destinies cross only to be separated later by chance. Both Rosario Bentivegna and Alberto Marchesi were part of the partisan unit that attacked a Fascist parade in via Tomacelli on March 10, 1944; two weeks later, the former would go on to be the protagonist of the action at via Rasella, the latter would be killed at the Fosse Ardeatine; yet, but for circumstances, their fates might have been reversed. In these streets, after a failed attempt to blow up the Fascist Republican National Guard, Carla Capponi got away but Umberto Scattoni, Guido Rattoppatore, and Armando Bussi were captured. Rattoppatore and Bussi were tortured and executed at Forte Bravetta; Scattoni was killed at the Fosse Ardeatine.

Carla Capponi. [A comrade and I] met with [Rattoppatore's] father in the church of Santa Maria della Pace, with money for the Red Aid to the families of the prisoners. And so in this church—which I remember was beautiful—he told her, "There's no hope: they'll kill him; they'll kill him." She says, "No, I don't think so, just wait . . . The Allies are coming, they'll be here in a few days, by the time they try him and all . . ." "There'll be no trial. He's wounded, they'll kill him, they'll torture him, they'll kill him!" He was desperate. And she was trying to console him. Then, after he left, she took me by the shoulders and said, "He's right, they'll kill him."

It was early March 1944. A few days later, Bentivegna and Capponi dropped by Alberto Marchesi's trattoria. They found the place empty, his wife Antonietta in tears. A few hours earlier, four SS had come in, ordered food and drink, and after they were finished took him away. "They took him to via Tasso. They beat him up almost to death. Not a name, not a word escaped from his lips. In the cell where he was locked, with his blood, he wrote a message to his son: 'Giorgio, think of your mother.' He was brought to the Ardeatine, eight days after his arrest, with his ribs broken and blinded in one eye."[13]

Tamara Eluisi. [My mother, Aldo's sister-in-law] said that she would go to Regina Coeli [to see him]. She says that he kept his hands hidden, beneath a sheet. "What's the matter, Aldo, won't you say anything?" And he wouldn't speak. So she pulled the sheet off his hands, and they had hung him up in the air, they'd beaten him with rifle butts in the chest, and they had pulled all the nails from his hands and feet to make him talk. The morning they took them all away, my mom had a [visiting] permit. When they got there, the guard says, "Look, it's no use you trying to find out, because they've taken them away in the middle of the night. But you've got this to hold on to, that Aldo didn't understand what was going on; he got on [the truck], but he was almost dead already . . ."

Ugo Scattoni. My dad went around delivering *l'Unità* [the Communist Party paper]; he'd put *l'Unità* in mailboxes, which, in those days, if they caught you with *l'Unità* in your pocket you were finished, they'd kill you. Nowadays, I look at *l'Unità* and I tell myself: for the sake of this paper my father risked his life, today they're turning it into a newspaper like all the rest . . . But I, when I became an adult, I wanted to now why he was fighting, what ideal he was fighting with. So I made up my own library of Lenin and Karl Marx, of [Palmiro] Togliatti, of [Antonio] Gramsci [founders of the Italian Communist Party], I made me a culture of my own to find out whether those ideals were worth dying for. And I agree, entirely: fight Fascism and Nazism, and don't listen to their blackmail.

3. Students

Massimo Uffreduzzi. Well, one was a Fascist because one happened to be a Fascist. Understand? They taught us Fascist culture in school; a consul of the militia would come in and explain Fascism, you understand? It isn't as if we could have listened to the other side, there was no such thing. If there had been freedom of thought and we could have heard their opinions—perhaps we might have changed our minds.

Vera Simoni. For us, everything was regimented. We didn't know the word freedom, we had to wear a uniform in school, we were supposed to think only in a Fascist way, we were not supposed to shake hands because it was forbidden, we had to give the

Fascist salute. Now even to talk about it seems absurd. But it's true; the letters we wrote to one another, the ending was always: Fascist greetings; [the date,] year eleven, year twelve, of the Fascist Era.

In letters home from Regina Coeli and from prison camp in Germany, Enrica Filippini Lera "describes herself as a young woman from a good family, raised according to the life style that was desirable then for daughters: a dabbling of culture expendable in polite parlor conversation; music lessons, mostly piano, sometimes violin; water colors, drawing, embroidery . . ."[14] "I played the piano, my sister played the harp; I studied the harp for five years, I even played in those concerts, 'Forty harps at the Teatro Quirino . . .'" (Carla Capponi).

Carlo Lizzani, later a major filmmaker, recalls "a long-haired, romantic-looking, pale young man who was interested in poetry, whose name was Mario Fiorentini. I would never have suspected then that he would turn into a warrior, into one of the most daring members of the GAP in Rome."[15] What was it that turned these well-finished young ladies and these romantic young men into armed partisans and warriors, that drove Carla Capponi from the harp to the gun, Enrica Filippini Lera from her piano to a concentration camp, Mario Fiorentini from poetry to armed struggle?

Of course, family background counts: Marisa Musu's mother was an active anti-Fascist, Carla Capponi's "was a follower of Maria Montessori, a feminist, highly emancipated. I'm almost entirely self-taught, because after they expelled the Jews practically I no longer went to school, and I was taught by my dad and mom" (Carla Capponi). Both joined the GAP that acted in via Rasella.

Many former partisans also recall anti-Fascist teachers: Maria Michetti mentions, among others, her Latin teacher, "Don Primo Vannutelli, who we all knew was an anti-Fascist, an incredible, extraordinary character," and Raffaele Persichetti, who would die a hero at San Paolo on September 8, 1943, "who is younger, just over twenty, when he comes to teach us . . ." "I have a photograph of my tenth grade class in the courtyard of the *liceo* Visconti, and you can recognize half the Party in it" (Carla Capponi). From the *liceo* Visconti, one of the top classical high schools of Rome, came future partisans and GAP members such as Carla Capponi, Laura Garroni, Giulio Cortini, and influential leaders of the Communist Left. On the wall by the main staircase, today, a Latin inscription composed by the anti-Fascist teacher and priest, Don Primo Vannutelli, commemorates a former student, Romualdo Chiesa, killed at the Fosse Ardeatine.

Mostly young people learned from each other—from classmates, from older brothers and cousins, neighbors, friends. Many future partisans came from the *licei,* the most academically demanding and prestigious public schools, as students (like future GAP members Rosario Bentivegna and Pasquale Balsamo) or teachers, like Pilo Albertelli and Gioacchino Gesmundo, both killed at the Fosse Ardeatine.

It makes sense then that the inscription for Romualdo Chiesa, one of the eight Roman students killed at the Fosse Ardeatine, should be in Latin. The classical tradition and the humanistic culture that Fascism used for its imperial propaganda would reappear on the walls of the Nazi prison at via Tasso, as a tool of resistance in the most extreme and literal sense of the word. Many of the graffiti left by the tortured and the killed are Latin or Greek phrases and classical quotes. For many of these young people, the rejection of Fascism began with aesthetics. "Fascism was despicable. Fascism was the phony voices of radio speakers, and then you opened the paper and the news was phony, the words were phony. That was Fascism" (Peter Tompkins).

Giovanna Rossi. For us it was a point of pride not to wear the uniform, to avoid physical education, and to scorn all that was physical appearance, buxomness. We didn't like all this exhibitionism, we dressed not just chaste, but plain ugly. On the one hand, we were sexually inhibited, with the sexual inhibitions we had learned at home; on the other, we were critical toward Fascism, because the Fascist propaganda toward women was so pervasive, it was so cruel it was frightening, especially against young women. The way they extolled the body, the woman's availability, the woman's beauty.

Before the war, Rome was a lively city from an artistic and cultural point of view, and the world of art and of intellectual pursuits became a breeding ground for dissent. The Fascist regime had found it expedient to give some leeway to youthful ferments, giving dissenters the impression that Fascism could be reformed from within. The filmmaker and partisan Carlo Lizzani recalls that "we discovered one another precisely by writing for *Roma Fascista* and spitting venom on the so-called 'white telephones' rhetoric" of Fascist cinema aesthetics. Dissent also took roots in the newly established Centro Sperimentale di Cinematografia and some theater circles. Some of the greatest painters of the twentieth century, like Emilio Vedova and Giulio Turcato, helped the Resistance; major writers like Vasco Pratolini and Franco Calamandrei, and future professors like Carlo Salinari, Valentino Gerratana, Giulio Cortini, and Mario Fiorentini would join the GAP. On the other hand, teenaged Marisa Musu was stirred to heroic fantasies and to the armed struggle by Buffalo Bill comics: "I was very young and had a practical disposition . . . I was interested in action."[16]

"Intellectuals felt the need to do something, in the beginning. We had this sense of being under Fascism, the psychological oppression, before it fell on July 25 [1943]. Then, after this, the need to do, to act, to participate . . ." (Valentino Gerratana). He quotes the last letter of Giaime Pintor, a hero of the Resistance:

"War has physically diverted men from their accustomed habits; it has forced them to acknowledge with their hands and with their eyes the dangers that threaten the assumptions of individual life; it has persuaded them that there is no salvation in neutrality and isolation . . . But for the war, I would have been an intellectual with mainly literary concerns. . . ."[17]

"Acknowledge with their hands:" to close the book and the piano, to take up a weapon. In her autobiography, Marisa Musu remembers Bertolt Brecht: "We / who wanted to create a ground for gentleness—we were not allowed to be gentle."[18]

4. Concentration Camps:
Gordiani, Val Melaina, Primavalle . . .

Goffredo Cappelletti. I lived at Donna Olimpia. They built these big projects, the [so-called] skyscrapers, and in my way of thinking these projects were not conceived in order to give a home to working people. They were conceived in order to concentrate the people who were adverse to Fascism in strategic places, where they could be controlled easily. This is my opinion. Because my father owned his own house [near] the Coliseum, where I was born, and practically he was expelled when they were making via dell'Impero in '30, and they gave him a place in these projects. Donna Olimpia was a hole, surrounded by three hills. The Germans, at the time of the Germans, dominated the skyscrapers with three machine guns, you see? They placed three machine guns on top of the three hills, and that gave an idea of what Fascism had done, and how.

After World War I, "bourgeois Rome drifts father and farther away from popular Rome." Until then, the classes had lived next to each other; slums and shanties vegetated within the recent middle-class neighborhoods with which they exchanged jobs and services.[19] This became incompatible with Mussolini's design of Rome as a monumental capital: "hygiene and decorum" commanded not so much the cleaning and sanitation of the slums as the removal of their inhabitants away from social, sanitary, and visual contact and contamination. As Fascism made way for the new imperial and ceremonial boulevards (via dell'Impero, from the Coliseum to the Capitol; via della Conciliazione, from the Tiber to Saint Peter's), the proletariat expelled from the gutted neighborhoods in the ancient center of Rome was deported to the so-called *borgate* (the closest English equivalent would be "hamlets"; the correct definition is "slums") at the margins of the city, where it mingled with the labor force expelled from the rural South.

The city government announced in 1931 that the *borgate* would be "invisible from the main thoroughfares" and yet be "under the surveillance" of *carabinieri* and Fascist militia. "Borgata Gordiani looked like a concentration camp with no guards," says Augusto Moltoni, a house painter who lived there until the 1960s: "Life in a *borgata* was worse" than concentration camp, says Angelo Fileni, who experienced both, "because in the camps we had one bed per person, and it was all men or all women; but where we lived, in a four-by-four meter room, slept eight, nine, people, and sometimes ten."[20]

Carla Capponi. I slept at Gordiani, which was the worst *borgata* of all. It was made up of shanties, with four families in each—wide open, I mean, and in the entrance space you could see beds lying on the ground, perhaps on boards, or nothing, on packed earth or concrete, and there they would lay mattresses and the children all heaped on top. By day they would roll it up, put it up, and when you went to lie down in them the beds seemed wet—they smoked, in the winter; I remember January, February, I only spent one night—and the bedbugs . . .

The transfer from the historic neighborhood to the new slums in the periphery was often traumatic. "Many held out, but not for long; they resisted because [they] had roots that were historical by then. There were families, generations. They cleaned it up: the ones that Fascism didn't like, they would get them and kick them out, they'd send them to Primavalle, in those crumbling little old houses" (Franco Bartolini). "I still remember when the trucks came, with the Fascists who loaded us up with those few rags we had; my mother screaming and us kids, on the trucks, thought it was a holiday. It was a long journey that seemed endless. They made us get off at a place that was a few scattered little buildings and mud all over. They said the name of the place was Primavalle" (Augusto Moltoni).[21]

———————————

At the end of the 1930s, Iva Manieri, her husband, and her nine children were moved from Trastevere to a huge housing project on the other side of town, in Val Melaina, "a fortress isolated in the fields. A huge eight-floor building, with no less than fifteen staircases facing the internal courtyard."[22] "This was a waste land, Val Melaina; it was only a square building with five hundred families. Then, during the war they made other buildings behind Val Melaina, but it was a place of hunger and poverty. In that building, people didn't lock their doors when they went out—not because there were no thieves, but because if they came in, what was here to steal? There was nothing in the house!" (Fulvio Piasco). After the war, this enormous building would become the heart of a working-class neighborhood, and receive a new, proud name: "Stalingrad." Next to its gates, a plaque commemorates Antonio Pistonesi and Renzo Piasco, who lived there until they were betrayed by an informer, arrested, and killed at the Fosse Ardeatine.

The *borgate* gave the Roman Resistance its mass popular base. The first armed confrontation took place in October of 1943 in Pietralata. Another *borgata,* Quadraro, would be the scene of the last mass deportation, in April of 1944. In the square at Torpignattara, a plaque commemorates thirteen men from the neighborhood who were killed at the Fosse Ardeatine; another, as one enters Quadraro, lists five more. The spirit of the *borgate,* a class aware-ness and identity often elementary but always intransigent, was best repre-sented by Bandiera Rossa. "All the periphery: Torpignattara, Quadraro, all the periphery of Rome, because that's where the fighting comrades were. [Immi-grants], poor folks, common people, people who barely eked out a living. Poverty was so thick you could cut it with a knife, and this is why so many joined our ranks" (Orfeo Mucci).

Two areas along the via Casilina (the strategic road that goes to Cassino, where the front was) were renamed "people's republic of Torpignattara and Cer-tosa": here, for most of February of 1944, Nazis would not dare come in, and the partisans acted openly. Uccio Pisino, later killed at the Fosse Ardeatine, trained partisans in the use of weapons openly in the square. Rosario Bentivegna recalls that "the Germans held Torpignattara, but in Centocelle they vanished completely, for about a month we had the run of Centocelle. The curfew was abolished, in the evenings we'd meet in the *osteria,* eat, drink, give the raised fist salute, the comrades would come in with red shirts or red handkerchiefs on. The police had placed themselves at our orders. This went on for twenty days or so, until the landing at Anzio failed; then the Germans raided the area and practi-cally they killed us twenty five comrades and deported others to Germany. [The GAP organizer] Valerio Fiorentini was caught, along with other comrades who later ended up at the Fosse Ardeatine."

The partisan hegemony in the *borgate* allowed them not only to keep the Nazis out but also to feed the population. Orfeo Mucci recalls that when the partisans began to organize raids to the bakeries for bread and flour, the local police chief would leave them an open field by deploying his men someplace else. "The women would go to the bakery, the baker was informed, he stepped aside and let them loot: flour, bread, everything. These women would take bread and all they could take. Afterwards, he'd go to the police and report it. The police chief would receive his report, pass it on, and the baker would get his flour back. Imagine that at Torpignattara [the partisans] went to a stable, where they had mules, pigs, sheep, they confiscated it all, and walked it down the street to Torpignattara. They gave the owners a voucher, and after the war they were reimbursed."

The anger of the *borgate* had other expressions, generated by the living conditions and by the awareness of violence and injustice, but more ambiguously oriented. I have been told that one of the Quadraro men killed at the Fosse Ardeatine was not a political prisoner but had been arrested for stealing copper wire from the telephone lines. Cutting lines, however, was a typical partisan activity: in times of hunger, where does theft end and sabotage begin?

The most dramatic incarnation of the oscillation between rebellion and unruliness, subversion and crime, is the myth of Giuseppe Albani, the "Hunchback of Quarticciolo," the leader of a gang "always on the edge between anti-Fascist struggle and common crime." "The Hunchback would go and steal stuff from the rich and give it away . . . to whores, and he helped people in need, that's all" (Fiorino Fiorini). He was killed by the police in obscure circumstances after the war, but he is remembered by many as a mythic "social bandit."

The killing of three Germans attributed to the Hunchback unleashed another dramatic German attack on the civilian population: the deportation of eight hundred men from Quadraro on April 17, 1944, led by the same Herbert Kappler who had directed the massacre at the Fosse Ardeatine a few weeks earlier. For the Germans, this was an effort to normalize a rebel neighborhood, a "nest of wasps" where partisans and rebels "disappeared" into hiding, and to round up a number of able-bodied men for work in Germany or at the front.[23]

Vanda Prosperi. In the morning, around seven, we heard banging at the door. It was Monday morning, April 17. We open the door, and there were two Germans and two SS. "Where husband? Men, where men?" We followed after my mother, holding onto her dress, we saw a truck, and the men loaded on it, and all the women screaming, shouting, and the Germans pointing their machine guns to keep them off. The parish priest came forward. He said, I offer myself in exchange for . . . you can't kill all these people, you can't condemn a whole population for [the actions of] one person, or two. But they weren't satisfied with the parson, and carried off more than eight hundred men, and took them to Germany . . . When he left, my father's hair was black; he came back and he was white, bald and white from fear. And this is the whole story.

5. A Street in the Center: Via Rasella

Bruno Frasca. The day they came here to film *Dieci italiani per un tedesco* ["Ten Italians for One German," a 1951 film on the Fosse Ardeatine], they filmed it here in via Rasella, and [my mother] came out just as they were doing the scene with the Germans lying on the ground, with red paint . . . Who knows what her mind brought up—she began to [scream], I had to carry her off . . . She had been reminded of something; she had lived that tragedy all over again.

In the center of the city, parallel to the elegant via del Tritone, runs a narrow street that goes downhill on the side of the Quirinale hill, then the king's and now the president's residence. From a family that lived there two centuries ago, it took its name: via Rasella.

Luigi Catemario. We must go back to the middle of the 1500s, when the street didn't exist; it was only a path, on this pleasant hill, the Quirinale hill, it was all orchards and vineyards. Cardinal Grimani, very powerful then, had purchased these orchards. This cardinal had begun to increase his vineyards, and as he did this he discovered some Roman remains that still exist, from baths of the time, I think, of [Emperor] Antoninus Pius. On top of these Roman baths, he erected the building we see [Palazzo Tittoni]. At first, it was just a little *vignola* [a country house with a vineyard]: just two floors, without the wings, that were built in the sixteen hundreds.

"The street: a popular neighborhood, all the children playing in the street, and I did it too. We all knew one another: my godmother lived across the street, and all the relatives, we lived right in via Rasella, we all knew one another" (Silvio Gigliozzi). "Via Rasella has always been the same: the buildings are the same, the historic center you can't change anything, so the houses are the same, maybe they've been repainted, the old shops are changed and gone. We redid the front of our building, but they made us leave the marks of the bomb" (Bruno Frasca).

The signs of the war are still visible in via Rasella. About halfway down its length, at the corner of via del Boccaccio, a short street that connects it to via del Tritone, the front and side of the building where Guido Volponi lived and was taken by the SS still bear the holes of the bullets fired at the windows by the Germans terrorized by the explosion. "Our building was all holes, and there are a few holes left still; then when we redid the front I guess they took off some of the holes but the arts commission required us to leave them, as they did with the ones down at the crossing" (Bruno Frasca). "Here at home, we have things that remind us: if you look, the casings of the doors are split in two, they were left like that by the explosion. For years, the decorations of the wall were peppered with slivers from the panes that had exploded. You can feel people walking in the next room because [the floor] was damaged" (Luigi Catemario).

"At the time I was ten years old. We ran a bar in via Rasella, which is still there, on the corner, a family-owned bar. My father then worked for the ministry of agriculture; he was thirty-five" (Silvio Gigliozzi). In Romolo Gigliozzi's coffee and dairy bar, with the sign "Ice for sale" and two entrances on the corner of via

Rasella and via del Boccaccio, on March 23, 1944, the day of the attack, three partisans of Bandiera Rossa were meeting to plan an act of sabotage. According to the historian and Bandiera Rossa apologist Roberto Gremmo, they chose to meet there because the bar belonged to "a socialist, Romolo Gigliozzi, who had some rooms in the back where (thanks to the owner's political leanings) anti-Fascists could meet." Romolo Gigliozzi's son and daughter proudly insist that their father was completely apolitical. Perhaps, being children, they were not aware of his politics. In any case, they have chosen to cherish the memory of their father as a mere unwitting victim of events.[24]

Liana Gigliozzi. I remember the house perfectly; I remember the bar, I remember it very well, perfectly. I tell you, I can still smell the bar, because we had a cellar underneath and the smell came up from the cellar, I can still smell that cellar . . . This has stayed with me. Also: our apartment on the first floor, with floors that shook when you walked on them, they weren't too firm—it was a brick floor and I remember that when you walked it shook, I can still feel it. Then the memory of the shutters ajar and the sounds from the street—cars . . . people . . . the fountain. . . . There was this drinking fountain where we children played, near the bar, we played with water all the time. . . . Yes, I remember perfectly these things; and then, of course, the bar and the possibility we had to eat candy, pastries, just go and take them.

Bruno Frasca. Here in via Rasella there are very few left [of the old residents]. We own this house; my mother owned the laundry store; many German soldiers came to have their laundry done there, so they knew my mother, my father, my aunts who also worked there. But those who were renting have left. One was Mrs. [Adalgisa] Pignotti, who I think has three at the Fosse Ardeatine: her husband, her brother-in-law, and her cousin, I guess—[Fulvio] Mastrangeli. Which mama always told me that this lady had married the same day as my mother, they were widowed the same day because both husbands died, and they even lived in the same house because before my mother it was Mrs. Pignotti who lived here . . . what a destiny . . . now she's dead, too . . . but as for other families, I am in touch with the relatives of those who lived in via Rasella, who by now are all dead. . . . For instance, there was [Romolo] Gigliozzi, who owned the bar down here; if you look out the window, I can show you. There was Miss Chiesa, who was my schoolteacher, and she, too, had a brother [Romualdo Chiesa] at the Fosse Ardeatine; when I see her, we talk about it. There are so few left, we always try to go [to the commemorations] . . .

"They could have done a more intelligent action elsewhere, perhaps out in the country: it was a rather unfortunate massacre, from the point of view of the local people" (Vera Yaria). Via Rasella is one of those old streets of Rome where the lower classes felt protected by the nearness of the palaces of the mighty: in this case, the shadow of the Quirinale, looming over their homes and shops. Although an armed German platoon walked its length every day, they thought that the war concerned other parts of Rome, not them. "We felt safe; because [the German roundups] weren't done here, in the back of the Quirinale, but a little further down, further away. But via Rasella was perhaps the safest place. [The air raids] were done on San Lorenzo, away from the Quirinale. When the alarm sounded, everyone ran to the tunnel [at the bottom of the hill], because we were beneath the Quirinale and were sure it would be spared. Via Rasella is parallel to the royal palace, so that area, like the Vatican, couldn't be bombed. So what was the point of coming here to do this job, to explode this bomb?" (Vincenza Gatti).

Another narrow street of old Rome, via degli Avignonesi, runs parallel to via Rasella. During the war, Piero Zuccheretti, eleven years old, worked as an apprentice in his uncles' optics store there. "He was such a lively child, and my father said, 'I can't control him: keep him for a while, give him something to do. . . .' My uncle was a bachelor, so practically my brother was his heir, so he put him there to work. And then it happened . . ." On March 23, 1944, Piero Zuccheretti, on his way to work, turned the corner of via del Boccaccio into via Rasella, and was blown to pieces by the explosion of the bomb. "[My father said] if I hadn't put him to work there, he wouldn't have died . . ." (Giovanni Zuccheretti).

Teresa Mussoni. *[Valle Aurelia] was like a village, they all knew one another, they clung, how can I explain . . .We [children] were not supposed to go to number eleven because they were all petty criminals and our parents told us, "when you go by there, for goodness' sake, don't listen to anybody . . ." It still exists, it's all there still, but it's been abandoned. All the people in those little shacks were petty criminals, good-hearted criminals, they would do anything for each other.*

The women worked, they worked for the rich folks, or they worked for the military, for the carabinieri: they sewed pants, uniforms. They worked at home, or they had a little stand in the market and a piece of orchard, raised everything in it and took it to Trionfale to sell at the market on a horse and cart.

Then the taverns, it was full of taverns. Some of the men beat their wives, it was known that this person beat his wife or that he was, how shall I say, mean to the children . . . For some, it was because of the poverty, having so many children . . . there was no shortage of children, I mean. Some cheated on their husbands, so on November 11 [the "cuckolds' holiday"] we'd go around with a clay head on a broomstick and we'd stick two horns in it, and beat drums, pots, and sing verses and all. That sort of things, and even if some family were some kind of rascals, yet we were all united.

My father was a brick maker, he was a kind of guard at the kilns. We had our own house, we kept chickens. As for me, I think I had a wonderful adolescence. I had a dad who—I didn't know it then, I guess—was the best of all, because the men there went to the tavern, they drank, they became a bit evil, maybe it was also the hard work they did, because back then they had what they call the cartmen, who carried bricks on a handcart, and they put them in the fire at the kiln and you had to be there at two A.M., work all night, with the heat . . . they became mean, they hardened. But my dad didn't. I remember we were five children, three boys and two girls, and my dad was always singing; when he came home from work, though he was tired, he didn't beat us, he was always cheerful. Because in those days the father figure was not like today: it was something to be afraid of. It was mother, instead, who was always stern, in fact when I was little I called her the she-lion because she had this big mane of hair and when she was in the kitchen she never laughed, she was always stern. She worked very hard, that's a fact. So, I've given you a perspective of what it was like in Valle Aurelia.

Then, when I was a little more grown, the war started coming and things were a little harder because the boys began to leave and be called to arms, and then we were in the middle of the war. Valle Aurelia wasn't bombed, but before the Fosse Ardeatine and the arrival of the Americans it went through a partisan period for a while. When Fascism fell, for some reason they stationed some soldiers at the kilns. [After the armistice on] September 8, the Italian army practically fell apart, all these soldiers were trying to get away, so some gave them clothes, something to wear; as they ran away, they left everything, even their weapons. And so the mothers would go and get the blankets, the pots, and the boys instead went for the guns. And they would bury them and wait for the time to come.

Among these boys, my brother also got involved; but dad realized that they were having these meetings beneath the kilns, conspiring, so he said, you all'd better leave. [My father was from San Marino, an independent state;] San Marino sent a proclamation that they would take in all who came back, feed and board us and all; so dad went to the consul of San Marino and said I'm sending them all off because they can't stay here.

My story with this boy, Alberto Cozzi, was a little story . . . I was, I think, fifteen; we liked each other, mostly we'd see each other in church, those groups of the Azione Cattolica, "I like this one . . . I like that one . . ." We had these children's sort of stories. When I had to leave . . . I remember vaguely that we were sitting together, "I have to leave, but I'll come back," things that children say, and we promised each other that we'd meet again. Afterwards, he spoke to my brother, and my brother told him: "This is not the time for that sort of thing, my sister is going away, we must stay here." So we said to each other, "When it's all over we'll meet again, we'll talk about it then, for now let's leave things as they are." Also, back then—you did as you were told. So mom and I leave with my other brothers, and they stayed here. We had exchanged photographs—"I'll wait for you," like that.

Then it happened that this boy got involved with the partisans. He was about eighteen or nineteen; he wanted to do something, like so many others. There was this friend of theirs who lived in the neighborhood and whose family they knew well (I won't say the name, he's out of jail and is doing all right, so I won't even speak his name) who was with them but then he'd go and inform on them. They planned some action, passing out some leaflets; when he came to where he was supposed to deliver his message, instead of his friend he found the Germans and they arrested him.

Then he was tried, and I've been told that he almost laughed the whole thing off, because the Americans were getting near to Rome. They sentenced him to I don't know how many years, but he laughed because he said, "I'll be out of here soon, the Americans are coming . . ." Instead, unfortunately, the Americans were held back, this smart guy [Bentivegna] put that bomb in the middle of thirty-three Germans, they made a selection in Regina Coeli and he paid the price— this is the story of this boy. When I returned to Rome I heard about it. And then, with this boy's mother, I said, "I'd like to see what's left." We went to this cave and there were things in it still, for goodness' sake, I could still see hair sticking . . . it hurt me. Then I got my picture back. He had it on him when he was in jail, and had given it to a priest who returned all his things to his mother—and a letter that I had written when I was away and [I thought] it had never reached him.

After that, we heard of other boys, friends of my brother, who we knew in the neighborhood, one of them lived by the brick works, and another in that notorious number eleven, who were executed [at the Fosse Ardeatine]. One of them was named Paroli, the other Casadei. So this is my personal tale.

. . . Pasquale Cocco, Saverio Coen, Giorgio Conti, Giuseppe Cordero Lanza di Montezemolo, Orazio Corsi, Guido Costanzi, Alberto Cozzi, Cosimo D'Amico, Giuseppe D'Amico, Mario D'Andrea, Arturo D'Aspro, Gerardo De Angelis, Ugo De Carolis, Carlo De Giorgio, Filippo De Grenet, Odoardo Della Torre, Giuseppe Del Monte, Raoul De Marchi . . .

CHAPTER 4

ACTS OF WAR

... Gastone De Nicolò, Fidardo De Simoni, Zaccaria Di Capua, Angelo Di Castro, Cesare Di Consiglio, Franco Di Consiglio, Marco Di Consiglio, Mosè Di Consiglio, Salomone Di Consiglio, Santoro Di Consiglio, Alberto Di Nepi, Giorgio Di Nepi, Samuele Di Nepi, Ugo Di Nola, Pier Domenico Diociajuti, Otello Di Peppe ...

Ada Pignotti. *Then, after that, they took them away, lined them up against the wall of Palazzo Barberini [in via Quattro Fontane], with their hands up—and kept them there.*

We couldn't see a thing because we were inside, in the house. We were on the ground floor, but they wouldn't let us open the windows. After a while, they came back, and took us away, too. So when we came out of the house, my brother-in-law's house, we walked along where they were standing, like that, with their hands in the air right against Palazzo Barberini, which there is a photograph, you've seen it . . . We, [they] made us come out—mistreated, no respect, for the children, for us—I mean, we were young then, but after all we were women, too, weren't we? We walked by [the men lined up against the wall]. So they saw us, that they were taking us away, too.

[The Germans] put us in a big room, all together, the women, the children, all in there. They kept us locked in there all night. No water, we had the children with us, nothing, not a drop of milk, nothing, nothing. All night we stayed there crying, screaming; we were locked in and couldn't even look out the window. After a while—actually quite a while, it was night already, they took [the men] away, to the Ministry of the Interior. And they put them all there together. During the night, around two a.m. or so, they came with these lists, and started calling the ones they wanted . . . to kill, actually. And my husband was the first to be called.

1. Race Laws

The Jews, they sure were persecuted, poor Christs.

—*Virginia Calanca*

Ester Fano. My father never was an active anti-Fascist—indeed, probably as late as '38 he was pro-Fascist. He was very conservative, he loved uniforms, the army—I have a picture of him in his uniform, another on horseback, he loved riding horses. He was a handsome 36-year old man, good-natured and, I think, charming . . .

Claudio Fano. He was very proud of being the first in the family to graduate from the university, to have a degree and, as was also very common among Jews of the time, of being able to serve in the army and being an officer. When the race laws came, they were supposed to give up their weapons; my father, as an officer, had a pistol; and a sword. And, as he went to give up his sword, he broke it in two, as did others, because an officer does not give up his sword.

In July 1938, a *Manifesto of Racist Scientists* proclaimed: "The time has come for Italians to frankly proclaim themselves racists." On November 17, 1938, the government issued the "Provisions for the Defense of the Italian Race": mixed marriages were forbidden, Jews were barred from a whole range of social and economic activities. From then on, prohibitions kept piling up, increasingly detailed, diverse and stringent. In 1943, the "Verona Charter," the constitution of Mussolini's Repubblica Sociale Italiana, declared that "The members of the Jewish race are foreigners; for the duration of the war, they belong to an enemy nationality."[1]

"In Italy we were all well integrated—not assimilated; it's different, it's completely different. One didn't think it could happen here" (Silvana Ajò Cagli). "Bourgeois family, perfectly integrated, perfectly assimilated—I thought I was a person like all the others; when they tell you no, you're another race, an inferior race, it's no small shock, I mean" (Maria Zevi). The emancipation of Italian Jews had taken place along with the process of national unity; many Jews, like other Italians, supported Fascism both for class reasons and because they saw it as a continuation of the Risorgimento.[2] "Fascists and anti-Fascists among the Jews were in the same percentages as the rest of Italians," says Claudio Fano, former president of Rome's Jewish Community: "Many had chosen careers working for the State as a form of emancipation. So it was that sort of petty bourgeoisie and middle class among which Fascism had made quite an impression, had got quite a hold." "In the first Mussolini cabinet, the underminister for the Interior was a Jew, Aldo Finzi"; he ended his life at the Fosse Ardeatine.[3]

"Yes, I remember that filthy rags like *Difesa della razza, Tevere,* already circulated a few years before the race laws—so my father was very, very much worried"; however, "We were citizens like all the others, we absolutely did not expect a thing like that" (Piero Terracina). The memories of the world before the race laws are stories of normality, familiarity, warmth: "In the ghetto—beautiful, look, beautiful. There was something in the ghetto that has always been there, it was the warmth. It was the warmth of the families, nearly all poor—a few were doing all right, but they didn't rub it in, it was a healthy, healthy community" (Settimia Spizzichino).

Suddenly, these normal people found themselves turned into second-class citizens: they were not allowed to serve in the armed forces, to be tutors of underage children, to own or manage businesses with more than a hundred employees or of military significance, to own land or buildings beyond certain sizes, to work in government, in government-connected or public agencies, banks, insurance, to own a radio, to be listed in the phone book. Fascist papers carried cartoons "with the ugly, hook-nosed, curly, nappy-haired, Negroid Jew" (Giulia Spizzichino), audiences cheered anti-Semitic movies like Veit Harlan's *Suss the Jew* (1940) .

The prohibitions grow increasingly exacting, detailed, and absurd. Jews cannot own radios, cannot raise homing pigeons; they were even barred from their traditional rag-and-bone trade. "The race laws were very tough, even though many ignored and violated them, individually. There were also administrative regulations—you couldn't have an Aryan maid, your name was taken off the phone book. People saved the '38 phone books to look up numbers" (Claudio Fano). "We were forbidden to go to [the beach at] Ostia. In our family, my mother sometimes used Jewish-Roman dialect words, so once she told me, 'go *resciud*,' which means be careful in Jewish-Roman, don't be recognized, because we're not supposed to be in Ostia—'don't make *davare*,' it means don't say a word" (Valeria Spizzichino).

Piero Terracina's father, a salesman, lost his most important account; Claudio Fano's father, a business consultant, tried to keep working in the back of some friends' office, but it didn't work out. The principal of Giulia Spizzichino's school summoned her mother: "Look, madam, unfortunately we have received an order from the Party that your daughter can no longer remain among Christian children."

Piero Terracina. I was literally put out of school—like this, and I was fully aware that I was a normal boy who took school seriously. It was a trauma, because my first thought was of what could I ever achieve in life if I couldn't get an education. Then, however, they organized the Jewish school—I had just started in the fifth grade, and I went to the Jewish school right away, so practically I didn't miss anything. I went to the Jewish school and basically I fit in right away.

Claudio Fano. Looking back, there was a discovery of identity, but it was also a moment of truth. Because some thought that with a quick conversion they could be spared and save themselves. This in itself gives a sense of dignity to those who didn't do any such thing—when it would have been easy, perhaps with a mental reserve, to get baptized . . . This is something that history has taught us to expect, that there are times when you must reaffirm your true identity. [I'm talking] about those Jews, and they are the majority, educated and uneducated, who in the time of persecution, when it might have seemed that by getting baptized retroactively, you could escape, they said no. That was a test of dignity. All right: my father was not active in the Resistance; [but] he had made his choice; I admit, he didn't have any other, but in '38 he had made his choice.

"I had never known any Jews, because in Sicily there aren't any, since 1492, when the Spanish eliminated them or kicked them out. So I didn't even know what the Jews were, and many of my friends were Jews, many girls were Jews . . . When anti-Semitism came, to me it was a very serious blow—but I'm talking about anti-Semitism in Germany, not even in Italy yet. And my first interest in politics began from the awareness of anti-Semitism in Germany" (Aldo Natoli). "There were reasons [for dissenting from Fascism], but, mainly, the basic reason was the action against the Jews. I saw that my Jewish friends were expelled from school" (Maria Teresa Regard). "In '37, when the campaign for the race laws begins, that is the moment in which I take sides and become firmly anti-Fascist; I was fifteen, maybe sixteen" (Rosario Bentivegna). Mario Fiorentini, whose Jewish father had lost all connections to the Jewish world, was so enraged that he went to the head rabbi of Rome and asked to convert: "'I would like to become a Jew out of solidarity with Jews, all right?' Now listen. He—very tactful, very subtle—didn't answer right away; then he began: 'Listen, tell me—have you been circumcised?' And I laughed: 'No!' I mean, I had to be circumcised, at twenty-two, it isn't such a cheerful prospect" (Mario Fiorentini). Fiorentini did not convert, but this did not keep the SS from arresting his parents (who managed to escape). Some time later, when he first saw the platoon march in via Rasella, he recognized "the same rotten-green uniforms" of those who had come to take his parents away and thought that something should be done.

2. Africa, Spain, Russia . . .

Cinque guerre cià dato re Vittorio più vent'anni de fascio obbligato- rio . . .	Five wars is what we got from King Vittorio And twenty years of obligatory Fascism . . .

—Domenico Savi[4]

In October 1934, on the eve of a great air show meant to publicize Italy's air power, General Sabato Martelli Castaldi, a World War I hero and an aviation ace, wrote to Mussolini that the Italian air force was no more than an array of old and ill-equipped crafts: "The nation's future is at stake," he writes; "Duce, what is needed here is some tough stick blows of the kind you alone can give." The blows arrived promptly: a few days later, Martelli Castaldi was discharged temporarily "for lack of military qualities and character." The next year, the discharge became permanent and without pay.[5]

We will run into him again: at Porta San Paolo, in the defense of Rome; in the military underground Front, with the battle name of "partigiano Tevere"; arrested and tortured at via Tasso; at the Fosse Ardeatine, where he will meet his death. One doesn't explain such an itinerary by personal resentment alone. Rather, Sabato Martelli Castaldi realized, at the peak of the regime's popularity, that Fascism was deceiving the Italian people. Perhaps, more than the defeat in the war, what opened the eyes of so many late but no less authentic anti-Fascists was the realization that they had been drawn to it by an irresponsible lie. General Dardano Fenulli wrote: "One does not lie to a people who bear with total understanding all the sacrifices of a war . . . leading them to believe in a superiority of means and in successes that do not exist." He, too, was killed at the Fosse Ardeatine.[6]

The Capecci family had six sons in the war, scattered between Russia, Italy, Yugoslavia. Two would be killed at Forte Bravetta and the Fosse Ardeatine. Aldo Eluisi's mother said that all of her four sons were in the war: two in Russia, and two in the Resistance.

Bruno Eluisi. I left [for Russia] on July 11 of '41. I caught my first snowstorm in October of '41; and we didn't have anything. Later, we were given winter clothing. For a rifle company of one hundred and fifty-three, fifty four people, we were given six fur-collar coats—of course, who got the coats? The officers—no way they would leave them to the soldiers, is there? Then, for the rifle company, they gave us fifty-three condoms . . . All the mules died on the road, they couldn't stand the cold.

"I think the military were perfectly aware of the how unprepared the Italian army, the armed forces, were to face this war; so, yes, they obeyed. They went to war because it was their duty to go, but they were aware of this" (Adriana Montezemolo). "My father had been to America when he was young and he had seen the planes that came out of these *factories* [in English], these plants—one every five minutes, the planes, one car every three minutes; so he had seen the efficiency of America, and when he saw that America entered the war and Mussolini said 'America can't hurt us' dad could already see all these boys dead, killed by irresponsibility. When the news came that his son had been killed in the desert battle of El Alamein, General Simoni said, 'I don't resent so much the hand of the New Zealander who fired against my son, as much as those who sent him without arms, without water, into the desert.'" (Vera Simoni).

Bruno Eluisi. So, when we marched forward, you lay perhaps for a whole day with your belly on the ground on the ice; then when you took these little towns all you found was old people and children and women—and maybe machine guns under the beds, you see? And then—these things, it wasn't only the Germans that did it, we did it too, I admit. You got there, you found the old man and two women—you took the old man and killed him. On the other hand, this is the way it is: at the end of a day with your belly on the snow, you get there, you kill and go.

The Italian military tribunal that tried Herbert Kappler did not find that massacres of civilians in retaliation were, per se, war crimes: its own army had perpetrated its share. In Ethiopia, after a failed attempt on the life of the Italian commander General Graziani, the Italians executed and otherwise caused the death of over a thousand monks of the Debrà Libanòs monastery and civilians in the space of a few days.[7] In December 1941, after a partisan attack on the Italian occupying troops in Yugoslavia, the mountain village of Plevlje in Montenegro "was destroyed and burned, the men were killed on the spot, the houses burned, the provisions scattered." After the massacre, "women, almost crazed, roamed and cried among the smoking ruins of their homes."[8] Carla Capponi recalls that Luciano Lusana, an army officer who fought in Africa and was later tortured and killed at via Tasso, told his young comrades about the Italian atrocities in Ethiopia, to teach them that Fascism was as much of an enemy as Nazism. Much of this memory, however, has been lost to the myth of the "good-hearted Italians" and the stereotype of the exclusive, intrinsic ferocity of the Germans.

Many good and kind-hearted Italians went to Ethiopia, during and after the colonial war. Some may have been attracted by the mirage of empire, but most were drawn by need. Celestino Frasca went to work on the streets and sidewalks of Addis Ababa; Cesare Tedesco also went, as did Romolo Gigliozzi: "When he left he was full of enthusiasm, because he said, when I come back, they'll give me the Fascist party card, I can get a job; in fact, he was hired as a clerk in the Ministry of Agriculture" (Silvio Gigliozzi).

Dardano Fenulli distinguished himself in the war against the "havens of resistance" to Italian colonization in Libya as early as 1912 or 1914, and earned a silver medal in Ethiopia.[9] Nicola Ugo Stame, opera singer and air force officer, fought in Ethiopia and in Spain. There, on the opposite side, was Vittorio Mallozzi, the Communist brick maker from Valle Aurelia. They all died, on the same side, in Rome, at Forte Bravetta and at the Fosse Ardeatine.[10]

"The day war was declared for me was a tragedy. The day Paris fell, I cried. Paris was Paris, it was the city of the French revolution, I cried like a motherless calf" (Rosario Bentivegna). The fourteen-year-old student Pasquale Balsamo was expelled from all Italy's schools for expressing doubts on the final victory of the Axis; he joined the Communist Party and the GAP unit that fought in via Rasella. In grade school, Goffredo Cappelletti wrote a paper about how Napoleon, too, had been victorious in Russia in the beginning. "They told me I was a Communist. I cried, because the word *Communist*, the way I'd been taught, I imagined I was a monster, what can I say, a criminal, a murderer. Yet, that's when it began to dawn on me. I mean, if this is what I think and they tell me I'm a Communist, what are the Communists, then?"

Vera Simoni. When my brother died, we went—mom, dad, my sister, and I—to the Holy Father to seek help, spiritual help. The pope received [us] immediately in his private study.[11] I can still see this scene like in a photograph, they hugged, my father and the Holy Father. And dad began to speak, to tell of this tragic situation; and then, I can still see the Holy Father's motion, with his hand he went like this to silence my father, and then the Holy Father, Pacelli, leaned over, unplugged the telephone on his desk, and said, "General, now you can talk," and, showing him the plug, "Here we are surrounded by spies." And then they began to talk, these two men of an equal stature, and they spoke the same language, and I remember the words of the Holy Father: "This is the evil that has come down upon the earth"—[he meant] Fascism and Nazism. The Holy Father felt for Italy's tragedy, and they were able to speak freely of everything, of this immense tragedy that they knew Italy was headed to.

3. War from the Air: San Lorenzo, July 19, 1943

The tragedy materializes in the sky of Rome on July 19, 1943, at 11:00 A.M. The city that thought it was exempt from the horrors of war found itself suddenly vulnerable. The first Allied air raid hit the working-class neighborhood of San Lorenzo. It killed between twenty-eight hundred and three thousand people and wounded over ten thousand.[12] Rosario Bentivegna, then a medical student, had just finished his shift at the university hospital, near San Lorenzo, when the alarm sounded.

Rosario Bentivegna. I ran up and we began to collect the patients and carry them to the ward in the cellars; and then the wounded, and the dead, began to arrive. Or people who died as they were carried in, and at the Policlinico [the university hospital, near

San Lorenzo] there were hundreds, and the scenes were heart rending. Each room in the Policlinico had been turned into an operating room. And those rags filled with plaster and blood, torn, piling up on the floor in layers of ooze, of blood, of dirt, of vomit, and it was a hellish thing. And we kept working that way all afternoon, all evening, we just lay down where we could to sleep on the floor for a few hours and then started again and while we slept the wounded kept coming, and it went on until the evening of the next day. And it was heartbreaking. The next evening, I was tired, exhausted; toward eight P.M., at dusk, I got my bike and started toward home. And I saw this endless line of people carrying their possessions, household goods, desperate, on carts, on any vehicle they could get hold of, children's prams, it was a—a heartbreaking thing. It was the image, the sequel of the shambles I had immersed my hands in until a quarter of an hour ago in the Policlinico, this line of desperate people who cried, who carried the few broken things they had managed to salvage from the ruins, it was—frightful."

Carla Capponi hurried to the hospital to look for her mother and stayed to help. "What struck me most was these dead from the bombs who had incredible coloring, pink skin as though they'd been painted over, they looked like puppets, because their legs, arms, were all in absurd positions, out of skelter [. . .] The orphan home in via dei Volsci had collapsed, the children were under the ruins, they said 'they're alive, you can hear them cry, you can hear screams and cries for help.'"[13]

Gianfranco Capozio. On via Tiburtina, on the bridge, I saw a horse with its legs up in the air, spurting blood, spurting blood from all over. It had been strafed. And then my father digging nearby, where you could hear, I too could hear these words—if you don't mind I'll repeat them—of a grandmother with a child, that she protected, the grandmother died and all you could hear was this child who screamed that he wanted to be brought out; my father digging, with his nails, along with the others. Digging, but they didn't make it. Beams, there were beams, I remember, iron beams, and they were stuck underneath. I still have this voice in my ears, in Roman dialect, that this child was saying—"it was the Americans, those sons of a bitches," excuse my language, OK? "It was the Americans, those sons of a bitches." This little boy. Then he died.

"I, my feelings toward the air raids in San Lorenzo were mostly apolitical, that is, of a great massacre, of a great . . . certainly not of hatred toward the Allies, the bombers, and so on. No, not hatred. I guess the immediate feeling was amazement, and horror—San Lorenzo was an open grave, a spectacle that . . . I mean, to see, not in a movie but in reality the ruins of the smoking buildings, the buildings cut in half, and so on, it's a thing that . . . (Marisa Musu). On a wall in via Casilina, the next day, someone wrote, in dialect: "Better the Americans on our heads than Mussolini on our balls."[14] The people of Rome knew who was to blame, knew that the Allied raids were the answer to the Axis' carpet bombing of England. After the raid, the pope was greeted in San Lorenzo with gratitude; but the king was rejected, and Mussolini thought best to come incognito.

However, it is not easy to ignore who it was that actually dropped the bombs. Antonello Branca, who was six then, remembered asking his father: "If they're coming to liberate us, why do they kill us?" Anti-Fascist memory has quite rightly blamed the Fascists and the Germans for the destruction of our cities; but it has skipped a passage and ignored an ambiguity that emerges between the lines of personal narratives: "They didn't care where they dropped them, they just bombed and that was all. Well, the Americans were no better than the Germans, I guess" (Rina Del Pio). Giuseppe Bolgia's mother was strafed and killed by low-flying Allied planes as she crossed the street to the shelter; his father was killed by the Nazis at the Fosse Ardeatine: "Who do I blame [for my mother]? I blame the Americans, I do: that thing, it was the Americans, not the Germans. They too did their part. And why did they bomb San Lorenzo, a popular neighborhood?"

"The bombing of San Lorenzo, of the railroad yard, it isn't true that it was a carefully aimed raid; it was a raid that was meant to terrorize," says Luciano Pizzoli, who miraculously survived the destruction of his building, two kilometers away from any military objective. The raids were aimed at railroads and war plants, but they were also intended to spread terror and anger in the population, and to send messages to the government. There is a relationship between the raid of July 19 and the fall of Fascism on July 25; between the raid of August 13 and the proclamation of the "open city" the next day; between the raid of September 8 and the signing of the armistice.

While Rome was under the bombs, Mussolini was meeting with Hitler at Feltre, in the North; Colonel Montezemolo was the interpreter.[15] The meeting was a failure; a few days later, on July 25, the Gran Consiglio, the supreme body of Fascism, voted against Mussolini's policy. It was the end of the regime. Later the same day, Mussolini was arrested by carabinieri under the command of Colonel Giovanni Frignani and Captain Raffaele Aversa. Both, like Montezemolo, would be killed at the Fosse Ardeatine.

Massimo Uffreduzzi. We expected that something would happen; many among us, in the [Fascist student organizations] changed, too, on the twenty-fifth of July. We were eighteen or so, with no direction, nothing to turn to. It wasn't that we were Fascists; it was the sight of how miserably we had ended. It was disbelief, you see . . . The fallen symbols . . . we believed, the most absurd idea, in the immortality of Fascism. The unbelief that the Fascist party, this giant, you understand, that it could fall—it was inconceivable. Truly, indeed, we were stupefied—stupefied.

"People began to shout: he's gone! He's gone! At first I thought, it may be a trap; then the phone began to ring. The next morning I was out in the streets of Rome: it was unbelievable, it was extraordinary, everybody was out in the street, speeches, leaflets, people shouting . . ." (Aldo Natoli). The symbols and signs of Fascism were destroyed and erased. Otello Leonardi, a waiter, climbed the front of his building and chiseled away the Fascist symbols; later, when the Nazis took over Rome, "he was marked, and he was easily identified. He was a partisan in Bandiera Rossa; he was arrested and tortured for over a month in via Tasso, and then executed at the Fosse Ardeatine" (Umberto Turco).

A few days after July 25, the new prime minister, General Pietro Badoglio, announced that the war would go on. On August 13, Rome was bombed again.

4. Death and Rebirth of the Homeland: Porta San Paolo, September 8, 1943

Pasquale Balsamo. Well, it was six in the morning, we came out of a meeting and stood at the corner of via XX Settembre, when we heard the sound of engines. It was the motorcade of the royal family running away. Twelve policemen on motorcycles opened the procession, then as those four black cars went by, each of us called the names of the personages they recognized—Badoglio, the king, the prince, the queen . . .

On September 8, 1943, an armistice was signed between Italy and the Allies; the next morning, the king, the government, the military command abandoned the city and their posts, leaving the army with no orders and the people with no leadership. Things fell apart. From then on, all would have to choose according to the idea they had of themselves. Many soldiers followed the example of their king: the war is over, let's go home. Others, military and civilians, felt broader and higher loyalties and a deeper pride that required them to fight a battle that was doomed from the military point of view but that was morally won by the very fact of fighting it.

Carla Capponi. The evening of the eight, from our windows, my mother and I were at the window, we saw flashes in the sky. And we heard this thunder, as it were, this rumble; and mom said, "This is no thunder: they're shooting, they're fighting . . ."

"The first shot in the defense of Rome was fired in the South zone, at 10:10 P.M. of September 8, by post number 5 in the sector manned by the First Regiment of the Sardinia Grenadiers."[16] A unit of German parachuters asked to be allowed to withdraw across a bridge; while negotiations were going on, they seized the Italian sentries and took them prisoners. The soldiers in the post reacted; the battle lasted all night, leaving thirty-two Italians and twenty-eight Germans dead. In the night, other army units resisted the German advance into Rome from the South.[17]

Carla Capponi. On the morning of the ninth, a group of people came walking along Trajan's Forum, shouting "Come, come out of the houses! Let's go to San Paolo and fight with the soldiers!" Some had hunting rifles, others a pistol . . . So I said, "Mom, I'm going!" and mom said, "Are you out of your mind? Where do you think you're going?" "Well, I want to see, I want to see what's going on." I threw on a jacket, a skirt, a blouse, and ran out, as I was. And I caught up with them on the via del Mare, I ran, and I kept asking, "Where are you going? Where are you going?" And one of them said, "Look what we've got—we called and called, and who came? a girl!"

Civilians came out to support the soldiers. Quirino Rosci and Pasqua D'Angelo, a baker and his sister-in-law, stayed with the soldiers in the grenadiers' field headquarters until it was captured by the Germans and they were shot in cold blood. Domenico Cecchinelli, Carminuccio and Maria Dieli-Barile were killed while tending the dead and the wounded. Sister Teresina, a nun, used her crucifix as a weapon to try to stop a German from taking a gold chain from off a dead man's chest; he beat her so badly that she died seven months later.[18] Twenty-eight women died in those days.

Carla Capponi. And then, at Garbatella, these nuns came out; the first wounded had come in, and they began to assist them. They lined them up—I don't know where they got them—a whole line of little dead bodies, and they wiped their faces, laid them down. The sisters had tucked up their skirts, up to here, to keep them clean, because of the dirt, the dust that was trailing; and they were odd, with these little black-stockinged paws, they looked like dancers. And then, I . . . I didn't know, I realized it was no use.

I ran into a group of women carrying those—you know, those pans you wash clothes in, they were made of aluminum them, filled with boiled potatoes. "For the soldiers," they said. So, you can see that they were already organized. I went with them, we distributed this food, we did what we could . . . Then the nuns told us: "Come on, girls, we've got to get organized, for these men here are fighting, they may be wounded, the Red Cross isn't around . . ."

Many narratives reveal the frustration of those who felt like unarmed and helpless spectators at a crucial event. Carlo Lizzani recalls that comrades came to him asking for weapons, and "all I had was a sheaf of [patriotic] poems inciting the [people] to the struggle, and they went away mad. They wanted rifles, not poems."[19]

"We were looking for weapons that we didn't find, and we even attacked, unarmed, an infantry barracks in viale Giulio Cesare and were pushed back by rifle fire" (Rosario Bentivegna). General Carboni delivered muskets and guns to the Communist Party. Cencio Baldazzi, the old leader of the Arditi del Popolo, seized a truckload of arms and distributed them, "helped by [Mario] Chierici, [Vittorio] Buttaroni and [Aldo] Eluisi," who would all later die at the Fosse Ardeatine. Fascists and German fifth columns attacked from behind; an army unit surrounded Baldazzi's armed volunteers. "It came very close to a tragedy, because I would never have given back the weapons, especially to those who I considered still fascists," Baldazzi writes; fortunately, General Martelli Castaldi managed to mediate and prevent bloodshed.[20] "We waited [for arms], we waited, until the afternoon of the tenth, then things fell apart and these weapons didn't come, so [we did] absolutely nothing, absolutely nothing" (Pasquale Balsamo).

The battlefront was pushed back to Porta San Paolo and scattered in myriad scenes and episodes. "There was gunfire, and you never knew who they were firing at; there is no line, there is no front, there is no barricade, there is no place, there just isn't" (Carla Capponi). To the doors of houses in the nearby neighborhoods of San Saba and viale Giotto "came Italian soldiers who were running away, across our garden, it was the Italian army falling apart in that moment; they took off their uniforms and we gave them civilian clothes . . . Then this poor boy came, who had lost his eyesight, he collapsed, died, right at our gate. And another came and died on our stoop . . . (Maria Marcelli). "The families helped out, the women helped a lot. Look, there was a great, great solidarity there, because the people came down from the houses and helped out, they fought to defend Rome. I didn't see the Party there; I saw brave people who just came—on their own, by ones and twos" (Maria Teresa Regard). Dozens of those who began the resistance that day around Porta San Paolo would die a few months later at the Fosse Ardeatine.

Many soldiers left their units to go home and cease fighting; others, however, came home to begin the fight. On September 8, Alfredo Capecci left his unit in Northern Italy and returned home "traveling any way he could, it took him two months—unrecognizable, with one woman's and one man's shoe on, ragged . . ." (Angelo Capecci). He and his brother Mario contacted a local partisan band: "And one night, on Christmas eve, 1943, the Germans caught them while they were carrying weapons. They had been tipped off, no doubt, by some citizen of Isola Farnese. They took one to Regina Coeli and the other to via Tasso." Mario was executed on January 31, at Forte Bravetta; Alfredo, on March 24, at the Fosse Ardeatine.

At St. John's gate, two career officers in the grenadier corps, Major Santucci and Captain Fago Golfarelli led a last defense, on a makeshift barricade across the ancient Roman gate. They had hardly any weapons and ammunition left: "We knew it was in vain, but it was a test of honor, of dignity; you die on your feet, you don't die groveling at anyone's feet" (Siegmund Fago Golfarelli). The battle lasted two hours; skirmishes went on around the Coliseum and at the central station. The surrender was announced on the afternoon of the eleventh.

Lucan Carpette. When the next morning we came back down Colle Oppio toward piazza Albania, we couldn't walk through because of the corpses—the poor soldiers, some even with their letters, their secrets—I saw postcards, letters, and blood on the trees. So we went around by the Aventino, to avoid having to go through Testaccio, and came down on the other side. And I saw corpses and blood, corpses and blood, a terrible thing.

Why did they fight? The military's reason for fighting, says an army historian, "is one and one alone: 'to obey the sacred laws of the Homeland.'"[21] For the Communist partisan Maria Teresa Regard, "the important thing was love of country; I didn't go because the Communist Party told me so." "But when the comrades who were fifteen, sixteen, twenty, thirty years old began to fight against the Nazis, they were not doing it to save the homeland, but to liberate it from slavery and from the oppression of the bourgeoisie and capitalism. We of Bandiera Rossa fought under this [ideal]" (Orfeo Mucci). Porta San Paolo may not have been a people's insurrection, but neither was it merely a military episode. Civilians and the military fought side by side. Antonio Calvani, a sixteen-year-old boy, "went out to Porta San Paolo, took a [fallen] grenadier's uniform, put it on, put the jacket on, and began to fire. They say they didn't know what road to take; but this boy knew, and took it" (Orfeo Mucci). The passing of the uniform from the dead soldier to the boy volunteer is symbolic: while so many soldiers were shedding their uniforms to don civilian clothes, many civilians in turn put on uniforms and took up arms. Among the combatants, rigid distinctions no longer hold: military and civilians are indistinguishable.

Aladino Govoni, captain of the grenadiers and military commander of Bandiera Rossa, killed at the Fosse Ardeatine, is one of these borderline figures. On September 8, he was on leave, in civilian clothes, having left his regulation gun at home: "My father, [Aladino's] brother, told me that he and my grandfather went to Porta San Paolo to deliver him his gun" (Flavio Govoni). "He was a revolutionary; his task was to begin the revolution in Rome, the insurrection in Rome" (Orfeo Mucci).

It would be meaningless to try to distinguish whether reserve officer Aladino Govoni, who might very well have stayed home, went out to fight, in civilian clothes, with the gun delivered by his father and brother, as a revolutionary or as a grenadier: perhaps, in those moments, it seemed possible to be both. How do we classify Sabato Martelli and Roberto Lordi, air force generals (ousted from the military) who reach Porta San Paolo "armed with two hunting guns"? Was Nicola Ugo Stame, wounded at San Paolo and killed at the Fosse Ardeatine, an air force captain or an opera singer, a grenadier or a militant of Bandiera Rossa? The three gold medals awarded to grenadiers who fell in the defense of Rome went to Luigi Perna, a career officer; Vincenzo Pandolfo, a reserve officer; and Raffaele Persichetti, a disabled veteran, no longer in service, a high school teacher of art history, who "in civilian clothes and summarily armed, rushed to the line of fire."[22]

Only at Porta San Paolo and at the Fosse Ardeatine do we find, in Rome, military and civilians together, not assimilated but equal. To speak of the ones without including the others would be to deny them both. They came with different motives, ranging from patriotism to class instinct. For some, it was the end of a cycle: Siegmund Fago Golfarelli fought heroically, was taken prisoner, escaped, and went home feeling that he had done his duty. For others, it was the beginning of another cycle, one that would continue with the Resistance. Conservative historians, thinking of the collapse of the state, have called this day "the death of the Homeland." Others, thinking of the volunteers who fought, called it instead "the new Risorgimento," a second resurrection.[23] They are both right, but one does not make sense without the other: a homeland that was not for everyone died, and a new one—from the vision and courage of many, if not from the consensus and participation of all—was trying to be born.

5. Portico d'Ottavia, October 16, 1943

Settimia Spizzichino. [About] the Fosse Ardeatine, I found out when I returned. A friend of mine, very close, her father was in there. And I was so close to his daughter, we used to go riding on our bikes, and her father would come along. He was a very nice man, very pleasant. She says, "Have you heard of my dad's end?" I say, "All right, I'll bring him some flowers." And I went. My folks, they scolded her—"She's just back from the extermination camp, and you take her to the Fosse Ardeatine?" And I said, "Do you think it'll affect me that much?" For one who's been to Auschwitz, it takes more than that . . .

Piero Terracina. Well, with the [German] occupation, that's when our big trouble began, because I guess at the moment we didn't realize—Rome had been declared an open city, the Vatican was here, it made us feel that here in Rome we were safe enough. The first blow was in September, when there was the request for fifty kilos of gold, from Kappler; and it was a big blow, because they revealed their real intentions right then.

On September 26, 1944, the leaders of the Jewish Community of Rome were summoned to the German embassy. Here, the SS Obersturmführer Herbert Kappler announced: unless they delivered fifty kilos of gold within thirty-six hours, two hundred Jewish heads of families would be deported. "My father and my grandfather were in the committee that was in charge of these things. My father's idea was: I don't trust them at all; [yet] this collection of gold is a thing we have to do to clear our consciences: I mean, the day something should happen and we haven't done it, they will ask us why didn't you do it" (Claudio Fano).

In those very tense hours, the Jews brought what they had: "I had a ring with a stone and I gave it, my husband gave his wedding ring" (Fortunata Tedesco). Some non-Jews also contributed: "I brought a brooch, I remember, that belonged to a grandmother, thin, but it was a very pure gold, because my grandfather had had it made, and two gold chains" (Puci Petroni). The Holy See, contacted informally, promises the loan (not the gift) of the missing balance, if necessary; it would not be needed.[24] The Nazis tried to cheat on the weight, Kappler refused to give a receipt: "When you take the enemy's weapon from them, you don't give them a receipt for their rifle," he explained later.[25]

Some felt reassured: "It was the word of a German officer" (Piero Terracina). Others realized it was just the beginning: "After they gave the gold to the Nazis, dad rushed home, in a hurry, he made up our suitcases, and took us away. Everybody said, this is too much, all they want is the gold. He said no, they don't just want the gold" (Giulia Spizzichino). Two days later Giorgio Fano took his family into hiding: "All those who heard about it told him he was crazy not to believe [the Germans]" (Claudio Fano).

So, when warning came, on the night of October 15, that the Nazis were preparing to raid the ghetto, it was not taken seriously. Yet, "That night there was a silence—there was always silence, the curfew was on, trams didn't run—this silence and the boots back and forth. We hear the first noises and we look out and we saw they were taking the Jews next door" (Settimia Spizzichino). "A relative of my sister's husband came, he said you've got to leave, run, because they're taking the Jews away. But my husband—I was in bed, I was pregnant—he kept telling me, don't worry, I'll go see what's going on, I guess they're taking the men . . . But when he got to Monte Savello he saw the trucks and he saw the Germans who were taking children, women. He came home half out of his mind: quick, hurry, get dressed, let's run, let's run. He had seen the disaster out at Portico d'Ottavia" (Fortunata Tedesco). "Back then we had a house that was very big, it was four rooms, huge, and it was a beautiful house, it was. But there were two rooms in-side each other; we hide in the last room and leave everything open so that if they come in they see [there's nobody home]. My sister, the youngest one, who knows what her brain told her, she was afraid, and ran out. She ran out of the house, went down the to the street door to escape, she was going down and the Germans were coming up, she saw them and turned back, she made them catch us all " (Settimia Spizzichino). The chase extended all over the city, from dawn to late afternoon. The roundup yielded 1,259 persons (363 men, 689 women, and 207 children); 237, recognized as non-Jews, were released the next day. Out of the 1,023 who were deported (including a baby girl born that night), only 15 returned. Only one woman, Settimia Spizzichino, survived.

The deportees were kept for two nights in an army college, near the Vatican. "My sister and all those who were taken away on October 16 stayed in the col-lege for two days—two days. I never heard that a nun had gone, that a friar had gone, that the pope had sent someone" (Fortunata Tedesco). The Vatican said nothing; "semi-official steps" were taken to obtain the release of converted Jews and members of mixed marriages. The German ambassador to the Vatican wrote to his government that "the pope has not yet abandoned himself to any demon-strative reprobation of the deportation of the Jews from Rome."[26] Meanwhile (with Vatican approval) priests and nuns in convents and parishes, to their own great danger, hid and saved no fewer than 4,500 Jews.[27]

<hr />

"Well, the raid on the ghetto was one of those stupid episodes that only the Ger-mans could have done. And in fact it was not done by the Italians, it was not done by our government" (Massimo Uffreduzzi). Actually, after October 16, the Germans left the task of persecuting the Jews to the Italian Fascists.[28] "There is no doubt that behind each Jew who survived there is a non-Jew who helped him, even at the risk of his life; but behind each Jew who was deported, there is a Fascist who turned him in. There is no doubt about that" (Piero Terracina).

The raid was the beginning of a story of hiding, escape, separation, uncer-tainty, fear. Fortunata Tedesco, eight months pregnant, hid in the house of non-Jewish neighbors in her building at via Marmorata; her son was born there. Then, to protect her hosts, she moved to the convent of the nuns of the Precious Holy Blood, from which she made a last-minute escape with the baby when the Nazis came to raid. Giorgio Fano's family lived for a few months in an apart-ment in via Flaminia. "We didn't have, as it were, the culture of hiding out. And the fundamental error that was made on that occasion was that we didn't estab-lish any kind of contact with the neighbors. If someone knocked on our door even, we wouldn't open, we stayed in, quiet as mice" (*Claudio Fano*). Then the family split: Ester stayed with her former teacher (she managed even to go to school for a time), the rest with a family doctor: "After a week, the maid, whose fiancé was a Fascist, she herself told us, look, they're coming, and we had to leave." The father went from one rented room to another, the family was harbored in a convent of Canadian nuns.

"I think that childhood is rather an invention. I don't think of those years as the years of my childhood, not at all. The transformation into adults took place around September eight, or on the twenty-ninth, when we went into hiding. From then on, childhood no longer existed" (Ester Fano). As they went through these experiences, children kept crossing the boundaries between reality, fiction, play. They were always changing places, and identities: it was a play of masks and representations, false I.D.s, assumed names, fictional identities. They had dangerous, telltale Jewish names and surnames: Ester became Giovanna, Spizzichino became Urbani. They hid their Roman accent to try to pass for Southern migrants: "I had become so adroit that once somebody asked: 'How did you manage, in the middle of the air raids, to travel from [Calabria] to Rome?' and I said, 'Madam! By makeshift means!'" (Ester Fano). Children learned rituals and languages; being able to recite a prayer in Latin might save one's life.

"It was also a game. It was a game because we had the family with us. If we had to do it alone it would have been quite different; but with the family it was a game that we did as a family group" (Ester Fano). Children sense that the boundary between play and tragedy is unstable; ironically, creating outright fictions is a way of setting things straight. Ester Fano recalls: "We did theater; we made up shows, we created costumes by transforming clothes, wearing them differently. And we made up all our own texts. And theater was also a metaphoric liberation from the reality we were living: you could have a situation in which fiction was fiction, play was play, and it made you feel better."

Informers and spies were the other side of this play of masks and identities. Giorgio Fano was betrayed, perhaps by a neighbor who discovered his hiding place when he had a radio brought to his rented room to listen to the BBC. An informer pointed out Cesare Tedesco to the Fascists as he walked down the street. The Jewish partisan Marco Moscato came back from the hills to look for his family; he was recognized by Celeste Di Porto—a young Jewish woman who had turned informer—and she pointed him out to the Fascists.[29] Ambition and frustration led Celeste Di Porto, a girl of the ghetto, called Stella for her beauty, to turn in dozens of her fellow Jews; yet the gray zones of interior ambiguity may also have more positive manifestations.

On October 16, Giorgio Fano had already taken his family into hiding, but his wife's parents were only just then getting ready to leave. Their suitcases were on the landing outside the apartment when the Germans arrived at their street door. It was getting late, and the Germans were few and afraid.

Claudio Fano. They had our names on the list, but it seems they didn't have those of our grandparents. But if they had gone upstairs, there were all those suitcases on the landing. And—this [neighbor] lady was coming down the stairs, who was the wife of a colonel who had joined the Black Brigades [Fascist anti-partisan units]; her son had also joined the Black Brigades, and all. And this lady spoke German. She found the Germans on the landing and asked them, "Who are you looking for? Look, they've all left." And the Germans didn't go up. So, the wife of the colonel of the Black Brigades . . .

What is the relation, within the same person, between the neighbor who saves individual Jews and the Fascist activist who supports the government that is trying to kill them all? Between this private virtue and public complicity or indifference, between the landing and the genocide, lies the impervious region that separates and connects the concrete and the abstract, the personal and the ideological, private life and history. Not all have the heart to cross this territory: it is hard and dangerous to see farther than one's own neighbor. But some do see the neighbor, at least: many who did not oppose either Fascism or the war took risks and paid prices to help runaways, draft dodgers, persecuted people. The Church set the example: not a word on the mass genocide, but help and protection to thousands of individual Jews.

As arrests and roundups continued, the Jews were taken to Regina Coeli or to the Nazi jail at via Tasso. From there, some, like Piero Terracina and his family, were taken to Auschwitz; others, like Cesare Tedesco, Giorgio Fano, and seven members of the Di Consiglio family, to the Fosse Ardeatine. Most families had both: "My sister, the one who they took her husband [on October 16], cried and said: 'They'll be envied, those of the Fosse Ardeatine. At least they died here, and they didn't suffer long.' But think: two days in the army college, five days on the train, God only knows what they must have suffered, my sister with that little girl, my father, sixty-nine years old, and all the others. And then, the things they had to see" (Fortunata Tedesco).

Piero Terracina. I remember my father's entrance to Regina Coeli, when we were lined up with our face to the wall at the registrar's office. Watched by an SS, absolutely forbidden to speak; but I remember that my father felt the need to say a few words to us. He must have had the, the perception of the abyss that was opening, no doubt about it. And I remember his very words, words that can't be forgotten, I mean. First he asked us to forgive him, for what I honestly do not know. Perhaps for not having defended us, who knows. And then—"Boys"—he said—"Anything may happen, but I have one recommendation for you: never lose your dignity."

Well—let's go on. And unfortunately—later—keeping our dignity, as human beings, it was not possible, in the end."

Giulia Spizzichino. My cousin was seventeen the day they carried them off, it was his birthday. I wonder why that boy that day told me those words, so, so terrifying. We were out walking, [and] he says, "You know, Giulia, today is my birthday; you know, I feel as if something is going to happen, I feel sad as if something bad is about to happen." That very night they caught him. That very night they arrested him. On his birthday. Two days later he was, he was dead at the Fosse Ardeatine.

I, when people tell me, "It's been fifty years, how come you are still thinking of . . ." I can't make you see it. You either feel it or you don't. No other way. Because I realize that for you fifty years is a mountain; but if I tell you that for me fifty years, for the pain I feel, so sharp, so violent, for me it's as if it had been two days ago, and I still cry, I still bear . . . I can't make you feel it, there's no way I can make you feel it. I had a six-year-old child that I lost. It was my only child, then I had this one a few years later—and yet many times, you don't know how guilty I feel—I tell myself, what are you saying? You're cursing against God!—I feel that the pain I feel for them is worse than this.

———•———

On March 21, 1944, the first day of spring, nine-year-old Valeria Spizzichino was hiding with her family in via Madonna dei Monti; other relatives, the Di Consiglio family, were hiding in her grandfather's hardware store across the street. Her mother had fried some fish; it was past curfew, but she sent Valeria out to take a plate to the relatives across the street. "I knocked on the gate—and instead of one of my relatives, a German opened the door. Inside, they were raiding the place, they were searching for gold and all. I walked in, carrying this plate, I laid it on the bed, acting very naturally and brazenly and made to leave. As if to say, 'I don't belong here, I'm just dropping in,' because I knew what was going on; I moved to go out but this German who had opened the door, with his musket, pushed me back in."

She asked her uncle, in Roman Jewish dialect, "'Should I go *resciud?*'—that is, run home to my father and mother; and he said, 'Are you crazy, you'll make them catch them all.'" The Germans opened the gate, she saw the truck outside and realized they were all being taken away. "And my aunt climbed in first with the baby in her arms, twelve days old, then I was supposed to be next." She climbed the first rung, then broke away and ran up the stairs screaming for her daddy. A soldier ran after her, gun in hand: "I was crazy, the instinct of self-preservation was so strong that I didn't realize that I was acting as a decoy, I was going to my father, to my father, and I would get them all caught."

"I sure put him in danger, my father, I put him right in the whale's mouth as we say, because my father could have really been killed." Her father, however, met her on the stairs and showed the forged papers that proved that they were not Jewish. "I guess this German didn't really look into it. I was lucky–when the Lord just wants to spare you. Because I was quick and I got away, or I would be in Auschwitz today, not even God could save me."

She was in shock. A refugee lady who was staying with them gave her a glass of wine; "After that, the blanket falls, I don't remember a thing. They said that for a week I was ill. But I don't remember: all the tension that kept me up to save me, to run . . . and then I don't remember a thing. While all the memories of that moment are very vivid: I remember my grandmother, I remember those Germans searching, the German by the door . . . I could draw the scene, if I were a painter."

The prisoners were taken to Regina Coeli; all the men were killed at the Fosse Ardeatine: "They killed my grandfather, three sons and a son in law of his, and three children of a son of his, so three generations in full. The women were taken to Auschwitz, and it seems that they were killed the moment they got there."

———•———

Piero Terracina. *Well, the sixth day, early in the afternoon, the train moved, it went in, into the station inside the camp of Auschwitz-Birkenau. They opened the wagons and we sensed immediately that we had arrived in hell. Among the, the shouts of the SS, the . . . the barking of dogs that were sicked on to the prisoners. We were supposed to get off the cars as quick as possible, and not all could do it. I was then a little over fifteen, and for me it was easy; but those who, elderly or ill, took too long were immediately struck with a series of random blows. This, this was the way we were—we were received at Auschwitz.*

Then a—a confusion, an indescribable confusion, a terrible confusion because many had their relatives who had traveled in other wagons—so it was natural to look for them, and see whether they were still alive, what state they were in. And so on. While Germans tried to make . . . order . . . with blows, I remember we went looking for my mother and my sister, until we met them as they came from the end of the train toward, toward the center.

And . . . we hugged. All. My mother . . . she had realized, right away, that this was the end. I remember that she gave, she gave us her blessing. She laid her hands on our heads . . . and then she saw some Germans coming with their sticks raised, she was afraid for us; and said go, go. And she added, we'll never meet again.

All right.

And . . . I guess that's the way it was.

They managed to make some order, with their ways, they made two lines, a line of men and a line of women. A group of SS officers lined up in front of the women, with their sticks in hand; the women's line began to move . . . and one of them pointed out, in that line, who was to go one way and who the other. The extermination had begun.

And, there . . . there were terrible scenes; because they tried to take from the mothers the children they carried in their arms, or by the hand. Because the mother, young, could go on, could work. The children couldn't. And so . . . those mothers who screamed, who were desperate, who ran after them, who tried to get hold of their . . . of their children, and sometimes they succeeded. They had to get back in the line, and when they went by the German officer, who was the doctor, he sent them the way most of the women had gone. That is, to die.

And . . . same thing for the men's line. My father and my grandfather one way; my brothers and my uncle and I the other. They took us to a—to a barracks, some prisoners there were already helping out the Germans for the arrival procedure, and there were some Italians among them. They told us right away that . . . maybe [the others] had already left the camp, through the chimney. Because they had been started to the gas chamber, right away, and from the gas chambers, then, to the ovens.

So there, the exhaustion from the, from the journey, the state of mental confusion, the hunger, the thirst . . . and then a degree of degradation, the blows we had received, the whole situation, the confusion, the state of confusion we were in . . . and completely naked—completely stripped, deprived of everything, literally everything, deprived of our clothes, deprived first of all of—of our loved ones; of the few things we had taken with us, deprived of our hair, even on our body—total depilation. A prisoner who dips a—a hand with a, a jute glove in a bucket which contains I think creosote, a pesticide, and runs it all over the parts of the prisoners' bodies, from head . . . to the private parts, to the feet. Next, standing in front of a German soldier who fills the form, completely naked in front of a clothed person, it's the most degrading thing there can be. The . . . the registration. They gave us a number which was also tattooed on our left arm; and we were told that we were supposed to learn that number by heart immediately in German because our name didn't mean anything anymore, didn't exist anymore. So we have nothing human left. So much that when the Germans counted us, afterwards, they didn't say, say, five hundred and twenty people. They said five hundred and twenty Stücke, five hundred and twenty pieces. We had become pieces.

Anything would do. Anything would do to, to get you killed. When they gave out food, prisoners made a circle around the Kapò who gave out what they called soup, waiting for him to finish to throw themselves all together on to that barrel that didn't . . . didn't have anything left in it. There was only a few, a few lumps stuck to the sides. And there sometimes there would be even . . . even very violent arguments. If it happened that a Kapò passed by and saw what was going on—always the same thing, he raised the arm, the sleeve of the left arm, and they were sent straight to the ovens, to the gas chambers.

Our work was digging canals, for the water to flow out when it rained. We reached the work site around eight, after a march of four or five kilometers; until sunset, the evening. Always under the drivers' whip, and with no water supply. So to keep from dying of dehydration, we placed a hose on the side of the canal we were digging; and the liquid mud would come, drop by drop, down through this hose. We put a bowl underneath, and that's what we drank. There was nothing else. So all this always with the nightmare of the stick looming, for any reason, but even for no reason at all—somebody might just walk by and start beating us. And unfortunately it happened very often that, in the evening, we had to carry back comrades, on our shoulders, who hadn't made it. Back to camp, we had to line them up for roll call—line them up at the end of the row, all perfectly in line, woe if some should have been a couple of inches out of line—an SS, a Kapò came along, raised the sleeve of the left arm, took a number, and after, after a few hours he was nothing but ash. Nothing but ash.

At the end of the month of June, convoys from Hungary began to come to Auschwitz. And then, room for those who were coming in had to be made by those who were already inside. And so they had the, the screenings; I think I went through one every two weeks from the end of June until September . . . And . . . I remember that—when one had made it through . . . at the moment you might be relieved; but then, when you realized that your friend, your bunkmate, or even those you knew from the barracks, were gone, well, then—you were overtaken with a . . . I guess a feeling of guilt. And this guilt feeling didn't end when we were liberated, it lasted for, for a long time. That is: who went to die in my place?

The crematories in Auschwitz, it was said, had a capacity to cremate ten thousand people a day. But in that period there were more than that coming in. So they couldn't manage this . . . this huge . . . amount of—of—of bodies; of corpses. So at the edge of the camp they had opened enormous ditches. From the gas chambers they brought them by the truckload, they were turned over into those ditches, and when they were full—they set them on fire. The . . . the . . . the smell, the stench from the crematories was already—terrible. Then those ditches, there, at the edge of the camp, and the wind carried this, this smell, which was a terrible thing. And you could see, you could see the activity, you could see them download the bodies, you could see everything. Think of what it means to live in a place where they kill ten or fifteen thousand people a day, where everything is known, everything is seen, everything is heard . . .

We were in camp D, separated from other camps by barbed wire with high voltage power. In camp E—it was an anomalous camp—there lived complete families. I mean, they had children; there were men and women who had kept their hair; who had kept their clothes, too. It was the camp of the gypsies. A camp full of life because there were children, children who maybe ran around, mothers who called them, clothes on the line . . . They had even kept their instruments so in the evening they made music, and to us it seemed an oasis of happiness, because there, there was life; on our side, there was nothing but death. I tell you, we were separated only by the barbed wire with the high-voltage power.

One night, it was the end of July 1944, we heard shouts, the SS giving orders; then we heard a great confusion, a bustle; and we heard the children crying because they had been awakened in *the middle of the night. Then suddenly silence. The next morning the first thing we did, we went to see what had happened . . . and that camp was empty. The camp was, was completely empty, it was a—there was nothing but silence, a chilling silence, I'd say. We realized immediately that they hadn't been transferred to another camp; it only took one look at the stacks to understand that during the night eight thousand people had been sent to die.*

In October there was a rebellion in the camp. In crematory number three, one day, there was a rebellion—they called it the Greeks' rebellion, because they were . . . Periodically, about every three months, the prisoners who worked at the gas chambers, at the crematories—the Sonderkommando, this is how they were called—they were in turn sent, made to go into the gas chambers. They had realized their turn had come, and—with some help also from outside the camp, I don't know how—they introduced into, actually into the crematory, into the gas chambers, some explosives. They blew up crematory number three. And, they took some weapons from the Germans; they . . . I think they held out perhaps half a day, no more; and then of course they were, they were all killed.

. . . Angelo Di Porto, Giacomo Di Porto [di Mosè], Giacomo Di Porto [fu Rubino], Gioacchino Di Salvo, Armando Di Segni, Pacifico Di Segni, Attilio Di Veroli, Michele Di Veroli, Salomone Drucker, Lido Duranti, Marco Efrati, Fernando Elena, Aldo Eluisi, Giorgio Ercolani, Aldo Ercoli, Renato Fabri, Antonio Fabrini, Giorgio Fano, Alberto Fantacone, Vittorio Fantini, Sabato Amadio Fatucci . . .

PART II

THE FOSSE ARDEATINE

CHAPTER 5

RESISTANCES

. . . Mario Felicioli, Dardano Fenulli, Enrico Ferola, Loreto Finamonti, Arnaldo Finocchiaro, Aldo Finzi, Valerio Fiorentini, Fiorino Fiorini, Angelo Fochetti, Edmondo Fondi, Genserico Fontana, Raffaele Fornari, Leone Fornaro, Gaetano Forte, Carlo Foschi, Celestino Frasca, Paolo Frascà, Angelo Frascati . . .

Ada Pignotti. *In conclusion, when it was the day after, that they let us go at about ten o'clock, I guess, ten, ten thirty, we went back to my sister-in-law's right away, to see if they had come back. Come back? Forget it. Well, I mean. It was empty: the house all messed up; they'd stolen everything in there that could be stolen. All the stuff thrown around, like that—a—a battle ground, it was. My sister-in-law: "It doesn't matter, who cares, let's just go find out what happened to them." We asked around, they said, "Yes, they've been taken to the Ministry of the Interior." So we started to the Ministry of the Interior; walking because, well, it wasn't far. On the way, we ran into those who were coming out, that had been released already. As for the others, they were taking them off to the thing, to . . . to the Fosse Ardeatine, to tell it like it is.*

And they asked us, "How come, haven't the Pignottis come back? How come, they were called out at two A.M. in the night, and we said, 'he must know somebody, that's why they're letting him out already.'" Instead, they were already picking those they were going to kill. When we reached the Ministry of the Interior, we had just arrived, we saw two trucks, all covered, coming out of the Ministry of the Interior. So we asked, this was, how do you call it, this guard; we asked, "Where have they taken them?" We were crying, screaming, wanting to know—he says, "Well, I guess they've taken them to work. We don't know, they didn't tell us." So we saw them as they were taking them away. Well, there we were, what could we do? We went to via Tasso. Via Tasso, nothing: "They're not here, they never were here." Instead, from there they had gone to via Tasso, loaded the others, and started off to the Fosse Ardeatine.

And so—after, after they took them out, every day we went to via Tasso, we went to Regina Coeli; I mean we made all the rounds but no one told us a thing. We hoped until the last that they had been taken to work; it was the hope that was the last to die. We had to write letters, twice in two weeks, to find out what had happened to them. After the second time, they sent us an envelope, with four pieces of paper in it, each with one of their names, that they were dead. In German. We had to look for someone to read it to us. And this is how the story ended.

1. Incipit

Massimo Uffreduzzi. My memory of that event is that on the twenty-third of March [the anniversary of the founding of the Fascist movement] the Germans had denied [the Fascists] permission to hold a demonstration, a spectacle, so to speak, in the streets. [Therefore the celebration] was being held in the Corporations' building in via Veneto. Which was then the headquarters of the Fascist Party. And while this ceremony was in progress, we heard the explosion, very clearly. We were, in a straight line, very close. So, all out, all rushing to see what was the matter; and we reached the place and I saw people, who were being held by the Germans against the railings of Palazzo Barberini, with their hands up . . . Surely the sight was not easy to describe, because the sight of these bodies torn to pieces, these thirty-three, thirty-two . . . I mean, it was unbelievable. I looked down via Rasella and pulled right back because it . . . it hurt me, I guess. Then, with others, we went through via del Tritone, those little streets around there. We heard nothing, and found no trace of the perpetrators. After which we went back to the Corporations' building and there I remember, in a whole other key, we held the commemoration of March 23, all deeply stricken, badly shocked, over this thing. I began to feel a state of overexcitement, a state also of fear in a sense, because it was the first time that an attack like that was staged in Rome, in the very center of Rome.

Massimo Uffreduzzi was surprised and skeptical when I told him that no, it wasn't the first time. In the center of Rome, there had already been a number of partisan attacks resulting in German casualties, and no retaliation had followed.[1] The belief that via Rasella was the first partisan action in Rome is, however, almost universal, and it is one of the foundations of the belief that the reprisal was automatic and inevitable—one attack, one retaliation. This is one reason the story, even when told by young people, always begins with via Rasella: "An ugly story . . . it began with the attack . . ." And: "What I knew was that there was an attack on a column of the German army. But I don't remember why " (Matteo Zapparoli, age twenty). "In via Rasella, in an attack by Italians against the Germans, I think, about thirty Nazi Germans were killed. And the Germans rebelled afterwards by killing at the Fosse Ardeatine, which honestly I don't know where they are, ten Italians for each German" (Simone Bova, age fifteen).

The young people cannot be blamed for their ignorance. This is how they have been told the story, even in history textbooks: ". . . after a partisan attack that caused 33 dead among the German soldiers, 335 Italians were executed (massacre of the *Fosse Ardeatine,* March 24–25, 1944"; "to every attack, the Germans responded with merciless retaliations; especially cruel was the one actuated in Rome in March '44 when, in response to an attack in which 32 German soldiers had found their death, 335 Jewish, anti-Fascist, *badogliani* prisoners were executed at the *Fosse Ardeatine.*"[2]

The belief that the retaliation was an automatic consequence of the attack implies a sense of fatality. Verbs are mainly in the passive form, the subjects are impersonal ("were killed," "were murdered"), as in an ineluctable tragedy in which there are no subjects, only victims. The eclipse of the personal subject is often functional to glossing over the responsibility of some and underscoring that of others: for instance, Right-wing sources tend to use active verbs and explicit subjects when describing via Rasella (the partisans "killed"), and return to the impersonal and the passive when they talk about the Fosse Ardeatine (the victims "were killed"): "Eighteen kilos of TNT mixed with shards of iron hidden in a street-sweeper's cart by the GAP, the Patriotic Action Groups of the Communist Party, tore to pieces 32 soldiers of the eleventh company of the Polizei Regiment 'Bozen' attached to the SS [. . .] In the German reprisal that ensued, 335 executed at the Fosse Ardeatine, the trial to the SS captain Erich Priebke is due to begin shortly."[3]

The blast of a bomb is a perfect narrative beginning. By definition, before the narrative begins, nothing happens: the retaliation "ensues." In the narratives of the June 29, 1944 Nazi massacre at Civitella Val di Chiana (Tuscany), where local memory also blames the partisans, the attack breaks the silence of a "small ancient world filled with soft and mysterious charm."[4] In wartime Rome it would be out of place to talk of soft rural silence; but its place is taken by the fiction of the "open city." The bomb is the beginning of everything because in Rome, the "open city," peace reigned and nothing was happening. Yet this was not the case.

"Via Rasella is an act of violence in a city that was the victim of war, of violence . . . violence was perceived as the violent response to a violent situation" (Valentino Gerratana). If we take into account the mass deportations, executions, air raids, arrests and roundups, hunger, and fear, then via Rasella is no longer a cause but a consequence: "We lived in a city where we could touch with our own hands that fact that every day there was either the informer who had caused the arrest, and thence the death, of a comrade who was in the underground; or the Fascist squad that took away a Jewish family that had escaped the raid on the ghetto; or the news, quote, 'he's fallen,' unquote, and it was someone you knew, and they had found the three-point nails and executed him . . . it was a situation—of more than terror—terror, there was—of constant violence, rather" (Marisa Musu). Perhaps, this is where we should begin the story.

2. Open City, Captive City

Yes of course it would be good to be able to die knowing why he dropped it in via Rasella. He says, "I gave Italy its dignity back." What's he talking about? Rome was an open city.

—Liana Gigliozzi

Giuseppe Bolgia. And then, Rome, the open city, which was not considered open either by the Americans or by the Germans—in fact, we were their slaves, nothing more. What do you mean, coming to rule Rome? Who are you, Hitler—the master of the world? And they kept us slaves, you couldn't talk, you couldn't say a word, woe if you listened to the BBC, all secret, all silence. A shame of a life, plus hunger, poverty. We were down to a hundred grams of bread a day. For potatoes, endless lines, and also for kitchen coal. And then, the fear of another air raid, after the first one we ran like gophers, scared of being buried under the ruins . . .

Unmberto Turco. Rome was livid, it was a Rome . . . in which it was a dissonance to see the uniform of the SS hierarch, of the Fascist lackey licking his boots, understand? . . . A dissonance, because all the rest was a grayness and sadness that you could see in the very air, you could breathe it . . . it seemed that the atmosphere was steeped in sadness, understand? It was this suffering, starving Rome. It was a Rome where you saw people on the run, gaunt, sad, understand? It seemed that the light had gone—and I say this, not as a feeling of today: a feeling I felt then. That is, you might see a body on the pavement, killed, but it didn't . . . it didn't strike you that much, such a thing. It was someone that the Germans killed, he was there on the ground, understand? And you dodged, you tried not to be involved. I saw many people on the ground, killed. Two days after September 8, you'd go out, and the [dead] soldiers were still in the jeeps, perforated by the German bullets, the grenadiers who held out at San Paolo . . . And Rome remained that way, all the time of the occupation, a sad city. It was a gray Rome. And that Rome, that is the Rome of the Fosse Ardeatine.

On August 14, 1943, after the second heavy bombardment, the Badoglio government proclaimed Rome an "open city," exempt from war operations from both sides. The Allies did not accept this declaration, though for a time they suspended the raids. On September 11, after the occupation of the city by the Germans, General Calvi di Bergolo, "commander of the open city of Rome," announced that "German troops shall remain on the edge of the free city of Rome."[5] On the same date, however, Field Marshal Albert Kesselring, commander of the Fourteenth German Army, declared that Rome was "war territory": the German war code was in force, "the organizers of strikes, saboteurs and snipers shall be executed," telephones would be under surveillance, and Italian authorities were expected to prevent "all acts of sabotage and passive resistance." The next day, police units under Obersturmführer Herbert Kappler set up quarters in Rome. On the twenty-third, German parachutists occupied the Italian headquarters of the "open city" and arrested General Calvi. His aide, Colonel Giuseppe Montezemolo, escaped in civilian clothes.

Adriana Montezemolo. General Calvi, the Germans arrested him, carried him to Germany. They told him that if he wanted to he could take along one of his officers, and he asked dad if he wanted to go with him. But dad didn't think it was right; if he went prisoner to Germany it would have been the end of all, and he instead felt that he could do things, he had an organizer's mind, he had everything under control . . . No doubt, the family's military traditions and love of country had an impact. And so he went underground.

"Rome, the open city" has become a kind of mantra with no relation to the history of an occupied city, never recognized as such by the Allies and never treated as such by the Germans, a way station for convoys to the front, a place of rest for German soldiers, a quarry of labor for the trenches and the German industries.

Vera Simoni. And then, this Italy invaded by these foreigners, by these invaders who had no respect for the population. On buses, I saw it myself, the invaders stopped the bus—Germans at the front door and at the back, and all, boys, old men, all had to get off, and were taken off in trucks; and they knew they would never return, because they were taking them to Germany, they couldn't warn their families, nothing. And we had to watch, my father and I, we had to see a tragedy like that.

Goffredo Cappelletti. One morning I went out and the Germans from viale Giulio Cesare began to push the crowd, I tried to hide somewhere but other Germans came and pushed and squeezed and carried all this mass of people: just like when they fish for tuna, for mullet, and they go with nets, like that. They take us all to piazza Risorgimento, began to screen us, and me, I looked younger than I was, they threw me out. The others, they loaded them up and took them all off, on the trucks.

The pushing, squeezing, snaring—Cappelletti's mullets, Bolgia's gophers—are both a concrete description of and a metaphor for a city smothered, one half hiding the other half. General Kesselring requests the delivery of sixteen thousand able-bodied male workers from this "open city"; only three hundred show up.[6]

Ada Pignotti. [My husband] was scared to death of the Germans, I'll say that. When he went out, in the morning, sometimes he came home and he was white in the face, like that; I asked him, "What's the matter?" "Well"—he said—"they made a roundup, we got off the tram, we were on the tram and they stopped it"—he said—"and they began to check. We sort of got away, and . . ." But he always came home agonizing. This is what he was afraid of, and this is what happened. What can we do about it?

On October 7, the Germans arrested and deported 1500 *carabinieri;* on the sixteenth, they raided the Jewish ghetto; on the twenty-seventh, one thousand people were rounded up in Montesacro, and one third was sent to forced labor. The war against civilians was waged relentlessly, with a sequel of roundups and mass deportations all over the city.[7] Many deportees would never return. None of these acts was related to partisan actions.

Giuseppe Bolgia. "Early March, March 8 of '44, dad didn't come home. Already we had lost mom; then dad doesn't come home—how come, what can it be, all day he didn't come back, what happened, could he be sick . . . He wasn't at the hospital, he wasn't dead, he hadn't gone back to work, what had happened? We went to the police, we went everywhere, at last we realized there had been a roundup near the central station and he had been picked up, see? He was taken as he came out of the station, on tram number eight, and all were brought to via Tasso. They kept him a day or two there, then sent him to the third arm of Regina Coeli. There, from that day he stayed at Regina Coeli until March 24, the day of the massacre.

Goffredo Cappelletti's father, a partisan, sent him with a loaf of bread to a family in hiding near Porta San Pancrazio. "I walked in, and [the father] turned this bread over on the table, the children elbowing one another like hungry wolves, they ate this bread and him standing by watching them like that, stern. He didn't touch a crumb. I still get goose bumps when I think about it: he was able, without touching a crumb, to watch his children elbowing one another, searching for the crumbs on the floor and on the table, with their tongues. And all because he'd married a Jew."

3. Let Them Know
They're Not the Masters of Rome

We in Rome were doing just fine. There was hatred for no one. Kappler wanted Rome to be a tranquil city.

—Erich Priebke[8]

"The Germans who in their jeeps ride arrogantly with machine guns through piazza Venezia: this is one of the most vivid memories" (Vittorio Gabrieli). On September 9, the Committee of anti-Fascist parties—Communists, Socialists,

Christian Democrats, Partito d'Azione, Liberals, Labor Democrats—renamed itself as National Liberation Committee (CLN, Comitato di Liberazione Nazionale).[9] The next day Mario Fiorentini and Lucia Ottobrini are at a street corner in via del Tritone: "The tanks pass, the Germans on them solemn and stern, there was silence . . . I take her by the arm—'*nous sommes dans un cul de sac*' [French: we're cornered]—and we rush anxiously to Pineta Sacchetti, Flaminio, Monteverde, to collect the weapons abandoned in the barracks, especially bombs and explosives" (Mario Fiorentini).

In the same days, Bandiera Rossa and the military also began organizing underground. The Resistance began almost spontaneously, with no rigid organizational distinctions.

Mario Fiorentini. It was a frenzy of meetings, a frenzy of seeing people in the strangest places. I came from Giustizia e Libertà and from the *garibaldini* of the Communist Party;[10] my first contact was with Fernando Norma, a cabinet maker from Giustizia e Libertà, who was arrested and then killed at the Fosse Ardeatine. And we piled up arms, arms, arms. We began to attack immediately in Rome, because Rome has the seven hills and if you choose your place well you can attack convoys as they go through. And we did many actions against convoys, with bombs [in the city center].

On September 20, a mine caused "several dead" in the Fascist militia barracks in via Eleonora Duse: "an action prepared and personally carried out by Pilo Albertelli and Giovanni Ricci of the Partito d'Azione."[11] Two days later, in the small town of Palidoro, on the beach north of Rome, the Germans were about to execute twenty-two men in retaliation for an attack that never happened; at the last moment one the hostages, the *carabiniere* Salvo D'Acquisto named himself as "the only perpetrator," and they killed only him: an event that would rise to mythic proportions. Three weeks later, still in Palidoro, they killed six draft dodgers. In neither case had there been any partisan action.[12]

Actions planned against the Fascist minister Buffarini Guidi and the Fascist torturers Bardi and Pollastrini failed at the last minute. At the beginning of October, the Communist Party formed the GAP (Gruppi di Azione Patriottica)—the underground cells for urban guerrilla warfare.

Mario Fiorentini. At the beginning of October, Giulio Cortini, Carlo Salinari, Danilo Nicli and I met, first at Ponte Sisto and then at Ponte Sant'Angelo. And one of the goals we had set ourselves was this: the Wehrmacht was no longer invincible; they were to feel that they were not the masters of Rome, that they are amid a hostile population. We would attack their communication lines, their transits, their truck routes, the truck stops, their headquarters; and especially this, they were not to march with impunity through the city. In other words: we wanted to force them to let Rome really be an open city. Therefore the action in via Rasella—not in itself, because it must be seen together with all the many, many actions we did before—was in a way the culmination, the crowning of a program that we had already outlined since October '43, which said that we were going to attack the Fascists and the Germans, make their life in Rome unsafe: they must not be the rulers of the city.

Then came October 16, the raid on the ghetto—once again, with no partisan "provocation." "At this point, since this was Kappler's way of keeping his word and respecting Rome's 'open city' status, the National Liberation Committee ordered us to organize armed units to operate in the city" (Pasquale Balsamo). The Resistance inaugurated its most lethal weapon: the three- or four-point nails. German convoys were left stranded on the highways, immobilized and vulnerable to Allied attacks from the air; on via Tiburtina, two German soldiers lost control of their sidecar when it hit a nail, and they died in the crash. The German command announced that "if such acts of sabotage should occur again, very grave sanctions shall be taken against those who live on the street or in the neighborhood."[13] In other words, the population was exposed to retaliation even for mere sabotage.

On October 20, partisans ("it was the comrades of Bandiera Rossa," Orfeo Mucci recalled) and residents of the *borgata* of Pietralata invaded an abandoned military installation, Forte Tiburtino, looking for abandoned arms and food, and clashed with the German guard. Ten men were arrested and, two days later, executed by the Germans. A boy hostage had a good pair of boots; they took them and let him go but made up the number by seizing an innocent passerby. The Germans posted a bill: ten members of "a Communist band" were sentenced to death for "attacking arms in hand members of the German armed forces. The sentence has been carried out." The language prefigures that of the Fosse Ardeatine, but with an important difference: the massacre is still justified as judicial punishment of "perpetrators," not as police retaliation on uninvolved civilians. Another foreshadowing of the Ardeatine is the passer-by killed for the bureaucratic purpose of meeting the number.[14] There had been no German casualties.

The GAP celebrated October 28, the anniversary of the March on Rome, with a number of actions against Fascist posts and barracks, and November 7, the anniversary of the Soviet revolution, with public speeches and demonstrations: "Franco Calamandrei made a speech in Piazza Fiume, protected by the first organized *gappisti,* and it ended with the explosion of hand grenades, those *balilla* grenades that can hardly kill a fly . . ." (Pasquale Balsamo). "On the side of the Victor Emmanuel monument, which was like an insult, we wrote, in big letters: death to the Germans and death to the Fascists. Below the Spanish Steps we drew a hammer and sickle—which remained visible for years, because that soft marble absorbs the paint, and you could see this shameful thing we'd done, and we were sorry, a huge hammer and sickle" (Carla Capponi). From the middle of November, the guerrilla movement grew stronger. On November 18, a bomb failed to go off under the stage of the Teatro Adriano, during a rally of Fascist military officers. Other parties set up their own armed units. Those of the Partito d'Azione, led by Pilo Albertelli and Giovanni Ricci, sabotaged lines, strewed four-point nails, delivered arms and explosives to partisan bands in Sabina; eighty-four of their members would be killed at the Fosse Ardeatine.[15] The Socialist armed underground (Brigate Matteotti) was led by Giuseppe Gracceva; Aladino Govoni was the military commander of Bandiera Rossa. The Communist GAP were organized in eight "zones" (four units, the *GAP centrali,* operated in the center of the city), under the Central Italy command of the Garibaldi Brigades and the regional military command. For security reasons, groups and units had few contacts with each other, and possessed a high degree of autonomy in choosing and carrying out their actions.

"Our commanders," Bentivegna wrote, "had indicated as our first objective the cleaning up of the city center from the Fascist squads."[16] To a large extent, these actions were entrusted to the initiative of the individual comrades. Maria Zevi's partner, a police officer who was also in touch with the GAP, "told me later: 'Look, I, every night, whatever I ran into, I shot it.' He had a good machine gun, he killed Germans several times." At his trial, Kappler testified that "often, corpses of German soldiers were found floating in the Tiber."

Bandiera Rossa was active mainly in the *borgate* and the periphery: "We had a kind of agreement: the GAP were at the center of Rome, they fought in the center; we fought on the edge" (Orfeo Mucci). They attacked German trucks, cut lines, subtracted arms and explosives: "I've gone into combat with the Germans carrying my thirteen-month old son, so they wouldn't understand . . . I went to Centocelle [airport] with Tigrino Sabatini and [Valerio] Fiorentini, we took the mines from the Germans, it was a frightful moment, in fact one of us, [Giulio Camiciani], was wounded" (Roberto Guzzo). Fiorentini and Camiciani, like Otello Valesani and Ilario Canacci, captured in a similar action, would be killed at the Fosse Ardeatine; Tigrino Sabatini, at Forte Bravetta.

On December 17, the GAP killed a Wehrmacht officer in via Veneto; he was carrying important papers that were then delivered to the Allies. On the eighteenth, the *gappista* Guglielmo Blasi hurled a grenade in a trattoria in via Fabio Massimo patronized by Germans and Fascists; ten died, two of them Germans. On December 26, in one of the most daring actions, Mario Fiorentini rode his bike by the German guards at Regina Coeli, got off, hurled a grenade that wounded many, climbed back on his bike, and rode away under gunfire. In response, the Germans prohibited bicycles and set an earlier curfew. However, neither this action nor the others were followed by reprisals.

"The Germans had barricaded in the area from corso Italia to via Veneto, and the area was surrounded with machine guns, checkpoints and such. I guess that this central area around via Veneto, we attacked it from all sides, because we blew up a garage in via Barberini, we blew up trucks in via Capo le Case. Our idea was to carry out actions primarily in this area that was directly under German control; and via Rasella was one of these streets" (Rosario Bentivegna). On the evening of the eighteenth, with the support of Mario Fiorentini, Carla Capponi, and Lucia Ottobrini, Bentivegna threw a bomb in the midst of the German soldiers coming out of the cinema Barberini; eight men died.[17]

Carla Capponi. And Lucia and I went back to see how many they were, and we saw some unbelievable scenes, because some of them had been hit in their behind and then you could see these uncovered behinds, of those who leaned forward screaming and the others pulling the pieces off them. And we were arrested right away, think what fools we were. But Lucia had grown up in France in the region where they are bilingual, she spoke German perfectly, and I'd told her, "You talk and I keep quiet, if they stop us." In fact, the Germans thought we were two street girls of those who slept under the tunnel. That night we walked across the tunnel, that was walled in, and inside it was all lights, lights, lights, and it was a big encampment of families of refugees that lived in there. So that was rather an adventure. Also, in practice there was no reprisal.

The next day, at the other end of via Veneto, the GAP attacked the hotel Flora, seat of the German general headquarters and military tribunal. "The bombs had come out of the laboratory of Giorgio [Labò, the GAP's explosive expert]," writes Franco Calamandrei: "It was an almost agreeable feeling, to hold in my hands their weight and their compact cylindrical volume." After the explosion, Calamandrei's diary goes on, "their roar swelled in the night, but there was nothing brutal and bitter in it, it was like a huge breath that had suddenly risen to illuminate the silent darkness. And I was filled with an elementary, childish joy. In panic, people ran here and there, the cars' headlights shone on running legs on the glittering asphalt. From the direction of the Flora, German and Italian voices shouted, pistol and rifle shots were fired at random."[18]

Again, the Germans choose to conceal their casualties; "but someone counts at least six uniformed corpses lined in a corridor."[19] There was no reprisal: at this point, the Germans still felt that the most important thing was to keep the city from realizing that there was guerrilla warfare going on, and to protect the myth of their own invulnerability. They succeeded so well that these events are hardly remembered or mentioned anymore.

4. Memories of War

"There was also another distinction that is mentioned sometimes: 'Oh, but I fortunately never killed, or I hope I never killed.' What does that mean? You were there, in arms, either ready to shoot and thus to kill, or anyway setting up something to make war and thus to kill—to make war is to kill: whoever takes sides, one way or the other, is willing to kill. And, they say, 'But I didn't do it'; and yet, you were there, and if the killing was done by the one who was standing next to you, he was able to do it because you were next to him, armed and ready to defend him, or at least you passed the ammunition" (Rosario Bentivegna).

Mario Fiorentini. Listen now. Franco Calamandrei, Carlo Salinari, and I, in the days immediately before March 23 and soon after March 23, we met every day—which we hadn't done before. And I could perceive the anguish in Calamandrei. Carlo Salinari didn't show it as much, because he was very controlled, as was Valentino Gerratana. And then—hear me now: in those days Carlo Salinari was almost struck dumb; that is, he never talked much, but he was even more . . . I really lived the, the . . . I lived the agony of Franco Calamandrei.

In war, one is ready to give one's life but also to take the life of others; willing to die, but also to kill. The partisan war is unlike all others less for the justice of its cause, always claimed by every war, than for the fact that it is fought by volunteers who renew their commitment with every action.[20] In the course of the war, partisans were also responsible for errors and wrongs; but no partisan ever excused himself by claiming that he was only following orders. "Ours was a choice. If one didn't feel like it because one might have moral problems, or political reasons, or disagreement—I don't know; each of us had chosen to do what they did" (Marisa Musu). "There were [some] who were pained very much by the actions against the Fascists: because the action against the Fascists is action against individuals, it's civil war. And I remember one, after an action, who told me, 'Listen, I'm not going to do these actions anymore.' It wasn't a matter of cowardice; one of these men later was parachuted in the North, he had an important role in the Resistance" (Mario Fiorentini).

Adolfo Fantini. One day [came] a comrade, and he carried a pistol with three bullets in it, and he says: "Go to piazza Fiume and wait for some Fascist to come along"—like that, with no preparation, no information . . . I go, with my trench coat on—I was sixteen—I go, fortunately no one got off the tram. After a while, just before curfew— "We've got to go home." I get on the trolley bus, and on the bus I hear two guys talking, they seemed Fascists. What do I do? Do I get off and shoot them? Then I gave it up, because how can you, like that, without a . . . I had never fired a gun, either . . .

"I had gone to medical school so that I wouldn't have to fight; I thought, if I'm drafted I, as a doctor, won't have to kill but I'll do what I can to save human lives" (Rosario Bentivegna). He was not drafted, but he found himself in a position where he had to kill, and in cold blood. After the first time, he writes, "we were in a state of shock . . . I had shot a man. I couldn't talk, I couldn't mix with my friends again. Between them and me now gaped a final fracture: I had begun the guerrilla war."[21] This fracture reappears as a conflict in memory and narrative: one the one hand, silence (heritage of the underground: "of these things we must never speak, not today, nor tomorrow, nor the next day, and who does them must know as little as possible," says Mario Fiorentini); on the other, the pressing need to narrate and explain.

In their just war, the partisans performed acts that can appear "unjust," in a time of peace, to the very conscience in whose name they were carried out: "In those very tense nine months, my life or your life, if I see one shooting at me, I shoot back; but then this kind of thing, which is justified in that moment, you have to give it up, or else you become, you become yourself a bearer of death" (Marisa Musu). Lucia Ottobrini muses: "During the Resistance I thought: it's as though I was transgressing; I was ashamed, to turn to Him. It was a different time. If I think about it now I say, how strange—was that really me?"

Maria Teresa Regard. Well, I didn't really dwell much upon it. I thought that we had to do these things to chase the Germans from Rome, this was the end, it surely wasn't that the idea of killing people pleased me. My daughters ask me, "How can it be, didn't you think these things over?" Actually, I didn't even want to think about it, because if I had, I don't know, I might not have the strength. We were like shielded, as if we wanted to protect ourselves from this, because it was such an abnormal thing for people like us. For me, it wasn't so much the fear, as the thought that if I let myself go a little, then I might have collapsed.

"So," GAP member Franco Calamandrei wrote in a 1941 diary entry, "I told myself—there isn't a war, but individuals facing the war; always individuals, always and only individuals."[22] In a famous page of his diary, the double, contradictory consciousness of doing something that is just and unjust at the same time takes an unexpected form in the tale of a young partisan waiting for the action in via Rasella: "The day I was waiting in piazza di Spagna for the German platoon to appear at the end of via del Babuino, and I thought that those men would soon die, I didn't care at all. But as I stood there in the warm afternoon sun, and I saw them march by, the aria of 'E lucean le stelle' sounded inside me . . . , and tears came trickling down my cheeks."[23]

The "divided memory," then, runs *within* individuals—between "I didn't care at all" and the unexpected tears. The partisans are bearers of a double consciousness; of the reasons for violence and the reasons for its rejection. Compare these two accounts:

Marisa Musu. When you hear [Giulia] Spizzichino, this woman, incidentally, who might be in films, beautiful, an outstanding woman, who tells you that all the Di Consiglio family died, a sixteen-year-old boy, one seventeen, one nineteen, twenty-one, the father, the grandfather, they were executed at the Ardeatine and then the rest of the family, a child of fifteen days, were gassed at Auschwitz—this even now fills me with such a—it's not even hatred; it's . . . forgive me, it may seem strange, but: we didn't kill enough of them; wish we'd killed more. I realize that it may sound cruel, but that's the way it is. If I think, say, that I contributed with a bomb to blowing up a German soldier, I don't think of him, say, as a mother's son, as the father of a little child, I don't experience it that way. I see torturers of via Tasso, raiders of Jews, extermination camp guards . . .

Lucia Ottobrini. War is war, there's nothing you can do about it. I remember on via Empolitana, the trucks filled with young boys going home [singing] "*In die Heimat, in die Heimat, es vird besser gehen,*" "at home all will be better." These are things that never leave you, I remember them always, all my life. For instance, the three hundred and forty they killed, they're always stuck within me. Because I don't like to even hear about it, it's not cowardice, it's an awful, terrible, frightful thing, I assure you. Some people write about it freely and easily. Not I, not for me: the enemy is a human being, too. And I'm very—infinitely sorry. These are very bitter things and I think it left a mark on me. For one thing, it made me more mature; I don't feel innocent, no one is innocent, and no one can call himself guilty.

These attitudes, though voiced by distinct persons, must not be thought of as opposed but as superimposed, overlapping: they imply the awareness that the same person is both the enemy and a human being (the extermination camp guards were also fathers and husbands, "ordinary men"), and the need to act and feel in consequence. After all, Lucia Ottobrini did contribute to blowing up those truckloads of homeward-bound young men; and Marisa Musu has an emblematic tale of ambivalence to tell.

According to her version, the partisans hit the car in which Giovanni Pizzirani, secretary of Rome's Fascist federation, was riding with his bodyguard; when they went, they found five wounded men and did not know which was Pizzi-rani. "I already had the bullet ready," writes Musu, "and was about to do what I thought must be done [that is, kill them all], when Franco [Calamandrei] stopped me: 'Come away: the order,' he explains, 'was to execute Pizzirani, not Pizzirani and all the others.' I think today that, as a more mature and responsible person, he was more sensitive than me to the subtle line that separates the execution of a torturer and murderer from the indiscriminate killing of enemies whose guilt has not been ascertained."[24]

Franco Calamandrei's diary skips the period in which this incident occurred; Carla Capponi and Mario Fiorentini tell it very differently. But beyond factual reconstruction, the tale is itself a significant fact. If Musu's version is accurate, it represents the partisan ethics toward unnecessary violence, and the difference between the partisans and their enemies. If it is not, then it means that this difference was so necessary that memory and feelings have worked over the years to stage a story to express it.

We speak of divided memory, but Franco Calamandrei's diary bears the title *La vita indivisibile*—"indivisible life." The sensitive intellectual and the armed fighter, the necessary indifference for the death one is about to deal and the suppressed pain of dealing it, cannot be divided. This is why Lucia Ottobrini is right when she rejects the categories of innocence and guilt: she and the others will not accept the guilt immediately laid upon them by the editorial of the *Osservatore Romano,* but they assume full and personal responsibility. To say that "war is war" does not mean that there are no distinctions, that reasons and feelings were suspended. It means: I had to take upon myself reasons that I will not deny, but that I do not want to see judged through the alien eyes of the innocents for all seasons.

Carla Capponi. For instance, we killed a German officer in [via Veneto]. Since I had not had the baptism of fire, they told me: "It's your turn this time." I felt like dying, my dear, because shooting a man, and in the back, too, I assure you it seemed a terribly cowardly thing to do. I wanted to call to him, to say excuse me, please, so he turns and at least he has the time to respond . . . So, after we crossed the first street, Bentivegna who was with me says "Come on, shoot," and I, nothing. When we come to the corner of San Nicolò da Tolentino, at his signal I shoot, just wildly at random, three or four times, he shoots too, and then we drop down. I remember it was raining, but he had a briefcase that we were supposed to take, and you know, taking this briefcase, tearing it, was as if we had torn the heart—think that I remained with the pistol in my hand, I didn't even put it in my pocket. We walked down, we reached piazza Barberini, and there I had a terrible crisis and said "No, no, it's impossible, we can't do this." It didn't seem fair. So Bentivegna reasons with me, "Look, they've already killed, Gesmundo has been tortured and Giorgio Labò [was killed], Gianfranco Mattei hanged himself [in jail], it's a struggle and you must see it this way, otherwise women ought to stay at home" . . . You see, he was trying to humiliate me . . . But I'll tell you the truth, it was a very hard thing to do. I think much of it depends on the fact that killing is against nature.[25]

"Otherwise women ought to stay at home." Maria Teresa Regard reads the motivation for her military gold medal: "'Arrested and taken to the prison in via Tasso, she always retained, under interrogation, a virile and exemplary attitude, not revealing anything . . .' That *virile,* I struck it off: I told them, look, take *virile* off, I can't stand it."

Lucia Ottobrini. I received the silver medal from [Paolo Emilio] Taviani, who at the time was Secretary of Defense. I was with two air force generals. He took me for the widow of a soldier, and asked me gently, "Madam, are you the wife?" He thought I was the widow of the honoree, that he was dead. I said, "Look, I'm the one who's getting the medal."[26]

Marisa Musu writes that when Valentino Gerratana sent her to Giorgio Amendola, the military commander of the Garibaldi Brigades, to be admitted to the GAP, Amendola told her: "In my opinion, your role ought to be to stand by Valentino and darn his socks at night." Amendola might have been thinking more of her age (she was eighteen) than her sex, but the phrasing is revealing. Of course, at the time, "Neither he nor I have the least idea that, several decades later, a feminist movement will arise. But I don't have the least idea of how to darn socks, either."[27] If there is anything to be learned from the Roman Resistance, it is that, although women can do the same things as men, war is other than the "virile" myth through which it is always represented.

Although the motivation for the gold medal awarded to Carla Capponi speaks of "cool determination against the enemy," Lucia Ottobrini says: "I have of her very tender memories. I remember that one night I slept at her house; it was cold, the bed was frozen, because it was winter, she had no heating, nothing. She got a flatiron, heated this iron—and warmed my bed, tucked me in—'Sleep now.' Another time, we were in a coal cellar, I had a high fever, there was no water; she gets up, picks up a flask, and comes back with a flask of water [at night, under curfew]. And that was another instinctive, spontaneous act."

Maria Teresa Regard. Yes, it's true, there were many women. But not, I think, as a feminist statement; no, I see that women are more practical; probably they saw that this war was run so badly, who knows, they reacted more. Clearly, there couldn't be a feminist mentality because it wasn't the time, but the idea of affirming women's right to participate, to count, maybe yes.

Marisa Musu recalls speaking to students in the 1990s in a school in Lucania, in southern Italy: "It was wonderful. The students were mainly interested in feelings. They didn't care how many people were involved, how many bombs were fired, how the action was conceived. Instead, they asked: Were you afraid? What did you think an hour before? If you could have canceled, would you have canceled? What were your feelings about death?" The former partisans are no longer young, and they are often removed from current politics; the young people are no longer those of the militant 1970s. It is possible now to look inside oneself and to speak of the Resistance as not only a military event but also as an intense personal experience.

Carla Capponi. We slept in a cellar and I was the only woman with all males sleeping in there. And imagine, my mother had given me one of those quilted wool blankets from the Marche, quilts that weigh a ton, and it was double size, so I folded it under me, selfishly, and then on top. Then when I saw that all the others were on the ground on packed earth, then I said, all right, let's put it on the ground, because it was so damp in there; and the four of us lay on top of it, in a row like so many salami. This sleeping like cubs next to one another gives you some relief, makes you feel warmer; then maybe one had brought a light blanket, another had something else, so we'd throw it over us, but it was very uncomfortable, you know. It was very promiscuous, but I must say, I received much respect from the comrades.

This is not to deny the "cool determination." But it had to be created and kept up in the presence of opposite impulses. Even the tactile quality, the "weight and the compact cylindrical volume" of the bombs, the metallic materiality of the pistol, represent a concreteness that defers anguish. Each found a form of inner defense: after each action, Lucia Ottobrini felt the need to bite a sandwich; Franco Calamandrei went back to work on his translations of French classics; Rosario Bentivegna played chess, Mario Fiorentini listened to classical music, Pasquale Balsamo made jokes "to break this gloomy atmosphere " (Maria Teresa Regard). They were all very young, hardly more than adolescents, and felt the excitement of change, of a new meaning to their lives, of the presence of death, of being alive. "My mother [Laura Garroni] told me that when they were GAP, [each] night they slept in a different hiding place . . . My mother tells it as an adventure, after all; besides, she was in love and . . . well, they were very young, it must have been this sense of danger, risking their lives—their predecessors had died, those who had come before them had been taken" (Anna Cortini).

Marisa Musu. Fear before the action, I don't think there was any. There may have been a great deal of tension, but fear, us young people, I don't think so. Nor during, because after, while you're shooting, there's a lot of confusion. The sense of death, certainly, yes. In the sense that once you'd been captured—they had taken me, they'd sentenced me to death—you expected to be killed, the regret of missing things that you hadn't known. That is, you had a clear sense that your life was breaking when you had hardly stuck your head outside the nest, and there were many things to see, to know, to do. This, yes. Great regret.

"Who can I talk about these things to?" asked Lucia Ottobrini. The urban guerrillas did not share the communal moments of Resistance in the hills; instead of partisan anthems, the GAP composed private thoughts, like the diaries of Franco Calamandrei or certain lost poems of Carla Capponi. Urban partisans hardly knew one another; they acted alone or in very small groups. They experienced hunger, cold, and fear, mostly alone. The partisan whom we call Giovanna Rossi says: "I'm even scared to remember how much certain physical hardships can degrade you. Hunger is terrible, look, truly terrible. Because you feel this body that weighs you down, the body requires you to eat—fortunately you don't find anything to eat, because you'd be ready to do something wrong, even, you understand?"

"We knew we could be tortured, imprisoned, dead, because they might kill us any moment, and I must tell you that on some occasions I was especially lucky—it's a very odd thing, we trusted one another, it's incredible" (Lucia Ottobrini). "Each of us has also very sad memories, of how a solidarity between friends, relatives, can be lost" (Giovanna Rossi). Solidarity had to be rebuilt around new relationships: the partisans could no longer go home, they had to break all contacts with their families (who didn't always know or agree); and they sensed that this could be communicated only to those who lived it.

Carla Capponi. Yes, there grew a solidarity which became affection . . . we were a very close group, understand, tight-knit. They put you together, you do actions together, you study together, have emotions together, there's living matter in it, you are involved with all your feelings. There is fear, there is courage, there is danger, there is death before you, you see it, you yourself give it. This wears you out, and you need a human relationship. The relationship with my family, for me, closed completely.

Part of Marisa Musu's "regrets" after being sentenced to death was "not having known love in its fullness."[28] It wasn't a time of sexual liberation yet, but the partisan women had already gone beyond the limits, put their bodies at stake, experienced unknown kinds of relationships. Family allegiance, Catholic education, Communist morals all stigmatized these new attitudes, but the intensity of the experience and the sense of uncertainty made a difference. Carla Capponi remembered the conversations with a comrade: "She wanted marriage, I mean, religious; and she told me all her doubts, that she had agonized over it but then had overcome all these things . . . It was a very intimate, very special thing, this conversation. And I, who was older, of course I told her, 'Look, listen, we don't even know if we'll make it through this month . . . forget all this nonsense. If you're in love, go ahead and love!'" "We didn't talk about marriage—of course, we went all the way, he was my first man. This is logical" (Lucia Ottobrini). "We were after all people who were having a very hard time, who suffered solitude, hunger, frightful conditions . . . in the end, it was a relief to have someone to love and to be loved. The humanity of Carlo Salinari was in understanding that this made the Resistance stronger, not weaker" (Rosario Bentivegna).

"I, for instance, marrying Franco Calamandrei was the last thing on my . . . I got married on June 13, because at one point he decided this way. He insisted so much I was distracted—'Ah, I can marry only someone who was in the Resistance . . . '" (Maria Teresa Regard). In a matter of weeks and months from the liberation of Rome, the *gappisti* married one another: Carla Capponi and Rosario Bentivegna, Lucia Ottobrini and Mario Fiorentini, Maria Teresa Regard and Franco Calamandrei, Marisa Musu and Valentino Gerratana, Antonello Trombadori and Fulvia Trozzi; Laura Garroni and Giulio Cortini had married before, others would follow. The outcomes of these marriages were not very different from all others: some fell apart with time, others were as strong as rocks. "And then this attachment, so strong, that there was between us lasted over time, this is the oddest thing, because one marries that way, a little adventurously . . ." (Maria Teresa Regard); "It is as though both of us [were] a force, it's strange, we were engaged before and after, we were a force and this held us up all our lives, all our lives" (Mario Fiorentini). It was always the men, however, who insisted on getting married:

Carla Capponi. Believe me, I was against it, I got married the night before Bentivegna left to join the Yugoslav resistance. Because I had always said no, I didn't want to marry, I didn't want to marry, didn't want to marry. Then, since I became pregnant around June or July—"Ah, you're denying me, I'm going to Yugoslavia to fight, I could die, I want to have the child, I want to give it my name." And this persuaded me, otherwise I didn't want to marry.

For the women, the partisan experience ended with the liberation of the city. The men continued—to the North, to Yugoslavia, with the Allies. They were devoted to the cause, but it was also a deferral of the end of an experience so total that its intensity could be preserved only in the relationship with a person who shared it. It's a need that men cannot acknowledge otherwise: "Mario says, 'When can you get some time off from work?' Well, you can get leave for summer vacation, to get married, or for a death in the family. He says, 'All right then, get some leave to get married'" (Lucia Ottobrini).

5. Long Heroism:
The Military Underground Front

Paolo De Carolis. The armed forces are filled with gold medals, are filled with heroes . . . [But] I believe that the heroism they suffered during the war of liberation was a more complex heroism than the one on the battlefield. There you are aware of what you are doing, but it comes and goes in the impulse of the moment; my father, though, achieved a heroism, I'd say, continued over time because . . . September 8 [1943]: the army dissolves. October: thousands of his colleagues [are deported] . . . After all, he had three children; silver medal, a boy of '99, he'd [fought in World War I], so he might have said that he'd done his part. He might have taken it easy, might have just waited [for the end of the war] and then come out in high uniform with all the braids, the stars, the scarf, the sword . . . But he didn't. Instead, he went to jail, he went ahead to be tortured . . .

The first German raid in Rome targeted the *carabinieri* [army police], suspected of being loyal to the king and, therefore, to the Badoglio government. On October 7, the Germans and the Italian colonial police (PAI) surrounded the barracks, overcame a weak resistance, and arrested and deported about fifteen hundred *carabinieri*.[29] Those who managed to escape the raid began to reorganize: among the leaders were Raffaele Aversa, Giovanni Frignani, Genserico Fontana, Romeo Rodriguez Pereira; they would all be killed at the Fosse Ardeatine. In November, the scattered bands were unified at the orders of General Filippo Caruso. The number of *carabinieri* underground, performing "a systematic work of information and surveillance," was claimed to be about nine thousand.[30]

Meanwhile, Giuseppe Montezemolo had reestablished radio contact with the Badoglio government in the South. He was placed in charge of reorganizing the members of the Armed Forces loyal to the legitimate Italian government and to the monarchy into the Fronte Militare Clandestino (Underground Military Front). Ugo De Carolis was his chief of staff. They would carry on their own resistance in Rome, at times in alliance with the partisan organizations.[31]

Adriana Montezemolo. During the clandestine period Rome was unbelievable. People started doing things, they helped, and he slept a week here and a week there, and in the last days he had to change every night because unfortunately there were so many spies. Of course we were absolutely forbidden to go near our house, because the house was watched, he was afraid that the Germans might arrest mother or us and blackmail him.

Paolo De Carolis. All I remember are a few flashes from the clandestine period, during which we went into hiding, because since my father was underground and wanted, the families were wanted too, for obvious reasons. We had a sense of the danger, because I was under orders, if they stopped me, to give only my mother's name. And I remember one night that we went to see my father, in the house of a distant relative to whom I am very grateful because he gave my father hospitality for some time, and my father had a forged document, dressed as a priest, with the first and last name of this relative. I remember only a warmed-up *polenta,* a terrible hunger, I remember the smell of mildew: it was a cold, cold winter, in 1943–44. We didn't go out much, we lived in two rooms in a very cold and damp convent—and after that, that's all I know, because I never saw my father again.

The underground military front's primary task was to keep the men together. Montezemolo wired the supreme command that "the hungry military bands tend to fall apart," and asked "urgent authorization to spend about a million a day" on wages. Also, he insisted that the government and the southern command do something to "make the bands feel they are participating in an Italian war" and "to credibly abolish the impression that the war continues only between the Germans and the Anglo-Americans."[32] Rodriguez, Fontana, and the *brigadiere* Angelo Manca were arrested by an SS unit led by Herbert Kappler in person while they were withdrawing funds to subsidize their men.[33]

Carla Capponi. I knew Carboni's address, and I went with him once to distribute money to the *carabinieri* at piazza della Libertà. I carried the briefcase filled with thousand lire bills, unbelievable! So I go with him, we walk and walk, we reach piazza della Libertà and I see all these clusters of *carabinieri* waiting around, dressed in the most absurd, crazy manner . . . depending on what they had found, because they didn't wear the uniform, of course. Some still wore military shoes, others had sandals, clogs, anything, as long as it wasn't military.

"At one point dad, when he was still here, asked the southern military command to appoint a general as head of the military front, because he was a colonel . . . In fact, they appointed General Armellini, but in practice it was dad who had everything under control" (Adriana Montezemolo). Even the supreme command had to recognize that personal "prestige" now counted more than rank.[34] "In that situation, it wasn't so much the orders that counted; it wasn't hierarchy and rank; it's not as if he had a general or a colonel to tell him 'Go and get arrested'" (Paolo De Carolis).

Adriana Montezemolo. Of course mother had a great desire to see, to know, to meet dad, and he told her, "Look, I am very busy, I have so many things to do, and most of all, it's very dangerous for us to meet; but look, let's try once a week to set a time and place, once here, once there, so that we can at least see each other." We also shared mother's apprehensions, and I remember very well that on Wednesdays at two she would go out and go to these friends' house, where she waited to meet dad; after which, also to keep from endangering these friends by staying in, they went out and strolled in villa Borghese, places like that. And mom, I think it was two or three Wednesdays that she was able to see dad; of course, she would live the whole week in expectation.

The military front existed in an unusual no-man's land, between the exceptionality of the times and the need for continuity. Loyalty to their pledge and the presence of officers guaranteed legitimacy; but the sense remained that now they were all basically volunteers. With a different culture and psychology, yet the military were in the same position as the *gappisti:* they were motivated only by their conscience, they could drop out any moment, they obeyed their officers only because their officers had earned their respect. Of course, while the *gappisti* thought they were subversive, the military thought they were legitimists. But the front's organization charts displayed odd reversals of hierarchies.[35] The front was a movement of colonels, captains, lieutenants rather than generals. Generals like Simoni, Martelli, and Fenulli accepted the leadership of a colonel, Montezemolo. Many of the generals who were involved with the Resistance were either out or at the edge of active service. Caruso came spontaneously out of retirement after September 8, to take command of the *carabinieri.* Piero Dodi, killed at La Storta, and Vito Artale, killed at the Fosse Ardeatine, were in the reserve. Simoni was retired ("he was out of it, he could have taken it easy; but he could not stand to see so many young people killed, massacred in this way by our own, not by the enemy," says Vera Simoni). Martelli had been removed from the air force; Roberto Lordi, also guilty of denouncing the inadequacy of the Italian air force, had been forced to retire in 1935 (for "reasons of age"—at forty-two), sent to a psychiatric hospital, and exiled.[36]

Montezemolo had earned a promotion while fighting in Spain on Franco's side; he had accepted World War II "with perplexity but in perfect obedience," earning medals and awards in Africa. In the same spirit of obedience and in the name of the same idea of a homeland identified in the monarchy, he joined the Resistance. The military underground front was held together by an ideology of "absolutely apolitical" patriotism.[37] After September 8, however, Italy's future social and political order could no longer be taken for granted; "apolitical" loyalty to the king, then, became in practice political support to one side and one political vision as distinct, or opposed, to others. The front's aims were "war on the Germans and preservation of law and order"; but this order was primarily a social order: the mission was to "secretly organize the force to take charge of public order in Rome, when the moment comes, in favor of the government of His Majesty the King."[38] This is one reason why the killing of Montezemolo was so unexpected: "All thought that the Germans would keep him and put him in charge of Rome when they left, because they knew he would be able to keep order in the city and allow the Germans to leave" (Adriana Montezemolo).

Paolo De Carolis. Rome was an open city, so the program was to destroy equipment, blow up trains, and so on, but without the primary objective of human losses to the Germans; and there was a function of preparation of law and order after liberation. There were grave dangers. Armed bands might have seized the opportunity to subvert the regime; and the *carabinieri* were a police force. As soon as the Allies came, they were to occupy the radio, the ministries, to keep the Communists, the GAP, from getting there first.

"In the cities"—Montezemolo wired—"the possibility of grave consequences and possible reprisals makes a very active guerrilla impossible."[39] The order to abstain from attacking the Germans inside the city was certainly due to the concern for the safety of the population, but also to the intent of keeping Rome peaceful and under control when liberation came. In fact, when the time for action came after the Allied landing in Anzio, less than half of the men nominally organized in the front would be available.[40] The political contrast between the monarchist army underground and the parties that formed the National Liberation Committee [CLN], however, did not prevent cooperation in the field.

Maria Teresa Regard. Montezemolo met with Amendola [the military commander of the Communist Resistance units in Central Italy], and told him: "On such-and-such a day, in December, two trains will ride the Rome-Cassino and the Rome-Formia line. Send people to blow them up." So we and the Partito d'Azione went . . .

Giorgio Amendola, then a leader of the CLN and later a prominent Communist official, writes that Montezemolo told him: "I would never have imagined—I, a monarchist and, I admit it, a passionate anti-Communist, that I would meet together with a Communist to plan such an action."[41] Perhaps Amendola would not have imagined, either, that he would be planning to blow up trains with a general staff colonel: perhaps, what was going on was also a process of mutual discovery between people who were, at the same time, on opposite sides and on the same side. At least some of the military were discovering new political vistas and a new autonomy, beyond uncritical obedience. Montezemolo met with Amendola, General Fenulli contacted the Communist Party because "it was the only Party whose reliability and ability he could count on."[42] Actually, "Many of the *carabinieri,* many of the military whom I met, with whom I fought, were for armed resistance" (*Mario Fiorentini*). Members or former members of the armed forces were organized in Left-wing groups, like Luciano Lusana in the Communist Party or Aladino Govoni in Bandiera Rossa. Partisans and the military underground exchanged information and arms—including the grenades that were used in via Rasella. In the National Liberation Committee, Amendola writes, some suspected that after Montezemolo had met with unexpected opposition to action after the Anzio landing among the military underground, his arrest was intentionally provoked in order to sabotage "the growing cooperation between the Left and the armed forces."[43] After liberation, in a rally at the Teatro Brancaccio, Communist Party Secretary Palmiro Togliatti invited his comrades to applaud the monarchist and military partisans: it may have been his famous "duplicity," but he moved even the proletarians from Torpignattara and the militants of Bandiera Rossa to stand up and cheer.[44] Whether in some army barracks someone invited the soldiers to applaud the Communist partisans, nobody knows.

On March 24, 1998, *carabinieri* in gala uniforms stood at attention by the graves of their companions at the Fosse Ardeatine. It wasn't easy to tell if they knew who they were honoring. The *carabinieri* on duty at the Priebke trial had never been told of their colleagues killed at the Fosse Ardeatine, either: "We had to tell them ourselves: Look, over there, there are twelve of yours, too" (Rosetta Stame).

6. Identities, Allegiances, Memory

"Other scholars suggest that the *gappisti* who organized the attack in via Rasella were aware that, by not delivering themselves to the Germans, among the victims of the inevitable retaliation, the Fosse Ardeatine, would be the leaders of Rome's Partito d'Azione, their political adversaries, who were in jail at the time" (*Archivi di guerra,* September 1998).[45]

"On a morning in October, 1943, I was having breakfast in an open air café in piazza Navona, with Gianfranco Mattei and Giorgio Labò. We were the three 'explosive experts' of the Communist Party. We spoke, among other things, of the risk of being captured by the Nazis, and Gianfranco said: 'In that case the wisest thing would be to kill ourselves. Only this way we could be sure we would do nothing dishonorable.' We would not betray the comrades, he meant.

"A few months later, Gianfranco hanged himself in jail and Giorgio was executed after holding out under atrocious tortures [. . .]

"Now, Your Honor, does it seem in the least way believable that young men hardly over twenty should face such terrible dangers, not in order to fight the Nazis, but only for internal quarrels between Communists and others in the Resistance?" (Giulio Cortini).[46]

Of course there were differences between the more libertarian Partito d'Azione and the Communist GAP. But they did not count much in the heat of underground resistance, and individuals moved from one group to the other often. Mario Fiorentini, who helped organize the action in via Rasella, came to the Resistance through Giustizia e Libertà (the underground organization of the Partito d'Azione), and was for some time a member of both the Partito d'Azione and the GAP. Franco Calamandrei, who was at via Rasella, was the son of one of the founders of the Partito d'Azione, Piero Calamandrei. The mother of the *gappista* Marisa Musu was a member of the Partito d'Azione. According to these "other scholars," a portion of the media, and a court case opened in Rome in 1997,[47] then, Fiorentini, Calamandrei, Musu acted in via Rasella in order to cause the death of their friends and comrades Fernando Norma and Umberto Scattoni, or of the comrades of their own father or mother.

In the end, in fact, the preliminary inquest judge of the Rome tribunal was compelled to acknowledge that there was no grounds at all to the allegation that the action in via Rasella was aimed at other groups in the Resistance rather than at the Germans.[48] Yet four months after the verdict had become public, a publication like *Archivi di guerra,* available at every newsstand, still spoke as if the verdict had never been handed down. Public opinion and the media still managed to ignore decades of public record and historical knowledge as well as recent judicial decisions, while continuing to credit and repeat fantasies, unreliable sources, and myth impermeable to fact. This attitude, in turn, is founded on another pillar of the anti-partisan master narrative: the Resistance was nothing but a war among rival bands, dominated by Communist plots.

The Resistance was, no doubt, also the ground of political tensions, hegemonic projects, and sectarian attitudes (for instance, the CP's hostility to Bandiera Rossa). But it is a mistake to think of it in terms of rigid partitions and monolithic and immutable identities. The Resistance was the work not of abstract political forces but of concrete individuals who had both serious differences and one common goal—the struggle against the Germans and the Fascists. We need only remember the Velletri train, blown by *azionisti,* GAP, and Bandiera Rossa, with explosives and information supplied by the military front, after a meeting between Amendola and Montezemolo.[49] "We of the Bandiera Rossa group fought along with the comrades of the Communist Party, they did actions, we did actions, and we did actions together, because the war against Nazism and Fascism was a total war, with no distinction of barriers. For us rank and file there was no distinction; the conflict was only between the leadership[s]" (Orfeo Mucci). Beyond the usual theme of contrast between sectarian leaders and sincere rank and file, however, we must also perceive another distinction—that between abstract political forces and concrete situations and individuals:

Mario Fiorentini. When I was in Quarticciolo, I was in charge of the sector, and under me I had the *garibaldini* of the CP, the Matteotti Brigades of the Socialist Party, the men from Bandiera Rossa, and also the military and people with no political color, and former Fascists—that is, there was a very fantastic situation and we all fought together, there were no distinctions.

This common ground is also confirmed by the impossibility of assigning each person to one and only one political and organizational identity. According to the claims of the various entities, those who died at the Fosse Ardeatine included 62 partisans from Bandiera Rossa, 40 Communists, 84 *azionisti,* 46 military, 265 Catholics, 75 Jews, 18 Masons,[50] a number of "apoliticals," many Socialists . . . in other words, the number 335 is too small to contain them all. It must mean that many among them were more than one thing, and that trying to divide them up and appropriate them is not the best way of respecting their complexity.

For instance: if we find Antonio Pistonesi, a waiter from Val Melaina, both in the list of the "martyrs" of Bandiera Rossa and in that of the "fallen" of the Partito d'Azione, and we know that he worked with Ferdinando Agnini's non-partisan student organization, our task is not to unravel this knot and label him once and for all, but rather to rethink the whole idea of party allegiance and organizational attachment in the context of the Roman Resistance—and perhaps in all contexts. To quote a less tragic case—how shall we label Don Ferdinando Giorgi: Salesian priest, collaborator of the military front, partisan of the Partito d'Azione, or all three, and more than their sum?[51]

What is true for individuals also applies to certain organizations. The ARSI (Associazione Rivoluzionaria Studentesca Romana, the Roman Revolutionary Student Association), founded by Ferdinando Agnini, organized young people from several parties, and from no party at all; Agnini himself was labeled both as *azionista* and as Communist.[52] The Partito d'Azione brought together the pre-war movement Giustizia e Libertà with groups of liberals, liberal-socialists, and republicans; it was always described as elite group, "very popular among intellectuals, professors and high-ranking professionals"[53], but in Rome it also had a popular following rooted in the tradition of republicanism, anarchism, and the Arditi del Popolo.

The Movimento Comunista d'Italia (Bandiera Rossa) gathered "old comrades . . . who oscillated between true democratic centralism . . . and anarchistic attitudes";[54] small clusters of Socialists and Communists who had lasted through Fascism; Left-wing libertarians and Socialists; anti-Fascist members of the armed forces (like Aladino Govoni and Nicola Stame, killed at the Fosse Ardeatine). According to one of their former leaders, Roberto Guzzo, even the name "Bandiera Rossa" was adopted less out of ideological persuasion than for its appeal to the proletarian *borgate*.

Joining the resistance, then, was also a step in a process of personal growth, a gradual discovery of self and of politics. Most of the partisans were very young, many hardly more than adolescents, who had grown up in the silence of politics. Their choices were influenced by circumstances, family contacts, neighborhood situations: "And then, sometimes it's only accidental whether they end up in the GAP or Bandiera Rossa or the Partito d'Azione; perhaps, they had a brother or a cousin who took them along" (Nicoletta Leoni). Raffaele Zicconi was recruited into the Partito d'Azione by his neighbor Luigi Pierantoni; Franco Bartolini joined the GAP because, on his return from the war, he could not resume contact with Bandiera Rossa; Umberto Turco leaned toward Bandiera Rossa because he happened to know Ornello Leonardi: "I wound up in Bandiera Rossa and I thought I was Communist Party, and I realized only after liberation that it was something else. And right after the liberation I joined the Communist Party, in 1945, which recognized my seniority as far back as '44 because in good faith I thought I was CP while I was Bandiera Rossa."

Death freezes at an arbitrary moment stories whose future developments no one could foresee. One has only to think of future biographies like that of Orfeo Mucci, heir to the memory and pride of Bandiera Rossa but finally a member of the neo-Communist Rifondazione party; or Franco Bartolini, who comes and goes between Bandiera Rossa and the GAP, joins the CP, leaves it after 1968, claims his Bandiera Rossa background, and is close to the young new-Left of Autonomia Operaia and the social centers. Many, who were Communists then, drifted away from the party, or from politics altogether, like Fernando Vitagliano, one of the *gappisti* of via Rasella; most monarchist officers, with the king's leave, swore allegiance to the Italian Republic. Those who died were frozen at the moment of death, and it is right to remember them as they were then—but it is wrong to deny them the possibility of changing, to imagine that they could only have remained what they were.

Out of the three major forces in the Roman Resistance—Bandiera Rossa, Communist Party, Partito d'Azione—two fell apart shortly after liberation. They left no heirs who could claim their memory: "I can't get the city to name a street after Fernando Norma, because he no longer has a party behind him to support him" (Giovanni Gigliozzi). Many activists and sympathizers of these organizations drifted toward forces that did not even exist as such during the Resistance; many more joined the Communist or the Socialist parties. Thus, when (existing) parties send representatives to the commemorations and ceremonies at the Fosse Ardeatine, nobody represents the Partito d'Azione, or Bandiera Rossa.

This pattern, of course, was reinforced by the practice of the Communist Party, which tended to absorb memories as it took in the individuals, encouraging its new members to think of their earlier experiences only as a prehistory of their Party membership. The recognition to Umberto Turco of the seniority acquired in Bandiera Rossa when he is "organized" in the CP is the individual application of a historiographic principle: the multiplicity of forms and experiences of the working-class and revolutionary movements in Italy was to be taken into account only as a disorganized prehistory of the Communist Party:[55] "My great-grandfather was an Anarchist, you know those old Anarchists with the big bow tie . . . Then, when the partisan war was over, each got organized, and my father because a fabulous Communist" (Gaetano Bordoni).

7. Anzio, Forte Bravetta, via Tasso . . .

I always advised my men to refrain from violence.
—Herbert Kappler[56]

Leone [Ginzburg] had died in jail, in the German branch of Regina Coeli, in Rome, during the German occupation, in a chilling February.
—Natalia Ginzburg[57]

The uniformed lieutenant who handled the whip on the upper floor was, in his heart, a patriot, and would today be a Senator.
—Luigi Pintor[58]

"When on January 22 [1944] they landed at Anzio, the order came for us to start the insurrection. We were told by the Allies, over the radio, to start the insurrection; they needed to have some strong action in Rome. They insisted on these actions, we didn't move haphazardly" (Maria Teresa Regard). Montezemolo had orders from the Allies: "The enemy must be sabotaged in every way, their retreat routes must be interrupted, every line of their communications destroyed, they must be struck wherever they appear."[59] "Montezemolo—Amendola writes—informed us that the Allied command requested the 'bands' in Rome to go into action as soon as possible. This was the last message we received from Montezemolo."[60]

Adriana Montezemolo. And then came that terrible Wednesday when she waited, she went to the usual place and dad didn't arrive and she waited, poor mom, you can imagine what state she was in, because she knew, she had realized. The last time she had seen dad, a week before, he told her, "Look, the Allies have landed at Anzio, it is a matter of days, because"—he said—"I have five police organizations on my trail," and, he says, "they're getting closer, and I can't hold out anymore," he says, "I think I can last another eight days but after that I'm sure I can't make it, within eight days they'll catch me, and if they catch me they will surely execute me": these exact words from dad, so he knew very well what he was facing. And after seven days they caught him.

Two days after the landing, the OSS agent Peter Tompkins came to Rome to establish radio contact between the Resistance and the Allies: "The order was to prepare the insurrection. It could have been done: if they had parachuted men over Villa Borghese, the whole city would have seen it, and they would have risen. From my radio post over via del Corso I saw everything that the Germans did, and they were getting ready to leave." Following orders, the partisans attacked. They killed Fascist militias in Prati and Torpignattara, two German soldiers in a jeep in Centocelle, six in trucks blown up in the city center. Maria Teresa Regard planted a bomb in the crowded German army rest stop at the central station, from which soldiers came and went to the front line: the number of casualties remained unknown.[61] On the twenty-eighth, Rattoppatore, Bussi, Scattoni were arrested after the attempt at the Aquila d'Oro failed. On the twenty-ninth (after a week of protests and demonstrations that had all but shut down the university) high schools went on strike. Outside the *liceo* Dante Alighieri, the student Massimo Gizzio was struck by a Fascist bullet in the back; he died after three days in the hospital.[62]

The euphoria over the Allied landing relaxed security.[63] "We had thought that the Allies were coming and the underground groups took risks, came in the open to do actions . . . And many were arrested" (Mario Fiorentini). But the Allies were held back, the Germans counterattacked, the front was stalled, and the Nazis regained control of the city. On January 22, General Simoni was arrested; the next day, Frignani, De Carolis, and Aversa were taken; on the twenty-fifth, Montezemolo fell, together with Augusto Renzini, Gerardo Sergi, Francesco Pepicelli, Angelo Manca, Filippo de Grenet; the next day was the turn of Placido

Martini and his collaborators Carlo Zaccagnini and Teodato Albanese. Martelli and Lordi had been captured on the sixteenth. They would all be killed at the Fosse Ardeatine.

A huge raid swept via Nazionale on the thirty-first; hundreds of men were rounded up and deported to forced labor at the front or in Germany. On the same day, ten partisans were executed at Forte Bravetta; among them were Vittorio Mallozzi and Mario Capecci. On February 2, eleven partisans of Bandiera Rossa (mostly from Valle Aurelia) were executed at Forte Bravetta. The execution was said to be a retaliation for the attack in via Crispi; however, the victims had already been sentenced to death. The firing squad, as always, was made up of Italians of the colonial police (PAI). Those who did not die from the first volley were finished by the SS with pistol shots to the back of the head.[64]

On February 3, the irregular Fascist Koch gang violated the extraterritorial status of Saint Paul's Basilica, Vatican territory, to arrest more than sixty anti-Fascists who were hiding there. The Vatican complained weakly. In the same period, a number of arrests took place in Montesacro: Ferdinando Agnini, Renzo Piasco, Orlando Posti Orlandi, and Antonio Pistonesi would be killed at the Fosse Ardeatine. Dozens of members of Bandiera Rossa fell in late February and early March: an informer turned in Marco Moscato, Pietro Ferrari, Antonio Spunticchia, Aldo Banzi, Pietro Primavera, and Ornello Leonardi; another led the police to arrest Ottavio Capozio and Domenico Polli. Aladino Govoni, Uccio Pisino, Nicola Stame, Ezio Lombardi, and Unico Guidoni were surprised during a meeting in a dairy bar in via Sant'Andrea delle Fratte. All would be killed at the Fosse Ardeatine.

"I unfortunately was in jail in via Tasso with Montezemolo. He behaved in an extraordinary manner, because he was beaten savagely, look—madly. Ours also behaved well, like Gesmundo and many others. But Montezemolo, too, is a hero for me" (Maria Teresa Regard). Montezemolo's courage, Kappler said later, "frankly moved us."[65] They expressed this respect by beating him almost to death. A woman fellow-prisoner later told his family that "his face was all swollen, he had a very high fever from the erysipelas he had got after they beat him like that" (Adriana Montezemolo).

Antonia Bianchi. Especially via Tasso, seeing those tiny rooms where they were kept— it was a very emotional thing for me. In that moment, in that very moment, it was heartbreaking to think that people there had been tortured, you know? Unthinkable. Unthinkable in the twentieth century, unthinkable that it happened fifty years ago, things that one expects in the Middle Ages, you know. But it did. In the twentieth century all this happened. So for me it was a very emotional impact. I kept seeing via Tasso, I saw it within me, and I imagined the people inside via Tasso . . .

In the seat of the German police under Kappler's orders, the walled cells of via Tasso—a street name that in Rome still signifies fear—Dardano Fenulli "was beaten savagely on the soles of his feet and was held with his hands tied behind his back for several days and nights."[66] Sabato Martelli Castaldi was "whipped on the soles of his feet plus enough lashes in soft parts and punches of all kinds," to which he responded with "a *pernacchione*" [a Bronx cheer]. But then he said: "What we miss most here is the lack of air."[67] In a cell of three by seven feet, Simone Simoni was hit until he fainted, then taken out to a fake execution; but all he said is: "I'm sorry I'm not younger, because I would have liked to do even more." He carved a crucifix on the wall of his cell, and wrote in a note to the family: "I am beaten but I suffer with pride, my thought to my country and family."[68] His wife and daughters sought help from his friend, Pope Pacelli, but all he could do was get them permission for one last visit.

Vera Simoni. And so we saw him, and I remember that dad's last words I heard—he had been tortured, he was in this closet-prison, and we were all around him—and he hugged my mother and while he hugged my mother that way, he looked at us, and said: "I am at peace with God and with men."

Lina Frignani, the wife of the *carabinieri* officer Giovanni Frignani, was arrested and forced to witness her husband's torture: "I found him leaning against the wall with his face bleeding from the punches and the lashes; eight or ten men were around him and each vented his beastly instinct on him: one held in his hands a big rubber ball with which he hit him on the stomach; another stuck long, long needles in his flesh and under his nails."[69] Giorgio Labò, the GAP's bomb expert, was held for eighteen days with his hands tied behind his back: "He is forced to lie on his stomach to keep the weight of his body from lying unbearably on his swollen and rotting hands [. . .] the lack of circulation has caused swellings and blood clots to appear even on his face. Around his wrists, a putrid furrow dug by the rope [. . .] To every question, he answered: 'I don't know and I won't say.'"[70] In this state, he was taken to Forte Bravetta and executed.

Luigi Solinas, a member of the military underground, is hanged from an iron rod and beaten with punches, kicks, lashes: "In came an SS officer, captain Pribke [*sic*] . . . Pribke gave me an evil stare, then vomited a series of vulgar insults and finally spat in my face." Priebke threatened to have him shot if he didn't talk; Solinas replied, "God's will be done," and Priebke answered, "here, it's only the Germans' will that counts"—underscoring this point with a blow on the prisoner's temple.[71] Erich Priebke, then a lieutenant, was in charge of external relations; he was the officer with whom the families of important prisoners dealt. But he also performed other duties: "They tied my hands and feet to the office door handle; Priebke kept beating me, he broke my nose, I still bear the mark"; "He was always in attendance, and he pounded me. Each time I fainted he pounded my chest with his boot and said, 'Speak . . . '"[72]

Maria Teresa Regard. Luciano Lusana isn't even registered in via Tasso, he isn't registered anywhere, because he died in prison; in the space of two days, they killed him, he was dumped in a common grave at the cemetery of Prima Porta. Gianfranco Mattei was dumped in the same place as Lusana. We went to look for them together, Lusana's sister and I and other friends, because we hadn't heard anything about them, he wasn't at the Fosse Ardeatine, we had no idea where he was, and instead fortunately we found him there.

Gianfranco Mattei was the other GAP bomb maker. "This Communist Mattei is terrible, he is awfully silent," Kappler said, "but now we are going to use Lieutenant Priebke to make him speak with physical and chemical means." For fear of being unable to resist and betraying his comrades, Mattei hanged himself in his cell.[73] To gauge the horror of via Tasso, in fact, we must not think only of the heroism of those who resisted, but also of the defeat of those who did not. The journalist Carlo Trabucco remembers "a poor being whom the blows had reduced to a shapeless object," until he finally named a few names. "He cannot be considered guilty [. . .] he was in such a state that he could not hold out."[74] This person, too, would be killed at Fosse Ardeatine.

Puci Petroni. All I know is that when [my husband Guglielmo] was taken [to via Tasso] he had all his teeth; when he came out he had to get dentures above and below, so his teeth, someone took them out, and I don't think they used anesthetics. For several years, we had to put very soft cloth on the inside of his shoes, because the soles of his feet had been burned, cut. His eyes were damaged: the wind, a bright light, and immediately they would fill with blood, and burn. And I remember the first night we slept at home; we have a liberty lamp, hanging from the ceiling in our bedroom, a round ball that isn't even very bright. He got into bed before me, and as soon as he got into bed, he said: "Turn off via Tasso."[75]

The stall at the front and the stepping up of repression caused a crisis in the Resistance. The military front was scattered. The activity of Bandiera Rossa and the Partito d'Azione was at its ebb. After the Anzio landing, the central GAP had been dissolved and their members sent to the periphery (Bentivegna and Capponi to Casilino, Fiorentini and others to Quadraro and Quarticciolo). The intelligence work continued, but in the middle of March the Koch gang broke Peter Tompkins's group, which had been signaling German movements and directing air raids via radio.[76] Of its members, Arrigo Paladini and Giuliano Vassalli were imprisoned and tortured at via Tasso; Luigi Mastrogiacomo and Maurizio Giglio would be killed at the Fosse Ardeatine. "Maurizio Giglio really gave his life for mine. He could have easily saved himself, and yet he chose to be tortured, to be killed at the Fosse Ardeatine" (Peter Tompkins).

The Allies at Anzio were in trouble, and the Germans almost succeeded in pushing them back into the sea; partisan support became essential. "Churchill, the radios, told us to strike the Germans always and everywhere" (Peter Tompkins). In mid-February, the central GAP was reassembled: "The Allies at that moment were saying: strike, strike hard. In the month of March the Germans almost push the Allies back into the sea, and so we must show that the city is hostile to the Germans; the Allies at Anzio must know that Rome is fighting" (Mario Fiorentini). For the first time, the Allies provided arms and supplies also to the Communist partisans. Paolo Emilio Taviani, a partisan in the north and later a Secretary of Defense in the Christian Democrat cabinets, recalled that Catholic partisan chiefs told him that "After the half failure of the landing at Anzio, the Allies urged the partisans to do something. This is very important. Not that I want to give the Allies the responsibility for what happened in via Rasella; but it's a fact that there was pressure from them" to attack the Germans behind the lines in occupied Rome.

"Toward February 15 we resume the activity of the unified GAP, and it's an awesome crescendo, that is, from February 15 to March 23 we are on the offensive and we attack almost every day, an awesome forcing" (Mario Fiorentini). On March 3, after a German roundup, a crowd gathered in front of the barracks in viale Giulio Cesare, where the men were being held waiting to be deported. Teresa Gullace, thirty-seven, pregnant and the mother of five children, saw her husband at a window; she ran toward him and an SS shot her and killed her. The GAP responded: in the afternoon there was an open gun fight, and the *gappista* Guglielmo Blasi killed a Fascist. The next day, the notorious Centocelle police commissioner Stampacchia was executed on his doorstep; on the fifth, a German officer was killed in piazza dei Mirti, in Centocelle.[77]

On the ninth, Carla Capponi blew up a German tank truck near the Coliseum. On the tenth, the GAP attacked a Fascist parade marching through via Tomacelli: some Fascists were wounded, a bounty was placed on the attackers, but the Germans forbade the Fascists from holding parades and ceremonies in the open from then on. The CLN parties congratulated the Communists for this daring action in the city center; Carlo Salinari heard favorable comments in the streets: "It's the Communists hitting the Fascists."[78] On the twelfth, thousands of people gathered for the papal audience in Saint Peter's Square, but Pius XII was vague and had words of condemnation only for the air raids.[79]

Death from the air, in fact, kept coming: "There was here in via Bodio a fountain, toward lunchtime all the women went there for water; they all died, all those women who went to the fountain" (Caterina Pierantoni). The hunt for the Jews was still on: these were the days in which Giorgio Fano and Piero Terracina's family were taken. And there was no lull in the roundups, the deportations, the arrests. On March 7, ten partisans, including Giorgio Labò and Guido Rattoppatore, were executed at Forte Bravetta. Informers caused the arrest of Pilo Albertelli, Enrico Ferola, a dozen partisans of the GAP and Bandiera Rossa in Torpignattara, and a group from Bandiera Rossa and the Partito d'Azione who, two days before via Rasella, were planning to blow up the city telephone exchange. They were all killed at the Fosse Ardeatine.

Via Rasella, then, was the culmination and the conclusion of this phase of the war. Afterward, the Resistance went on, but the retaliation, arrests, and executions, left a mark. Also, a comrade's betrayal broke up the central GAP.

Valentino Gerratana. One of those who were in via Rasella was Guglielmo Blasi, who—while usually the [central] GAP members were mostly students, petty bourgeois, I mean—he was one of the few who were instead of a proletarian background. He had an infallible aim, and so he was appreciated for this talent of his. He was with the GAP, at via Rasella; then, on his own, he'd go and rob stores. He was caught, during a robbery; then he immediately changed sides and turned everybody in.

Blasi's defection also caused the arrests of Carlo Salinari and Franco Calamandrei. Capponi and Bentivegna managed to get away and go on to fight with partisan units in the hills behind Palestrina; Fiorentini and Ottobrini moved to the Tivoli area. Marisa Musu, Pasquale Balsamo, and Ernesto Borghesi were arrested on April 7, after a failed attempt to kill Mussolini's son Vittorio; they managed to escape from jail, but were now known to the police and could no longer be of use in the underground.[80] Between the end of March and the beginning of April, however, the partisans still attacked Fascist posts and German cars and trucks, causing several casualties.[81] On April 17, hundreds of men were deported from Quadraro. After a mass to commemorate Albertelli, Canali, and Gesmundo, in Santa Maria Maggiore, a Fascist started an argument and was killed. There were attempts to raise the conflict from guerrilla to mass struggle; workers rallied and marched in San Lorenzo; on May 3, the CLN called for a general strike, which failed.

The most effective form of struggle, however, was another: the women's attacks on bakeries and mills for bread and flour.

Giovanna Rossi. The women comrades from Valle Aurelia, unbelievable, unbelievable. They marched down to Trionfale to attack the bakeries. At the warehouses at Campo

Parioli, at Villa Glori, it was the women of Ponte Milvio, which was a desperately poor *borgata* then, and they were capable of anything to get a piece of bread. I was a little different, I was a girl and I was much younger. The wildest were the women who had children. The women who had children were wild.

Ester Fano. A thing that I absolutely don't forget is the tale of a maid we had, who told with enthusiasm, with joy, as if it were a battle in the *Orlando Furioso,* of an assault on a train in San Lorenzo or Tiburtina to carry away [food], and who got a sack of flour, who got some other thing. And she said: "And then, mom made *pasta e fagioli!*" As a sort of undreamed synthesis of all that is good. Mom made *pasta e fagioli!* Around this girl's tale there was such a joy . . . the way someone might speak who has just torn down the Bastille, this is how she spoke.

On April 6, in front of a bakery in Tiburtino, a guard killed Caterina Martinelli. The next day, an inscription appeared on the sidewalk, dictated by the partisan poet Mario Socrate: "Here the Fascists murdered / Caterina Martinelli / a mother who could not stand / to hear the hungry cry / all together / of her seven children." The next day, in Ostiense, Fascists and Germans executed in cold blood ten women who participated in a mass invasion of the Tesei flour mill, supplier to the German army. There had been no German casualty, and no partisan attack.[82]

In mid-May, the Anzio frontline finally moved. Until the last, the decision to call for Rome's insurrection hung open. The partisans waited for a signal that did not come: the Allies and the conservative forces wanted to avoid the damage that a battle might cause to the city, but were also concerned with keeping the city of the king and the pope quiet and safe for the return of the government. However, as they entered Rome on the evening of June 4, the Allied troops were welcomed by the armed partisans of the Communist Party and Bandiera Rossa.[83]

Scattered fights continued until the next day. On the morning of the fifth, Ugo Forno, twelve years old, fired upon the retreating Germans to stop them from blowing up a bridge on the Aniene; they fired back, and the boy was killed. "It was a day of great celebration but also of tension. There had been in the morning a clash at palazzo Sciarra and another in corso Rinascimento. In fact, the last partisan casualty in Rome took place at five in the afternoon: it was Pietro Principato, who was a comrade from Bandiera Rossa and, while he was on patrol in Torpignattara, was killed by a Fascist sniper" (Rosario Bentivegna).

In this atmosphere, Bentivegna was involved in an incident that would also weigh on the memory of via Rasella. This is his story: "I was on patrol as a partisan officer, and I had a gunfight with two people who were tearing up bills. I ordered them to halt, and they responded, one by shooting, and the other by pulling his gun out of his holster . . . I was faster . . ." The victim was Giorgio Barbarisi, a lieutenant in the Finance Guard, a collaborator of the Allies.[84] After a trial held by the Allies and intended to be exemplary, Bentivegna was sentenced to eighteen months for excessive self-defense; a month later, in a revision of the trial, he was acquitted on self-defense. The incident, however, left him with the aura of an "easy gun," which would contribute to the construction of Bentivegna as the "monster" of via Rasella.

To the last, Fascists and Nazis continued to kill. On June 3, with the Allies at the gates, the Italian colonial police executed six prisoners in Forte Bravetta. As they prepared to leave, the Germans loaded the prisoners left in via Tasso on trucks to take them north with them. One of the trucks wouldn't start; the German soldiers ran and let the prisoners go (one of them was Carlo Salinari). Another truck, carrying fourteen prisoners (among them was Bruno Buozzi, a Socialist union leader) stopped, possibly for a mechanical breakdown, in via Cassia, between via Trionfale and La Storta. The next day, in a grove by a fountain, all the prisoners were killed. It was the Nazis' last farewell to Rome. There had been no partisan attack.

<hr />

Carlo Castellani. *My father had a sister, his sister had a husband, this husband was a partisan, Brigata Garibaldi. The evening of April 3, 1944, he came over to our house and said: "You know, I'm here because I've been warned that tonight they're coming to arrest me, and I don't want to be found at home . . ." They scolded him a bit: "If you are being watched, they'll come to your house, they don't find you, they'll look for you at your relatives." "Well . . . in that case, I'll get out from the window, and besides I'm armed, I'm not afraid." "Well, you are armed, but I'm not!" The morning of April 4 comes, nobody came to look for him, during the night my father goes out with him to try to set him up in a convent and [he says], "I want to say goodbye to my wife!" "Skip it, I'll see her and give her your message." "No, I want to see my wife and my children!" So they went to viale Trastevere to see his wife; on their way out, they were caught, loaded on a car, taken to Regina Coeli.*

Later in the afternoon some SS came to the house, and told my mother: "Your husband has been arrested!" They pushed her aside very rudely and did a summary search. But they didn't say either where he had been taken, or under what charges: he's been arrested, period. They made a mess of the house and left. And here comes the wisdom of the women of Rome. My mother was not the only one whose husband was arrested. She talks to one, talks to another, they advise her to go to Regina Coeli on a given day with a load of clothes and food; if he's there, he'll get it. In fact the next day they gave her back his dirty laundry and we found out that my father was there, in Regina Coeli, cell 279. It was a month and a half of agony, of climbing mirrors . . . and my mother, the last recollection she has of him, his face through the lattice of the wicket of the second-floor gate and she was below, then the German caught her arm and pulled her away.

*One fine day, one sad day, my mother takes the change of clothes, and the next day it is re-
turned: he has been moved, no one knows where. We go through the same routine, and we find out
that he is in via Tasso. And via Tasso wasn't the quiet, pleasant boarding house where you go on
holiday. With via Tasso, no contact; all you could send was two hard boiled eggs a week, and I heard
from someone who later got out of via Tasso that these hard-boiled eggs were divided among the
four, five men who were [in the cell]. Then June 3 came, June 4 came, and the anxiety to go see . . .*

*Then the news came that these fourteen bodies had been found, abandoned at La Storta. They
arrived there early in the morning, or during the night; they kept them all day tied in this farmhouse; they said they had stopped there because the truck wouldn't go. Then in the afternoon of
the fourth, in coincidence with the entrance of the Allies from Porta San Giovanni and Porta San
Paolo, someone decided they must be killed.*

*[We heard] around June 6 or 7, with a pounding sun so hot it split the stones, that year. And my
sister, my father's sister, went to the Santo Spirito [hospital], where the bodies had been taken, thinking she would identify her husband, instead she had to identify her brother. We went to the funeral,
went to La Storta . . . every year on June 4 we would go and it was completely abandoned, abandoned for ten years. There was only a cross by the road—[which is not where they were killed] because they took them out of the farmhouse, made them walk down a ravine, and there was this little
sort of glen in the interior, surrounded with trees, and there they killed them. What made us mad was
that for those poor wretches of the Fosse Ardeatine they did up the place real nice; ours were completely
forsaken. The corpses were taken to the Santo Spirito and then to the Verano cemetery and buried in
the shrine of the fallen of World War I, that white monument that I remember you go down some
stairs . . . Anyway, the tenth anniversary comes around, and like every year we go, where normally
every year there's a Mass, a few perfunctory words, and then everybody went back to their own
business—and we find a whole ceremonial apparatus, a stage, flags, the* carabinieri *brass band: "This
year we're making it solemn, we're doing the whole thing up here . . . ," practically, by the road. "But
the dead died down there, what are we doing here?" All the relatives, my brother, my mother, my aunt,
the widow of Bruno Buozzi, Pennacchi, De Angelis, we all go down where they were killed, down that
horrible road that was still a dirt road; we say a few prayers and come back up. On our way back, we
hear the loudspeaker, a whole panegyric, unfortunately only one way—I have nothing against the
person, but frankly we were sick and tired of always hearing "Buozzi and his companions."[85] Why don't
we say, the fourteen of La Storta. They died the same, they suffered in via Tasso in the same way. All
right—we rebel against this panegyric. We begin to shout, to try to talk to the journalists, to the
mayor of Rome, Rebecchini. This led to a meeting with the mayor and to the redoing of the place the
way it stands today—with all the problems that have emerged, there's no fence, there's no light . . .*

. . . Giovanni Frignani, Alberto Funaro, Mosè Funaro, Pacifico Funaro, Settimio Funaro, Angelo Galafati, Antonio Gallarello, Luigi Gavioli, Manlio Gelsomini, Gioacchino Gesmundo, Alberto Giacchini, Maurizio Giglio, Romolo
Gigliozzi, Calcedonio Giordano, Giorgio Giorgi, Renzo Giorgini, Antonio
Giustiniani, Giorgio Gorgolini . . .

CHAPTER 6

VIA RASELLA

. . . Gastone Gori, Aladino Govoni, Umberto Grani, Ennio Grieco, Unico Guidoni, Mario Haipel, Domenico Iaforte, Sebastiano Ialuna, Costantino Imperiali, Mario Intreccialagli, Sandor Kereszti, Boris Landesman, Gaetano Lavecchia, Ornello Leonardi, Cesare Leonelli, Epidemio Liberi, Amedeo Lidonnici, Davide Limentani . . .

Ada Pignotti. *And then, while we were out looking for them—one day, we were on the tram, which back then went by the Coliseum. A man, he had a paper,* Il Messaggero, *and in box characters on it—"Justice has been done." I don't remember the exact words, because, at the sight, it made me ill, and my sister-in-law after me; and we got off the tram, because we could do nothing but leave. And so, then, we began to believe they were dead.*

Alessandro Portelli. *And you, afterwards . . .*

Ada Pignotti. *Despair. Despair. I still talk about it—and I can't speak. Which has been like this for fifty-four years. Because that wasn't the end. They say, "Well, he's dead now, you've got to . . ."; they say, "Well, you adapt, because he's dead now and he exists no more . . ." But how he died! And it keeps coming back; and now they've stirred it all up again, from A to Z, and it's been terrible. And then, I found myself alone because my folks didn't live in town, I'm from the Abruzzi—and besides, what could they do? Even they, there wasn't a thing they could do for me. So I found myself alone, I stayed with my brother-in-law's wife, I stayed three months, but then, what was the use? I was there, I wasn't doing anything. I couldn't find a way to . . . because I had to find work. And my husband hadn't left me a thing because, first of all it was wartime, there wasn't much anyway; plus—[married] three months, what could I expect, after all? It was inevitable, we were just beginning. Anyway. In conclusion, I stayed there three months, then I saw it wasn't . . . what was the use of me staying there? I went home.*

I. That Day

Bruno Frasca. That day, I don't remember it, because I was a year and a half . . . I can tell you all the things that afterwards I heard tell from my mother, from an unfortunate person who lived a tragedy. She said that it was two-thirty in the afternoon and they always came by, this platoon of Germans, they came every day. At one point, she heard a big explosion, a blast, all the panes were shattered, in the confusion the Germans began to shoot like mad . . . They shot up the place because I guess they thought that the bomb had been thrown from a window, and instead it was in that cart . . .

"The success of the action in via Tomacelli" writes Giorgio Amendola, "encouraged us to increase the intensity of our activity. We decided, thus, to plan a new and bigger strike on March 23, the anniversary of the foundation of Fascism." The plan was to attack simultaneously the jail in via Tasso and the Fascist anniversary parade. The Socialists, too, were "getting impatient . . . and asked us to plan a joint armed action."[1]

At the end of February, at the corner of via Rasella, Mario Fiorentini had seen the platoon of the Bozen regiment, a police unit attached to the SS in Rome: "I see them march by, I am immediately on guard: I saw the rotten green [of the uniforms] of those who came to take my parents. On the eighteenth, we meet on the spot, and discuss the plan. And when Sasà [Bentivegna] sees them, he says, 'we must attack them.'"

The action was planned for the 21st but was postponed because of problems with the preparation of the explosive. On the twenty-second, the column doesn't come. "The command tells us: you must attack on the twenty-third": a symbolic date, the anniversary of the founding of the Fascist Party. The usual Fascist parade has been forbidden by the Germans ("marching the Fascist banners with music through the streets, while the population of Rome was going hungry," writes the German consul Möllhausen, would have been "an unnecessary provocation").[2] "And on the twenty-third they came" (Mario Fiorentini).

On such a date, even the parade of a company returning from rifle drill might look like a provocation. Therefore, the routine of the Bozen battalion (military police attached to the SS) was altered: they went back to quarters later than usual, security was reinforced, the noncoms marched at the head of the platoon rather than, as they usually did, in the middle; and "They told us not to sing. Usually, we were always supposed to sing. But that morning we were told not to" (Sylvester Putzer). After drill, "We started back with our rifles loaded, and it had never been done before" (Franz Bertagnoli). The streets were empty, the city deserted: it was a special, tense day. But nobody explained why; for decades, the Bozen survivors would see these deviations from routine as the cues to a plot in which all—Germans, partisans, Romans—were in collusion against them.[3]

Silvio Gigliozzi. And, nothing; that day . . . I at the time was ten, and my sister two. Every day, dad gave us a croissant and told us, go eat it out in the gardens on via Quattro Fontane. That day, too, around two, dad told us, all right, go and play in the garden.

The events of that day have been told countless times, but always in pieces: the partisans, the neighborhood, the Nazi officers, the soldiers, each from their limited points of view. Sometimes the stories shrink to worn out anecdotes; often they are loaded with a formless and terribly intense emotion. Thus, that wooden garbage cart, with the explosives inside, stands incongruously at the core of all narratives, as a mere local-color detail for some, as a powerful visual icon for others, symbolizing perhaps the discrepancy between the humble means and the enormous consequences, or even to suggest somehow a peculiar dishonesty in those who used it.

On March 22, Carla Capponi received the explosive from the military front. The next morning, Rosario Bentivegna took the long walk to via Rasella across the city center, wearing a streetsweeper's smock, and pushing a cart with twelve kilos of TNT in a steel box, six kilos of other explosives, and loose iron fragments, all under a thin stratum of garbage. He ran into two real street sweepers, who knew he shouldn't be there, and prevented them from looking into the cart by making them believe he was carrying black market goods. Carla Capponi, carrying on her arm a raincoat Bentivegna is to wear over his smock after the action, walked back and forth between via del Tritone and via Quattro Fontane. The Germans were late. Bentivegna, halfway down via Rasella, by the gate of historic Palazzo Tittoni, waited and chain-smoked, until he had hardly enough matches left to light the fuse.[4]

In the collective imagination, in the tales of the passers-by, of the neighborhood, of the soldiers, everything happened in the flash of the explosion: a blast, period. In the narratives of the partisans, however, the time was long and agonizing: preparation, waiting, false alarms, more waiting, dead time. "Via Rasella wasn't as tough as many other [episodes]; but it was very, very tough from the point of view of neuro-psychic endurance, because it lasted so long, it lasted so long" (Rosario Bentivegna). The Germans and the neighborhood didn't realize what was going on before the explosion; the partisans never saw most of what happened after; Germans and civilians were only afraid of each other. And their narratives have hardly ever been placed next to each other.

At a quarter to four, siesta time was over, the street was no longer as empty, the partisans were about to give up and fall back, when at last the platoon appeared at the end of the street. Franco Calamandrei took off his cap: it was the signal to light the fuse. Carla Capponi writes:

> As the signal was given we realized
> That the hour of judgment had come,
> At each corner a face was upon us
> Leaning as if waiting,
> And away passed, swept by fear,
> The young shyness
> Of our twenty years.[5]

Arthur Atz. March 23, that day, after we'd been to the shooting range, we were an hour late, and we turned into via Rasella. When we came up, a bomb exploded and we believed that it was an airplane bomb, and we soon saw that it was not so and at that moment the partisans also started shooting at us. I was the first in the row, the first before me was . . . nothing else happened to me, I came out unscathed. We had . . . there were so many wounded and dead, we didn't know what to do, and so ended all the story, I believe, of that day.[6]

As they came up the street, the Germans again started to sing; children followed after them. Liana Gigliozzi recalls: "We saw two men come back up the street, they were dressed like street sweepers. One of the two, I found out later, was Rosario Bentivegna. 'Go away, children,' they told us. Somebody pushed me, they threw us, my brother and me, into a shoemaker's shop" around the corner.[7] Bentivegna warned off a group of men who are working on the street ("'Go, run, because in a minute here, with the Germans, it will be a havoc,' and they too ran off"). One man, Orfeo Ciambella, didn't understand or didn't take him seriously; he would be hit by the fragments of the explosion and bear the consequences for the rest of his life.[8]

Pasquale Balsamo. Ferdinando Vitagliano and I were standing at the entrance of the tunnel; we were supposed to cover the retreat of our *gappisti* who were stationed on the steps, on the steps that went up to the Quirinale. There were some children, and they were following the column that marched, singing, so it was a cheerful sight; fortunately they had a ball, so Fernando gave it a kick and I another; and the children— "You son of a bitch . . ."

The children ran after the ball; "and among the insults of these children we heard the roar of the explosion" (Pasquale Balsamo). Halfway up via Rasella, another child was not as lucky. Probably, while Bentivegna was walking away toward via Quattro Fontane (with his back to the cart), 11-year old Piero Zuccheretti turned the corner of via del Boccaccio close to the where the cart stood. His body would be found in pieces, next to another body that was never identified, either another victim of the bomb or of the random fire of the Germans.[9]

"As we turned the corner, there was this enormous roar that I still remember, that still thunders in my ears" (Liana Gigliozzi). "When the bomb exploded, at the height of the second floor windows it created a ceiling of glass, all the window panes, a roof of glass, that suddenly—as if it had been suspended in mid-air—crashed down upon the German column" (Pasquale Balsamo). "I was hit by a volley of fragments," says Sylvester Putzer; "I had neither time nor presence of mind to wonder what had happened: I was bleeding all over . . . Something cut an artery, I was bleeding . . ."[10] From the steps in via del Boccaccio, Raoul Falcioni, Silvio Serra, Francesco Curreli, and Pasquale Balsamo attacked with hand grenades and engaged the rear guard in gunfire toward the tunnel; Capponi and Bentivegna disengaged along via Quattro Fontane, pursued by Fascist fire: "We reached piazza Vittorio, [Carlo] Salinari was there waiting for us, he had got there before us, and he said it's all right, everybody okay, you're all safe" (Carla Capponi).

Konrad Sigmund: The explosion . . . there wasn't only one. There were several. We all carried five or six hand grenades on our belts, and many exploded, either because they were hit by the fragments, or from the heat that grew out of the explosion. This is how many died.[11]

Karl Andergassen had "his head cut off; [Eugen] Oberlechner bled to death because the blast tore off both his arms" (Franz Cassar). "The cart with the explosive was two or three meters away from my shop," says Guido Mariti, a printer in via Rasella: "The blast threw us to the ground. I was wounded, my face was covered with blood." Everybody went berserk. The platoon's commander, Major Dobbrick, "ran up and down screaming: 'Run, you pigs!' We were in pieces, many already dead, and he kept calling us pigs . . . And where on earth were we supposed to run?" (Joseph Praxmarer).[12]

The shoemaker at the corner of via Quattro Fontane called Silvio and Liana Gigliozzi into his shop: "Come right in, kids, they're bombing" (Silvio Gigliozzi). At first, the Germans also believed it must be an air raid but soon realized they'd been attacked. Their guns were loaded, and they started shooting around. Annetta Baglioni, sixty-six, a maid in Palazzo Tittoni, looked out of a window: "From below, the Germans fired, the bullet bounced on a shutter and went into this poor woman's head" (Luigi Catemario). She died a few days later; German fire also resulted in another dead (Pasquale Di Marco, aged thirty-four) and eleven wounded.[13] "Yes, we shot around . . . here, behind, because the partisans kept shooting at us. We didn't see them, whether they were on the roofs or where, and so the story ended I believe" (Arthur Atz).

Eugen Dollman, head of the SS in Rome, recalls human limbs scattered here and there, big pools of blood, the air filled with groans and screams, and shots still coming from the rooftops.[14] This last detail is a figment of the Germans' panic and confusion.

"The scene was beyond description: dead bodies, wounded and ruins," writes Herbert Kappler: "The general confusion was very intense." The Germans still thought the attack was coming from the houses: they knew the city was hostile. General Mältzer, military commander of Rome, "was excited and wished to blow up the whole neighborhood. At that moment the house search and the evacuation of the dwellings in the vicinity of the scene were in full swing. Mältzer informed me that these orders had been issued by himself ."[15]

The SS, the Finance Guard, the PAI (Italian colonial police), and "a few of us of the Tenth Mas," a Fascist brigade (Massimo Uffreduzzi), broke into the houses and shops and pulled out whomever they found: "We went into this shoemaker's shop, stayed a couple of hours, then the Germans came and took him away" (Silvio Gigliozzi). In Palazzo Tittoni, Bice Tittoni, an eighty-year-old lady, "was trying to figure out this explosion, less than ten minutes after, and eight Germans broke into her room screaming in German that she had planted the bomb, and they were going to arrest her. She answered in German that it's ridiculous to think that an eighty-year old woman may go around throwing bombs under her own window" (Luigi Catemario). They took her away any-how; she would be released the next morning. Armed Germans broke into An-gelo Pignotti's house, where they found his brother Umberto with his wife Ada, his cousin Antonio Prosperi with his wife (also named Ada) and three little girls, and his nephew Fulvio Mastrangeli: "They tore my sister [from my father's arms] and gave her to my mother"; they take away all the men, who will never return (Ada Prosperi).[16] Houses and shops were sacked.

Silvio Gigliozzi. They kept shooting all afternoon; in the evening I finally managed to get through. Our bar was filled with Fascists, Germans, who were all drunk, the bar destroyed, they stole the till. We had a cellar under the bar, where we kept wine; they shot up the barrels, all the wine on the floor, the lights were out, I saw all these shad-ows in there, all dark, and them drinking, drunk . . .

They came into the porter's lodge at Palazzo Tittoni: "They dripped blood all over, and my mom got out all that she could find [to take care of them]; she prayed to the Lord that they hadn't come to take my father. Yet, the officers wouldn't listen to reason, though she'd taken care of them, and took away dad, my uncle, another lodger, it was despair, despair" (Vincenza Gatti). These men would be released; others were not so fortunate. Celestino Frasca was picked up off the street ("He'd come out of the barbershop to go pick up my brothers in kindergarten, and he wound up at the Fosse Ardeatine instead," Bruno Frasca says), like Ettore Ronconi, who had come bringing wine from Genzano; they were killed at the Fosse Ardeatine. Umberto Ferrante, who worked in Mariti's print shop, recalls: "As soon as we came out of the printshop, with our hands up, we were faced with a scene I'll never forget. That child's trunk had been blown halfway up the street, twenty or thirty meters away from Palazzo Tittoni. Instinctively, I stood still and began to pray: 'Ave Maria . . . ' 'Raus, raus,' a shout and a gun barrel in my kidneys pushed me forward. A little further lay another victim: you couldn't tell what she was, man or woman, young or old, she was just pulp with a coat over it."[17]

"Three comrades were meeting [in Romolo Gigliozzi's bar] to plan an attempt, organized by I don't know who" (Orfeo Mucci). It is not clear why they were in that place at that moment. Antonio Chiaretti and Enrico Pascucci, telephone workers from Bandiera Rossa, "seeing the Germans put all the passers-by against the wall [. . .] pulled out their guns to defend themselves, but Tommaso Chiaretti fell immediately, cut down by machine gun, while Enrico Pascucci was arrested (and, later, beaten savagely)." Giovanni Tanzini, a mason, was arrested nearby with a Bandiera Rossa card in his pocket. Deported to Germany, he was thought to have died at the Fosse Ardeatine, until he returned, years later, broken in mind and body.[18]

The chauffeur of the Chief of Police Pietro Caruso was running toward piazza Barberini with a gun in his hand; the SS took him for a terrorist and killed him. Not knowing where the attack came from, the Germans panicked and saw terrorists everywhere: "The street doors were bolted from the inside. I think they were all in cahoots. The Germans broke them down. In the houses, they found sixteen partisans who later were executed at the Fosse Ardeatine. One was hiding in a closet with a hand grenade in his hand" (Arthur Atz). Kappler would later claim that three of the men arrested in a house via Rasella were caught in the act of taking a Communist flag off a wall.[19]

Actually, only one door was bolted, by the frightened residents, on the corner of via del Boccaccio. Inside, only peaceful and frightened citizens; but the Germans shot at the windows (the marks are still visible), then broke down the gate with hand grenades and went in.

Sergio Volponi. When they started shooting, we all ran out. All the men brought the women and children, me among them, out in the stairwell . . . When they threw the two hand grenades, the curtain of smoke came up the stairwell, and we couldn't breathe. At last someone remembered that the gate was barred and my mother, still living and well—she's eighty-three—fortunately she looked out the top floor window, which had a cornice, together with this other lady. Together, they began to scream, "Don't shoot, don't shoot, we're opening."[20]

Four men came down the stairs: among them were Ferruccio Caputo, an eighteen-year-old student, and Guido Volponi, who was in bed with the flu and came to the gate in house coat and slippers. But the Germans are in such a terror that the SS Boran Domizlaff "sees" a completely different scene: "There was a great confusion. The house was barred and I believe, but I am not sure, that two Italian parachutists attempted to break down the door. Four or five men were brought out of that house. All the Italian population went toward them and beat them. They were leaned against the wall and it looked like they wanted to lynch them. One was already on the ground. I was the only officer on the scene and I felt it was my duty to step in. I took those men and led them away to via Quattro Fontane. They were placed in a truck and driven away. A member of Unit Four was near me, and he said that those men had been saved from lynching by my intervention."[21]

No one else recalls attempts to lynch anyone; if anything, a number of witnesses recalled acts of violence by German officers toward the population. Far from saving their lives, Domizlaff sent those men to die at the Fosse Ardeatine.

Meanwhile, Kappler arrived on the scene. "I approached General Mältzer. He was excited and in tears. Look, he told me, what they have done to my men, and he pointed to some of the dead."[22] The image of General Mältzer "waving his hands like a madman," screaming "Revenge, revenge for my poor comrades!" (Eugen Dollman) is another of the icons handed down from that day.

Kappler took the situation in hand. He made sure the wounded were picked up and taken to the hospital; ordered his men to stop shooting against "non-existent targets"; collected what was left of the partisans' grenades. "I thought I would examine the debris myself, but when a saw a little girl's thigh and arm I left the task to others. I felt the same resentment as on other occasions after bombardments."

Liana Gigliozzi. They sealed via Rasella; I know for certain that my father managed to get out of via Rasella, because as soon as he heard the explosion he got out and ran to the garden to see if my brother and I were there, because there was talk of civilian casualties; so my father looked through the debris and didn't see us, so he ran to the garden because in that moment I think there was a great chaos at the garden, didn't find us because we were in the shoemaker's shop. He went back into via Rasella. There was this Fascist policeman he knew: "Look Romolo, if you go into via Rasella you'll never get out . . ." And the last words he told him were, "I must go, I must find the children . . . they're not at the garden, they may be dead . . ." So I think my father died believing this, too.

"I've been told that from the windows they saw him, with his white jacket on—he was a bartender—searching among the German dead, if we were there, too" (Silvio Gigliozzi). Hans Plack, quartermaster in the Bozen battalion, says that among the men arrested "there was a guy in a white jacket, like an ice-cream vendor. He addressed us as 'camerati' but carried three grenades in his bag."[23] Perhaps, this quartermaster's paranoia was the reason why Gigliozzi, rounded up with his father and brother and taken for a terrorist, was sent to die at the Fosse Ardeatine.

Bruno Frasca. Finally they made us all come out and lined us up in front of Palazzo Barberini . . . you can see that famous photograph . . . and my mother said that with one arm she held me, and she kept the other one up . . . and it seems we were all supposed to be executed . . . all the neighborhood blown up, and instead the order came to send the women and children away and keep only the men . . .

"At gunpoint, they lined us up all the way to via Quattro Fontane in front of Palazzo Barberini," says Guido Mariti; "Kappler told us: 'Comrades kaputt, you kaputt.' But he also told us that we would be freed if the perpetrator of the attack had come out."[24] No one else remembers any such words, nor did Kappler ever claim that he said them—though it would have been to his credit if he had. The other prisoners remember only shouts, orders, and threats; other witnesses saw men beaten with rifle butts, women grabbed and hit with fists by German troopers and high-ranking officers. Then the women were released and the men were locked a few blocks away in the Viminale, the seat of the Ministry of the Interior, "all in one room, lying on the ground, among urine and excrements."

Elisa De Santis. My father-in-law always talked about how he happened to be at via Rasella, going by via Rasella on business just at the moment of the explosion, practically in the moment of the reprisal, so he was arrested along with a lot of other people who were in the area, about a hundred, and was locked up for several hours, overnight I think, not knowing what would happen. So there were scenes of panic, he tells me of a huge room, a night spent where there were also people who had been wounded, hit with rifle butts, without a chance to use a bathroom, nothing, so there were persons who were ill, in every sense. The next day, he was, with very few others, ordered to clean up the room and then, inexplicably, he still doesn't know why, released; the others, I think most of them, were then taken to the Fosse Ardeatine.

"All the people that were rounded up that day were piled up in the cellars of the Viminale. It was more than three hundred people, and we had to go through the background of each, make lists, checks, phone calls. A job that lasted until morning, and we did it very scrupulously, I guarantee, so that no innocent would be caught" (Hans Plack). Toward two A.M., some were called. The others thought it was because they had some kind of protection or recommendation; instead, they had been selected to be killed. Hans Plack does not remember, and no one asked him, what the charges were against Angelo and Umberto Pignotti, Antonio Prosperi, Fulvio Mastrangeli, Guido Volponi, Celestino Frasca, Ferruccio Caputo, and Romolo Gigliozzi.

———•———

"My cousin Benedetto [Gigliozzi] and my uncle [Domenico] came back to my house that night; black and blue, a frightful sight . . . They didn't dare go home, and came to me. They didn't know where Romolo was . . . my uncle said, 'I left him at the Viminale, he was there . . . '"(Giovanni Gigliozzi). "Then, the next day, my grandfather and my uncle and my mother came back. She says, 'What about Romolo?' They say, 'He stayed at the Ministry of Interior to clean up.' I think it was an excuse. My grandfather said, 'Look, Romolo stayed behind to clean up.' And we never saw him again" (Silvio Gigliozzi).

Vincenza Gatti. Me looking out the window and mom picking up the pieces of human bodies, I think that was a sight that—I was eight, nine—left its mark on me. I still remember that truck, black, that pitiful black coach, that came, to collect these remainders, and down the street flowed water and salt . . .

2. The Germans Who Sang

[. . .] they marched, fifty or a hundred of them, for their "friendly" entrance, unarmed and in tight ranks, bare-headed, the blond thin hair caressed by the autumn breeze [. . .] and they sang in chorus, in their silvery German voices, the national-socialist anthem, the "Horst Wessel Lied."

—Aldo Zargani, *Per violino solo*[25]

Carla Capponi. About those who carried out . . . who did the executions in the Fosse Ardeatine, there is an important detail, which is that Kappler offered the commander of the Bozen [regiment] . . . of the special SS police from Bolzano, to give them the satisfaction of avenging the attack, to be the ones to carry out the reprisal; and instead the commander refused, they refused, and this I must say, in all truth, was a brave gesture, if you wish, of these special troops that had survived the attack.

They were not special troops: it was the Eleventh Company of the Polizeiregiment Bozen, in training for public order duty in Rome. Though they were attached to the SS and depended on Rome's military command, they were not at that point combat units (later, the Bozen regiment would be employed in anti-partisan operations in the north). Rather, they were in charge of the kind of "order" that Nazi occupation meant in Rome: round-ups, deportations, and repression.

The men came from the German-speaking Italian province of Bolzano (Bozen), denominated Alto Adige by the Italian state but known as South Tyrol to its population. In 1939, in the framework of the special relations between Fascist Italy and Nazi Germany, the South Tyrolese were given the option to become German citizens, and a number did; later, when the whole Tyrol and parts of north-eastern Italy were annexed to the Reich, German citizenship was automatic. Until September 1943, only those who had opted for German citizenship (*optanti*, "choosers") were recruited; after German occupation and annexation, nominal Italian citizens were also drafted—under the pretense that they were all volunteers (most of them were only to the extent that if they had to be drafted at all they would rather serve in these units, better paid and farther from the front lines.[26]

Arthur Atz: My name is Arthur Atz from Caldaro, I am a farmer, and an Italian, and I did my military service in '39 in Italy, in Sardinia. After, I went home. In '43 I had to serve as a German soldier, and we went to Bozen, stayed three months in the barracks, and after we went to Rome. We stayed there three months, and had the attack on March 23, '44, and after that we went to Piedmont. We were always on guard duty, because they were all partisans in the mountains. When the war ended I was a prisoner of the Americans, they captured me and I remained a prisoner six months, and after that I came home.

The regiment was divided into three battalions: the first was employed in security and anti-partisan duties in Istria; the second took part in a number of actions against the Resistance and at least two mass reprisals in the north-east (including the massacre of forty-six civilians in the Bois valley in Cadore and the hanging of fourteen prisoners in Belluno). The survivors of via Rasella would also go on "to fight against the partisans, of course. In Piedmont, around Susa" (Arthur Atz). They were not just an innocuous defense guard, as they have been often represented.

In February, the Third battalion arrived in Rome. It was made up of three companies: Company Nine, deployed to the south of the city; Company Ten, on police duty in Rome; Company Eleven, in training. They did not wear the gray uniform of combat SS but the lizard-green dress of the roundup specialists. They were neither select nor very fresh troops, although the anti-partisan myth exaggerates in describing them as old men: the ages of those killed in via Rasella range from twenty-seven to forty-three, averaging thirty-eight (Arthur Atz, who survived, was twenty-five; Francesco Curreli, a member of the GAP unit, was fifty-five). Many had families and children. Their German officers and noncoms despised and insulted them for their lack of martial spirit and their rural South Tyrol background, and subjected them to a training which to them seemed exceedingly and unnecessarily harsh.

The most absurd requirement, in their eyes, was the obligation to sing while marching: "They required us to march through the streets always singing to the top of our voices, like so many roosters, chest thrown forward, shouting a rhythmic cock-a-doodle-do" (Franz Bertagnoli). The German authorities, however, knew what they were doing. The singing evoked a whole mythology of the relation between Germans and music, which generated both sympathy and fear.

To children, singing soldiers are an attraction rather than a threat: "Some of my friends that night asked their mothers if they could come out and see these marching soldiers" (Vincenza Gatti). Some would grow up to believe that this army unit with loaded guns and hand grenades at their belt was only a musical corps: "It is not true that they were armed with machine guns, they were harmless. They were going to the Quirinale; it was a music band; they were going for the changing of the guard" (Liana Gigliozzi).

For adults, however, the martial singing is an exhibition of identity and power, almost a part of the uniform. "The column, announced as always by a Nordic song, turns into via Rasella," writes Franco Calamandrei;[27] "They marched onward singing, in a language that was no longer that of Goethe, the songs of Hitler. One hundred and sixty men of the Nazi police, with the insignia of the Nazi army . . . They marched onward singing, macabre and ludicrous . . . (Rosario Bentivegna).[28] That day, they had been told (with no explanation) to march in silence, but none of the expected trouble developed until they were almost home, so just before they reached via Rasella the singing resumed. In one of the last rows, Josef Praxmarer only pretended. Bentivegna and Calamandrei did not realize that they weren't enjoying the singing at all; on the other hand, the men of the Bozen regiment did not understand what impact even their reluctant singing had on those who heard it. By forcing them to sing, the German authorities had turned them into a walking message, a proclamation of imperial and racial domination, of which they were not aware but which the partisans took at face value.

This double-voiced singing that the singers alone didn't understand was a metaphor for their status of unconscious oppressors and unconscious victims—as if their bilingualism placed them beyond the pale of both languages ("We were all Italians, as nationality we were Italians [. . .] but we all spoke German, we're not Germans, only the language we speak," Arthur Atz says). One of the men killed in via Rasella bore a last name that is common in South Tyrol, the emblem of "a people who inhabit a perennial border, now Austrians, now Italians, now Germans": *Dissertori,* or "deserter."

The fact that the Nazi police were former Italian citizens is constantly evoked against the partisans. However, they didn't call themselves "Italian" when it came to killing ten Italians for a German; from the beginning, the German press release spoke of them only as Germans. Their Italian-ness is a late discovery, subsequent to the outcome of the war. On the other hand, some of the perpetrators of the Fosse Ardeatine (Gunter Ammon, Wilhelm Kofler) also came from South Tyrol, but their previous Italian citizenship does not seem to have influenced their behavior there. Ironically, at least ten of the Jewish victims of the reprisal had been born in Germany.

The Resistance was also a war among Italians, a war in which Italians killed each other. Thus, the fact that these ex-Italians were wearing a foreign uniform only made them guiltier in the eyes of the anti-Fascists. "Years ago, the mother of one of the soldiers that had been killed called me, and said: 'Do you understand, Balsamo, that my son was Italian?' 'Madam, don't tell anybody! Because, if you do, it's high treason! Not only was your son Italian: he was wearing the German uniform, occupied an Italian city, and persecuted Italians with his German uniform on, so he was a traitor'" (Pasquale Balsamo). Balsamo, embittered by the controversy, was perhaps ungenerous. But there is some truth to what he said: when one wears a uniform, one is on one side only.

True, not all had chosen to wear that uniform. Many had only done as they were told: "They were innocent. They were doing their duty in a town that was not a battleground, they were doing their normal service in a territory where there was no war" (Don Giovanni Fagiolo). In those times, indeed, thousands of men were refusing, at the risk of their lives, forced enrollment in the Fascist and Nazi armies; even in South Tyrol there were episodes of resistance and draft-dodging. The men of the Bozen regiment might have known this—after all, as we are constantly reminded, they were grown men. Yet, it seems they neither understood nor tried to understand, what kind of war they had been thrown into. Taken out of their valleys, they were dumped in a hostile city that spoke another tongue, quartered "like prisoners" (Franz Bertagnoli) in the attic of the Viminale, forbidden from fraternizing with the natives: "We liked Rome very much, we never spoke to private people . . . we never had contact with them, never" (Arthur Atz).

This is the background of their "refusal" to carry out the reprisal. "There were discussions, agitated phone calls, bursts of anger. But our decision was clear: they could not expect Christians like us . . . (Luis Kaufmann). Kaufmann is the only survivor who mentions this detail; others are not even aware that the question was raised.

Question. Were you asked to participate in the reprisal?

Arthur Atz. No, that they didn't ask of us, no, because we were not able to do a thing like that . . . because the major also said those soldiers are not able to do . . . because they are too Catholic, because we had never killed even . . . the whole company, not even one throughout the war, not even then.[29]

"Because we were not able": an ambiguous phrase. Kappler never spoke of a refusal by the men, but rather of a decision of the officers: the commander, Helmuth Dobbrick, "insisted on the fact that his men who were religious could not be expected to carry out the execution *in the short time at their disposal*" [my italics].[30] Dobbrick, whose low esteem of his men was well known, did not say that they refused to execute the massacre, but only that he did not think they could do it in time—or, as Kappler reported his words on another occasion, that they wouldn't have the heart to shoot point-blank: "My men are old. They're partly very religious, partly full of superstition, and come from remote valleys in the Alps." Religion per se does not seem to have made a difference in all cases; Erich Priebke, for instance, insists that he was "a believer," but his faith did not prevent him from participating in the massacre. In the case of the Bozen, their religious feelings are represented less as a paradigm of noble spirituality than one of rustic simplicity. Also, their religion was not expected to interfere with the execution in principle, but only in expediency: "Dobbrick put forward the fact that his men were not trained in weapon use and were advanced in age."[31]

All this is reworked into the oft-told narrative of the Bozen battalion's "refusal." It is a narrative that is functional for all sides: the Church, because it implies a superior spirituality of Catholicism (all these narratives are imbued with the persuasion that only Catholics are Christians); the Right, because it makes the partisans guiltier by illustrating the "innocence" and forgiveness of their victims; and the Left, because it underlines the guilt of the executioners by showing that others were more humane and that, contrary to the standard defense line, it was possible to object to the order.

As we have seen, it was less the men's conscience than their commander's low esteem of them that exempted them. However, their military inadequacy is also the sign of a cultural otherness from the SS superman myth. In such a context, being unwarlike is a virtue that must be acknowledged. Yet, to endow the Bozen with a sharper awareness and higher consciousness than they really possessed is another way to use them as the vehicle for ideological messages that float above their heads—just as when they were made to sing as they marched in the streets of Rome.

3. The Sleeping Dog: Cause and Effect

Everyone knows that the Germans are a bad race . . . that they are cruel . . . Why did you have to mess up with them? Listen—here's a lion, and he's fierce, but he has already eaten; why do you mess up with him? He'll eat even if he's not hungry! He's fierce!

—M.C., Civitella della Chiana, Tuscany[32]

Vengeance on a dumb brute . . . that simply smote thee from blindest instinct! Madness! To be enraged with a dumb thing, Captain Ahab, seems blasphemous.

—Herman Melville, *Moby Dick*[33]

"Authentic mechanical monsters passed—among shivering and dumb crowds [. . .] in their camouflage suits of green and yellow [. . .] like the bellies of snakes," writes Corrado Govoni, Aladino Govoni's father.[34] His intention is to intensify his invective; however, the coupled metaphors of the Germans as machines and as beasts place them outside the pale of humanity and therefore beyond the range of moral judgment. Machines and beasts do not know good from evil and cannot be blamed for what they do. It is up to human beings to exercise judgment: "These partisans knew that they were dealing with beasts more beastly than themselves" (Liana Gigliozzi); "They should have known that those were beasts, that in that moment they were beasts and if the Germans were defeated, they turned into animals" (Teresa Mussoni).

The stereotype of the German as machine or beast, then, portrays the massacre as a natural event and shifts the guilt onto the partisans. According to this narrative, the reprisal was an automatic or instinctive reaction, and therefore the partisans should have expected it (in some variants of the myth, the partisans are supposed to have acted precisely to provoke it). But this is not the way things were. It is not true that, as even some history textbooks repeat, that "to every attack the Germans responded with merciless reprisals" (and that therefore every massacre was a response provoked by some partisan act).[35] The massacre of the Fosse Ardeatine had, in fact, no precedents in Italy; it was neither a knee-jerk reaction nor the application of a pre-established policy and procedure. Rather, it was the outcome of a complex decision-making process that set a precedent for the massacres to come.[36]

Says Herbert Kappler: "I remember that the afternoon of March 23 I had lunch with General Mältzer, commander of the open city of Rome, at the Hotel Excelsior. I was on my way back to my office, driving along via Nazionale, when

I heard a loud explosion. I had just sat down at my desk when I was informed by telephone that an attack had been perpetrated and my presence was required immediately in via Rasella. Actually, I did not realize immediately the gravity of the event."

In other words, the explosion of a bomb in the middle of the day in the center of Rome seemed to Kappler nothing out of the ordinary. Rome was not a pacified city: at his trial, Kappler himself listed fourteen attacks before via Rasella, some of which resulted in German casualties. Rather than reprisal, however, the Germans had chosen silence. The myth of the invulnerability of the German war machine was essential to preserving submission in the occupied city; and the Nazis protected this myth by hiding their own casualties: "At this time a state of emergency existed in Rome, although no declaration was issued to that effect, because almost every night there were actions in the City against the German troops" (Erich Priebke).[37]

Before they were attacked in via Rasella, the Germans had already shot dozens of prisoners at Forte Bravetta; on two occasions, the shootings followed partisan attacks. However, although this in no way absolves them, these were not indiscriminate reprisals against uninvolved civilians, but the execution of death sentences, issued after at least a shadow of legal proceedings, against persons charged with specific violations. Aside from the sheer size of the massacre, then, the Fosse Ardeatine was the first case in which the victims were other than the authors of the anti-Nazi action that was being punished. Also, while in all cases the public was informed only after the fact, yet the connection with the partisan attacks had been sometimes suggested by contiguity but never formally proclaimed.[38]

Via Rasella was not the first partisan attack—but it was the first that could not be publicly ignored. Massimo Uffreduzzi, then a member of the Fascist combat groups, says: "It was such a grave thing, so gigantic, and then, I repeat, with an influx of people . . ." From the opposite side, the Communist leader Giorgio Amendola makes exactly the same point: "On other occasions, they had absorbed the blow without losing their composure. But this time the outrage was too strong, the partisans' boldness and efficacy too evident."[39] This combination of gravity and visibility was what made via Rasella unbearable. Thirty-three victims were a serious blow to the Reich in themselves; but thirty-three German dead under the public eye, an armed unit marching in formation, attacked in open and protracted combat by an enemy whose very existence they were bent on denying—this was intolerable. The more so when it took place in a city that did not cooperate, dodged the draft, did not supply manpower, did not turn in Jews and anti-Fascists, and did not support Mussolini's "republic." Therefore, the Germans' priority was not to capture the perpetrators, to punish them or to avenge the dead, but rather to punish the city and publicly restore with a show of inflexibility their own wounded power.

4. Lists, Posters, Orders, and other Missing Texts

The reprisal of the Fosse Ardeatine was carried out with the utmost respect for the law. In the end, the only ones included were Jews, Communists, and such other people; no innocents.
—*Hans Plack,* quartermaster of the Bozen regiment, 1979

The partisan action at via Rasella generated a frenzy of emergencies, contradictory orders, voices in confusion, even more inextricable since the only descriptions we have today are judicial self-defenses. It was a sequel of negotiations and compromises that only the stereotype of German precision and ideological opportunism transforms, in memory, into an automatic, ineluctable—indeed Teutonic—chain of events.

Via Rasella was a new situation, and the mechanisms of reprisal had not been oiled yet. Only after the Fosse Ardeatine would the chains of command of the Wehrmacht and the SS be unified under the control of Field Marshal Kesselring.[40] Thus, while Kappler and Mältzer were on the phone trying to reach Kesselring, one of Kesselring's staff officers, Colonel Dietrich Beelitz, gave the news to the supreme command in Germany. From there, a General von Buttlar called him back with Hitler's orders: blow up the neighborhood, evacuate it, and execute fifty civilians for each German. Beelitz played for time; he realized that "this was not Hitler's final order: he was only venting a momentary anger." He asked his chief of staff, Major Hauser, to contact von Buttlar, who spoke to Hitler again. Hitler, "still very much agitated," says that "the reprisal belongs to the supreme command in Italy"—that is, to Kesselring.

Meanwhile, Kappler, Mältzer, von Mackensen, and Kesselring had agreed that "the ratio between German dead and hostages executed shall not exceed ten to one. The victims shall be selected among people already under detention for actions against German law," sentenced or liable to be sentenced to the death penalty. Mackensen claimed that Kappler assured him he had enough persons under a death sentence to fill the entire order; Kappler in turn said that he suggested that "given the great number of victims, the usual proportion of one to ten could have been published in the press but, on the other hand, there was no necessity to shoot the entire number," and Mackensen agreed.[41] They knew very well that no one would verify. As Kesselring himself later testified, the number of victims was less important than the message, a warning to prevent the repetition of similar attacks.[42]

At eight P.M., however, another order came from Hitler to liquidate ten Italians for each German. What had been conceived as the maximum rate has now become peremptory. Hitler's final dispositions come in at eleven P.M.: the execution was to take place within 24 hours, and had to be carried out by the police—that is, Kappler's men. Kappler, however, gave another version, claiming that he received the order only the next morning from Mältzer, after Dobbrick's refusal. No matter what the actual sequence was, however, certain elements stand out in all versions.

In the first place, everyone concerned assumed that a massive reprisal would take place. However, there was controversy and negotiation over its actual dimension: the first figure mentioned is fifty to one, then it appears that Hitler "would definitely not be satisfied with a shooting of less than twenty times as many hostages as there were victims of the bomb" (Mackensen). The ten-to-one ratio is mentioned first as the maximum, then becomes peremptory. In other words, the number of victims is not the result of the ineluctable mathematics of an iron law of war, but rather the outcome of compromise and revision. Yet, the phrase "ten Italians for one German" has become a kind of mantra in Italian commonsense, thanks to the fearful symmetry of that round figure that facilitates the count and fits so neatly into the myth of Teutonic rationality and automatism. Thanks to the fluid and complex nature of this decision, indeed, the executioners would even attempt to present themselves as saviors of human lives—it could have been worse. By agreeing to the ten-to-one ratio, Mackensen claims, he was "freed from an insufferable conflict of conscience" because "in that way I actually saved as many innocent persons. I could then use the others, whose liquidation was inevitable and over whom I had no influence" to report to his superiors that the order had been carried out.[43]

Even the famous iron-clad "Führer's order," supposedly unthinkable to disobey (an assumption on which a number of court verdicts hinged), appears to have been negotiable. Hitler changed his mind at least three times within a few hours, did not concern himself with verifying whether his order had been carried out, and was in fact actually disobeyed: Mackensen says that his command to raze the whole neighborhood was a "nonsensical demand," Beelitz saw it as a mere venting of anger, Kappler claimed that he sabotaged Hitler's order to evacuate the city, and Kesselring insisted that he consciously contradicted Hitler's order concerning the mode of the reprisal.

In fact, like the mythic edicts requesting the partisans to deliver themselves, the Führer's order is one of those invisible texts on which the whole narrative is founded. Not only, unlike other circumstances, did Hitler issue no formal written order;[44] but there is not a single testimony from a person who heard it first-hand from him. All the testimony is second- or third-hand, or mere inference.

Finally, and most importantly, nowhere, except in belated and doubtful self-defense statements (and in the anti-partisan mythology), does it appear that the decision to carry out the massacre ever depended on the arrest or self-delivery of the partisans. This eventuality is not mentioned in any version of Hitler's order. From the beginning, the intention was not to punish the perpetrators but to punish and terrorize the city; even if the partisans had turned themselves in they would not have prevented the massacre. This is why there was no serious search, nor any poster or public announcement. This has been a matter of record since Kesselring's 1946 trial:

Prosecutor. But you could have said, "If the population of Rome does not deliver within a certain time the perpetrator of the attack I will execute ten Romans for each German killed"?

Albert Kesselring: Now in tranquil times after three years past, I must say that the idea would have been very good.

Prosecutor. But you didn't do it.

Kesselring. No, I didn't do it.[45]

"For the event in via Rasella," Kappler said, "I made no request to the population, I had no jurisdiction to do so."[46] The 1948 verdict concludes: "The search for the perpetrators was not the primary concern of the German police, but was carried out blandly, as a marginal activity, after preparation for the reprisal was already under way."[47] At his trial, Kappler repeated unconvincingly that "the Fascist radio announced every fifteen minutes that if the gappisti of via Rasella did not turn themselves in, the Germans would execute 320 civilians." Yet, this was not the case. The day after the massacre, the journalist Carlo Trabucco wrote in his diary: "The radio has made no mention [of the attack] and the newspapers are mute."[48] Had the radio said anything, it would be hard to explain how the Vatican was informed by a phone call only in the late morning of the next day (after which no known action was taken).[49]

Kappler's next task was the nocturnal drawing of the lists. "The whole of that night we searched the records and could not find a sufficient number of persons to make up the number required for the execution," Erich Priebke stated.[50] "We realized that the number of those sentenced to death was not 300, but three or four," Kappler confirmed. He was the chief of police, so it is strange that he didn't know. At this point, the circle of the "candidates to death" widened without bounds. On the suggestion of his superior, general Harster, Kappler included the available Jews; he obtained from the military tribunal the names of "persons sentenced not to death but to terms of detention out of clemency," and added them to list. The number of German dead had reached 32, and all he had was about 220 names: 176 charged with crimes liable for the death penalty, but not yet tried; 22 tried for similar violations but not yet sentenced; 17 sentenced to long terms of hard labor; 4 sentenced to death (actually 3: one had been acquitted), 4 (but they were actually more) arrested in or near via Rasella.[51] "At this point I was in the necessity of having to include Jews. As I recall, the number of Jews was 57. If I had not included the Jews I should have had to include other persons whose guilt was not as clear." The Jews' guilt was, apparently, intrinsic.

He spent the night going over the lists—but apparently did not notice that they included old men and minors. He was still fifty names short, and asked the Italian police to deliver them. The next day, the Chief of Police Pietro Caruso, after an informal meeting with the Minister of Interior Buffarini Guidi, drew the list and had it delivered. Kappler said later that "the order of carrying out the execution weighed upon me more than, the night before, the task of compiling the list [. . .] I had never witnessed an execution, my profession notwithstanding." After receiving the order, he spoke "as a friend" to his officers announcing that they were to kill three hundred and twenty people. "All agreed with me that, for the sake of discipline, all unit commanders should take part with at least one shot in the execution [. . .] If someone had refused, I would have listened and discussed."

"If someone had refused." "He said that this thing was a horrible thing to do and that to show the men that they had the backing of the officers, all the officers were to fire a shot at the beginning and a further shot at the end" (Erich Priebke).[52] No one demurred.

There was no time to "create a cemetery," there was no time to execute the victims individually, tied to the chair, with religious comforts, as in a normal execution. In order to accentuate the terror and cover up the horror, the SS had to find a "natural death chamber" that could function as a place both of execution and burial. "With the creation of the death chamber, I thought that the corpses would no longer need to be removed" (Kappler). Captain Köhler suggested certain quarries he knew on the via Ardeatina; Kappler sent him out to prepare the place, and went to via Tasso to alert his men: "He warned us to procure our arms immediately and hold ourselves ready because that afternoon we were going to avenge the deaths of our comrades killed in the Via Rasella " (Günter Ammon).

He learned then that another man was dead, and had ten more names added to the list: Jews who had been arrested that day. "About mid-day on the 24th March 1944, between 80 and 90 men from Department III and IV went to the Ardeatine Caves, Rome" (Erich Priebke).[53]

5. Personal Responsibility and Collective Guilt

"This 'order has been carried out' is a phrase that had stayed in my mind, concerning the Fosse Ardeatine. Another phrase has stayed, of the some kind: the one uttered by the defendants in the trials at Nuremberg, which goes: '*Ich bekenne mich in Sinne der Anklage für ünschundig*'—'in the sense of the charges I do not recognize myself as guilty.' It is a phrase that for me has the same import, and I repeat it once in a while, like a magic formula, black magic, because these two formulas are the same thing" (Vanda Perretta).

The philosopher Giorgio Agamben notes that "the confusion of ethical and legal categories is a very common misconception." In the story of the Fosse Ardeatine, this confusion concerns primarily the tendency to contain the debate within the category of *Befehlsnotstand,* the impossibility of disregarding an order received.[54] However, the legal possibility of disobeying the order concerns only the judicial evaluation of personal responsibility; it leaves out of the picture the person's subjective relation to that order and the historic, ethical, cultural context that acts upon the subjectivity of the individual and his or her interaction with institutions. The legal sphere concerns the individual's personal responsibility; but the Fosse Ardeatine, as Lutz Klinkhammer points out, must be recognized "as a war crime [. . .] independent of the question of individual responsibility" and of the possibility of reaching individual verdicts.[55]

The court trials against Nazis, then, are not the same thing as the historical judgment on Nazism. The illusion of a transparency between individual legal guilt and the historical responsibilities of Nazism generates, in fact, a complex play of mirrors at the end of which all come out more or less clean. The more we insist that Kappler or Priebke are guilty because they had a right to disobey, the more we tend to represent Nazism as a rule-of-law state. When, with the best of intentions, the German historian Gerhard Schreiber proves that the refusal was allowed by German law, the risk is that we might look at Priebke, ironically, as a violator rather than as an instrument of Nazi law—as if mass murder were a disobedience, an exception, rather than the system's ordinary practice.[56]

From trial to trial, the Nazis played upon this misconception, bouncing responsibility among themselves or unloading it all on one dead man, Hitler. In 1945, in his interrogation by the Allied authorities, Priebke made no mention of any protest or opposition to Kappler's order to kill; in 1948, as we have seen, Kappler said that "if" someone had protested he would have persuaded them, but none did. In 1974, Kappler actually boasted that he lied in court in order to save his men: "I told a lie at the trial [. . .] I told one of them: 'You must state that you carried out the order to shoot because you knew that I would have you executed with the others if you hadn't.'" Only in 1996, after his extradition, did

Priebke claim that "We all protested, but Kappler said that the order [came] directly from Hitler and it was up to us to carry it out. Who refuses shall be sent to the SS military court."[57]

The fact is that it never occurred to them to protest. "There was not in us"— Priebke himself adds—"either the culture or the *forma mentis* to enable us to disregard those rules, and it was totally unimaginable to judge the decisions of the high commands." "The essence of the armed forces is discipline," Kappler said: "It is the duty of every soldier to obey orders without discussing them."[58] Whether or not they could have disobeyed the orders, then, they did not intend to do so. Karl Hass, Priebke's comrade and co-defendant, put it this way: "In war all orders are legitimate."[59] In 1948, the Italian military tribunal actually recognized as an extenuating circumstance the fact that Kappler was a Nazi: his "mental habit [was] oriented toward immediate obedience," and therefore he might have believed that the order was legitimate.[60]

The armed forces are not the only institution founded on obedience. Priests, too, take a vow of obedience; however, they have never been ordered to exterminate three hundred thirty-five persons in cold blood. On the other hand, no partisan, even one charged with serious crimes, has ever claimed exemption on the grounds of having carried out orders. The question then is, how does a person place himself in a position to receive such orders? With what institution has he elected to align himself? Priebke joined the Nazi Party voluntarily in 1933, Kappler in 1931; Priebke's affiliation with the SS was a much less automatic consequence of his joining the police than he has asserted. And "remaining in that corps meant consciously taking the risk of one day having to face and obey criminal orders."[61]

The question is not only why one is in a position to receive the order, but also why is he chosen to receive it. Nothing prevented Dobbrick or Mältzer from issuing to the Bozen battalion the same ineluctable "Führer's order," or threatening court-martial: the *Befehlsnotstand* applied to them, too. If they didn't, it was because they knew they had abler and less reluctant executioners at hand: Hitler knew what he was doing when he specified that the order was to be carried out by Kappler's police.

Not that the SS necessarily enjoyed it. Priebke now says: "Carrying out this terrible order was for me a horrible thing, a personal tragedy [. . .] I had never killed before that day and, fortunately, never had to do it again [. . .] I was, as I am now, a religious believer [. . .] If I could have avoided that order I would have [. . .] This feeling I live within myself, the tragedy of the Ardeatine accompanied me all my life."[62] In his behavior, there was no trace of such feelings; but others were ill, fainted, had to be helped and exhorted before they were able to kill. Nevertheless, there is no evidence that anyone challenged the order.

Before an unacceptable order, there are more alternatives that a heroic no or an immediate, blind, and unconditional yes. There are countless ways to negotiate, delay, and hinder the execution while minimizing personal exposition and danger—especially when, as in this case, time is of the essence. Someone might have misplaced a list, punctured a tire, forgotten to pass on an order; thirty, rather than one, might have felt incapable of shooting; and the timing might have been thrown off, something might have happened . . . But instead:

Mario Fiorentini. Kappler was a demon, he was quick, he was determined, he was a force of nature; he gathered his powers and carried out all this in very little time. Even a small delay—that might have come from the Fascists, from the Germans, from circumstances—might have sufficed: if the massacre of the Ardeatine had been postponed even for a short time, then the Vatican would have stepped in, at least to mitigate. Mussolini could not remain passive. The partisans in the north might have said, "We have this colonel, we have these officers. Watch out, don't do this or we'll kill them." And then, we could have attacked the jail, we were about to attack via Tasso [. . .] [But] neither the Vatican nor we had the time to do anything, because Kappler destroyed us, as far as the possibility of negotiation was concerned.[63]

No one ordered Kappler to add ten victims to the list after the death of the thirty-third soldier; it was his own choice to give to the order a broad interpretation (in order, according to the military court, "to increase his prestige in the eyes of his Nazi superiors with a very energetic and daring action"). The "frantic rush to carry out the execution with the utmost rapidity" resulted in the murder "by mistake" of five extra victims.[64]

6. Politics of Time

I say, what did their brain tell those people, why? Yes, all right, there was this attack, right; but is that the way to react? Will you at least take time to breathe, to look for someone? No, you just go and shoot.
—*Ada Pignotti*

I was talking to Daniele Parrotta and Nicola Centi, first-year university students, and the latter's parents. I asked: how long was the time between via Rasella and the Fosse Ardeatine? "A week" (Nicola Centi); "No, a week is not enough—a month" (Mauro Centi); "I'd have said a year" (Daniele Parrotta); "A month" (Daniela Centi).

I put the same question to dozens of people of different generations, social and educational backgrounds, political leanings; nearly always, the answers ranged between "three days," "maybe a week" (Sara Leoni), "a few months" (Simone Bova). "I guess a . . . a short time: fifteen days" (Rosa Castra). Massimo C., a young Right-wing activist, said it was nearly a month, and when I told him he was mistaken he replied, "This is not what I know, this is not what my document says." It isn't a matter of ignorance, but one of perception and imagination. At a high-level training seminar for foreign service diplomats, I asked the same question, and the answers ranged from two days to six months, averaging two weeks.

It was less than twenty-four hours. This expansion of time in popular belief is the most fascinating memory construct concerning these events. It most immediate consequence is to reinforce the belief in the partisans' guilt, by imagining that the Nazis had time to publish an appeal to them.

Marco Maceroni. The Germans for a week went around doing reprisals, capturing prisoners, especially in the Jewish quarter, and warning, warning that if the perpetrators of the attack in via Rasella hadn't come out, they would take for each dead German eleven Italians, eleven or thirteen, I don't remember now.

"How long was it? I don't know. If it had been done right away, it would have been, how shall I put it, a passionate reaction; if it was done later, as I suppose it was, how shall I put it, a cold and calculated reaction, so I suppose it was quite a long time" (Francesco Bonini). Those twenty-four hours are both an incredibly short and a criminally long time. The Fosse Ardeatine differs from other massacres precisely in the separation between the place and time of the attack and those of the reprisal: the organization, the transportation of the victims, the hiding of the bodies are not the bloody acts of an angry and scared army running amok, but an efficient and "civilized" military operation. "You want to retaliate? All right, then, along Palazzo Barberini, with a machine gun, trrr—this is how you retaliate, under everybody's eyes, not in secret. Otherwise, what reprisal is it? A reprisal for your own use only, at your whim?" (Ada Pignotti). "Twenty-four hours isn't such a short time, to think about what you are going to do . . . To think about something for twenty-four hours, to stand there and shoot five people at a time sixty-seven times—it's no easy thing to do" (Nicoletta Leoni).

Don Giovanni Fagiolo. In the first place, they gave warning: for each German, ten Italians will be killed. They posted bills, of course not all over Rome, but they did post some. From the newspapers, the radio, it was known immediately. I saw the poster, and others did, too. But the important thing is this: that the author was invited to turn himself in. The Germans wouldn't have killed, at least they had promised that they wouldn't kill anyone. "Unless the author, the real one, turns himself in, we go ahead with the threat we have made."

Ironically, the memory of Nazi massacres in Italy has prompted countrymen of the victims, citizens of the wounded and victimized country, to go out of their way to invent excuses for their oppressors and executioners. As we have seen, the Germans, whose best interest would have been to say the opposite, admitted that they never posted any bills or made any announcement. Hundreds of Italians, on the other hand, insist that they read or heard them. No one has ever been found, however, who claimed that he had written or broadcast them. In the German and Italian archives, not even the most painstaking Right-wing researcher has succeeded in unearthing a single copy. No specimen was ever produced in court.

Not only was there no announcement after via Rasella; there was none before, either. None of the many bans and ordinances issued before via Rasella included the fatidic phrase "ten Italians for a German" or any such thing. Kesselring's public orders of September 11 and 21, 1943, are often cited to prove that the reprisal had been announced. They, however, said something else entirely. The former announced that German military law is in force and therefore the "organizers of strikes, saboteurs and snipers shall be summarily tried and executed." The latter confirmed: "Whoever attacks and wounds or kills a member of the Germanic Armed Forces or a Germanic Office or in anyway perpetrates acts of violence against the occupation forces is punished with death. In less severe cases he may be tried and punished with internment or prison." Further on, the edict reads: "Any action, punishable according to Germanic law, that comes to attention of the German military courts, is judged according to Germanic laws." Sanctions, therefore, were provided exclusively toward those who were directly responsible for the actions; there is no mention of repercussions for the civilian population, hostages, and such. Also, punishment was to be preceded by judgment by the German military courts—something no one even dreamed of doing in the case of the Fosse Ardeatine.

The most immediate factor in the creation of this misconception is, of course, ideological manipulation: the legend of how the partisans could have prevented the massacre by turning themselves in to the Germans was inaugurated by the head of Rome's Fascist Federation, Giuseppe Pizzirani, in a briefing of the party cadre on March 30. The motif is picked up a few days later by an the underground monarchist paper, *Italia Nuova*.

In July 1944, *Italia Nuova* again wrote that Bentivegna and his comrades, "instead of dumping the bomb, or the bombs, on the Nazi platoon from a window" should have attacked it in the street (which in fact they did), and that, when they heard of the reprisal, they should have turned themselves in, saying "we killed the oppressors of the people of Rome." The next day, *Il Tempo* (then controlled by the Social Democrats), explained that "the after-the-fact announcement of the reprisal was given simultaneously with the news of the attack" and concluded that via Rasella "is the most important event that happened in the nine months of German occupation in Rome. Let us reverently uncover our heads to the martyrs of the Fosse Ardeatine, and not insult them with the suspicion that their sacrifice was in vain." By 1948, *Il Tempo* (returned to its antebellum owners) had forgotten what it knew four years earlier, and was writing that Bentivegna "ran to hide in a convent leaving the 335 to be massacred."[65] This theme was to be a staple of Cold War election campaigns for a couple of decades.

"This story came out several years later, but always from our side, from the Christian Democrats, who said this bomb wasn't necessary" (Teresa Mussoni). "When I came to Rome," recalls Paolo Emilio Taviani, a Christian Democrat politician who had fought in the Resistance in Genoa, "I was amazed that in Rome there should be people who questioned this. In Genoa we did worse, because we blew up a cinema where the Nazi soldiers went, and five Nazi soldiers died."

Gemma Luzzi. And then I remember an argument between my grandfather, in the street, and a man who talked about "they ought to have turned themselves in." And my grandfather was from Trieste, and he had done armed actions against the Austrians in Trieste [before it returned to Italy after World War I], and of course he transferred this experience of his, he got all heated up, and said that of course there had been a reprisal, but surely those who did the attack in via Rasella had also put their lives at stake.

Umberto Turco. I saw the first poster, on a white background, written in black, where the Communists were accused of the massacre of the Fosse Ardeatine. It was the Comitato Civico [a conservative Catholic movement]. I was deeply indignant; I felt it was a bleeding outrage, to those comrades who had dared the Germans, and the Fosse Ardeatine was a consequence of a sacrosanct, just battle, and the Germans were the murderers . . . And these people instead called the Communists murderers.

Ugo De Carolis's sister wrote to *Il Tempo* that Bentivegna "hid behind the pile of the bodies of the 320 and came out only to brag about what he had done." There were, however, also vibrant responses of support and solidarity with the partisans. Gaetano Agnini—who had been tortured at via Tasso together with his son Ferdinando, later killed at the Fosse Ardeatine—wrote: "If such a poster could be affixed and read without a feeling of rebellion, this . . . simplifies things. Either here or there, either for the laws of humanity or against the laws of humanity. As far as I am concerned, my choice is made."[66]

The controversy flares up periodically: in 1976, during the campaign for the liberation of Kappler, and his escape from military prison; in 1982, after the delivery of the medals awarded to Bentivegna thirty years earlier by the Christian Democrat prime minister Alcide de Gasperi ("a veritable rain of medals was returned [in protest] on the desk of [Defense Minister] Lagorio"); and, of course, after 1994, following the extradition and trial of Erich Priebke. In 1996, the Right-wing journalist Giampiero Mughini dares write in *Il Tempo* that there were no posters nor announcements; a flood of letters from readers comes in to contradict him. A reader swears "in front of God and men" that he saw a bilingual bill posted not in Rome, but as far as Valentano, a small town in the province of Viterbo. Mughini points out that no history book says there was any such thing; a reader replies: "We know very well who wrote the history books." Mughini mentions the supreme court sentence that defined the partisans as "not criminals but combatants"; his readers reply that "we know very well how that verdict developed, in a political climate hegemonized by the Communist Party" (that is, the '50s: in the middle of the Cold War, Christian Democrats administrations, anti-Left repression, and discrimination). As Mughini rightly concludes, such interlocutors "are very hard to reason with."[67]

There are, however, other factors that help explain the transformation of what began as an intentional Fascist lie into a widely held public "truth." The most important is the assumption that when a "crime" is committed, the logical thing to do is to seek out and punish the perpetrators, using the threat of reprisal primarily as moral pressure on the perpetrators and on the population. This is not, however, the logic that the Nazis followed: the culprit to be punished was the city of Rome itself. The very fact that so many people believe that the Germans acted otherwise than they did indicates that the German rationale for the reprisal is inconceivable to many ordinary people, who therefore are ready to accept or invent narratives that make the "absurd" more understandable and reasonable.

The belief in the German proclamations and the expansion of the interval between action and reprisal are truly impermeable to factual verification; they pertain more to myth and folklore than to historic memory. As late as 1996, the maverick (but consistently anti-Communist) politician Marco Pannella could still claim that "Someone asked the chiefs of the Resistance to turn themselves in to the Germans to avoid the reprisal."[68] The more one explains and informs, the more one senses that "superficially they say you're right, but then you realize that they still think as they did before" (Ugo Scattoni). A lady told me that the partisans should have turned themselves in; I explained how things went, and suddenly she recalled that she already knew—but had forgotten: information that counters the myth is not retrievable, cannot be remembered. I asked a group about the length of the interval between the two events; most said it was at least three days. I corrected this error, but at the end one approached me and repeated that the partisans should have turned themselves in. I repeated: there was neither the time nor the request, and she replied that they should have done it spontaneously. A student in the liceo named after of one of the victims, Manfredi Azzarita, objected: "You said it was twenty-four hours from the explosion of the bomb to the Fosse Ardeatine. But why didn't the attackers turn themselves in to the Nazis of their own spontaneous will after the attack? He who does the attack then turns himself in" (Marco Maceroni).

In 1949, a small group of relatives of the victims sued the partisans and the leaders of Rome's National Liberation Committee. Their brief to the court stated that the order to attack had been given "with full knowledge of the reprisals announced, threatened, and carried out by the Germans" and that "after the mass arrest of the inhabitants of via Rasella and the announcement of the collective reprisal, the authors of the attack had remained in the dark and had allowed the collective reprisal to go on."[69] In support of these claims, they refer to the proceedings of the Kappler trial—which, as we have seen, say exactly the opposite. But mythic persuasion is untouched by logic, factual evidence, or the letter of the record: a thoughtful legal brief can "prove" a claim by citing a document that flatly denies it.

However, the mythic quality of these narratives and beliefs does not authorize us to ignore them. They could not take such firm roots in popular imagination if they were merely an ideological lie or a logical misconception. Myth, whether factually true or not, is always a response to a deep necessity; in this case, it is only the rudest and most ideological form of an ineludible question on the relation between cause and consequences and on the nature of responsibility.

Thousands of people were killed in Rome, by the Germans and by the Allies. The Germans killed often without provocation; many of those who were killed at the Fosse Ardeatine might have died anyway; perhaps, without via Rasella, there might have been other deaths. All this is true. But it is also true that without that action at least some of those individuals would not have died. They died after that action, not another: "If that criminal didn't lay the bomb, the monument wouldn't exist" (Vincenza Gatti); "If it hadn't been for the *gappisti*, there would be three hundred and thirty-four more granddads" (Daniele Limpido). When Priebke says that "the responsibility for all those deaths belongs to the Communists: if they hadn't done the attack in via Rasella there wouldn't have been the Fosse Ardeatine"[70], he mines a deep lode of commonsense: the Nazis are the criminals, but they committed that crime as a response to that "outrage."

Throughout this book, I endeavor to broaden the context and to distinguish between the attack and the reprisal. But this is not to drown everything in the context, or to deny that a connection exists: the micronarrative that begins with via Rasella and ends with the Ardeatine is short-sighted and deceiving, but it does have a meaning and requires explanation.

7. Should We Have Turned Ourselves In?

Alessandro Portelli. Have you been there, at the Fosse Ardeatine?

Rosario Bentivegna. Yes, right after the Liberation of Rome, I went alone, I got on my bike, I stayed there for a long time. It was a thing . . . well, there are problems, very personal ones, that you can't tell everyone; you don't talk about it, it's your own business . . . forgive me, I think that this question is . . ."

Portelli. Intrusive.

Bentivegna. Yes, intrusive, let's put it that way. Don't get upset—but I can't be an exhibitionist of my feelings.

After getting away from via Rasella, Carla Capponi and Rosario Bentivegna went to her mother's house. "Bentivegna wasn't feeling too well and my mother gave him [a sedative]; he had had like a small breakdown; you know, the tension" (Carla Capponi). A lady at Capponi's mother's house offers them her house for the night:

Carla Capponi. We stayed at her house that night, and there were these two boys who were her children and lived in this apartment. Bentivegna began to play chess, I didn't know what to do, first I watched their game for a while, then I was thoughtful because I was thinking of all the pros and cons, what would happen after, what was happening in Rome. We tried to listen to the radio, but there was nothing on, just music, always the same songs of the Fascist era, and then I began to mull it over, to think about what might have happened in that street . . .

I began to write, to jot down some thoughts, and I felt very depressed because you know, there's a letdown after, you know? Because we didn't know how many had died nor what had happened. And so I began to write this poem. Rather than a description, it was the sensation of the action; for instance, the weather was fine, [but] I saw bad weather, like a cloudy day, with no sun. First I was blinded by the sun, then this sense of a storm. This is part of a sensation that must have seized my soul while I was waiting, probably, because it was two hours and more.

It wasn't their first action, but they realized that it went beyond their expectations. Ironically, the perfect organization generates results that surprise the authors;

moreover, as we have seen, the number of casualties is increased by the explosion of the grenades the Germans were carrying.

Valentino Gerratana. It exploded at the right moment, and so actually it was a thing [you did not expect] that would turn out so well, I mean. You might have calculated that you'd get two, I mean, and that would have been enough of a success; it went that way. And so, the reactions, no one expected it. We thought there would be a reaction, but one of this [magnitude], I mean, hadn't happened before.

Marisa Musu. This was really a big, a big trauma; because no one expected it. We had done some fairly significant actions; though we never knew how many had died, because the Germans never told. Sure, we'd never killed thirty at one blow; but I mean, there had been no reprisals yet. That is, they had killed, they had executed, and all, but actually they had never made the connection. So for us I'd say, no doubt, it was a great, a great shock, we were deeply troubled because it was something . . . we certainly hadn't foreseen it.

"When we started, we knew we might meet with a reprisal. How would we act? How would they develop? But we thought of a negotiation, we thought of a phase of negotiations" (Mario Fiorentini). Maurizio Pacioni, preliminary inquest judge in the 1997 case against the partisans, wrote in his final conclusions: "While a strong German reaction to the attack was certainly foreseeable, the forms and ways through which it would have been implemented were not, since the reprisal (and especially the reprisal upon prisoners) was only one possibility among many."[71]

There are other considerations, too. Giorgio Amendola writes: "To accept the blackmail of reprisal meant to give up the struggle from the beginning [. . .]: We fighting partisans had the duty not to turn ourselves in, even if our sacrifice might have prevented the death of many innocents. We were a unit of the fighting army, indeed we were part of the command of this army, and we could not abandon the struggle and go over to the enemy with all our information on the organization. Our only duty was: to continue the struggle."[72]

"The idea wasn't to surrender ourselves after shooting, because each of us, more or less, did have some secret information, and you never know how far you can resist under torture" (Rosario Bentivegna). "It's absurd for the combatant to turn himself in. He admits that he shouldn't have done anything. If you risked your life and then after you've risked you surrender, [expose] your breast—absurd. To make war is to risk one's life, and the partisan war is a war. It's as though one went to the front, went into action, and then turned himself in . . ." (Valentino Gerratana).

These rational answers, however, do not ring entirely satisfactory to the partisans themselves. We have seen the state of mind of the gappisti after the Fosse

Ardeatine: Calamandrei's agony, Salinari's silence; and the pain, the "bewilderment" (Valentino Gerratana), and frustration of all. Beyond the duty and the right not to surrender themselves, and beyond the fact that there was no occasion or demand to do so, the awareness remains that if the partisans are not legally nor morally responsible for those deaths, yet they are not separate from them. And with this awareness comes the question: what would I have done, if they had asked?

Carla Capponi. Not to turn myself in would have meant to die every day for the rest of my life. I would have delivered myself even knowing very well that the Germans would not act like gentlemen, would certainly not be satisfied with only one victim. They would have just killed me, along with all the others.

During Kappler's trial, a woman assailed Bentivegna, screaming: "Why didn't you turn yourself in? My son was killed!" He answered her that if there had been an appeal "none of us would have refused to deliver themselves, because each of us, when we joined the GAP, put his life at Italy's service."[73] In 1964, Bentivegna told an interviewer: "I don't know . . . I think I would have reacted by not turning myself in . . . I would not have accepted the blackmail. Anyhow, I think I would have obeyed orders. I guess so—I'm not sure. It's too easy, and also too irrational, to answer now. Actually, the only possible answer is: I don't know."[74] In 1983, he wrote: "It is possible that, faced with the shocking threat of that crime, some of us might have chosen to die in the place of the Martyrs of the Ardeatine"; however, "Today we know that it was our duty not to respond to the enemy's call." He thus solves the contradiction by imagining another heroic death: "We would have unleashed a furious battle, putting all our lives at stake, to take from the enemy the designated victims"; "I would have gone over [to the Germans], but armed to the teeth, ready for war!"[75] In his 1998 interview with me, he concluded: "And yet you know, faced with such a shocking thing, your life today is worth three hundred people, I don't know what we might have chosen to do. My hypothesis is that the response would not have been surrender, but a military response, hard, desperate, even against orders—with the hypothesis, even if microscopic, of being able to save some of them, at the cost of losing our lives."

These oscillations and discrepancies register not insincerity but rather an inner search: the different replies that, at different times in his life, the same person can give to a question that he is always asked, and always asking himself, and that cannot be answered once and for all. I hope I am not being intrusive if I think that the public battle that Rosario Bentivegna has been fighting for the last half century to defend his actions is also the sign of a tension between the reasons for those actions and the feelings of which he will not speak.

8. What Was the Use?

Aldo Natoli. I heard about it in the street, when I saw the poster . . . the poster in which they announced that there had been an attack . . . and that there had been an execution of ten for one and the verdict had been carried out. I felt an . . . impotence to the verge of self-destruction. More than once in those years I did feel impotent, but not like that time. I remember that I went home and I didn't tell [my wife], nor my mother, nor my father. Then that night I met with [some comrades], we were together awhile, and we began to rationalize . . . the horror. You see, in that moment we didn't even know the names; and I knew of comrades, of friends, who were in Regina Coeli, and in fact some of them ended up [at the Fosse Ardeatine]."

"One of our regrets was that we were unable to turn the piercing pain of the people after the massacre of the Fosse Ardeatine into an impulse of rebellion against those who were its real perpetrators" (Lucia Ottobrini).[76]

———•———

In an often quoted passage in his diary, Franco Calamandrei notes the negative comments he heard in the neighborhood soon after the attack. But he also recalls that members of other, non-Communist Resistance groups were "impressed" and congratulated him.[77] Rosario Bentivegna recalls two *carabinieri* of the military front who boasted that the attack had been carried out by their organization. Mario Fiorentini says that when he described the action to General Alphonse Juin, commander of the French allied corps in Italy, the general said "formidable! formidable!." "General Alexander, speaking informally with [partisan commander Arrigo] Boldrini, said, look, our attitude toward Italians has changed, because a city that dared attack, in the middle of town, an armed German battalion, and a city that sacrificed so many human lives at the Fosse Ardeatine [is admirable]" (Pasquale Balsamo).

In those days, the Fascist police recorded a number of phone conversations ranging from concern to approval of the reprisal: "It was a horrendous crime [. . .] The reaction was terrible and just, although it's a harsh law of war"; "They are madmen who throw bombs; but they gave them their due; 320 who won't come back to make trouble anymore . . ." The historian Aurelio Lepre interprets these transcripts as a sign that the partisans' action found no legitimacy in the collective thinking of the population. However, it is hard to consider these wiretapped conversations representative: phone owners were few, and they were concentrated among the upper and upper-middle classes; the lines were tapped and no one would voice a different opinion over the phone.[78]

Yet, there were many authentic voices of concern: "The attack in via Rasella impressed us very much; but I'd say that there was then a sharp awareness that it would cause retaliations, and therefore we were unable to rejoice in it. We understood its import in the struggle against the Germans, but we worried over the consequences" (Vittorio Gabrieli). Often, the reactions to the attack change after the retaliation. Let us take two activists of the same party, the Partito d'Azione, in the same neighborhood, Trionfale: "We applauded the attack because it had killed the Germans. That is, in practice for us it was an act of combat, though it hadn't been done by Giustizia e Libertà, it had been done by the Communists" (Lucio Bruscoli); "At first, *especially after the events at the Fosse Ardeatine* [my italics], in practice we thought that if there hadn't been via Rasella, all those friends of ours would have stayed alive" (Alberto Baldazzi). This sorrow and concern, however, hardly ever imply approval for the reprisal: as a Right-wing writer says, "the Germans were surrounded by chill, distrust, hostility ."[79] One reason why Kappler made no appeal to the population to deliver the perpetrators was, as he testified, that he knew that the population would not help.

Marisa Musu. We were perfectly aware that we lived if we had the silent solidarity of the population; that is, if you don't have a network around you, even an unconscious one, made of the one who pretends he doesn't see if he sees you with a gun, or the one who warns you—"Look, there are Fascists around" . . . Without all this, we knew we were a tiny minority, very very small. There was an attitude of "Let's lend these good young people a hand, they're trying to kill our torturers," no doubt; yet surely, when the thing burst like that, people were afraid.

To ask what was the relation between the Resistance and the city is to imagine that the Resistance and the city were two separate things.[80] The Resistance, however, is also part of the city: "The Resistance is not an army marching through, or a busload of tourists locked inside the same bus. When I think of the beds I slept in, or the streets I walked on, I should mention hundreds of names" (Maria Michetti). Around each partisan "there had to be ten active sympathizers; then there had to be a hundred who agreed; then there had to be a thousand who might have been agnostics but they didn't care to bother us because they hated the others. That is, the partisan was the center of a series of widening circles" (Rosario Bentivegna).

The limit of sympathy is self-preservation (though so many risked their lives to protect Jews, refugees, draft resisters). "[I've been asked], what did people say when you placed bombs under their houses? They told us to take them some place else; that is understandable. But they never ratted on us" (Rosario Bentivegna). The Resistance was all right, but its activities were best done elsewhere:

above Ada Pignotti and the author (from the collection of the author)

right Rosario Bentivegna (Courtesy of
Rosario Bentivegna)

Michele Bolgia, killed at the Fosse Ardeatine, and his wife, Maria Cristina Palmi (Courtesy of the ANFIM Archive)

Nicola Ugo Stame, opera singer and partisan, killed at the the Fosse Ardeatine (Courtesy of the ANFIM Archive)

left   Guiseppe Cordero Lanza di
Montezemolo (Courtesy of the
ANFIM Archive)

right   Mosé di Consiglio (Courtesy
of the ANFIM Archive)

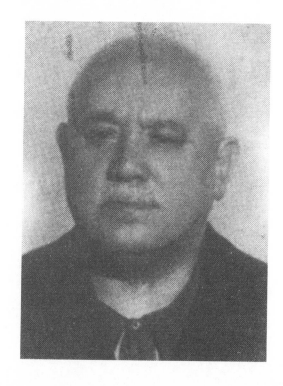

left Enrico Ferola (Courtesy of the ANFIM Archive)

right Angelo Pignotti (Courtesy of the ANFIM Archive)

left Domenico Polli (Courtesy
of the ANFIM Archive)

right Umberto Scattoni (Courtesy
of the ANFIM Archive)

Mario Fiorentini and his wide, Lucia Ottobrini, partisans, 2002 (Courtesy of the ANFIM Archive)

Carla Capponi (Courtesy of Carla Capponi)

not in the "open city" of Rome, not in the center of Rome, in the backyard of the Quirinale, via Rasella.

Of course, Bentivegna adds, "If you take the action elsewhere, you take the retaliation with you." When the partisans of Centocelle moved to Monte Tancia, in the rural hills of Sabine, well away from the center of Rome, the Germans reacted to an open battle on the mountain (not a "terrorist outrage" in the city) with a massacre of old men, women, children. The closer the defeat loomed, the more the German occupying army felt surrounded by a hostile population, and carried out a policy of war on civilians, in which massacres were intended to rid the territory from this hostile presence whether or not there was partisan activity. The basic misunderstanding, in the memory of these events, is to conceive of each of the countless Nazi massacres from Sicily to the Alps as a distinct and separate event that can therefore be explained only by local causes and responsibilities, rather than as the practice of a political strategy that linked the Fosse Ardeatine to the Nazi massacres at Caiazzo, Civitella, Marzabotto, Sant'Anna di Stazzema, Leonessa, and countless others.[81]

On March 26, at a meeting of the military committee of the National Liberation Front (CLN), Giorgio Amendola asked for formal approval of the action in via Rasella. The Christian Democrat Mario Spataro opposed the request, saying that he had not been forewarned of the action: a surprising argument, considering that, for security reasons, actions were not subjected to previous approval by the committee but were decided and organized autonomously by each partisan unit, within a general strategic framework. Sandro Pertini also complained of not having been informed, but for another reason: that day was supposed to have been designated for joint actions by GAP and the Socialist brigades. Later, when he became Italy's most popular President, Pertini declared: "The actions against the Germans were covered by conspiratorial secret. The action in via Rasella was carried out by the Communist GAP. Naturally, I did not know about it. However, I totally approved of it when I was informed."[82] A proclamation of the GAP's military command dated March 26 announced that "partisan guerrilla actions shall not cease until the Capital's total evacuation by the Germans"; more cautiously, the multiparty CLN recognized, on March 28, that via Rasella was an act of war carried out by Italian patriots, and condemned the "unspeakable crime" committed by the Germans against "men guilty of no other crime than loving their country"; but the CLN expressed no approval (or condemnation) of the action in via Rasella and made no mention of future partisan actions. [83] The last word, then, was left to the Germans.

Rosario Bentivegna. On the twenty-fifth of March the Germans at noon announced that "the verdict has been carried out." So, we immediately got ready for counterattack, for an action that was almost suicidal—not that we wanted to die, we never looked for *la bella morte,* the "beautiful death"—but we were so mad that we didn't give a shit about dying. We decided that this action would be an attack on another military police unit, in largo Tassoni; but at the last moment, when we were already in place, we were stopped because perplexity had arisen in the National Liberation Committee. I think it was a mistake. We should not have allowed an ignoble action like the massacre of the Ardeatine to take place [unpunished]. We should have met violence with violence. Otherwise, frankly, the victory was theirs.

According to the historian Enzo Forcella, certain members of the CLN, in later years "did not hesitate to give false witness in court, in order to hide the contrast that took place then between the Communists, the *azionisti,* the Socialists on one side, and the Christian Democrats, the Liberals, the Democrat Labor party on the other."[84] Of course, the Communists, the *azionisti,* and the Socialists represented virtually all of the active, fighting Resistance in Rome: the split was not so much within the Resistance as between the forces of Resistance and those of political conspiracy. Even the latter, however, had never objected before, when other armed Resistance actions had resulted in German casualties in Rome. The conflict flared not after via Rasella, but rather after the Fosse Ardeatine: it was the German reprisal that—retroactively—made via Rasella morally and politically controversial in the eyes of the conservatives.

We should not overestimate, however, the import of these Roman debates. All over occupied Italy, it never occurred to the CLN to condemn attacks on the Germans or to order the partisans to stop fighting, notwithstanding massacres and reprisals. The problem, then, was not the reprisal per se as much as the special nature of Rome. The need to protect the city's civilian population and art treasuries mingled with the political intention to avoid social and political turmoil in the capital of the state and the Church, anticipating the restoration of power after the war. In this sense, we might look at the controversy over via Rasella after the Fosse Ardeatine as part of the preparation for the future Cold War between these very same political alignments.

"The Allies were at the gates, they had landed at Anzio—I don't think that attack was really necessary" (Liana Gigliozzi). With the front stalled at Anzio, the Germans were still thinking of holding out and counterattacking rather than leaving, which is why the Allies insisted that the partisans step up their action. Of course, "who placed the bomb didn't win the war" (Silvio Gigliozzi). This, however, applies to the great majority of war actions: were *all* the air raids over Rome and other Italian cities, with their thousands of casualties, each and every one of them equally appropriate, equally necessary to winning the war? No single action or battle won the war: modern warfare is no longer fought in open field battles, and this applies even more to the Resistance, a war of multiple armed and unarmed, active and passive attitudes and activities. No individual action can be said to be decisive—which is why it makes no sense to think of any action individually, apart from the rest: "Via Rasella isn't the survivors of via Rasella. Via Rasella is the partisan war" (Valentino Gerratana). "Well, it was the resistance. We're the ones who suffered for it, so we're sorry about it. But there was a chance that perhaps, with these attacks, they [the Germans] might have left earlier" (Ada Pignotti).

Thus, while some historians denounce via Rasella as an irresponsible action that resulted in the death of hundreds of innocent people, others see it as an assertion of the role of Italians in their own liberation and the redemption of the country's image and identity. Yet, questioning the legitimacy of via Rasella is tantamount to questioning the legitimacy of armed Resistance and the nature of the democracy that grew from it after World War II.

Giulia Spizzichino. I who speak to you am one who has seven [loved ones] in there [at the Fosse Ardeatine], so it's not as if I said "Thank you very much," all right? Please. Yet, it wasn't as if we could give them [the Germans] free rein, "Go ahead and do as you please." In a way or another, Rome had to react, didn't it? Or should we have waited, like good little children, for the Allies to come—"Here, please come free us, meanwhile we do nothing"?

Goffredo Cappelletti. My aunt said: "My husband is dead, but he [Bentivegna] should never have turned himself in, because my husband was for the armed struggle and [he] knew that he was going to die when his turn came, and that they had to know how to die." She reasoned with me: "If, after the attack, he had turned himself in to the Germans, what kind of armed struggle would that have been, against the Germans? All they'd have needed was one German, to sit there and wait for the Italians to turn themselves in and execute them. I don't resent the Germans who executed my husband at the Fosse Ardeatine; I resent all the people who shut their windows and let the trucks go by and let the Germans shoot those poor people. I resent the cowards who stayed at home, because if all had acted like my husband, or like Bentivegna and the others, the Germans wouldn't have remained in Italy, wouldn't have killed anyone, because they'd be the ones to die."

"If we all acted like sheep all the time, staying at home, then a man would come with a whip and order us about, 'Do this, period!'" (Fulvio Piasco); "Did we always have to be nothing but sheep?" (Ugo Scattoni). The Axis would have lost the war anyway, and Italians could have waited for the liberators to liberate them. Perhaps it would have been a longer wait, with more destruction, more bombardments, more dead. The Resistance allowed Italy to be recognized by the Allies as a co-belligerent; otherwise, the terms of surrender and peace would have been much harsher.[85] Most importantly, Italy would have been only the object, not the subject, of its liberation—which is not a good start for the foundation of a free country.

———•———

Giovanni Zuccheretti. *We twins were separated as soon as we were born, because as soon as I was born I was supposed to be dying. The doctor came to the house, [we were] in the two cradles, he covered me up, and said, "this one is gone, perhaps we can save the other." After my mother's grief and tears—they'd tried everything, they'd bathed me in vinegar . . . —"Try putting him out to nurse." So they went to this agency in Porta Maggiore, there was this woman who came from Ciociaria [in Southern Latium, renowned for its wet nurses]; she had the courage to take me up. Later in fact she told me that on the train people kept telling her, "This one's going to die on you," because I weighed a kilo and a half, something like that. Instead, thanks be to God, I lived.*

So what happened—when I returned, my mother gave my brother to my grandfather. We were always apart; so either he ran away to come see me, or I ran away to go see him, and we'd meet halfway. We [did] everything together, everything together—considering that of the two I was the follower because he was very strong minded, he was very smart—for instance if someone wanted to beat me up he'd come, he protected me from everybody.

You understand, I was thirteen, I remember we heard the news that this child hadn't come home. So they looked for him in all the hospitals, because the fact of via Rasella didn't become known immediately, it became known only later in the evening, "There was an attack there . . ." So my parents ran—because the child was around there—they went to via Rasella and—at least from what I've been told, there are photographs, too—that the body was torn into seven pieces: one piece was at the morgue and one was there in via Rasella. In fact, the identification was made by two people, by my uncle and by my father; one recognized him at the morgue and one in via Rasella, this child.

My grandmother had knitted him some undershirts, and at some point she had run out of thread, and these shirts, from white that they were, she finished them in red. On his arm, they saw the red of these shirts, which was unmistakable; dad saw his head, it was unmistakable because the face hadn't been touched, you've seen the photographs? It wasn't touched at all because the blast hit him from below, it lifted his overalls, cut him in half from below and the face was spared. Actually I remember that they told me when I was a child that he was buried without his feet, that his feet and shoes were never found, either; actually, when they did the first autopsy, they couldn't figure out whether he was a boy or a girl. [On the grave, they put a picture of me, because we didn't find any of Piero; I also sat for his bust. It's as though for fifty-two years I'd had my place all set for eternity].[86] He was the other myself.

Apart from the fact that I was still small, but my father and mother never wanted to stress this fact too much, never wanted to exhibit this loss they suffered. [Bentivegna] came often to hold meetings and rallies in the Party local across the street from the butcher's shop our family has had for three generations . . . Never a word of consolation; no one ever came to us. And to think that when I was young I went dancing in that local—where else was there to go? But when I thought of via Rasella, I've would have choked them one by one, with my own hands. We didn't even hear about the trial of Bentivegna—which now, apart from the fact that I don't want to judge because this is what judges are for, but how can they give him a gold medal, a being like that? He has three hundred and sixty-five people on his conscience, because if there had been no via Rasella there would have been no Fosse Ardeatine. No use of him talking about it was an act of war: you can't plan an act of war at via del Tritone at four in the afternoon, where a hundred people may be walking, what, do you kill those hundred people to kill thirty-three Germans, who actually were from Alto Adige, do you realize? Who was he trying to kill?

And then, I don't know what brave action is that, push a button and run; and in court I always accused, and always will, that he had seen my brother. One can make, let's say, a distinction of his moral or ethical reasons, whatever they may be: that they would have killed them all anyway; that if you had turned yourself in you might have given away the whole network because under torture you might have spoken. But the direct thread between you and me is that I accuse you of killing my brother, that you did see him: this is where I accuse you. The evidence are those words of his about the moment before the attack: he had to calculate the middle of the platoon, and when he saw the platoon march by and the child was near it, he saw him. They claim they sent some children away but that my brother had the ill fortune of turning into the street, near the cart, just at the moment [of the explosion]. [But] the conditions of the body show that he was leaning on it, perhaps not actually sitting on the cart but leaning on it, because his legs [were] broken and all.[87] If he'd been farther off he would have been hit by the fragments; [instead] he's torn to pieces.

Childhood until then had been wonderful. Unfortunately, when he died for me it was terrible, the loss was so sharp, it influenced all my life. Because—this is a thing I shouldn't even say—my mother turned against me, she even said "It was better if you were dead, not your brother"—maybe in a moment of anger, but she did say it.

As soon as my father died I went to work. [My parents] can't be blamed, I guess, the way things were then I can't blame them; but I had an eighth-grade diploma, I could have had any job in Rome because of what happened to my brother, and it didn't occur to them; my father brought me up in his trade. I can't hold them too guilty, because you know . . . in time of war, I remember very well that white collar families came begging for a piece of fat, for a little bit of meat over the rations. Though butcher shops were closed, we managed somehow because my grandfather traded in what is now called and was called then the black market.

In my heart I felt that I always wanted to do something about it, but didn't know how. Then, when Priebke's lawyer asked me to testify—because I had seen the posters on the wall, here, that said, "Achtung! For each German citizen ten Italians shall be executed"—I signed the papers to sue [Bentivegna, Capponi, and Balsamo, for the death of his brother]. The man from Alleanza Nazionale [the ex-Fascist party] calls me up. So I told him, "Listen, I'm not a fool, I know you *have political motives. I'm not interested in politics, but I want the light of truth; but I want [you] to sign a paper that I don't have to pay."I always worked, I got up at six in the morning, I spent the last thirty years in the shop, I never saw the sunlight because I was always in there, so politics . . . He says, "Of course, Mister Zuccheretti; you will be assisted by seven or eight lawyers."He signs a paper—otherwise, how could I [afford it]?*

[I want] compensation, and justice. I think this is logical, because justice follows compensation, it's automatic. If I am going to get involved, not having any interest in politics, part of it is for the sake of truth, but if I can also gain something, it's welcome.

Alessandro Portelli. *What kind of compensation would you like to ask for?*

Zuccheretti. *I don't know. That's what the lawyer said.*

Portelli. *Symbolic compensation, financial compensation?*

Zuccheretti. *Financial, I think.* [88]

. . . Giovanni Limentani, Settimio Limentani, Ezio Lombardi, Giuseppe Lopresti, Roberto Lordi, Giuseppe Lotti, Armando Lucarelli, Carlo Luchetti, Gavino Luna, Pietro Emiliano Lungaro, Ambrogio Lunghi, Umberto Lusena, Everando Luzi, Mario Magri, Candido Manca, Enrico Mancini, Alberto Marchesi, Duilio Marchetti . . .

CHAPTER 7

THE MASSACRE

. . . Antonio Margioni, Vittorio Marimpietri, Angelo Marino, Angelo Martella, Sabato Martelli Castaldi, Placido Martini, Fulvio Mastrangeli, Luigi Mastrogiacomo, Giuseppe Medas, Umberto Menasci, Ernesto Micheli, Emidio Micozzi, Cesare Mieli, Mario Mieli, Renato Mieli, Raffaele Milano, Tullio Milano, Ugo Milano, Sisinnio Mocci . . .

Ada Pignotti. *It was during the war, I didn't have anything. So after a couple of months or so, there was this man from my village who traveled back and forth from the village, he and his wife came and went to get food and things, because back then it was rationed, you bought on the black market. He called me up, he said, "Ada, listen, if you'd like to come, come with us; if we find some means, we go. Otherwise, we walk." I say, "Oh well, all right"; I wanted to go, the folks at home didn't know yet . . . Because—not even the radio, they didn't have a radio, who could afford a radio back then? We didn't have anything, anything. They didn't know anything. So, all right. So part of the way we found a truck—a German truck, imagine; I didn't want to get on it, this man said, "Look, if we want to get there . . . think about it . . ." "Let's hope for the best."*

And so we arrived. It took a whole day. By the time I was below the village, they saw me dressed in black, because—back then, we wore black. Actually, I wore it for four, five years. And so, these girl friends of mine from back when I lived in the village—"Ada, how come you're dressed in black, what happened . . ." And I told them: "Umberto, poor man, has passed away." When I arrived home, the scene when I got home—dad, mom, were stunned. Say, "How come, what happened?" Say, "What happened?" "It happened like this; it happened. Like this."

And so it went on, even there, the story. I stayed two or three months, then I came back to Rome because I had to look for something to do, because I had to live, what did I have to live on? The pension I didn't have?

1. The Jail

Il ventiquattro marzo alla mattina	March 24, in the middle of the morning
A Regina Coeli presso le porte	They gathered these unfortunates together
Presero questa gente poverina	By the gates of the jail, Regina Coeli
Innocenti li portano alla morte.	And innocent lead them to their death.
Neanche fosse carne selvaggina.	As if they were animals, wild game.

—Egidio Cristini[1]

"On the twenty-fifth of July [1943]," Remo Pellegrini testified, "Those of us who were in jail broke the slats from our cell windows": a symbolic gesture intended to celebrate Mussolini's fall and the end of Fascism. Those broken slats were the narrow loophole through which, on March 24, 1944, Pellegrini was able to see the roundup of the prisoners bound for the Fosse Ardeatine.[2] No one was supposed to see: as soon as it began, the Germans and the police "started shutting up all the wickets" on the cell doors (Roberto Guzzo).

The scene of the massacre is the opposite of the scene of the battle in via Rasella. There, a public space provided a setting in which everybody seems to have been a witness, making for a proliferation of anecdotes and tales; here, jails and caves enclosed a space into which no one could see and no one could enter, and from which those who returned had every reason to hide and erase what they had done and seen. All we have are the stories of those who stole glimpses of things they were not supposed to see. "From my spy hole I can see some of what is going on," wrote Enrica Filippini Lera; "Through the wicket that served as window for my cell," Eleonora Lavagnino could see the Germans as they took the prisoners out. The partisan Andrea De Gasperis broke the wicket of his cell and monitored the hallway through a strategically situated mirror. Looking through the slats of his shutters, the student Giorgio Fiordelli saw the trucks leave via Tasso. Crouching in a field across the road, the field hand Nicola D'Annibale saw them arrive at the quarries on via Ardeatina. Through the spy hole of his cell in via Tasso, Riccardo Mancini heard about the massacre, after the fact, from a Polish fellow prisoner.[3]

At the gates of Regina Coeli, Rosetta Stame thought she recognized a message from her father, in a departing truck loaded with prisoners: "We were waiting, and I started screaming—'Daddy, daddy . . . ' And then the third truck—I was gazing at them—from the upper part of the awning I saw a motion, a visible motion, like a head leaning—it isn't my imagination, I did see it, I can't prove it but I am persuaded, I am sure, that daddy recognized my voice and he couldn't call back at me because the Germans were sitting on the bench beside him, but he shifted his head against the awning and moved it."

THE MASSACRE / 175

The SS marched into Regina Coeli around 2:00 P.M. Eleonora Lavagnino saw them, papers in hand, going from cell to cell, opening the doors, calling out prisoners' names. "The first to be called was Major Talamo, he was on the ground floor, almost directly beneath my cell. He came out without his coat on, he wanted to go back in to get his coat, but no, it wasn't allowed" (Roberto Guzzo). Eleonora Lavagnino noticed that they were not allowed to collect their clothes, but the impression was still that they were being taken out to work.

Luigi Pierantoni, a doctor and a political prisoner, was dragged away from the infirmary, without being allowed to finish giving a woman an injection. Lavagnino attempted to speak to him, but he was "pushed back by the Germans into his cell, with their usual words: '*Komm, komm, los, los.*'" Other names were called. Pietro Paolucci, Raffaele Milano, Genserico Fontana, Romeo Rodriguez (his wife Marcella, also in jail, saw him go by: "He told me they were taking him to work, but I knew what it was about"). Alberto Fantacone was carried away "on a stretcher, because he had lost his knee cap in the war in Albania, and couldn't walk without a stick" (Remo Pellegrini). Seeing him, Pellegrini realized that they were not being taken to work: "I started screaming: 'Murderers!' I realized right then that they couldn't be going to work, it was a slaughter, not a retaliation. And all the jail echoed back: 'Murderers . . . ' The jail called out: 'Murderers!'"

The one trait in common between via Rasella and Regina Coeli was the frenzy and confusion of the Germans: "*Komm, komm, los, los!,*" "*Schnell, schnell!*" Lieutenant Tunath gathered prisoners from the third branch, under German control, and waited for the Italian police to supply a list with fifty more names. But the list was late, so in his hurry and zeal "he began to round up prisoners at random"; some were taken even as they were signing release papers in the registrar's office. When the list came at last, the director of Regina Coeli, Donato Carretta, replaced eleven names of political prisoners with those of men rounded up at random.[4]

"I endeavored to peek through the wicket, and I saw that in fact they had gathered a number of prisoners on the ground floor," writes Giovanni Solinas.[5] "The group of the prisoners selected by the Germans kept growing," writes Eleonora Lavagnino: "Then the Germans separated the Jews from the Aryan prisoners," and called the roll: 192 names. Among them, she could make out Pierantoni's white overalls and "his ascetic figure, his fine-featured face made oddly tender by the blond beard [. . .] I recognized the following men among the two groups of prisoners: Della Torre Odoardo, Gelsomini Manlio, Piattelli Cesare, Astrologo Cesare, Carola Federico, Carola Manlio, Pula Spartaco, Pula Italo, Pierantoni Luigi, Pietrucci Paolo, Di Consiglio Mosè, Di Consiglio Marco, Di Consiglio Franco, Di Consiglio Santoro, Di Consiglio Salomone, Di Consiglio Cesare. The oldest must have been eighty, the youngest about fourteen."

Michele Bolgia was dragged out of the cell he shared with Lieutenant Solinas, as Manlio Bordoni passed by in the hallway. Enrica Filippini Lera saw, for the last time, Luigi Gavioli, Gerardo De Angelis, Vittorio Marimpietri, Mario and Federico Carola, Candido Manca, Edoardo Della Torre. Roberto Guzzo heard the guards calling Manfredi Talamo, Uccio Pisino, Arturo D'Aspro, Guido Costanzi, Aladino Govoni.

After roll call, an SS noncom asked who was willing to do heavy work, digging ditches and trenches. A long silence followed, then one by one all volunteered. Around 11:00 A.M. that day, Domenico Polli had told his wife, on a visit: "Don't come tomorrow; they're taking us to work, I think it must be some kind of quarries, we're leaving at noon" (Gabriella Polli). The roll was called again; Franco Di Consiglio, aged seventeen, had not been called, but he stepped forward to join the rest of his family, and his name was added to the list. "When this was over, they shut the iron doors of the cells, so that I could no longer see. It was about five o'clock P.M." (Eleonora Lavagnino). "After the call, all the wickets were barred and we could not see anything" (Enrica Filippini Lera).

"The sky is darkening," she writes, "and I feel something move in the yard. I climb up to the window, and through the slit of a broken pane I can see a group of SS with a machine gun and two city policemen. Further back, I see a few street sweepers, watching; the Germans shout them away." The prisoners are not led through the main gate, but along the inner yard wall. "There is a frightful silence, considering how many men are there; only low whispers, silenced by the shouts of the SS. It's like living in a nightmare. By the time all are gone, it's dark already; the wickets are still barred, and there is a fearful silence in the branch, broken only by the screams of a woman." It's Genserico Fontana's wife: she knows.

Similar scenes had unrolled in via Tasso. Riccardo Mancini recalls: "And then, what happened? March twenty-fourth, we were in the cell, seven in a cell. At two-thirty in the afternoon, it happened: they emptied the cells—at random, like. And the SS noncom, who held the personal files of the prisoners—he appeared, with two other men with machine guns on their shoulders—I'm sorry for the children, who have to hear these tales[6]—and started calling names. They went down into the yard, they tied their hands behind their backs, and took them to . . . to, to the Fosse Ardeatine. We didn't know a thing. [After] all the row, there came a silence—they had taken away so many. We wondered, where did they take them? Why didn't they call us, too? They took them away around three P.M. or so—they must have been seventy or so. We were one hundred and twenty prisoners, and fifty were left; and this huge silence came, the place was empty."

The next morning, in Regina Coeli, "the awakening is frightful, not a voice is heard" (Enrica Filippini Lera). "The next day, the Germans sent a list of the prisoners who had been led away, to the kitchens of the jail. This was

in order to inform that food for them would no longer be required"
(Eleonora Lavagnino).

2. The Road

Parte l'autocolonna, si distese	The motorcade departs, it rolls away
Giunse all'imbocco de le Sette Chiese	And reaches via delle Sette Chiese
Alle ore dieciassette sono scese	At five P.M., the men stepped down
Le Esse Esse fecero un confino	The SS made a ring around them
Presso le grotte a squadre sono prese.	And led them in groups toward the caves.

—Egidio Cristini

Gabriella Polli: I think that the moment they left Regina Coeli was the beginning of emptiness, of annihilation. This is one of the things that torment me: to think that my father, in that moment, must have become a nothing, he was a number—that, was my father.

Rosetta Stame: It was early afternoon, they were leaving. I saw three trucks, and we stood outside waiting, with others, because we were supposed to visit the prisoners. They were the kind of trucks they use in the army, or in slaughterhouses, covered above and on the sides with awnings . . . The people waiting began to call their loved ones' names; but the Germans seemed crazy, they came forward with their machine guns—"Go, go, *kaputt*"—they were mad.

The first trucks from via Tasso left around 3 P.M. As he left Villa Massimo with his comrades, the Nazi Lieutenant Gunter Ammon saw a covered truck filled with about twenty prisoners, with their hands tied behind their backs. While the prisoners exchanged silent looks, a policeman said to another: "They'll make manure out of them."[7]

Giorgio Fiordelli, who lived across the street, saw the trucks leave. "From my window, on the second floor above the dairy bar in via Boiardo, from behind the shutters ajar, I heard two Italian policemen announce through a megaphone that all windows must be shuttered tight because a German convoy was gathering on the street and they would shoot anyone who looked out of the windows. In fact, after a while the convoy was ready, led as usual by a motorcycle with sidecar and a machine gun. SS sat on the tip-up benches in the back, keeping their guns aimed at the poor prisoners squatting inside, ready to shoot if anyone made a move."[8]

"Before I went to the Ardeatine I oversaw the preparations for the departure of the victims," Herbert Kappler testified: "I asked Schutz why he had tied their hands, and he said it was to keep them from escaping . . . I asked him if he had informed the victims, and he said he hadn't, lest they should cry out the news in the street and cause the convoy to be attacked." No one must see, no one must hear. "They were common police trucks, covered on top and open behind."

"And I say, in all of Rome, didn't anyone see those trucks go by? Didn't anyone follow them? You know, this is a question I've been asking myself for fifty years. No one asked questions, no one tried to find out—why are they blocking the streets?" (Rosetta Stame). Later that night, in the Hotel Excelsior, where the German officers were quartered, a noncom talked about what he did that day: "I was in charge of driving the men to be executed from via Tasso to the place of the execution. The prisoners' hands were tied behind their backs, and their feet were tied, too, so that they could move only in short steps and jumps. They were lifted and thrown into the trucks like baggage. Many bore the marks of torture on their faces."[9]

Around 3.30 P.M., Nicola D'Annibale saw them arrive on via Ardeatina. Sentries stopped cars and pedestrians up and down the road from the caves. In a field across the road, Celeste Rasa, a seventy-four-year-old refugee, was gathering grass for rabbits; she came too near a German sentry; he fired his gun at her—she was old and unarmed, but might see—and she died of a heart attack.[10] D'Annibale saw the trucks turn around and stop with their back toward the mouth of the cave: "This cut off my view of the entrance altogether and in consequence I was unable to see any of the occupants dismount from the vehicle."

It is right that D'Annibale should speak of impeded vision: from the moment they left via Tasso and Regina Coeli, the victims were no longer seen by anyone—with one exception, which we'll see later—except by their executioners, who perhaps didn't see them at all, unless as *Stücke,* pieces, names to be crossed off a list; who would stand behind them in the dark to shoot them; and who never describe them in any of their numerous memoirs, autobiographies, interviews, testimonies. No one saw them, nor can we know what *they* saw. No one can tell the story of his own death; all the living can do is imagine it.

Gabriella Polli: And how can we forget how our fathers died—and we imagine these men climbing down . . . often I imagine like a movie, I see these people walking, desperate, perhaps looking around them wondering, some trusting that they're going to work, maybe some more pessimistic who say they're taking us to get killed . . . What did their brains tell them in those moments, what did they think of—their children, their wives . . .

Ornella Tedesco. Each time I go to the Fosse Ardeatine and I see that place, when I go in, I always tell myself: here, my father thought of me for the last time. And then I think of how he must have felt.

Fortunata Tedesco. Desperate—he must have thought of me, of these children. He died desperate. Like that, in the hands of the Germans hidden, drugged with hatred, what that man must have suffered in that moment God only knows.

Amedeo Tedesco. That was a time, a moment of terrible desperation—what has always been on my mind, I told you, didn't I, is: when they walked into those caves, what did they see?

Kappler explained that "trucks were to arrive in such a way that they should-n't have to wait outside." He arrived at the Ardeatine shortly after the beginning of the execution, "in a state of excitement." He did not remember when the ex-ecution began, but was certain that "the first to be executed were those who came from via Tasso." The order of the executions is not irrelevant: the first to die did not have to go through the long wait, did not have to hear and see. "We always hoped at least that [my brother] had been the first, which was at least a consolation" (Caterina Pierantoni).

Silvio Gigliozzi. I'm thinking of [my father's] last moments, of what he saw, because he was the last to be killed, one of the last, the last wave. I think he must have lost his mind, because he thought we were dead, too. I don't dream of my father, but I think of the moments he went through, horrible. He saw this sea of dead, all this blood. Then, on your knees, and they shoot you.

Kappler didn't remember who led the first firing squad; he took charge of the second. "I noticed"—he says—"that as they stepped down from the trucks the men's names were crossed off a list. The list was held by Priebke. I cannot say whether he held it all the time. I have heard that he performed this task all the time and was replaced only briefly." According to Karl Hass's testimony, "Priebke was there with a copy of the list. He made the people get off the trucks and crossed the names off as they came down [. . .] On one of the trucks that came later on, there were some prisoners whose names were not on Priebke's list." Lieutenant Tunath, who brought the last, hurried contingent from Regina Coeli, was unable to explain; so Kappler said: "What shall I do with these five men who saw everything?" The decision was: kill them, too.[11]

In court, Kappler would later claim that he only heard about this the next day; the official press release mentioned 320 victims rather than the actual 335. "And among those extra five they gave him, there was my husband, because he was taken out of the jail's infirmary" (Fortunata Tedesco).

Gabriella Polli. Can you imagine when they stepped onto this clearing, they saw this cave—those eyes, what do you think those eyes were like, what did they look at? They

saw nothing, I think, I think they saw nothing because, you see, grown up people become like children in moments like that. What drives me mad is, I think my father in
that moment—a strong man, a fighter—in that moment I wonder what he had become, a child, scared, full of fear, who knows, maybe like a trembling, scared worm—
look what thoughts I have, can you imagine the shame for a man, the shame of feeling
like a sheep among wolves?

At least one person came back from that voyage: Joseph Raider, an Austrian
deserter who had been arrested, taken for an Allied spy, locked in via Tasso, and
loaded on the trucks to the Ardeatine, his hand tied to Don Pietro Pappagallo's.
As he came down off the truck, "a group of prisoners were already entering the
cavern, followed by another, and so on [. . .] The cavern must have been already
full, because at one point there was a jam." A group gathered around Don Pappagallo: Colonel Rampulla, General Simoni, the lawyer Prospero Martini, the
carabiniere Forte, and "a certain Montezemolo," bruised and swollen, "whose
tired and yet martial and heroic aspect could not hide the suffering he had been
through." A voice asked Don Pietro for a blessing. "Everyone's hair was on end,
some had turned white in that crisis for their lost hopes, assailed by terror or
taken by sudden madness."[12]

Gabriella Polli. Look, what strange sensations, when I close my eyes and go to thinking . . . It bothers you to think that in that moment your father, so fragile, so defenseless, they had taken even his personality, they had taken even his strength, his
manhood—these people must have said, Holy Virgin, what are we? Nothing, look at
us, like sheep: five by five, you know, like when they take beasts to slaughter, and then
one on top of the other, my uncle, my father, one on top of the other, what do I know,
can you imagine it?

Some have something to hold on to: the officers shout "Viva l'Italia"; a priest
riding his bicycle along via delle Sette Chiese relates, implausibly, that he heard
the singing of a patriotic hymn, "Si scopron le tombe," the rising of the dead.[13]
Others are helped by religion, or so it is hoped: "My brother [Luigi Pierantoni]
was very religious, imagine, we found a rosary in his pocket, because when he
was in jail every night he would recite his rosary . . . And it consoles us to think
that his faith may have helped him in those moments, in those hours—because
it wasn't moments, it was hours" (Caterina Pierantoni).
    In his defense, all based on the humanitarian kindness with which he orga-
nized the slaughter, Herbert Kappler testified that he and his collaborators did
consider providing religious assistance to their victims. "I was told that in the case
of an execution the victims will try to speak [to the priest] as long as possible, so

I chose not to call in a chaplain, rather than have to force the victims to be parted from him after a few instants . . . When the chaplain makes contact with these human beings, it is very hard to drive him away after a few seconds. I thought it was best not to have him." From the back of the courtroom, a voice shouted, "How kind!" It never occurred to him that some might have wanted a rabbi.

A priest, however, was on the scene. An Italian SS who took part in the massacre (yes, they were there, too) told later how Don Pietro Pappagallo had been given the option of being taken off the list and had declined.[14] There is no independent confirmation of this story. However, Raider relates that "in that moment, something more than human happened. The hand of God must have acted, because Don Pietro managed to free himself from his ties and uttered a prayer, giving to all his paternal blessing." "To all": seventy-five of the victims were Jews; others were Communists, atheists, Masons, free thinkers. Perhaps, in those moments, they too received that gesture in a more universal sense; but we have no way of saying so for certain, nor can someone else say it for them. In the caves, "most of the Jews were found lying near one another."[15]

The real miracle was that, as he freed himself, Don Pappagallo also freed Raider, who said that, in the general confusion, he managed to jump aside and escape. He did not enter the cavern.

3. The Black Hole

Others did enter the cavern. Erich Priebke: "I went in with the second or third party and killed a man with an Italian machine pistol. Towards the end I killed another man with the same machine pistol."[16] Gunter Ammon: "I entered the caves and walked along the tunnels. When I reached the junction of the tunnels I saw a heap of bodies apparently dead lying on top of one another on the ground. All had their hands tied behind their backs and lay prone. Four or five Germans were standing by the stack of the bodies." It was dark, "the lighting was so dim that one could not see" (Kappler), and there were only a few candles to make out the targets.

The execution proceeded according to Kappler's humane guidelines: "I ordered that all members of the commando should fire at least once, and I instructed Schutz as to how the execution was to be carried out. Although time was scarce, we must retain as far as possible the usual procedure for executions: the firing order was to be given by an officer; the squads must alternate. The same for the form of the execution. I ordered to aim for the brain. The proportion between the number of victims and my men was such that we could not possibly fire more than once on each victim. The only sure target was the cerebellum. In order to avoid damage to corpses, and out of concern for the physical and psychic sense of the victims, I ordered that the guns should not touch the victims' heads, and yet should be fired as close as possible so as to be sure of the effect. I suppose I cannot avoid speaking of this . . ."

A noncom entered the cave "out of curiosity," to see what he could see. After he witnessed the killing of "about sixty hostages," he was overcome by nausea: "Later, some of the SS soldiers teased me for this 'weakness' of mine, and one bragged that he had 'liquidated' about seven thousand people in the same way, in the course of his career."[17] Not all can boast of such expertise. Gunter Ammon breaks down: "A few minutes later I saw five more civilians escorted along the tunnel by five Germans. These civilians also had their hands tied behind their backs, they were forced to kneel beside the heap of corpses. And then captain Clemens, who was there, ordered me to stand behind one of the prisoners to shoot him. Four other Germans stood behind the other four. Captain Clemens then ordered us to raise our guns and fire on the prisoners. I raised my gun but was too afraid to fire. The other four Germans each fired one shot in the back of the other four prisoners' heads, and they fell forward. Seeing the state I was in, another German pushed me aside and fired on the prisoner whom I was supposed to shoot."

We have no way of knowing what passed through the mind of that prisoner in the few instants in which the executioner hesitated—perhaps, an unreasonable hope. What we do know is that in that context the solidarity and cooperation among comrades consisted in helping one another to kill. The group compensated for the weaknesses of its members.

As he returned to the caves, Kappler discovered that the troops were "in a state of agitation, and words had been bandied about such as: he gives the orders but doesn't carry them out." Second Lieutenant Wetjen had refused to fire. In a fatherly manner, his arm around Wetjen's shoulder, Kappler helped him by his example to carry out his duty: "In the interest of Wetjen and of discipline, I spoke to him, I did not blame him, I gave him no orders. I just pointed out to him what effect his behavior was likely to have on his men. He explained his state of mind to me, and I asked him whether he would be able to carry out the orders if I stood beside him. He said he would, and then I collected myself and joined the execution squad once again." This is the culmination of an ironic tale of good feelings: the barrels slightly removed out of concern for the bodies and feelings of the victims, the priest not called in order not to interrupt him, the young subordinate helped by his kind superior—a humanitarian massacre after all.[18]

Some of the executioners missed, and it made things worse, because not all the victims died immediately. One of the bodies revealed at least four bullet holes: apparently he just couldn't die. Thirty-nine heads were never found: they had been blown away by the bullets and by the gunpowder gases that penetrated their crania. Some of the corpses, however, had only relatively minor wounds. The anatomo-pathologist Attilio Ascarelli, who examined the bodies, writes: "As to these, one cannot discount the possibility that they had to await death by the side of an already dead companion." Those whose bodies were found in better state were the ones who died hardest. The only comfort is that the shot fired at close range may have caused such a shock and loss of consciousness that "it was impossible for the wretches to see the cruel scene perpetrated beside them."[19]

"Since the corpses were found close to one another, and given the multiple strata in which they had been stacked," writes Ascarelli, "it is evident that as the *morituri* came in they had to be forced by their executioners to climb on the bodies of the companions already killed."[20] With his usual humanitarian attitude, Kappler denied that such a thing happened: "I was informed later that after the execution the entrance to the caves was to be closed off, and the technicians had already set the mines [. . .] The explosions might have mutilated the bodies, and this is why they were removed and placed on one another [. . .] In the course of my experience, I did not see this shift." It is unlikely that such an operation could have been carried out without the commander noticing; and it makes little sense to speak of respect toward bodies that were going to be hidden and whose heads had been blown off. The position of the bodies (many prone, their legs folded against their stomachs, as they fell after being shot) and their relation to one another (victims still tied together, relatives near one another) suggest that they were not moved after being killed. They were probably killed while kneeling on their comrades' bodies.

At his trial, Kappler said: "Aside from Wetjen, there were no other cases of general loss of morale. The men were under the weight of a great spiritual depression [. . .] I offered my men a bottle of cognac, and I have already explained that this was done at my urging, to prove that the men suffered from the same depression I felt." Fifty years later, addressing the court, Erich Priebke includes in his memoir a detail he had somehow forgotten to mention in all his earlier statements: "As I already said many times [after extradition; never before], the participation in this terrible execution was for me a personal tragedy."[21]

"That same evening—Ammon testifies—"at ten p.m., Kappler again addressed his commando in the Villa Massimo dining room." He was still in his paternal mood: "He said, 'The reprisal has been carried out, I know it was very hard for *some* of you [my italics], but in cases like this the law of war applies. The best thing you can do is get drunk." Kappler said later that he did not remember saying this, but could not deny it. In via Tasso, Marshal Steinbrink told a prisoner: "After what I saw at the Fosse Ardeatine the only way I can get to sleep is get drunk."[22]

The bodies were still to be disposed of. Someone suggested burning them. Kappler says no, "to avoid offending the population's religious feelings." These feelings, evidently, were not sufficiently outraged by the killings themselves.

Nicola D'Annibale. On the twenty-eighth of March '44, I was again working in the same field, when I saw two German military vehicles approach the entrance of the caves and stop. Several of the soldiers alighted. One of the vehicles then was driven up a path that leads over the top of the Ardeatine Caves, where it stopped. I then saw several soldiers commence to dig two large holes in the ground over the roof of the caves. They finished at about 17:30 hours. I then saw them place what was apparently a barrel of explosive substance in each hole and fill the holes in.

They withdrew some distance and I heard the sound of two terrific explosions. I saw earth and smoke arising from the explosion. The Germans then left the locality.

The natural death chamber was sealed. No one saw, no one must see. The order has been carried out.

4. Women Who Seek

> Alas! Who shall carry the news to the plain?
> Alas! Who shall advise the family?
> And who shall weep for you, my husband?
> —Funeral song, Piana dei Greci, Sicily[23]

Carla Gabrieli. I think my mother went with other women to the caves that very day— as they were then, of course. And there are, you know, very—very physical impressions, of smells; of smells and—now this gets distorted in time, but my mother always told me things that were true, without distortion. I don't know whether it was on the same day or the next, that they returned to the cave several times. One of the things that shocked her most was the sight of these SS, laughing. Now, whether they laughed because of an anxious state of their own, or . . . who knows. And then I think the next day, or a few days later, they formed a sort of procession of women; she went, and I think Pilo Albertelli's wife and Pierantoni's wife, or maybe his sister. They went, this small band of women, again, there, to see.

"We grope our way under the heavy roof,"—Lia Albertelli wrote later, remembering that day; "the greasy air fills our mouth / and stunts our breath":

> We hold on to one another
> Hand in hand.

A few brides
And with us is a sister and a mother.
At the end of a cave rises a tall heap.
We climb
And the earth opens under our steps.
From the broken clods a bursting wind assails us
Its heavy breath harder and harder.
One of us gathers a blood-clogged strand of hair.
Her desperate scream hurls us to the earth.
We are there, underground, and we tread with our feet
Upon the fathers of our children.[24]

Anxious rumors follow one another, Rome is criss-crossed by women seeking husbands, sons, and fathers. "Figure it: [my mother's] brother and husband had disappeared, so chance had both grandmothers out there looking for the fragments. The next day, my mother went to Regina Coeli and didn't find him, of course. For three months, she went around asking about her husband, some told her he was at Forte Bravetta, some said somewhere else, figure that my mother in those days didn't even have money for transportation, she covered all of Rome on foot" (Gabriella Polli). "For a month, my mother kept going back to Regina Coeli, because they said that maybe he had been taken to Regina Coeli; she went to Regina Coeli every day to bring his clean change of clothes, but they wouldn't return her the dirty ones. They would take what she brought, but no one could tell her anything—whether he was there, whether he wasn't, no one told her anything, until my father's corpse was found, at the Fosse Ardeatine" (Liana Gigliozzi).

Meanwhile, brothers from the two Salesian homes across the street from the caves realized that something has happened there.[25] "We noticed a number of cars and then the next day we saw the German ambulances, you know, going inside. We suspected something—what are they doing there? Since after via Rasella they said they would take and kill ten Italians for each German, we suspected that something sinister was going on there" (Don Giovanni Fagiolo).

A lay Salesian brother named Van der Wijst saw the preparations and was sent off by a German sentry; another, Luigi Szenik, saw the trucks arrive. The next day, the twenty-fifth, he invited the German soldiers to visit the catacombs; they told him about the massacre, and one added: "This is only the beginning."[26] He overheard a noncom, who had asked to use the phone at the catacombs' gift shop, announcing to his superiors that the order had been carried out. He informed the priests, and in the afternoon three of them went to the caves.

Don Giovanni Fagiolo. We went further in, and for ten or fifteen meters there was nothing new. We didn't know what to do, and then [a boy] said, "Don Fagiolo, look, there's a wire, an electric wire, on the ground." I went, picked it up, and it was covered by the dust that had fallen from the roof. I followed maybe ten or fifteen meters further, and I was stopped by a heap of earth, of dark sand. It was sealed off, because the explosion we heard had caused all this sand to fall. There was a ladder nearby; I leaned it against the sand heap and, with a candle—because we carried candles as we walked—I climbed the ladder and I saw on the other side a stack of corpses. It must have been two, two and half meters wide, about as high, and one could see arms hanging, legs hanging, heads hanging, I mean. I crossed myself and then I climbed down and told the others to look. I didn't tell them what: go and see.

The next day, Don Valentini informed the Church authorities of the discovery. In the following days, the caves were visited by Antonio and Vincenzo Gallarello, who were acquainted with Nicola D'Annibale and with the partisan priest Don Giorgi, who told them what happened. They were looking for their father. For several days they kept coming, with other people; they dispersed the mobs of scavenging little boys from the Garbatella and Tormarancia and managed to see some corpses: a man in his mid-twenties, with three fingers of his right hand raw to the bone from previous torture; a young man clinging to the side of the wall, his hands still dug into the sand; another whose "hands were dug into the breast of a comrade next to him, as if in a desperate effort to rise." They had not died easily. Farther in, they discovered a corpse that must have been at least three months old, perhaps a hobo or a refugee who had somehow come to die in those tunnels.[27] The police watched over the site, a German post threatened death for those who went near it, but the news was out and people still tried to come and see.

Giovanni Gigliozzi. We kept hearing about "Ardeatine, Ardeatine." One evening, recklessly, because there was a curfew on, my cousin Laura [wife of Romolo Gigliozzi] and I tried to find where these Ardeatine were. We came out of Porta San Sebastiano, and there was a little shack, I remember, we went inside, there was a little old woman, she had braids of garlic hanging from the ceiling. I asked for water for my cousin, and she gave it to her from a ladle. I said, "Where are these Ardeatine?" She gave us a frightened look, and said, "They'll kill you, they'll kill you!" and pushed us out the door, and we turned back.

Vera Simoni. Well, on March 24 this thing happened, we heard about it, and so we went with Mrs. De Grenet, her son worked at the Foreign Office, a very remarkable person, and he was [killed] at the Fosse Ardeatine, too. So, with this mother, I and my mother went, to the Fosse Ardeatine, but we didn't know where they were or anything; I remember we knew they were outside the city, and we kept asking where they are, "The caves, where are they?" "Maybe they're out there, go a little further." It was a pilgrimage, rather a long one, too, and we went and we did see something, because the place had been closed off by the mines.

In order to halt the pilgrimage, the Germans blew off the tops of the tunnels. But people kept coming. "Daddy came with some friends, partisans, they went to the Fosse Ardeatine to see if among the corpses there was someone alive that could be saved. Instead when they got out there, they found the Germans who put bombs on top and blew up everything and they couldn't get a look" (Goffredo Cappelletti). The partisans of Bandiera Rossa attempted the first commemoration: on April 2, "nine men and two women [. . .] armed to the teeth, approached the Fosse Ardeatine to lay red flowers and a commemorative poster." The place was under surveillance; they had to wait until dark. They tried again on May Day (led by Orfeo Mucci), and again on May 5, when the ceremony ended in an armed confrontation with the Germans.[28]

Orfeo Mucci. I went on the first of May 1944. I had this team of ten, eleven comrades. There was this stack of corpses, there was a stench, from three hundred and thirty corpses. I made a little speech, to the comrades; I expressed the sacrifice of those comrades, who gave their life for the idea, and we must fight the Nazis and Fascists in the name of the idea. The comrades returned once more, without us. There was a truck with a flat tire, two Germans came out, and they started shooting at each other. Then they got back on the truck and left.

Fantastic rumors abounded: there was talk of seven, eight hundred dead; the Germans were said to have gone back inside to kill four prisoners who were still alive and had been heard moaning; a wounded man was supposed to have escaped at night and be hiding at the Garbatella; Allied sources spoke of hundreds of people killed inside the Coliseum.[29] Lists of names circulated, some apocryphal, some authentic, all partial. The most credible was the one that the Salesians of San Callisto obtained through the Church authorities, but it included fewer than two hundred names. "At this point, the problem was to find out whether the name was on the lists. And there were so many lists going around, with variants. And from the ones we got, we could understand that [my father] was there. Partly because there was a fixed order in the names, they had emptied the cells in a certain order, there were a few names that always went together—two of them were distant relatives of my mother, named Milano. Two brothers, elderly. And a man named Alberto Di Nepi, whom he knew, and who was older than him. I think they were in the same cell, and they were found next to each other. So his name appeared and disappeared, because there was a margin of uncertainty to these lists" (Ester Fano).

More than a month went by before some of the families received a laconic note in German, dated April 22: your relative is dead; you may collect his belongings at the police offices in via Tasso. "It was my daughter's birthday, and I was giving a little party when someone called and said that my sister-in-law had received a letter that said Doctor Pierantoni *kaputt*" (Caterina Pierantoni). "About a month went by, and the telegram came, the famous telegram you have probably seen, written in German, which of course none of us knew a word of, of German. My mother took and went out to piazza Verbano, near here, where a teacher of German lived; she told her, impassively, 'He is deceased . . .'" (Sergio Volponi). Luis Kaufman, of the SS Bozen commissary, remembers: "These women came to our office with pieces of paper in their hands. It said that their husbands, their fathers, their sons were 'fallen,' and they were required to come and withdraw their things, their personal effects [. . .] They were crying [. . .] Only after a while did I realize that they were the relatives of the people who died at the Ardeatine."[30]

"The Jews didn't receive anything, because they weren't at their regular addresses" (Claudio Fano). In the occupied city, many families were in hiding; not all received the letter immediately, if indeed at all.

Bruno Frasca. [My mother] hadn't been told that they had been executed; later, the postcard came—which I still have. In fact, my mother had some money saved, which she wouldn't touch, because, "Who knows, someone may help me free my husband." She thought they had been taken to Germany to work. The postcard didn't arrive here; it was sent out to the village, perhaps because they found a village address, Veroli, the countryside near Veroli, in his pocket. So this news that my father had been killed was sent there, and my aunts, mom's sisters, came to Rome to tell her, and when—when, in other words, when they had to tell her, and she dropped down like a stone. And the tragedy began . . .

Even the families who received the letter were confused by conflicting news, by voices that kindled their desperate desire not to believe. "This note came and it said: on March 24 Giuseppe Montezemolo died, his property may be withdrawn, and so on. The letter that everybody got. After that, they told us that [the Germans] had written this way so we wouldn't try to set him free—you put your heart at peace, don't try to free him. So it was up and down, a see-saw, unbelievable" (Adriana Montezemolo). "They sent a letter, everyone got it, saying he's dead—we have it still, it's a document. At the same time, they sent a German soldier to tell us, yes, the massacre did take place but your relative was not included, so . . . so we waited for him until the end, we did. Until the end of the war, and then we kept waiting for months" (Vera Simoni).

"We didn't know the number, didn't know how, didn't know . . . and then we actually heard that my brother, because the German commander had taken a liking to him, had been brought to Germany, and we continued in this delusion until the beginning of September, optimistically, but we believed it, we clung to this hope" (Caterina Pierantoni). A stranger told Guido Volponi's wife that her husband was detained in via Tasso, and persuaded her to give him money to have him released. "So they met, she gave him five thousand lire. And my mother and [my uncle] went to the appointed place, and nobody came" (Sergio Volponi).

Claudio Fano. The other thing my mother did, there was this person, who was a Jew, but he was an egregious rascal, who had a German lover, and he was the brother of a sister-in-law of my father's brother—who, incidentally, was deported. And since he was known to be an ambiguous character, who hung out with the Germans, my mother managed to get in touch with him, saying, "Do something if you can, help him escape . . ." And she gave him, I think, quite a lot of money. This rascal went back to my mother and said: "I've been to the front at Anzio and I saw the prisoners digging trenches, and I saw your husband there, I gave him all the money you gave me and added some of my own, so please give me the difference." So through the following months, there was on the one hand the belief that he was safe, also he wasn't in the lists, we thought he was who knows where, who knows what had happened, and all those months, until—until the liberation, we lived like this, in doubt, hoping he had been deported . . .

5. Burying the Dead

Silvio Gigliozzi. And this is what is left of my father: this was a tooth, and it's flattened on one side, because my father had tried to crack a nut with this tooth, and my mother recognized the corpse from this tooth, which is flattened on one side. And this is what is left of my father.

Rosetta Stame. [In this urn] I keep some of daddy's things. Look at his hair. When we moved, the glass broke, I opened and touched it—it's alive, you know what I mean, alive . . . This is a piece of the coat he wore; and if you look at the handkerchiefs, you can still see the blood. His crucifix and his nail scissors are in [the museum at] via Tasso, and so is a little medal he wore around his neck. Then there's a piece of his overcoat; and this greenish thing is his socks. These are the stars from his uniform. See these stains? This was blood. Then I took a little vial, and filled it with some of the earth . . .

The struggle over memory and meaning begins with the act of burial. Burying the dead, Ernesto de Martino writes, is to make them "pass" within us, turn the loss into value, overcome the crisis of mourning.[31] But here everything went wrong: the Nazis' attempt to make the bodies disappear forever beneath a mass of earth was an erasure of death, which prevented the dead from dying for the living. They were interred, not buried. From the beginning, this was a difficult mourning: the time, the place, the very fact of death were uncertain; there were no bodies to weep over and to work through the loss. In this void, pain froze in rigid shapes that would be hard to thaw later. This is why, at the Fosse Ardeatine, burial began with the opposite gesture: exhuming the bodies back from under the earth, to identify them and deliver them back to the earth in true burial. Only then would the *cave* Ardeatine be called *Fosse*—no longer quarries or caves, but graves.

After the liberation of Rome, the Allied authorities planned to leave the bodies as they were and build a monument over them. "They thought, there's nothing we can do, because the mines have destroyed everything. And then, it had been months, and [it was believed that] they had sprinkled acid over them . . ." (Vera Simoni). But unless the dead were recognized and identified singly, one by one, the monument would be just another stone over those corpses left to molder underground. "They wanted to make a big concrete thing and seal everything, because they said, it will be—impossible to identify them; after all these months, the explosion, they were turned into soap . . . But all the families rebelled: this way, we will never know whether our loved ones are under there or we must still wait for them" (Giulia Spizzichino). And the women organized.

Vera Simoni. So, that's where my mother steps in. My mother said no, unless we do this we'd still be waiting for our father. She said no, I want recognition for each and every one. She spoke to the authorities, they said, "Madam, we want to do all that you wish, but it's materially impossible, it cannot be done." Very well. So my mother, and my sister and I with her, we went to see [Colonel John R.] Pollock, who was the head of the Allied forces, and he too received us right away. And my mother said: "Look, we came to ask you this: we know you want to make this monument, and we refuse to accept it, we want identification, body by body." At this, the general looked at us—"My God, I'm dealing with people who are somewhat . . . perhaps the sorrow has [deranged them] . . ." And he said, "It will not be easy." But my mother had already talked to Professor [Attilio] Ascarelli; he had gone over there, and said: "It's a mad idea, but all can be done, when there is such a powerful need . . ." So my mother said, "No, it can be done, we talked to Professor Ascarelli, it can be done." He said, "Let me think about it," and led us to the door, and—I, too, said these words, as did my mother: "Look, we insist on this, we don't want anything, we don't ask for anything, we only want them to be recognized. Because all the others are in the same situation, and [in English] *we don't give up.*" So he looked us in the eye, and saw that we would not yield, and a few days later he came over with his aide and said: "We're going to do it."

Attilio Ascarelli, an anatomo-pathologist from the University of Rome, was responsible for the exhumation and identification of the bodies. He visited the caves with his aides at the beginning of July. The bodies had been underground for three months. "As we went deeper into these lugubrious tunnels,"—Ascarelli writes—"a sense of chill invaded the visitor, also oppressed by a sickening stench that it was hard to resist, a stench that caused nausea and stimulated vomit."[32]

Professor Ascarelli's report on his incredible work is an extraordinary effort to write the horror. He says: "To give an exact idea and a representative description of the appearance of these two human shambles is something I cannot express in adequate words."[33] But he tries: "Among the miserable scattered limbs insects swarmed, thousands of larvae fed on the tortured, broken flesh, and many large rats were running around, in and out of the unburied and unwatched remains and the shattered skulls! Tightly embraced were the corpses in the tomb that heaped their sacrifice and coldly they awaited the merciful hands that would at last rejoin the scattered limbs, that would return them to the tears of their loved ones and to the glory of their suffering martyrdom!"

Ascarelli uses a high, lofty language that conveys an aura of classical drama: literary words, the poetics of sacrifice and martyrdom, adjectives and exclamations verging on the emphatic, alliteration, Latinate poetic inversions. But a few lines further down, the register changes, and he presents his data in a neutral, objective medical terminology that is able to call *common* the process of putrefaction and *normal* the liquid issuing out of the "tortured, broken flesh": "Contrary to what has been claimed by many, no caustic substance was strewn over the corpses, unless one takes for such the normal liquids of putrefaction that still soaked the clothes and the ground . . . On the dissection table, a great majority of the individual corpses displayed a typical thanatological transformation known as *adipocera;* that is, a special stratum of teguments turned into soap-like matter, visibly changed into lard-like masses, greasy at the touch, of grayish coloring and pearly reflexes. In other bodies, we observed varying degrees of mummification along with the common processes of putrefaction."[34]

A humanistic, classically educated and professionally accomplished doctor of the old school, Ascarelli is forced by history to test the limits of language. The equal inadequacy of both the lofty and the technical rhetoric exposes the powerlessness of language: there are no "adequate words." Established language can go only as far as the brink of the horror. But now it is necessary to look inside (the most terrible part of Ascarelli's book is the photographs), and those who look are mostly women and children.

Bruno Frasca [showing photographs]. And the worst day of all was the day of recognition, when they went to the place and the slime oozed out . . . you know this, what came out . . . look, I shiver just to think about it, because I knew my mother and what she was like, and I think of what she had to go through. Those killed in March were found in July, in the heat, you know, they were all drenched, they had got that famous *adipocera,* that had turned them all into soap. Just imagine, the mothers, the wives, and all, who watched as these corpses were dug out . . . Look at these pictures: this one is all turned into soap . . . a frightful, frightful thing . . . a heap of sand, of mud, of people . . . Think of their patience, prying them apart, one by one . . . look here, how do you identify anything here . . . Just think of the courage of these doctors, professor Ascarelli . . . Think about it . . . the sand had eaten away the flesh and he was left all skin and bones . . . a mummy . . . turned into soap . . . look, look, a person who found a brother, a father, like this . . .

The bodies were painstakingly separated, and numbered in the order of exhumation. This procedure caused some resentment among the families of the military, who would have preferred a different arrangement,[35] but was retained both for technical reasons and because—as Ascarelli writes—it confirmed the equalizing role of a death suffered in common by many different persons. The families were given a questionnaire to describe those physical traits of their relatives that might not have been erased by the execution and by time; the bodies were ranked by height and age groups. "For instance, my mother said, we'd find a hand: clearly, a farmer's hand is different from that of a scholar . . . So he began to make a distinction by professional categories, before he could even attempt to do it by names" (Rosetta Stame). The state of the bodies was such that only about 20 percent could be classified in this way. With the help of the police laboratory, individual dossiers were put together for each body, including data on clothing and objects, documents, and papers found upon them.[36] All these objects were placed in "disinfected deodorized degreased" envelopes marked with the body's number. Individual cards were drawn up with all the data concerning each body. "It was circumstantial identification at best" (Paolo De Carolis), which in fact left eleven bodies unidentified, but managed at least to give a name to the others.

"The recognition, I didn't see it; I saw all the rest: the caves in the state they were in then, with the prints of the hands in blood, strands of hair; I remember all the coffins lined up, in the dark, we went into these caves by candlelight. Which kept going off" (Giuseppina Ferola). "We would go almost every day, but it was not easy to arrive all the way there. It was a pilgrimage of love and prayer" (Vera Simoni). "My brother, the second oldest, was a boy, he was nineteen, he went every day to help, to do, to see; he would ride his bicycle from

Rome, and in fact at a certain point they realized that [a body] could be dad, and my brothers recognized him" (Adriana Montezemolo). Giuseppe Bolgia was thirteen; his mother had been killed in an air raid, it was he and his sister who had to inspect their father's body and identify him.

Giuseppe Bolgia. It was a thing I had better not describe, no one can understand it, only who has . . . It wasn't easy, because this stack they had made of two layers of dead, on top of each other, a row of seven corpses on top of each other . . . We had given Professor Ascarelli the information, what he was wearing when they caught him, and all that. We go, my sister and I, in the fall under those ugly caves, for me it was a truly negative experience, now fifty-three years later it stays in my mind as if it were yesterday, seeing all these dead, butchered . . . I remember a big box full of skulls, skeletons everywhere, the ones no one could recognize. We recognized this body, our dad's, his head was missing—many were headless, because they were shot in the back of the head, understand? We recognized daddy from his clothes, and he had a German watch that was issued to railroad workers. We recognized him from that. And he had an address book with telephone numbers and we could still read some names of friends, relatives . . . Then the shirt he wore, my sister recognized the clothes, and so even without the head we were able to recognize that it was he.

In the photographs and films of the time, one can see the wooden coffins carried on the relatives' shoulders, with the women in black; and in the background, next to the boards ready for more coffins, children in the awkward coats of those years, watching the carpenters work.

Sergio Volponi. There were all those famous wooden coffins lined up inside the caves and the candles, and we were children and I . . . today nothing upsets me anymore, because . . . Perhaps [Bruno] Frasca, who knows me, remembers still—we used to play hide and seek inside those caves, imagine. In the heat, we stood there in the open, on that big clearing, and I remember very well the aluminum tables with all these remains that gave off a smell . . .

Ottavio Capozio's mother recognized him "from little things; you know, mothers know something about their sons' bodies" (Gianfranco Capozio); Domenico Polli's mother and wife recognized him from the watch, stopped at 1:33, perhaps the time of departure from Regina Coeli, and from the shoes: "When they dug him out my grandmother wanted to lay his head down, the head fell off, it came off from the body, so try to imagine this old woman who holds this, it poisoned my mother's blood, she was breast feeding me at the time so she fed me poison milk and I was dying too, my mother was dying . . ." (Gabriella Polli). Romolo

Gigliozzi was identified by his white barman jacket and by a belt his wife had given him; Mosè Di Consiglio, from his pipe, his dentures, and his walking stick; Giorgio Fano from a patch on his coat, an eyeglass case, blurred photographs; Giuseppe Montezemolo from the initials darned on his shirt and from his ring: "I remember that my brothers recognized him. We [daughters] of course didn't [see him], and I remember that mother had sewn a flag and we laid this flag over him and covered him with it" (Adriana Montezemolo).

6. Sacrifice, Martyrdom, Consecration?

Martyrs, who had done nothing against the Fascists, who had fought in World War I, had given to the homeland what they were supposed to give . . .

—V. C., Civitella della Chiana,
Tuscany, on the Nazi massacre of June 29, 1944

Not culprits on one hand, but fighters; not mere victims of a harmful act on the other, but martyrs fallen for the homeland.

—Rome Court of Appeals, verdict, May 5, 1954

The *Osservatore Romano* described the dead of the Ardeatine as "persons sacrificed." From that moment on, the metaphors of sacrifice and martyrdom dominated the voices of memory. In the 1944 issue of the progressive magazine *Mercurio,* dedicated to the occupation of Rome, an author identified as F. G. writes of "dark days of terror, somewhat brightened by the light of heroic sacrifice." He then goes on to associate the dead of the Ardeatine with the saints and martyrs lying under the ground of the surrounding Roman countryside.[37] Gianfranco Capozio, who lives nearby, confirms: "They are martyrs—Pius XII says: there is no better earth to rest in, because this is a land of martyrs. Martyrs among martyrs, in other words. Even right here, underneath where we are. Two hundred meters from here, they had to stop all construction because they found a branch of the catacombs." A bill posted after liberation proclaimed: "Next to the graves of the Christian Martyrs, other graves have opened for the Martyrs of the Homeland. Both died for the freedom and dignity of the human spirit against the pagan tyranny of brute force." With a revealing mental association, the Fascist department of the interior announced that the victims had been killed in the Coliseum.[38]

In another article of those years, Giuseppe Cambareri commemorated the partisan Edmondo Di Pillo, who "was sacrificed along with Bruno Buozzi, and the others, in the ditch of La Storta, by the useless cruelty of the Germans."[39]

In the name of the "nobility of sacrifice," a plaque in the building of the Revenue Service commemorates Ezio Lombardi and Edmondo Fondi, revenue officers, killed at the Ardeatine: "Their spirits hover among us, heirs and guardians of freedom recovered, the ideal for which they died to live again in eternity."

This convergence of the same figures and words, sacrifice and martyrdom, suggests a conflict over the meaning of the massacre and the words used to describe it. In the first place, the effect is to draw the event into the realm of the sacred, as confirmed by the designation of the site as a "shrine" (*sacrario*). This is understandable: a "sacred" aura, in the most soundly etymological sense of the word, always surrounds death, especially a violent, sudden, mass death. This is why memory *consecrates:* it makes sacred what it shields from time.

Giovanni Gigliozzi. Those who move me most among the martyrs of the Ardeatine are the defenseless ones, the fourteen-, fifteen-year-old children, the old, these who were really murdered and led to the slaughter . . . Maybe this is the sense in which we could use the word "sacrifice": victims sacrificed to Moloch, this angry god of blood . . .

Words like "martyr" and "sacrifice" derive their intensity from the association with the narrative of the death of Christ. The day after Rome's liberation, in a clearly fanciful report, *Il Messaggero* described the state of the bodies in the caves: "One is by itself. Apart from the ranks, held up by some irregularity in the wall, his hands untied and wide, as on the cross. He is in the attitude of Christ, and represents the sacrifice, the holocaust, the martyrdom of all."[40] The association rests on two motives: it is an especially cruel death (the torture on the cross), so much that the word "martyrdom" loses its connotation of "witness" to designate instead extreme suffering and pain; and it is a chosen, voluntary death (Christ comes to earth to die). This construction is instinctively, often unreflectively, applied to all unjust deaths.

Sacrificing and consecrating, in fact, designate two phases of one process: making sacred. But who are the subjects of this process? Who is the depository of the sacred—he who can confer it by the ritual act? In the sacrifice, the are two subjects, the victim and the officiator, and much depends on the point of view: to sacrifice is one thing, to be sacrificed is another, and to sacrifice oneself another yet.

In the language of the *Osservatore Romano,* for instance, the accent seems to fall on the function of the sacrificer: the executioners make the victims sacred as they sacrifice them in order to restore and redeem, with the symmetry of retaliation, the order violated by the "culprits." That the victims are innocent and are killed for the act of others reinforces the association with Christian imagery of redemption. Thus, martyrdom fuels the light of spirituality in the prose of the world: "When after the storm we feel that we are stagnating in a livid motionless swamp [. . .] in the gray prosaic struggle for life [. . .] the images of those who fell at the Fosse Ardeatine may appear to us like the ancient saints and martyrs appeared to their companions left on earth, to give them comfort and hope."[41]

Both F. G. and Cambareri insist on the awareness, the agency of the killed who made themselves sacred by accepting the possibility of death. But the drift of language betrays them: Cambareri writes that Di Pillo "was sacrificed," as though he had received his holiness from his murderers. This drift is important, because it indicates the viscosity of linguistic commonsense encrusted upon the figure of sacrifice: when there is a sacrifice there must be a sacrificer, who tends to become the principal actor. On the other hand, when the victim is granted an active role, it is that of a voluntary offering. Even in its nobler and sincerest forms, the figure of martyrdom tends to turn a murder into a gift.

Gianfranco Capozio. Anyhow: the blood that was shed, the tortures they went through, so to speak, maybe served to save mankind, from what? From other, other curses, other tragedies, because it was as if this was a gift, a donation to God on behalf of human kind, in other words—as a holocaust, this sorrow presented to God to redeem human evil, to redeem human violence. It was a ransom, this sorrow, a redemption of humankind.

"The Christian [martyrs] chose. These instead—the word *martyr* is not connoted in this way; it is connoted rather as innocent victim. I don't want to be the daughter of an innocent victim" (Ester Fano). On the first coffin in the crypt at the Fosse Ardeatine, the persons buried there are described as "volunteers of danger / and of death." "Volunteers of danger" is a good description for many of them; "volunteers of death" seems to me a rhetorical mistake (that also diminishes their murderer's crime). The stone at La Storta reads: "We gave our lives for liberty." I don't think it is to diminish the role of these resisters in any way if we say that they did not *give* their lives; their lives were *taken*. Through their involvement in the Resistance, of course, they had accepted the possibility of death ("To make war is to risk one's life, and the partisan war is a war," Valentino Gerratana said); but they did not *seek* it . The ideology of the "beautiful death" belonged to the other side. As the attitude of the bodies shows, their fingers dug into the sand or even in their comrades' bodies "in the effort to rise"—some tried unto the last to survive. The substance of their heroism is the way in which they consciously put at stake their own lives, which they dearly loved and did not willingly give up.[42]

Another word stands out in Cambareri's article: "the Germans' *useless* cruelty." Indeed, while the anti-partisan narrative insists on proclaiming the "uselessness" of the action in via Rasella toward winning the war, the massacres at the Fosse Ardeatine and elsewhere did not give victory to the Nazis either. However, while it accentuates the senselessness of the Nazis' crime, the figure of the useless massacre also underlines a necessary trait of the sacrificial victim: innocence. The massacre is useless because the victims had not done anything to provoke it.

Indeed, the object of sacrifice must be ritually pure of the evil it is meant to redeem. This throws further light on the opposition between "culprits" and "persons sacrificed" and subtracts agency from the latter (on the other hand, by being defined as *victims,* the SS killed in via Rasella acquire an implicit innocence). Now, we know that things did not stand exactly thus. One of the foundations of the symbolic power of the Ardeatine is the fact that united in the same massacre are persons killed for what they had done (partisans and supporters of the Resistance), for what they were (Jews) and for where they were (men rounded up at random in the street and in jail). In order for the Ardeatine to function as the unifying symbol it is, we must resist the temptation to erase the manifold subjectivities of the killed: in their diversity lies their symbolic power. In this sense, the overlapping of the figure of the victim with that of the martyr is equivocal. Unlike the victim, the martyr is not *innocent:* he consciously violates the oppressors' laws, and in the oppressors' eye he is always guilty: not sacrificed, but sacrilegious.

Carlo Castellani. For me, it is an absurdity to say that they died innocent. Innocent is he who has committed no crime. Those fourteen [killed at La Storta] had done something, maybe good for one side and evil for the other. They were combatants: my father is not the poor lost lamb; the jail's records for him speak of espionage . . . My father is a victim, indeed; but innocent, I don't know. He committed no crime, nothing against humanity, patriotism; but he fought his war, he suffered jail and torture, he fought his battle. And paid with his life.

It is not easy to distinguish between victim and martyr. They are not mutually exclusive terms, but rather the polarities in a continuum that includes a number of in-between figures, roles, and subjectivities. This is why any memory that reduces these diverse stories to one ideal type is inadequate and unfaithful. The enormity of the event can be gauged only through the multiplicity of the stories: the "innocents" picked up at random or killed because of their Jewish identity prove the absolute injustice of the murderers; the "conscious martyrs" who came through Resistance, jail, and torture stand for the subjectivity and agency of the murdered. The Fosse Ardeatine are such a powerful symbol because they include them all, together and different.

Nicola Stame "was a member of the Resistance, he was determined and was perfectly aware of the risks he was taking; yet, he felt it was his duty to do what he did." But Guido Volponi "was not a prisoner in Regina Coeli, via Tasso, or anywhere. In practice, up to the moment of explosion of the bomb, he was anonymous . . ."; when he was taken, "He was at home with the flu. He was in bed, in his pajamas."[43] It takes work and pain for these differences to become articulations of a common history.

It seems to me that the highest moment in the Priebke trial came when Giulia Spizzichino, who had lost seven relatives, gave a memorable answer to the prosecutor who asked rhetorically whether "these relatives of yours were in any way involved in the attack in via Rasella." First, she responded that they were totally harmless and had no politics at all: "No, absolutely not. The only weapon [my cousins] knew was their butcher knife, because they were all butchers. They were goodhearted boys who loved their family; besides, those were times in which they could only think of saving their lives, there was no way they could think of doing terrorism." But then, instead of relying on their innocence to separate them from the partisans, she goes on proudly: "Actually, I wish I could say that they were fighting to liberate Rome, unjustly called 'the open city.' I cannot take this credit."[44] In this way, she does not mean to belittle their memory—quite the opposite. When they were taken, the brothers Di Consiglio were not part of the Resistance. They are part of it now, thanks to the conscience and memory of those who lived to remember them.

I wish we had new words to designate them all together. *Martyrs* has too many religious undertones, it implies a hope of otherworldly reward that not all shared. *Heroes* is more secular, but its connotations are larger than life, macho, military. *Victims* diminishes their subjectivity and agency. Will we ever find secular, civil words to designate these founders of our conscience, words that do not deliver them, in the very act of naming them, to the flag and to the cross, to the churches and to the armies, perpetual administrators of death?

Fortunata Tedesco. *No, I wouldn't believe it afterwards; until they found him, I wouldn't believe it. Then, gradually . . . but I, until the last, until the last, I wouldn't believe it, absolutely, I absolutely would not believe it. In fact, when my sister went out there—we lived together, we helped each other, she washed, I ironed, I mean, we did everything together—she'd gone out there and had recognized something. So one days she says to me, "Listen, there isn't anything there, look, but you ought to go." And I, "No, I'm not going, no, he isn't there, he isn't, he isn't, he isn't."*

She had told everyone, "Look, I recognized, I recognized his things, I recognized all the things . . ."
So they all told me, "Go, go, go, go." And then one night I dreamed of him, he was in a crowd and
[beckoned] like this, went like this, and said, "Go."

And here I go one morning with my sister, and mom, I go, I go in, there were all these doctors,
Professor Ascarelli was there, I go in a room, a big room with a U-shaped table with all the things
on top, because they had taken maybe a piece of cloth from a coat, a piece from a suit, a piece
of, of, of what they wore, with a number, as the corpses were found. So when the professor saw me:
"What's your name?" He says, "Come here, come here my pet, because—it has happened, it has
happened, unfortunately, but it's a pity that they should remain unknown." He says, "Come here."

And would you believe it, I was feeling, I may be a fool, but I felt that something was get-
ting hold of me, two hands were pushing me; and I, the first spot I stood at, I recognized my
husband's things, right away. And then, I had never cried yet . . . I never could make a tear, but
when it was that moment, when I recognized him, the professor looked at me—"Madam,
you . . ." "This is my husband: this is a piece from his shorts, this is his handkerchief," the hand-
kerchief was white trimmed in yellow, the piece from his shorts was cotton, the cotton they used
to make men's shorts, and his pullover was the one he'd bought while we were in hiding; and
the suit, he wore a pin-striped suit that he was married in, it was a blue suit with white stripes,
but it had turned brown all over, so I told the professor: "The suit was blue," here it is, this one
[in the wedding photograph], the suit he was married in. [Turned] brown, brown all over. So he
says, "Are you sure?" "Yes, quite sure." "Come here, then." He took me to a, a safe or something,
he opened it . . . he says, "In his pockets, what did he have?" I say, "Look, in his pocket he had a
wallet that he had bought in Africa," and which now [immigrant peddlers] sell here, too, those
pressed leather things, with those patterns . . ." Plus, he had a little metal box that after he had
smoked he'd put all the stubs in there to make another one later," and in fact . . . "Oh," he says,
"What about the belt?" I say, "The belt, look, is tubular leather, it was." Then what else? Oh, he
asked me if he had something in his mouth, I said, "Yes, he has a few caps, made of steel, he did."

And so, when Ascarelli, professor Ascarelli, opened the safe, he hugged me, and he said,
"Madam, so many are still unknown, I wish all were as brave as you are at recognizing your hus-
band." And I recognized him. After, I cried, I cried, I cried, but after that I felt better . . . but I
cried so much, cried so much that all that bad feeling, that nervousness, went away, all of it. And
this is the story.

. . . Augusto Moretti, Pio Moretti, Santo Morgano, Alfredo Mosca, Emanuele Moscati, Pace Moscati, Vito Moscati, Carlo Mosciatti, Agostino Napoleone, Celestino Natili, Mariano Natili, Giuseppe Navarra, Sestilio Ninci, Edoardo Nobili, Fernando Norma, Orlando Orlandi Posti, Armando Ottaviano, Attilio Paliani . . .

PART III

MEMORY

CHAPTER 8

A STRANGE GRIEF:
DEATH, MOURNING, AND
SURVIVAL IN ROME

. . . Pietro Pappagallo, Alfredo Pasqualucci, Mario Passarella, Ulderico Pelliccia, Renzo Pensuti, Francesco Pepicelli, Remo Perpetua, Angelo Perugia, Amedeo Petocchi, Paolo Petrucci, Ambrogio Pettorini, Renzo Piasco, Cesare Piattelli, Franco Piattelli, Giacomo Piattelli, Luigi Pierantoni, Romolo Pierleoni, Angelo Pignotti . . .

Ada Pignotti. *Him? Let me show you his picture. He was a little taller than me; a person—as far as I'm concerned, elegant, you know, a pleasant person. He liked everybody, especially old people. He really had a weakness for them. I remember that when he went to work I'd make him a sandwich because back then they stayed morning and afternoon, with a lunch break. So he wouldn't have to come home [for lunch], which was far, I made him a sandwich. What I had, I used, that's all. He was a sweet person, kind; sensitive. He liked to joke, he was good in company, he liked to talk, you know, to discuss things. He was a—complete—man. Most of all, he was good, that's it. Good. I was married three months, but we courted three years. So I knew who he was; the family, too, honest people, faultless, absolutely. And yet . . . Well, forget it, what can we do, that's the way it is.*

Portelli. *Have you ever thought of remarrying?*

Ada Pignotti. *No. I never gave it a thought, I'll tell you why. You may say it's silly. But I've got to tell you. When we were engaged—you know, we talked, we said things—he says:"If something should happen to me and I die, what do you do, do you remarry?"All the time. I say, "What thoughts are these?You're twenty-nine.""Well, but, you know how it is, it may happen, may it not? There's a war on . . ."He says:"What do you do? Do you remarry?"I say, "No, I don't remarry." Maybe this was why—I said so, and so I never remarried. Or perhaps because I didn't find the one who . . . but no, it was because the very thought was gone . . . Now—things went wrong; I've heard of so many who remarried and then they regretted what they did, because they say, "I wish I hadn't, because after all, I was alone, and I was better off alone than in company."As for me, I didn't suffer too much about it, because I knew I wouldn't. I stayed this way—alone. Fifty-four years.*

1. Survivors

Gabriella Polli. See how it is: he didn't just kill a man; he killed a man, a woman, and all the children with them, so the dead are not three hundred and thirty-five, behind those dead there are . . .

In books, monuments and ceremonies, the *history* of the Fosse Ardeatine ends with the massacre; if it continues, it does so, as historical and political controversy. But the *stories* of the Fosse Ardeatine go on; indeed, many stories begin at this point and are not over yet. The city's relation to these stories is a sign of Rome's relation with itself: it is the history of death in a key time and place of cultural transition—postwar Rome, a city at the junction of north and south, a phase of change between traditional society and a modernization that changes even the ways of dying.

Gabriella Polli. My childhood is this: when grandma would take me to see the caves and I'd say, grandma, where did daddy die, can you show me where, and grandma would say, in a hole; but how did they put him inside that hole, I couldn't figure that out. And then the sense of fulfillment when I opened that golden book [in which the names of those killed at the Fosse Ardeatine are listed], I stood there and as soon as I was able to read I opened that book and I said, well, my dad is written in the gold book—it isn't gold, but when I was little it was all bright and shining, now it's got old . . .

Giuseppina Ferola. When we'd go to the Fosse Ardeatine—the transport authority gave us a bus every Sunday, you know? On the bus, every Sunday, it was the same story: the mothers said that the wives couldn't understand a mother's sorrow. The wife said, the mother couldn't understand the wife's sorrow. And I, little and small, within me I wondered: what about the sorrow of the children?

Gabriella Polli. It's been so many years, I remember all these women bent over those coffins, crying, children playing, I remember that I played with so many little girls there, little orphans like me, that was my childhood, to the Fosse Ardeatine to play. Other children went to gardens, went to parks, to merry go rounds, and I went to the Fosse Ardeatine, these were my Sunday outings. Then we got married, the other brides out to enjoy themselves, us with our pretty bouquet to the Fosse Ardeatine to bring flowers, after the wedding we went to the Fosse Ardeatine, and the day before I married, my father, I sent him a bunch of roses and the next day I went with my bouquet . . .

2. Memory in Pieces

Oh lo voglio sapere ad ogni costo	Oh, I want to know, at all cost
Se lo verrò a sapere chi t'uccise!	I shall know it in the end, who killed you!
Se vivo ancor, ormai mi tiene in vita	If I still live, what keeps me alive
Solo l'odio e il furor della vendetta	Is only hatred and the furor of revenge.

—Corrado Govoni, *Aladino.*
Lamento per mio figlio morto[1]

When I began to think of this book, someone gave me a collection of pieces from a partisan journal, *Patria indipendente.* There was a poem by Corrado Govoni, a poet I knew only from school anthologies. The title was *Aladino,* after his son killed at the Fosse Ardeatine:

Quanto poté durare il tuo martirio	How long did your agony last
Nelle sinistre Fosse Ardeatine	In the sinister Fosse Ardeatine
Per mano del carnefice tedesco	At the hand of the German executioner
Ubbriaco di ferocia e viltà?	Drunken with cruelty and cowardice?
Come il lungo calvario di Gesù	Like the long calvary of Jesus
Seviziato deriso e sputacchiato	Tortured, jeered at and spat upon
Nel suo ansante sudor di sangue e d'anima	In his heaving sweat of blood and soul
Fosse durato, o un'ora o un sol minuto;	Had it lasted, either an hour or just a minute;
Fu un tale peso pel tuo cuore umano	It was such a weight upon your human heart
Che avrai sofferto, o figlio, e conosciuto	That you must have suffered, son, and have known
Tutto il dolor del mondo in quel minuto	All the pain of the world in that one minute.

[*Aladino,* VI, 78]

A few weeks later, as the epigraph to a Right-wing book—Pierangelo Marurizio's *Via Rasella. Cinquant'anni di menzogne*—I found other lines. The author was the same, Corrado Govoni, and so was the title, *Aladino:*

Il vile che gettò la bomba nera	The coward who threw the black bomb
Di Via Rasella, e fuggì come una lepre,	At via Rasella, and then ran like a rabbit,

Sapeva troppo bene quale strage	Knew even too well what kind of slaughter
Tra i detenuti da Regina Coeli	Among the prisoners of Regina Coeli
A via Tasso il tedesco ordinerebbe.	And via Tasso the German would command:
Di mandante e sicario unica mira.	For principal and killer, only one aim.
Chi fu l'anima nera della bomba?	Who was the black soul of the bomb?
	[*Aladino*, XLVI, 65].

The concept of "divided memory" is today a staple of the discourse on war, resistance, and Nazi massacres[2]. Memory, however, is not divided only *between* different persons and alignments: a poem about a partisan martyr in a partisan journal and one about the cowardly murderous partisans in a Right-wing pamphlet. Memory divides, more painfully and dramatically, also *within* persons and within texts: the lines above are not from two poems in opposition, but *one* poem by the same author in the same book. One sure way of missing its meaning is to carve it into pieces, divide it up, and use those the pieces that serve our purpose.

The fathers of the dead at the Fosse Ardeatine were old—they had grown-up sons. Patriarchal identity entrusts to the son the task of continuing the father's life and youth (how many children and grandchildren bear their names!) and guarantees the father a role of protection and guidance. The son's death wipes out the investment in the future and sanctions the failure of protection. It is too late to start again; men have no set role in the rituals of mourning, and they are ashamed to cry. Mothers and wives leave the house to perform the tasks that death assigns to them; the fathers shut themselves, literally or metaphorically, inside the house (a credible source told me of a father who, for years, kept his son's skull on his desk). When he heard of his son's death, Ugo Baglivo's father "leaned his head on his arms on the desk, and spoke no more" (Antonio Nicolardi). He never returned to his medical practice and his psychic balance. The main forms of male mourning, thus, are silence and furor; its main expression is revenge.

Caterina Pierantoni. My father, when he heard about it, first thing he did he shut himself in his room for four or five days, and he wouldn't come out. Like a caged animal, and none of us could go to him either, because he wouldn't open the door, I guess he needed to vent his sorrow unseen. And then, when he found out who had betrayed him, he started looking for him, and we were afraid, because for almost a month he went around with a pistol in his pocket, from morning till night. Almost a month, then he gave it up, he didn't find him, because he would only have gone to jail, and then what?

The two books Corrado Govoni wrote after his son's death—*La fossa carnaia ardeatina* (The Ardeatine charnel ditch, 1944) and *Aladino. Lamento per mio figlio morto* (Aladino. Lament for my dead son, 1946)—voice the desperate and furious invective and complaint of a man struck by an unacceptable personal tragedy. Known as a poet of nature, Govoni begins by denying his very poetics: the bucolic scene is contaminated by horror, the nightingales are as drunk as the executioners, the intoxication of spring and the madness of the massacre are one and the same thing. He insists upon that terrible word—"charnel"—as though his son's death achieved both the highest peaks of spirituality (like Christ's martyrdom) and the most horrid abyss of physical decay. The poems of the *Fossa carnaia* (1944) are dominated by figures of decay, shambles, slaughter, "foulness," corruption, excrement, vomit. The poem is a universal curse against the Germans, against Mussolini, against the Italian people, and, finally, against the partisans who wanted their flag "red . . . with your accusing victim's blood."[3]

One might exorcise these lines by making a count and finding out that, out of the forty-six sections of the *Fossa carnaia,* only one is aimed against the partisans. But the very fact that there is only one reveals its function. Here there is no question of political alignments, but of wrath; the curse must be total, no one is exempted: the whole world has killed Aladino and betrayed his father, Italy, and humanity. No one is exempt from guilt.

Two years later, the curse is even broader. In *Aladino. Lamento per mio figlio morto,* the poet rants against the fugitive king, the inept pope, the city of Rome, all of the Italian people, but he also calls vengeance and curses upon "all wretched humankind"; on "the icy breast" of poetry; on a monstrous God oozing "anguish and disgust"; and even on his own murdered son ("because you knew well, my son / how much your heroic wanting to die / would cost me in atrocious pain"). Here, again, a fragment against the partisans of via Rasella (one out of one hundred and four) serves primarily to integrate a universal condemnation.

The function of mourning is to protect the survivor from the excesses of his own sorrow, to find meaning and order in despair.[4] In Govoni's poetry, this is accomplished by the transition from the Whitmanian free verse of the earlier book to the regular meter and rhyme of the second, as if to control his self-destructive mourning within boundaries of form. Aladino is no longer an epic hero but a son, an intimate, tender memory. Perhaps a new meaning will arise from the symbol—Bandiera Rossa, the red flag—with which Aladino is identified: "The flag that now wraps your remains," that "was unfurled over liberated Rome" with "its embrace of hammer and sickle."

But the effort fails. The final lines still beg for annihilation and end. And the inscription reveals a double, dramatic unfinished work: "To the three hundred and thirty-five pitiful and glorious martyrs, unburied and unavenged, of the Ardeatine charnels ditch." It is men, mostly, who are left to brood and waste away in the impossibility of avenging the dead. The task of burying them, as always, falls upon the women.

3. The Forms of Grief

The choice of the quarries on the via Ardeatine is a denial of burial. The intention of Kappler's "natural death chamber" was to hide the corpses, not to bury the dead: later, the idea of building a monument on top of them ignores the mourners' need to identify the bodies and weep over them. In order to be truly buried, then, the dead of the Fosse Ardeatine must be first exhumed.

Rosetta Stame. Then rises the problem of where to find the material to lay these poor remains away. Then, of course, some relatives—I say this with pride, sincerely, frankly: my mother was great; she climbed so many times the stairs of the Capitol, she even went to the Vatican for help, because they didn't have anything . . . Keep in mind that we had just come out of the war, Italy was destroyed, there was even a shortage of wood. Also, the Ardeatine were sand quarries, and they kept caving in, too; and more than once those poor remains were martyred again, because the whole thing caved in, everything opened up . . . And they were left in that state for so many years, it was an awful sight, all lined up against the walls of the cave . . . my dad, I remember, was on a corner, and we'd go and bring him flowers . . .

In the first year after the massacre at the Fosse Ardeatine, at least seven thousand people visited the "mausoleum of sand" each Sunday.[5] Soon after liberation, "from Porta San Sebastiano, on the Appia Antica, every day, from morning to night, a constant and sad pilgrimage took the Roman families to lay a flower at those quarries along the via Ardeatina."[6] Thousands of Romans, like the ladies I met on a visit to the Fosse, still remember what they saw then: "I was, I guess, almost grown, almost a young lady; my father and I came here, to see them. And they had been put in boxes, and there were, on the poles that supported the roof, there were all the photographs. The boxes were on the ground . . . Shoes, things, scattered every which way . . .

Vanda Perretta. We didn't have anybody at the Fosse Ardeatine—yes, there was Pilo Albertelli, whom my mother had met, and there were others—but for us little girls, it was the flowers—the sorrow—the tears—all this subdued weeping, no screams, the candles, with all this funereal Italian folk devotion, which on the other hand was completely different because they were in a different space, and because there was this si-

lence, this terrible sorrow, that touched even three little girls, three children, and this
is the longest memory. There was this . . . enormous sorrow . . . because the place
was full; full of people, who I all saw dressed in dark colors; so many, that my mother
had to watch us all the time, or she would lose us in that crowd. And we were all
united, all together.

Ester Fano. And then there wasn't only the risk of seeing what you shouldn't see, because
the chambers were, I mean, the way they were, it wasn't that—that nice clean thing—
that you see now. There was a constant danger of cave-ins. And then, many of the bodies hadn't been identified yet, or anyway it was all coffins on the ground, some of which
were still open. And what was truly terrible was that all these families would go, spend
hours and hours there, and fill these coffins with flowers. These flowers always rotted. I
still have problems with cut flowers; I know that sooner or later they will smell that way.

Only in 1949 was the space rearranged, and the crypt and monument were
built. But the formal burial was only the visible form of an elaboration of
mourning that, as the emotional intensity of the Priebke trial revealed, is still
unfinished half a century later.

"Sudden death," writes Philippe Ariès, "was very much feared, not only because it did not allow the time to repent, but because it deprived man of his own
death."[7] In via Tasso, the prisoners had time to prepare for death, to leave messages, spiritual testaments, today jealously guarded and protected on the walls of
the jail turned into a museum and in the books of letters of the martyrs of the
Resistance. But at the Fosse Ardeatine all took place in a few hours; there was
no way of writing, their hands were tied, the last "Viva l'Italia" was heard only
among themselves; not all were aware at first that they were going to die. They
were deprived of the possibility of living their own death.

The survivors try to imagine the "shame" of desperate men, maybe crazed,
imagining them as children once more or as beasts led to slaughter. They are like
those extermination camp inmates who were dubbed "Muslims" because even
before dying they were in a sphere other than what we call life—so that "the injured dignity is not that of life, but rather that of death."[8] And then, the corpses.
Giorgio Agamben, in his discussion of Auschwitz, remembers the pages of *The
Brothers Karamazov* in which the corpse of Father Zosima emanates an unbearable stench, an "evident lack of dignity on the part of the dead man" that seems
incompatible with his sanctity.[9] I would add the body of Addie Bundren, bub-
bling audibly as it decays on the edge of death, in William Faulkner's *As I Lay
Dying.* Stench looms over the Fosse Ardeatine, incorporating even the flowers
intended to counter it. How do we sanction these deaths, if their smell will not
go away? How to spiritualize them, if the flesh is so tangible?

Claudio Fano. And, the Fosse Ardeatine, I remember this, this terrible stench you could smell all over the place. And then these lined-up coffins, these caves in a thin light . . . where at the same time there was also a kind of . . . I don't know how to define it— a village gathering, all the people—riding in on a battered bus, who brought flowers to these lined-up coffins, arranged them, shifted them, maybe they'd set the bag on a coffin, or sit on it . . .

The village atmosphere is understandable: Rome is still a southern city, containing a huge village on the verge of modernity. People sit on the coffins not only because they are tired, or to mark their own, but also because rural mourning is different, more extreme but also more ordinary. In Ernesto de Martino's *Morte e pianto rituale,* a peasant woman from Lucania explains: "Both us peasants and the gentle folks, we go to the graveyard and cry over our tombs . . . The gentlefolks come to the cemetery but they don't cry . . . In their heart they cry, but the mouths, the mouths don't cry . . . The rich folks cry, they do, but not like us peasants. We who are peasants, we cry more. The rich sometimes cry too, but they say a few words, then they have the consolation of the other gentle folks, and are reconciled."[10]

At the Fosse Ardeatine, as we have seen, the dead include "gentlefolks" and poor people, Piedmontese aristocrats and Southern peasants. Before those still open graves, the ancient Mediterranean keening coexists tensely and suspiciously with the new urban middle-class restraint. In the scenes filmed at the time,[11] one can see authentically ethnographic images, women in black who faint, cry, mourn without restraint. Carla Capponi accompanies Alberto Marchesi's wife: "Then she went in and when she came out she half fainted, she screamed, all her relatives were around her, her son, I realized that in there it was a mad, hellish scene because the relatives had to recognize them from those fragments." Ada Pignotti, the daughter of Abruzzi peasants, remembers: "A frightful thing there, the screams, as these dead were being brought out, it was—what can I say? It was a tragedy [such that] you didn't know how you could stand the sight of that horror."

I think the word *tragedy* must be taken literally: the gestures, sounds, and voices belong to the same universe as the ancient Mediterranean theater. On the first anniversary, a journalist notes: "We glimpse a nearly centenary peasant woman whose clayey hands, on the wood of a coffin, caress the photograph of a twenty-year-old boy [. . .] Further away, a young woman kneels and repeats the same syllables, the same verses, in the same monotone as the early Christians."[12] These are the gestures and sounds that de Martino would recognize in the keening for the dead in Lucania, "performed according to a well-defined gestural rhythm [. . .] iterating indefinitely the gesture, verse by verse, in a sort of automatic motion that makes it as regular as the orbit of a planet" and thus organizes and controls grief.[13]

Luciano Chiolli. I was very young, and I remember perfectly this scene of a father who throws himself upon two graves and hugs them, and he wasn't crying so I thought he was laughing, "Mom, that man is crazy! He lies on the graves and laughs!" "No, those are two brothers—that father has run out of tears."

These ancient expressions of grief seem incomprehensible to the children of the urban middle class. Says Ester Fano: "All the people there were out of control; the sounds I heard were sobs, which sounded like laughter. I disconnected, and compared them with the other sounds there that didn't sound like sobs." They had other rituals—for example, the bustle around the decor of the grave ("Clearly, there was already a defense mechanism on. And there was this, that the first time I was there, or the second, I had the illusion of a sort of normality, that is, of doing something together with mom and dad"). The restraint that keeps everything inside replaces the externalization of emotion: "And then, a sense, which has stayed with me for many years; a sense of reserve, of not showing your grief."

Flavio Govoni. We're not a family that shows their feeling easily, like that; there is a restraint in exhibiting certain feelings; and my father went once or twice a year and was always very moved. I was impressed at how my father was moved each time by his brother's grave, perhaps because I couldn't understand such an intense emotion in a person who instead, toward his own son, was a much more controlled person, from the point of view of the expression of feeling.

There were, however, mediations and exchanges between the archaic rural forms of mourning and the urban middle-class ones. In her "earthen" hands, the old peasant woman held an object of modernity, a photograph, which was gradually becoming part of the ritual: "All brought photographs, then they wrote the coffin's number on them . . . back then a photograph was still something rather special . . . most of them were, maybe, a wedding photograph where the head was cut off because, who knows, they didn't want to expose photographs of people who were still living; or photographs of people in bathing suits, in undershirts, things like that" (Claudio Fano).

And they brought the children: it was not yet customary to keep children away from the sight and knowledge of death.[14] "It's a southern tradition, too, if you wish: death is part of life, so . . . the children participate" (Vanda Perretta). The mothers had no other place to leave them, and anyway they wanted them to know the meaning of those deaths. Some remember it as a violence they never fully overcame: "And I never dared say that I didn't want to go, nor did my brother, and I didn't have the courage of telling my brother, either, because if I had we would have stood by each other" (Ester Fano). For others, instead, it was a lesson in identity, like her father's name on the gold book for Gabriella Polli, or the flag for Adriana Montezemolo: "I was a child; I was much taken with, with the glory of the thing, I guess— it was a gift of life to the homeland. I was still a child, and I thought it was a truly splendid thing, a heroic thing, a beautiful thing, and I was very much impressed."

"I remember seeing other children who were in our same condition. And realizing that, like us, they said nothing, about where their father was, how come he was dead, and so on. I never spoke about this story, I stopped talking about it even then. I was never able to cry until I was twenty. Never, it never happened. Only once, because I had a little plant on the window sill, and somebody, rolling down the shutter, inadvertently broke it. And so I had a great crisis of tears, this was at the end of '44, the beginning of '45, this was the only occasion. After that, never; after that, never" (Ester Fano). The psychoanalyst and historian David Meghnagi said once that for years he had a patient who was a relative of a person killed at the Ardeatine, and that this person protected herself from grief by means of a very intense political activism—until one day, after another loss in the family, she broke down completely and was finally able to acknowledge the suppressed grief for the Ardeatine. [15]

In intergenerational relations, restraint can defer the acknowledgment of a looming and untold pain: "We asked my grandmother no questions about this story, we knew it was almost a taboo subject, that you couldn't touch. I remember that she had this gold brooch with my uncle's picture, she always kept it pinned to her suit, so the pain of this story is something that was passed through to us, too. I think there was a great deal of restraint in telling this story, yet at the same time the memory was kept very much alive" (Elisabetta Agnini).

"My son asked me about it recently—he has a problem with this unlived, undeclared, unelaborated mourning. And he told me: there's something here that happened before I was born, and I wish we would talk about it, that it weren't a censored ghost; and he asked me, some months ago, to go with him to the Ardeatine. Where I hadn't set foot in a long, long time." [16]

The extreme form of restrained emotion is the refusal to acknowledge the death: "My mother was paralyzed, and they kept telling my mother that he was in Germany. She never knew; but she always imagined it, because she always said: my son would have sent me a signal if he were in Germany" (Caterina Pierantoni).

Flavio Govoni. Then [my uncle's] death occurred, and his mother's reaction was, in practice, a neurotic removal from death, a denial of death, so that even though she had some moments in which she was aware of it, most of the time [she] tried to deny it, and so she thought he was abroad, she thought he was away. She knew, but she had developed this neurotic of denial of death—my grandfather wrote about it in some poems—where on holidays she would set the table for him, when the season changed she would bring out his winter or his summer clothes; so that this agony was revived also for those who had come to terms with the problem of this death.

The mother's denial and the tangled anger in the father's poems, a memory that refuses to be born and one that refuses to go away, turn Aladino Govoni's death into both an identifying presence and a psychic risk. Each time the family moved, the husband and the surviving son got rid of some of Aladino's things in order to protect his mother; his brother, the last bearer of this memory, would not talk about it. The generation that comes after, then, feels that it is possessed by a memory it can no longer possess.

Flavio Govoni. My position is painful because I have been deprived of a part of my family's history, a part that I'll never be able to reconstruct and that I won't be able to pass on. As long as my father was living, I never inquired much, because it was there as a historical memory I could reach any time—though one doesn't want to inquire, to avoid hurting the person who should be able to tell you. I always experienced this as a tragic thing in the family, that could be faced only to a certain extent; many of these memories were so personal, such a personal and intimate life experience [that my father] hid them anyhow. Then there was an even worse agony when I realized that I hadn't been able to understand all this situation, and that therefore my life experience was incomplete—because I had this family problem, this family tragedy, but I was unable to rationalize it in full, because I took for granted that it was all contained in this casket of memories jealously preserved in the family, and then I realized that the person who holds it can never open all of it.

4. Out of the House

"And then, for a long time the anniversary was a day of silence; in the first years, I would embrace my mother and remain that way for hours, without speaking. Then it changed, but still . . . The unspeakable is unspeakable, no use trying to embroider it" (Ester Fano).

"I used to visit my sister-in-law's, and take the new baby, who wasn't two years old yet; I'd spend the night at her house, and I used to put a sedative in her soup—unseen by her, I put it in her soup, and secretly she was putting it in mine" (Caterina Pierantoni).

Gabriella Polli. One day [I call my mother], I ask her, "What are you doing, mom?" "She says, I'm crying because, you know, after thirty years now I have time to cry for your dad." I was stunned. She says, "Yes, because now that I'm left alone, that I've retired, I'm remembering my poor Domenico, now I'm crying for him, I never had the time before." Terrible. My mother always said, "I don't have time, dear girls, to sit down and cry. Around here, everybody cries; but I have to go, I have to run . . ."

Portelli. The terrible thing is that, this mourning, there was no way to . . .

Polli. Let's say the monster word: to enjoy it. There was no way to cry for these dead in peace, because they couldn't afford to. How could a woman sit in the house and cry? What would she eat, bread and tears? They couldn't, these widows, these widows could not cry, it was impossible, they had to run . . .

"And so this tragedy began, and my mother had to go to work . . . to work to support her family, because she had three children, and then since she couldn't run the store alone she sold the store and bought this house she lived in, which is why we have this house today . . . then they gave her a little pension, but you know the pension was very small, so she just had to go to work . . . In fact, as a war widow, they gave her a job at the government mint office, but she would come home with her legs all swollen, because to earn a little more she tried to get on the night shift that was a little better paid" (Bruno Frasca). Soon after the tragedy, the women began to leave the house: "Back then women didn't work . . . because the mentality was different . . . we came out of Fascism, and we know well what our dead Duce said: sons for the homeland, the woman had to be the rabbit that made the children, for him to send off to die . . ." (Rosetta Stame).

"In July, 1944, some widows, heartbroken with sorrow but filled with courage and willpower, climbed the stairs of the Capitol . . ."[17] They left the house, climbed the stairs of city hall, the ministries, the Vatican in search of a pension or a job, confronted bureaucracy, organize to help one another. The ANFIM (Associazione Nazionale delle Famiglie Italiane dei Martiri: Association of the Families of Italian Martyrs of Freedom) began this way, an organization for assistance. Though it was always chaired by men, it was primarily a community of women ("it was the younger ones especially, but there were also some mothers," Rosetta Stame says) who helped one another and proclaimed the public, collective nature of their personal grief.

Nicoletta Leoni. My grandmother [Lucia Stame] was one of the founders of ANFIM, she spent a lifetime in these rooms. She was the secretary until she got a job at the min-

istry; she always told me of the problems they had over everything—not being recognized, having to beg for cars to carry to relatives to the Ardeatine . . . And these
people—women didn't work then—had been left with nothing; so, they made up
packages . . . In June '44, long before they began exhuming the bodies, the city gave
them a room and there it began as [the committee of] the Three Hundred and
Twenty—they didn't know that the victims were three hundred and thirty-five. Actually the children, the victims' children, wore a black band that said three hundred and
twenty. This people were in need of everything, absolutely everything. Some of these
women didn't get a job until as late as '48, for four years they were without a job, with
children to support. There was the Light of Fraternity, which organized concerts, did
some assistance work, and then [they did] all the work to collect the data, to pass on
to Professor Ascarelli all the physical connotations so he could give the right name to
the right body. It was also a way for these women to meet, to talk about their lives.

Ada Pignotti. In fact we love each other very much, because it seems that our family is
this; the family of all those. Back then, when it happened—so many young people; so
many brides, more or less my age, some even younger; and they were left like that. As
we began to meet, we exchanged phone numbers, we called each other, then perhaps
for the holidays we'd exchange greetings. We called each other, we talked about how
we had struggled for recognition, to be able to see them—everything, I mean. Among
women, of course, all among women; the men—the men weren't around. All among
women. Then each told about her things, her stories, how it had happened, how he
had been taken, how . . . that's all. What a bad story.

With their presence in public places, in offices, in workplaces, these women
won't let the city set its mind at rest. The city was in sympathy with them, but only
as long as they stayed in their place. All the city's emotions converged at the Fosse
Ardeatine; but it was one thing to go in procession to what had become the designated site of death, and another to have to face this excessive death in the everyday space of ordinary life. Here, it became "a pain too visible" that "inspire[d] not
pity but horror." In a city that was slowly going back to life, there was solidarity,
but the temptation to close the book was also very strong; and these women
loaded with death stirred the "unease and emotion" caused by "the mere presence
of death in the midst of cheerful life."[18] Gabriella Polli recalls that her grandmother thought she was ushered to the head of the line at stores out of respect and
kindness, until she recognized that it was because they wanted her to leave as soon
as possible: "It's a strange grief, I'm telling you: for a couple of years they were better off not saying anything, you mustn't tell, you mustn't talk" (Gabriella Polli). As
Ada Pignotti recognizes, even the rush to blame the partisans was a way of avoid-
ing the subject: "And then this fact of the Fosse Ardeatine, nobody talked about

it. I guess it was still a hot subject, really. I told you, I'm old, and still—and still I have to hear people who say, 'Ah, but . . . ' Even now, you know. If you talk about these things: 'Ah, but he should have turned himself in, if he did they'd have taken only him . . . '"

Another way of exorcising the subject is to reduce all the killed to one single understandable category: they were all Jews, all Communists, all criminals . . . "Then there was always a part that was in bad faith: at the Fosse Ardeatine, it was all scoundrels that died . . . they were all spies . . . they were Communists and it's right that they should die; or, they were all criminals taken out of Regina Coeli" (Nicoletta Leoni).

Modesto De Angelis. I found a steady job, at the Mater, that famous metal plant, out here near the Appio bicycle track. On a Saturday, I go to work, and they say, "Don't come back on Monday." "Did I do something wrong, did I make a mistake somewhere?" He says, "No, no, it's all right." "Then why?" "Mmm . . . look, don't come, forget it—you're also a son of—you're a war orphan." "That ought to be one more reason to keep me on this job!" He says, "Yes, I guess you're right, but the children of Communists are not welcome here. Goodbye and thank you."

De Angelis's father was not a Communist. His mother, he recalls, accompanied her daughter to a work interview in a public office. The man told her: "'Why did your husband, with four children, have to go and get in all that trouble?' She came home and she cried like a baby."

Gabriella Polli. Because at that point Rome found itself with three hundred and thirty-five widows who were invisible; at the Kappler trial, they didn't let them sue; so there were three hundred and thirty-five widows, how can I tell you, what adjective can I find, three hundred and thirty-five non-widows, absent; childless mothers, absent. It was an absent grief, a grief that wasn't there. A grief that was washed white, pressed, darned, folded, wounded."

Carrying this strange grief, they go out to work. The jobs they took were are almost a cross-section of the unskilled labor market in the public sector in postwar Rome: the government mint, the ministry of defense, the city government, the welfare office, public hospitals, the state tobacco plant. "I was called over [to the tobacco plant] in piazza Mastai: 'But madam—he says—all we have room for is a cleaning woman'. I say, 'listen, sir, whatever it is, I have two children to feed, whatever it is, take me on'" (Fortunata Tedesco). The jobs were secure, but the functions were humble, the pay low, the working conditions hard.

Bruno Frasca. My mother died of cirrhosis of the liver and she never drank a glass of wine, we think it was because she worked at the Mint, she touched so much ink, so much lead, that she may have been poisoned. I remember, yes, how awfully swollen her legs were, because she worked nights and then she came home to do all the house chores.

Giuseppina Ferola. Then, our calvary began. She was five months pregnant, my mom; in that state, she would go do the laundry in rich people's homes. Then she got the job at the tobacco plant, and thus began a working-class mother's life. With sacrifices, because the baby that was born after, she had a rash all over, she couldn't take her to kindergarten. So then she'd leave the baby at home, and every three hours I would bring her to her from via della Pelliccia to the tobacco plant that was in piazza Mastai; she fed her, and I'd bring her back home."

Gabriella Polli. So the first job that they got her, at the Forlanini [hospital], because all these soldiers were coming home with TB, and she had to wash the floors. Now, it's not that I want to give my mother credit, but my mother was a very serious, very careful person, and she managed to take an exam at the United Hospitals as a seamstress and was hired at the sewing shop. She'd start at seven A.M., got off at two-thirty, came home, stayed three or four hours, made dinner, took care of us daughters, and then she went all night to the [hospital's] switchboard; she got off from the switchboard, she'd go straight to the sewing shop, that was my mother's life. She never slept, only those two or three hours, with me on top of her, too: all night, at the switchboard, to keep us from going around—I'm sure you remember, in the fifties, those children with the big round holes on the heel of their socks, they called them apples—to keep us from going around with apples on our feet, she'd knit us cotton socks; with my uncle's used shirts, she made underpants, she'd sew the lace on them, all night she sewed and knitted, to keep us always clean tidy and neat. And then, life paid her back so well that she died of Alzheimer's disease—I guess because in her life all she'd done was work, because she was only thirty when she became a widow, so in her old age, when she could take it easy a while, she had to get Alzheimer's disease.

"My mother was married five years in all. But she was very young, she must have been thirty-two, thirty-three. My mother never remarried. But I actually believe that—this is a little hard to say . . . she lived in the thought of that man and he remained, look, in her heart all her life. Imagine that for several years my mother told me that she dreamed of my father every night . . . Not only did she not remarry, but she never had a companion, never had a friendship" (Amedeo Tedesco). "This was my mother's life, she never remarried: how could she get another man, who would go near such a madwoman, because she was mad, mad in that her brain ran three hundred miles an hour with all the worries she had, four daughters, you think it's easy to raise four daughters, four girls? But ours was a strange grief, I always say so: these widows were strange widows, absurd widows, because look, out of so many widows those who remarried are very few, look, you can count them on the fingers of your hand" (Gabriella Polli). "And my mother was a woman who adored him, you know those old-fashioned women . . . the husband is everything . . . he died, and she never saw another man in her life; because once her husband died, she died along with him" (Bruno Frasca). "My mother's cousin was left a widow at twenty-six. And she actually said, I never remarried because—that was it: my husband—the way she said it, the Roman-Jewish way—as he left me, so I am. That is, he was the last to touch me and no other touched me after that" (Giulia Spizzichino).

Rosetta Stame. And what about a woman who was alone, in terms of hormones, of affection, a good-looking woman . . . striking, desirable . . . She needed to have a romance, but she didn't want to. I feel a great sense of guilt toward my mother because I blackmailed her; each time I realized that [someone] was courting her . . . one, I chased him away with a broom—and he was a victim's brother. "No one must take my father's place; you're free to do it, but remember that if you do I'll go live with my aunt, because I can't stand to see another man in my father's place . . ." It was later, after many years—after I was married and a mother—that I understood how selfish I had been. A daughter's sorrow—you go your way, live your life. But for her, it was a physiological itinerary that was broken; my mother had an early menopause, of course. Later, one understands.

Fortunata Tedesco. I fed [my son] in that time of suffering, and in fact he got those big abscesses in his behind, when I took them to the doctor he said, madam, you didn't feed milk to this child, you fed him poison—because you couldn't buy milk like you can now, there wasn't anything, and he drank all this poisoned milk of mine .

Giulia Spizzichino. I bear the pain on my flesh, I felt the consequences on my health, I felt it the way I went through my life, because it isn't true that it makes you stronger. People see me as a combative person; but inside, what do they know of how fragile I am? What do they know? It's a more intimate thing, more your own. Yes. Something that when you really think you can say "Now I can make it, I can fight," then you realize that when you're alone, alone with yourself, alone, alone with yourself, you realize that you want to cry like a child, like a little baby, and find someone who takes you by the shoulders and says "Here I am, come here." You'll never find him because—this pain, I'll carry it to my death; and I'll die with this pain. I know that my last, my last thought will go to the people I loved and whom I saw killed so barbarously. I can never, never separate myself from this pain; I never will, never. Maybe I'm all wrong, maybe I'd like to have again my grandmother's tenderness, to have my grandfather's tenderness and sweetness, to have my little cousins' affection and enthusiasm . . . And you can't find it all in one man.

Ada Pignotti. Because wherever you'd go, they knew that I had lost my husband, I and the others, the other women—and then all tried, wanted, tried to give you a line, a talk all of their own, because—who knows: you had to be at their disposal. You were a woman, you had no husband anymore, so you could very well . . . Can you believe it? If you knew how many arguments, how many arguments each time I went some-where—because you had to defend yourself. You had to defend yourself. Both in the [offices] you had to visit, and in your workplace, where you worked. You always had to have your feelers up. This was the worst of all; really, the worst thing I had in my life.

Solitude and hard work were not enough: they had to face harassment on top of it all. "My aunt told me: 'You know what it was like—maybe your mother never told you—to be left a widow then. Widows were looked at like whores, this is the truth . . .'" (Nicoletta Leoni). It is the ultimate arrogance of office, the insult inherent in being women, young, alone, in a place and time where male imagination perceives them as legitimate prey, available, unprotected. "My mother was a good-looking woman when she was left a widow, and she was ha-rassed all the time; this clerk at the tax office in via della Conciliazione made some passes, so once she tells me, 'Adolfo, come with me.' My mother took me along to show that fool . . . You understand: a woman who fought her own way alone . . ." (Adolfo Fantini).

Ada Pignotti. I mean, it's happened, all right; you're by yourself, you don't bother any-body—why do they have to bother me? For what reason? Why? Just because I had this misfortune, you're trying to take advantage, too. So it was in the offices: when you went, they started ogling, wheedling you. But the things they were supposed to do for you, that they didn't do. So it was with this pension. "This is a gift from the state." What do you mean, a gift—a gift for a person who died at twenty-nine, who left you by yourself, at twenty-three . . . A painful thing; it was a painful thing. You were sorry about it because beyond the loss you've had, they try to take advantage, too. You're a widow, so you must be at their disposal. What? See how it was? "On top of all the tragedies, do you have to come along, too, to torment us?"

5. Orphans with One Leg

Amedeo Tedesco. I did dream of my father, of course, but I'm only talking about a few times, because I have no recollection [of him]. This shows how certain things are still alive. I don't like to talk about it much anymore, because afterwards I feel bad again . . . Once I dreamed that my father was caressing me; he was young . . . Then of course, once I got older—now my father could be my son, you see?"

Valeria Spizzichino. One night I dreamed that my father was in Testaccio, in his trench coat, very handsome . . . because my father was very handsome, slender, he had been a boxer . . . And so I dreamed that he wore this fluttering trench coat and I ran to him, in slow motion, like these love scenes in which she runs, and I was running toward my father and I laid my head on his neck, and I felt the warmth; I woke up abruptly, there was an old winding clock that didn't run, a legacy of my father, and it started, tick, tack, and ran all night.

Gabriella Polli. A strange grief, ours, a very peculiar grief—my mother, for instance, wasn't a normal widow, you see, and she all but avoided talking about dad; perhaps she was afraid that we would scold her, that we would scold our father—there is this cover-up, this protection of these dead by the widows, who just don't speak. It's a strange grief, this, it's a grief outside of all other griefs, this is a peculiar grief for the widows and for the children, because it's all a peculiar story that perhaps might have been avoided—"If you hadn't meddled . . . ," all those ifs, all those hows, "Why did you do it . . ." The wives on the one hand, who covered up for the husbands, who loved the husbands and therefore exalted them—but the daughters . . . Here, these are strange griefs; this father, this mother is a strange grief because you keep asking, you keep seeking—one dies, but why?

"I said immediately: but then my father loved his comrades more than me. It's understandable, isn't it: you feel it just like a betrayal" (Rosetta Stame). Vera Simoni recalls how, soon after the war, the son of one of the men killed at the Fosse Ardeatine "went out one day, and didn't come home for a day, for twenty-four hours, and the mother was desperate. So at a certain moment we found ourselves with a sense of rebellion. I would have wanted to rebel but I couldn't, because I had my mother, there was this effort to keep us all alive, we had to help each other in the family." The effort to survive keeps the wives from falling; but the sons and daughters are lost, bewildered; they rebel against death, against the mothers who do not explain, against the fathers whose choices left them to carry the burden.

Gabriella Polli. I had a life with so many problems, I married young and so many times when I was a thousand lire short, then—it's a shame—this led me even to be aggressive many times toward my father, and then I regret it, I regret it so much I could die, but I still do it, I always say, but why, I wish I could know why, why did he have to meddle with these things so red, so absurd, what kind of a life may he have had, carrying these weapons around, how could he live this life, this I'd like to ask him, didn't you think of your children? A father can't walk all day in the midst of fire, fire burns, he ought to avoid it sometimes. Why didn't you put on a black shirt, on Saturdays you'd stand there like a dolt, listen to their nonsense, and think of your family, with four little girls, what's the sense of you meddling with these things . . .

"Then I also lived a few years in a boarding school: this sadness of being sent away, I didn't know why—now I understand that I didn't understand why. I knew it had happened, I sensed only this great sadness in the family, everybody cried all the time, the grandparents, the uncles, my mother were desperate, all this despair, but I was small, I couldn't understand, being sent away from home like this seems an injustice" (Ornella Tedesco). The loss of the fathers they hardly knew (many were a few months old; some were actually born after) is followed by the separation from the family: working mothers can't watch over them, so they make whatever arrangements they can. "When . . . it happened—my brother was fourteen and my sister twelve; they were young, too, and we were abandoned somehow. So my mother had the idea of putting us in an orphans' home. Once in a while she'd come see us, and she always tells me that they called her the weeping willow, because she went up the stairs laughing and came down crying, because of course . . . she'd left us two behind" (Anita Ferola).

Liana Gigliozzi. I was put in boarding school when I was four. Then I suffered so much, because I stayed in boarding school all those years and I hardly ever saw my mother, it's not as if she could come see me every Sunday, and so many years of solitude . . . First they sent me to a boarding school in Frosinone, where I really starved: my mother found me one day on top of a tree, eating fig skins . . . No wonder my health was bad. Then they sent me here in Rome to the nuns in via Aurelia, where I was a little better; but it was still a boarding school, I saw my mother once every two, three months . . . so what love did I have, the nuns'?

Gabriella Polli. That is the age when you have small children, so we are orphans both of father and mother. [Priebke] threw families out in the street, he left orphans in boarding schools, people who ate the plaster off the wall, my sister made little balls of newspaper and ate them, that's the legacy of this egregious gentleman. And then the complexes, you're right: it drove me crazy, that I couldn't have my father sign [my report card]. It was the Epiphany, I must have been ten; this little girl comes up, she says, "My father bought me a doll carriage, a toy car—what did your father get you?" "Nothing, he's dead." My mother had bought me a lot of presents for the Epiphany, because she worked much too hard so that we wouldn't lack anything; but the fact that it hadn't been bought by my father, that doll, that pram that I too had got . . . I don't remember a kiss from my father, I don't remember a slap, look, even a quarrel—you know when you begin to grow up, and I see my daughters once in a while have an argument with their father . . . Well, I could never have this pleasure, and it's been a long time, and yet sometimes I think, "Holy Mary, I wish I, too, could have quarreled with my father"—I never quarreled, he never scolded me, nothing, it was all taken from me.

During the first Priebke trial, when it was in the news, I thought that the media's description of the families of the victims as "elderly orphans" was a sign of paternalism that froze them to the moment of grief—as if from that time on they had stopped existing, or at least had existed only as orphans, not as whole persons. But I found that terrible oxymoron, "elderly orphans," in their own words. "I am an elderly orphan," says Gabriella Polli. "We are perennial orphans; we are people who are without a leg, we carried on through life with this handicap, this absurd grief. We are persons who are without a leg; we put on a nice wooden leg and we walk, all these orphans, a nice wooden leg and we walk, we go on."

"Professor, I'll tell you one thing. I didn't live through these things in person, because when daddy died I was four and a half months. I am living through them now, it's as though they had happened, believe me, a week ago" (Amedeo Tedesco). There is an image that represents this relationship with time: the stopped watch that starts again, in Valeria Spizzichino's dream or—perhaps invented but nevertheless striking—in a newspaper story on the Priebke trial: "Michele Bolgia's head was gone; but at his wrist he still had his watch [. . .] Yesterday, suddenly, the German-made watch of the partisan Michele Bolgia started again. After being stopped for fifty-two years, it began once again to mark time; but it was the time of sorrow. Yesterday, too many wounds which in half a century had never become scars, because a lifetime is not enough to heal them, started bleeding again."[19]

In the story of Michele Bolgia's watch, the idea is that time was suspended on March 24, 1944, and stood still until the Priebke trial set it in motion again. In Valeria Spizzichino's dream, however, it is the dream itself that sets the clock in motion. Though they bear the weight of the frozen time of loss, these orphans were forced, were able, to live adult lives, to become citizens. Not for all did grief freeze in an insurmountable trauma. Wives and mothers hired as cleaning women took exams, got office jobs, raised their families. Sons and daughters and grandchildren who grew up surrounded by grief have worked, gone to school, become technicians, secretaries, merchants, clerks, professors, lawyers, even psychoanalysts. The motionless time of unelaborated loss and the historical time of everyday life flowed alongside each other. The visible strength and the inner fragility of which Giulia Spizzichino speaks are each a condition of the other, and they cannot be contained either by compassion or by a reassuring admiration.

6. Explanations

Actually it's no accident, that they wound up there, at the Fosse Ardeatine . . .

—Elisabetta Agnini

Oh well, if he did it I guess that it . . . it was worth it . . . That if he believed in it so much . . .

—Anita Ferola

The central question—*why* did they die—is raised on two distinct and related planes: the reasons for the event as a whole, from via Rasella to the Fosse Ardeatine ("it would be good to know why he threw it in via Rasella," Liana Gigliozzi observes); and the reason for each individual destiny: "If my father had been in the Resistance, it would be different. Because it could have been part of the game, see? See how I talk . . . It's a risk you take, I mean. But a person like that, taken like that . . . it created an agony to last me a lifetime" (Amedeo Tedesco).

Giulia Spizzichino. I didn't say that my relatives were second class [victims], absolutely not; I said, however, that if they too had been fighting partisans I would be even prouder: they fought for something they believed in. Instead, they died like lambs, without a weapon in their hand, see what I mean? There they were, running from the Nazis, that's all they could concentrate on; they're on the run because the Nazis take their children and deport them; you come and kill me anyway, then I might as well have had a weapon in my hand, at least I'd know why I was dying.

For the children of the combatants, the reasons at least are clear. They may be disappointed ("My hero father did us no good, because he was not granted an adequate pension, not awarded a gold medal, no jobs . . .") but pride remains: "My father got himself killed; if our rulers, including the Fascists, remembered today that that's where their freedom comes from . . ." (Gabriella Polli). This pride can also be a responsibility: "Dad's figure—I lived only a few years with him but blood is not water, no doubt, and with his example he gave us much, we are proud and glad of it; it's an exceptional legacy, so one must try to live up to it" (Adriana Montezemolo). "Do you know what my grandmother used to tell me when I was beginning high school? 'Remember whose granddaughter you are.' You were not allowed a false step. We belong to those years also of sexual liberation; so what grandma said was also a warning about certain things. But it also meant: you must have dignity, you must study at all costs . . . I lived it with pride" (Nicoletta Leoni).

Elisabetta Agnini. It's part of my life, from my earliest childhood memories: the study, in my grandmother's house, was really the image of my uncle, everywhere; something, I don't know, of which I've always been very proud. The word *heroism* has perhaps rhetorical connotations, but there was something strongly idealistic in these people, which is something I feel proud of. I had an uncle who was tortured no less than twelve times, who was young and who managed to organize a student movement, the student association, so he is one of those minds who brought us to have a democratic system. In other words, I don't think his death was accidental.

Things are more difficult for those whose death can be perceived, instead, as "accidental": those taken from jail at the last moment or picked up in via Rasella. The Jews can have a context for it all ("If my father instead of the Fosse Ardeatine had been taken to Auschwitz for him it would have been much, much worse," Claudio Fano says); but for those who have no cultural or ideological tools of interpretation, blaming the partisans becomes a way of angrily reaching for an explanation.

Liana Gigliozzi. My mother told me. "Ah, because an irresponsible person, a wretch, a son of a . . . got up one morning, went and threw the bomb, and because of him your father died." This is the simplistic manner in which my mother told the story, so clearly, this idea has been rooted in me since I was three.

I think this is an understandable reaction, especially inasmuch as it tallies with commonsense. Speaking with some of the few survivors who share this point of view, I often felt that they would speak this way even if they were not directly involved, because this is how their environment thinks. This attitude appears from the very beginning: Govoni's poem, the mother who attacked Bentivegna at the trial, the relatives who sued the partisans in 1949 . . . If anything, it is surprising that there are so few of them.

During the Priebke trial, I was intrigued by the relatives' lucid rebuttal of the anti-partisan argument. I imagined that this attitude was not unanimous, that it had been reached only after a long, difficult, painful process. But I was surprised at how prevalent, firm, and clear the final awareness was.

Ada Pignotti. Now—I understand it; I've thought it over. In the beginning I didn't reason, because I didn't understand it, I'll tell you the truth: after all, what did I know about the Resistance? Later, need made me understand, woke me up a little. At home we never talked about these things. Besides, when you're twenty-three, you don't think about politics. As for me, back then, in my time, at twenty-three we were still children, and didn't understand much yet.

"The wives, the mothers [of the fallen partisans] told us: 'See what you've done—you drove our sons to it, you got them killed'" (Orfeo Mucci). Carla Capponi recalled her first encounter with Alberto Marchesi's wife, after he was killed: "When I went to see her, she initially reacted, how shall I say – 'For me, this partisan struggle, it took my husband from me'—in other words, she resented the partisan struggle somewhat; later she became one of the most active." "Carla Capponi came into my house—and she was thrown out by yours truly, poor woman. Yes, because—I was little—I didn't understand; it's normal for a child, the first thing she does . . ." (Rosetta Stame).

Giovanni Gigliozzi. But that is instinctive . . . I guess it's a gut reaction; but we are made of guts and brain. In the beginning, yes—you must understand: they tell you, "He set off a bomb and because of all that they . . ." Even sources above suspicion, like the *Osservatore Romano,* who put the partisans and the German reaction on the same plane . . . there really was a process, a work of misinformation. I'm ashamed that I, too, felt this resentment. Then I thought it over . . .

This rethinking, as Gigliozzi explains it, is based on an awareness of the context ("This wasn't the first and only attack, and no matter where they did it there would have been a reaction . . . But if these partisans hadn't acted, what would Italy's image have been in the eyes of the Allies?") and on the constant recollection of who it was that actually pulled the trigger, and how ("It wasn't a retaliation, it was a slaughter, there was no respect for anything, the most elementary laws of humanity were broken . . . a mad, mad thing").

Claudio Fano. I have a very clear idea, which I told many times, no matter how they try to twist it: the guilt for the Fosse Ardeatine falls on the Germans, not the partisans; it was an act of war, it was the partisans' duty not to turn themselves in. For a very simple reason: what is the goal of the retaliation? Its goal is that there must be no acts of war against the [occupying] army. So if they had turned themselves in, the Germans would have got what they wanted. As for this idea of justifying such a massacre on the basis of so-called laws of war, I won't even discuss it. The partisans should not, should not have turned themselves in.

It is not easy, however, to reconcile "guts" and "brain." "I don't feel much resentment toward them. Of course, I wouldn't have given them a gold medal, that's for sure. Yet, I don't feel a great resentment toward them. I never in my life thought, 'It's their fault.' Never did I have that thought, and I don't think I ever will; and I hope I never will" (Giulia Spizzichino). Ada Pignotti has reached a clear understanding of the reasons and meanings of the partisan action, and of how the anti-partisan discourse has been used against her; yet she will not meet with Bentivegna and Carla Capponi. On the other hand, General Ayroldi's daughter chooses to ask Bentivegna to commemorate her father in his home-town, Ostuni. Giuseppina Ferola is convinced that "if he had turned himself in, there would just have been one more [killed]. If it's true that there's a God, he'll deal with him. But I sincerely still don't feel I can blame him." However, find-ing herself in the same room with Bentivegna (without his knowledge) is a trau-matic experience: "I looked at him—and afterwards it was so tiresome, and a very long road to walk out of that room. My legs were shaking something awful. And even then, I said, 'No. It would have just been one more.' It hurt me so much. But I still say, he would have been just one more."

There is, then, a distance between political reason and personal emotion that is overcome in older or more direct personal relationships. "Many were comrades of ours: Gesmundo was our political commissar, Scattoni had been loaned to the GAP from Bandiera Rossa, Alberto Marchesi was a comrade . . ." (Rosario Ben-tivegna). Some of the victims' relatives chose Bentivegna as their family doctor and received from Carla Capponi precious moral and tangible support: "I was in touch with Carla most; a woman with guts, very brave and also very suffering. She was my teacher, she drove me [to get involved]. As for Bentivegna, it was mom who knew him best; he worked at the Fleming [clinic] and mom would go there for her tests" (Rosetta Stame). "Bentivegna was a doctor for the Romana Gas [Rome Gas Company], and at the gas company they had three who had been killed at the Fosse Ardeatine, so through these families . . . Then many of them were partisans, so we took care of their papers for partisan recognition, because many wives didn't even know sometimes that their husbands had done actions with us. Gesmundo's sister, for instance, didn't know about her brother, because she wasn't in Rome, she was in the south" (Carla Capponi).

These, however, are individual processes. I think that the real difference be-tween the attitudes of the survivors of the Ardeatine and other communities in which a tight anti-partisan memory has prevailed[20] derived primarily from the urban, pluralistic context in which memory and mourning were elaborated. The diverse background of the victims prevented the formation of a single narrative; and the fact that it all took place in the heterogeneous context of a big city ex-posed the individuals to a plurality of discourses and interpretations.

Also, memory and mourning were elaborated collectively as well as individu-ally. The families of the Fosse Ardeatine appeared from the very beginning as a collective public subject that did not delegate to others their common material and emotional needs. Although this did not mean that they subscribed formally to one interpretation over others, it certainly made the anti-partisan polemic a secondary concern for them (besides, they were less susceptible to the false and wrong tales, because they had lived through the events and knew exactly what had happened). Furthermore, because they were primarily a community of women, they were kept together more by deep personal emotions than by ideological controversy; they did not brood in solitude over their individual grief and recriminations.

This, of course, did not happen instantly and painlessly. There were also moments of conflict among the different groups of survivors, tensions over symbols, attempts to create alternative associations. But the consciousness of what united them prevailed; what the families wanted most was to be together.[21] The interaction between this need for unity and the actual differences did not generate a tight homogeneity, some kind of political line; but it kept most of the more emotionally or culturally fragile persons from sliding into reactionary attitudes and behavior.

Gabriella Polli. We were third class orphans, fourth-class maybe, because behind our grief there was hunger, poverty, despair; we were fourth-, fifth-class orphans because we were the poor orphans, rejected by all because we were the children of Communists—because, for the others, they were all Communists. Really, look, it's a grief that only served to fill your bodies with anger, because my father died for a flag, and this flag wrapped none of us in it.

———◆———

Rosetta Stame. *When those Nazi villains came to search our house at night—also, there was an Italian with them, remember this, always: the Fascist spies, informers . . . Mom knew that daddy hadn't come home, we didn't know where he was, but we knew he had been captured by the Germans. My father was arrested in piazza Mignanelli, near the revenue office; a man who worked there and lived in our building saw his arrest, he saw my father getting into a car with two Germans at his side, at gun point; and that evening he came over—mom was [walking the floor back and forth like] the she-wolf of the Capitol,[22] because dad hadn't come—and he says, "Madam, look, I hope I'm wrong, but I saw as he was being loaded like that . . ."*

But where he'd been taken, we didn't know. Mom began to search, but we didn't find out anything. Three days went by. Then at night a great screeching of jeep wheels. Those jeeps, those cars that the Germans, the Nazis drove, when they arrived they screeched like that, all right? In fact, for years, the sound of boots, any uniform—it stopped me in my tracks—not with fear, though: with hatred. "Bang . . . bang," on the door, loud. My grandfather opens; they come in and ask for

mom. We were asleep; that screeching, I only half heard it. They came into our bedroom and literally rolled us over with the mattress. Awakened in the middle of the night, seeing these men in
uniform, sticking the mattress with the points of their bayonets . . . My grandmother, who slept
in the bed next to mine, was paralyzed on her bed; one of them leaned his gun on her belly, and
she lay face up, motionless; I can still hear his sneering laughter, they were enjoying themselves . . . Grandma stayed like that, eyes wide, motionless, you couldn't even see the throb of this
poor woman's breath . . . They were looking for weapons . . . My father had a pistol, a knife,
which I think were from back in World War I; but, more important, my mother had all the military plan [of Bandiera Rossa], with the names . . .

Life was turned around, unstrung. They didn't kill only daddy; [his mother] too. Because when
my grandmother heard of her son's death she gave out a scream like a beast . . . you know, a
wounded, hurt beast . . . She gave out this great scream, and never spoke again. She lived another
nine years; just think, when she was able to speak again all she could say was "Nicolino, Nicolino," and she was like an automaton. They even gave her electroshock, poor woman, I remember
her in the psychiatric hospital . . .

A few years before [my mother died]—I did her so many wrongs—[I told her]: "You would-
n't let me give my father a last kiss, I can't forgive you for this . . ." I was driving, crying. "Listen, mom, this is a thing you shouldn't have done." Then she, who hardly ever cried: "Stop the car!
How could I let you see him? When I opened his shirt to kiss his chest, his chest was crushed
in . . ." Because when dad was found his head was missing; they sent her away while they tried
to put him back together, to make him presentable. She had told me about it, but she hadn't told
me that his head was cut off from his body . . . a hand was broken off . . . and this bloody
rope . . . I remember the bloody rope very well, what happened to this rope I don't know . . .

In the beginning I felt somehow betrayed by my father. When he died, I said, "He died because
he wouldn't go back on his word to his comrades; so the comrades came before his love for us; he
didn't love me enough . . ." For years, after I no longer saw my father, I went around looking for
men of my father's age, dark haired, with thin whiskers, tall and strong, like him. When I was
twelve or thirteen, I looked like a girl of eighteen; outside my school—suddenly, I stop in my
tracks and stare at a person . . . My classmates look at me and look at each other . . . and I was
gazing, staring, he felt the stare, turned around . . . and I was staring and he was looking at me.
They say, "Rosetta, what are you doing . . . ." "Be quiet, be quiet, don't say a word . . ." So one,
gently, says, "Rosetta, I know why you're looking at that man like that: you think it's your father,
but it's not so." "Ah, be quiet . . ." So one said, and she did right: "But don't you understand why
that guy's looking at you?"

This happened in the eighth grade. I had good grades, I am reading the results, and this class-
mate, I remember it very well because these are things you never forget—"Of course, she gets
[good grades], she's an orphan . . ." I was standing behind her, I felt like dying. And coldly, worse
than a blade: "I hope you become an orphan like me soon, so you too can get [such good grades]!"
Such a life—Mister Priebke won't hear about these things, but I told them . . .

I visited my daughter on a Sunday and went to mass. A priest I'd never seen, at the reading *of the Gospel, says: "Look at all the hatred that is going on at the Priebke trial . . ." I was unable to take communion. I heard the mass and then I went into the sacristy. "Father—I say—today you kept me from taking communion." "Me?" "Yes, because at the Gospel you said . . ." He looks at me and says, "I'm very sorry about this, I didn't know there was a daughter [of a victim of the Ardeatine] in the church." "Excuse me, but the sermon is not supposed to be according to who's in the church . . ."*

And yet, if there's a will, out of the great pain, the great sorrow, out of this being cheated out of a life, one may be enriched, one may understand human sorrow, and struggle for this injustice to end. Death is death, but there are deaths and deaths; violent death, and violent in this way . . . I hated, and how I hated, my Lord! I couldn't understand, I couldn't do anything, because I basked in my hatred. There was I and my sorrow, the injustice that I had suffered, and the rest didn't count. It was a great sorrow for me, as sorrow goes; however, if you overcome the impact of sorrow, and your individual selfishness, you do reach some point . . . this is how things are.

. . . Umberto Pignotti, Claudio Piperno, Ignazio Piras, Vincenzo Pirozzi, Antonio Pisino, Antonio Pistonesi, Rosario Pitrelli, Domenico Polli, Alessandro Portieri, Erminio Portinari, Pietro Primavera, Antonio Prosperi, Italo Pula, Spartaco Pula, Beniamino Raffaeli, Giovanni Rampulla, Roberto Rendina . . .

CHAPTER 9

POLITICS OF MEMORY

. . . Egidio Renzi, Augusto Renzini, Domenico Ricci, Nunzio Rindone, Ottorino Rizzo, Antonio Roazzi, Filippo Rocchi, Bruno Rodella, Romeo Rodriguez Pereira, Goffredo Romagnoli, Giulio Roncacci, Ettore Ronconi, Vincenzo Saccotelli, Felice Salemme, Giovanni Salvatori, Alfredo Sansolini (b. 1897), Alfredo Sansolini (b. 1917), Francesco Savelli, Ivano Scarioli . . .

Ada Pignotti. *And yet, they were dead: three hundred and thirty-five people! And they killed those extra five because they were there and saw what they saw, so they had to eliminate them, too.*

Because he testified, the criminal, the executioner, he testified about everything: how they did it, what they did, the way they did it, how—they said that they had to do it that way, one bullet apiece, to save [time] . . . Talk about memories! This is what they ought to do, what they ought to talk about, in schools: what the Germans were capable of. They put us under siege, they came over here and acted as if they owned the place. And they destroyed us a life. I'm sorry, but I have to say it. All the rest, you already know it; what happened, everything else, you already know. But I lived through it, and it was horrible, a horrible thing. Which I never thought, I'll tell you the truth, that it could happen.

Because when they took him to court, him, Kappler, that was a memorable trial, soon after the war. It was a tragedy, all over again, because the thing was still fresh—I mean: it was two or three years, maybe five, but it still . . . We were allowed to attend because we were the injured party. The crowd, [thick], like this: the relatives, the children, the mothers, the fathers, and the wives were all there.

Now there's only a few of us left, who attend the trial, at least. We're old, it's been fifty-four years—I was only twenty-three, but now I'm getting on in years, ain't I?

1. Hunger and Anger

Su comunisti della capitale	Come all ye Communists of the Capital
È giunto alfine il dì della riscossa	The day has come to rise again
Quando alzeremo sopra al Quirinale	When we raise over the Quirinale
Bandiera rossa	The red flag.
Questa città ribelle e mai domata	This rebel city that was never tamed
Dalle rovine e dai bombardamenti . . .	By ruins and bombardments . . .

—sung by Marisa and Alfio
Menichetti, Val Melaina [1]

O Roma Roma, città tanto cara	Rome, Rome, such a dear city
Dove se magna, se beve e poco se paga	Where you eat, drink, and don't pay much
E se c'è qualche disoccupato	And if someone is out of a job
Che non ha magnato,	and didn't get a meal,
c'è San Cosimato	can eat at the convent of San Cosimato
C'è Villa Borghese p'anna' a diggeri'	digest in the Villa Borghese
Reggina Cèli p'annacce a dormi'.	and sleep in jail at Regina Coeli.

—sung by Renato Trinca, Rocca di
Papa (Rome)[2]

Virginia Calanca. As soon as the war was over, by the year '46, '45, the people were, how can I explain, gaunt, they needed fats. So we made the Turin Bomb, a cake that is a cannonball of fat: coconut butter, egg, Strega liquor, very very good. And we sold it, that cake, you have no idea how much, by the ton: the Turin Bomb. The very word, *bomb*—nowadays, people wouldn't eat it if you gave it out for free, but in those times everybody ate these huge balls of fat, because all it was was butter.

Anna Menichetti. I remember that my father, as soon as a building site was completed, was left out of a job, and before he found another it would be up to a month, and during that time at home we fought all the time, we fought, because we were hungry . . . And then, cold, inside and outside . . . physically, I suffered very much, because, no blankets, which among other things had been sold for a piece of bread, and so in winter we'd throw our coats over us; with worn out jacket sleeves we'd make half a pajama, and then, we'd warm the bed with a brick – which eventually crumbled off, so you can imagine . . .

In occupied Rome there was no food, and there was no air. When the war was finally over, the city vented an anxious yen for excess in a context of penury, a craving for material and immaterial needs—food and dance, a yearning for justice, an urgency of revenge, the expectation of quick and deep change. Rome was turbulent, frustrated, excitable; its political consciousness was yet largely un-formed. Furiously, it wanted to remember; and furiously, it wanted to forget. Popular culture oscillated between ironic fatalism, cathartic expectation, excite-ment over new things and ways, disappointment over lack of real change. Social rebellion mingled with petty crime and the underworld.[3] In December 1944, when the controls on the price of bread were repealed, "Hundreds of women and children from the *borgate* and the popular neighborhoods poured into the center of Rome and started looting food and clothing stores."[4] Much of this ex-citement focused on the memory of the Fosse Ardeatine, on the role of the vic-tims' families, on the political activism of the former partisans.

The Church and the political parties gave out soup and food; the Socialist Party's kitchens were named after Giacomo Matteotti (killed the by the Fascists in 1926), Bruno Buozzi (killed at La Storta), Pilo Albertelli (killed at the Fosse Ardeatine), and the Three Hundred and Twenty Martyrs of March 23. Hand-written signs changed street names: via Savoia (named after the royal family) was renamed after a victim of the Ardeatine, Armando Bussi (but the police imme-diately restored the old name); another street was re-named after Pilo Albertelli. In July the exhumation of the bodies began; the area around the Fosse Ardea-tine was filled with monarchist flags, many relatives complained, and Alberto Marchesi's widow tore the royal family's symbol off a flag with her teeth.[5]

The struggle over memory culminated on the first anniversary. A mass was celebrated in via Rasella; a wreath was dedicated by "The survivors of via Rasella to their martyred comrades." The official commemoration was held in the basil-ica of Santa Maria degli Angeli: at the sound of solemn classical music, the prime minister, the crown prince, and other authorities were ranked in front of a "tall catafalque draped in velvet and red, white, and green flags." Only some of the victims' families were in the church; most had chosen to attend another mass, at the Fosse. As soon as it was over—"lest this ceremony may take on an undertone of protest against the staid and official rite being held at Santa Maria degli Angeli"—the police loaded them on trucks and sent them off to the Basil-ica, where they found the doors "inexorably closed." Excluded from the rite in honor of their own loved ones, these "invisible widows" started a vocal protest that soon turned into a near riot. Those relatives who had been inside left the church in solidarity and joined them. At the end of the service, the authorities left among hostile shouts, and the families forced the church authorities to re-open and to celebrate another mass only for them (meanwhile, among of all these masses, the Jewish widows and children are even more invisible). All day, an "interrupted pilgrimage" flowed to the Fosse; at the end of the day, "the en-trance to the Fosse was covered with black palls; on the sides, two partisans stood guard wearing red scarves."[6]

During the "riot" at Santa Maria degli Angeli, Fernando Norma's widow recognized a policeman who had refused to let her see her husband in jail, and slapped him: "many, at the moment, were reminded" of the most tragic episode of those months, "the lynching of Donato Carretta," director of Regina Coeli.[7] It had taken place earlier, on September 18, 1944, at the trial of the former Chief of Police Pietro Caruso (who had given Kappler the extra fifty names to complete his list). That day, the widows of the Fosse Ardeatine had been the spark and catalyst of the horrendous anger of an excitable crowd, which had no experience of rules and procedures and was frustrated by the slowness of change and the omens of restoration.

Here, too, all began with a crowd by a closed gate. The courtroom where the trial was to be held was too small. The crowd milled outside, it made way in silence for the relatives of the dead of the Ardeatine ("The women all in black, with black hats and veils"), but roared resentfully at the authorities: bureaucrats and police seemed and often were the same as before.

Suddenly, the crowd broke through the police line and the gate, erupted into the courtroom, stopped the trial: "The group that protested most loudly was made up of women, relatives of martyrs of the Fosse Ardeatine, clamoring for immediate justice." The exhumation of the bodies was not finished yet, their eyes were filled with that horror. A woman screamed to Donato Carretta, "You're the one who got my husband killed!." Carretta had not been the worst person in the wartime machine of repression; but now he was surrounded by angry women (including some widows of the Ardeatine), kicked, slapped, insulted. The police pulled him out of the courtroom, but the crowd took him back and dragged him into the street.[8] "He got away and ran toward the bridge and then, in a paroxysm, he jumped into the water. They went down to the river bank, got an old boat that was sitting there, and beat him with the oars on his head, they killed him that way, then picked him up, beyond the next bridge, in front of Regina Coeli, took him out and hanged him upside down by the gate of Regina Coeli" (Franco Bartolini).

Three weeks before the riot at Santa Maria degli Angeli, General Mario Roatta, who was on trial for failing to organize a defense of Rome on September 8, escaped. The next day, twenty thousand people rallied by the Coliseum and marched toward the center.[9] A demonstrator was killed by a bomb he was about to throw at the police. "Of course, the demonstrators thought it was caused by the police, so they took this body, carried it to the Viminale [the Ministry of Interior] and laid him down on the chief of police's desk" (Carlo Castellani). It looked as though the day announced by the song of Rome's Communists had arrived: "They had a red flag, and you could see this red flag climb from floor to floor, because as they occupied each floor they hung the red flag out the windows" (Aldo Natoli). The Communist Party tried to calm the crowd, the police did not attack: "I remained outside on the square; Carla [Capponi] and I, we tried to calm the comrades" (Rosario Bentivegna). But the State had learned a lesson: "I remember that the head of the office where I worked had the door barricaded; and each time there was a strike, a demonstration, you could see the machine guns sticking out of the windows, on the ground floor toward the square. See those iron bars? They're open at the bottom, so the machine gun can range freely . . ." (Carlo Castellani).

On July 14, 1948, the secretary of the Communist Party, Palmiro Togliatti, was shot and wounded in front of the Parliament. Italy was on the verge of revolution. "I was the secretary of the Aurelia local; in less than an hour, I gathered two hundred comrades together and organized them to go to the center of Rome. And when I got to piazza Colonna [near the Parliament] there were many more; we tried to break into the Parliament, the comrades were already digging the paving stones from off the street . . ." (Franco Bartolini).

Rosario Bentivegna. At noon, I hear the news and my first feeling is a choking in my stomach: here we go again. So I rushed to the headquarters, and I found some comrades who told me, "We give you a taxi"–which was driven by an ex-GAP comrade, Raoul Falcioni, who was a taxi driver—"and you get the GAP back together right away." Target: the Viminale. In two hours I put the GAP back together, and about twenty of us, armed, we meet at the partisans' association, in via Savoia.

The attempt on Togliatti's life took place while Kappler was on trial for the Fosse Ardeatine; Pasquale Balsamo, former GAP member, covered it for the Party's paper, *l'Unità*. He recalls: "[Edoardo] D'Onofrio [the Party's city secretary], on July 14, told me: 'All right, tomorrow morning when you go to the Kappler trial, you shoot him.' 'What? Are you out of your mind? They're going to arrest me.' 'No problem, it's a retaliation.' 'But we don't make retaliations, Comrade D'Onofrio.' 'All right, then let's off some factory owner.' And he gave me the name of a factory owner. I talked about it with some comrades from the GAP, I said, forget it, we've been through all those troubles, we're not going through it again for Kappler's sake, I don't give a damn . . .'"

Rosario Bentivegna. Then, fortunately, I said, "All right, before I do anything let me find out what's going on" so I went to city headquarters where I found D'Onofrio, and he jumped at me, "What are you doing?" "What do you mean, what am I doing? I'm getting the GAP back together, I've been told to get the GAP back together." Meanwhile, another order had been dispatched for [former GAP official] Carlo Salinari, who goes to Torpignattara, the strongest partisan area, to unearth the war hatchet, and they unearthed not only the war hatchet but a whole other lot of stuff: mortars, machine guns, and so on, and they march toward Rome. The target was always the Viminale [the Ministry of the Interior]. And D'Onofrio saved my life that day. He told me, "You're confined, you and those other turds you got together, don't move, stay where you are unless we tell you something else." Then he ran out to stop Carlo Salinari, who was marching with a column to the center of Rome. Well, I must admit that he did save our lives, because we would have fallen into the dirtiest of traps, we'd have wound up in jail, unless we got killed first.

2. People of the *borgate*

May 13, 1970, via della Serpentara, a new middle-class development under construction. Homeless families have been squatting in a building. At dawn, the police comes to evict them. People gather in the street, looking. "They carry tear gas, they wear helmets, who knows what they think they're gonna do," a woman says. They remember the war, and the scene reminds them: "The Germans—the Germans, they sure beat us up!" says another. And a third: "Like the Germans! They killed ten Italians for a German!" A policeman, as if on cue, replies: "We carry out orders . . ."[10] Thirty years later, the memory of the Fosse Ardeatine is still the symbolic yardstick for the violence of oppression.

Rosario Bentivegna. For a year, I was an editor at *l'Unità;* then I went back to medical school. After a year I graduated; for a few months I was a municipal doctor in a village near Siena, then I was taken on as [company] doctor for the gas workers. And I covered the area where I had been a partisan, from San Giovanni to Borgata Gordiani, and Pietralata; and I saw, and I lived through, the events of those terrible postwar times.

In order to understand the meaning of via Rasella and its memory, it is important to realize that the protagonists of that episode were also protagonists of the postwar struggles of the Roman working class. The former *gappisti,* who had carried out the resistance in the peripheries and the *borgate,* went back as political leaders and organizers: "I discovered this extraordinary, fascinating Rome, Rome of Trastevere, Testaccio, Pietralata, Tiburtino—a great love for this city. Because it was an extraordinary city, filled a will to live, to change, to rise from ignorance—a great city, I think" (Marisa Musu).

Carla Capponi. I had a pleurisy I had neglected, [which I caught] during the nights I slept in Centocelle after the landing at Anzio. But you know, that's a whole other story: in the hospital, we founded the ULT, Unione Lavoratori Tubercolotici [Union of Workers with Tuberculosis] . . . These are incredible stories. After I got out of the hospital, I worked with the Consulte Popolari [People's Conferences], and I remember that at Borgata Gordiani they would set up boxes, you know, the kind you use for fruit; I'd stand on them and harangue the women; the police would come, the women insulted them, they defended me . . . We did so many demonstrations, with the women . . . We would seize a bus and tell [the driver]: "Take us to the Prefecture, or else!" And he'd take us down to piazza Venezia. And I remember the great floods of [the working-class slum of] Pietralata . . . And I remember, that time, we protested at the Prefecture, and a pregnant woman had an abortion, she hemorrhaged [on the street]. They loaded her on a jeep and carried her away. And we all screamed, "Prefect, murderer, you killed a baby! Prefect, murderer, you killed a baby!" Then we managed to obtain for Pietralata, after great battles, two hundred council apartments. And we also got the trucks to carry their possessions . . . Imagine: the city of Rome made a donation of mattresses because theirs had been soaked by the water and were no good anymore.

In 1953, a little girl was nearly drowned in one of the collective latrines of Borgata Gordiani. In protest, the women tore it down; the next day, *l'Unità* wrote: "So now the inhabitants of the *borgata* will be one common latrine short and shall have to walk half a mile to reach another just like the one that was torn down." [11]

Rosario Bentivegna. You'd go in, they were all shanties: out in via del Mandrione, by the Acquedotto Alessandrino, behind Torpignattara and all the way to Centocelle—you can still see the signs there—the arches of the [Roman] aqueduct had been used as bases to built shanties on. I was a doctor in those parts, Borgata Gordiani, Borghetto Latino, Acqua Bullicante and though my clients were gas workers, that is, people with jobs, with pay checks, yet conditions were unbelievable, a heavy social hardship. At the Acquedotto Felice, you actually had open sewers running down the middle of the street, and on both sides were these shanties, and the filthy water ran in the midst of all these children—which I won't even try to describe, they were a frightful sight. You'd go into those houses, you'd find families that slept ten, twelve in three or four rooms, people slept on the ground, the children slept in the commode drawers. And yet they made an effort to retain some degree of civilization.

So' fanello e so' de Pietralata	I'm a young kid and I'm from Pietralata
Tredici anni co' quarche mese in più	Thirteen years old and a few months
E da quanno la scòla m'ha cacciato	And since school kicked me out
Co' la vita me trovo a tu per tu . . .	I'm face to face with life . . .
Respiranno 'st'aria avvelenata	When you breathe this poisoned air
Sempre duro è er prezzo da paga'	You always have a hard price to pay

Tante mejo lenze de la strada	So many of the best hustlers from the street
Stanno drento a piagne' libbertà . . .	Are in jail and crying for liberty . . .
	—Armandino Liberti [12]

Rosario Bentivegna. In '51 there was trouble in the Pietralata local, so the Party asked me to go and act as secretary there. Pietralata had a population of about five or six thousand, solid red. And there I learned a great lesson. Once we called a reverse strike; those of us who were working, we all came out, including the tram drivers, the shopkeepers, all the Party and all the *borgata*. So I look around and I see that the unemployed are not here. I say, "What, we're doing the reverse strike for the unemployed, and the unemployed don't come?" And someone told me, "Look, Rosario, you don't know anything, do you? The unemployed are sleeping, at this time." He says, "The children have to eat, so those people go around at night, to hustle something for the children to eat." And they were all ultimately decent people, honest: it was the Roman lowlife of those times, odd characters, thieves, pickpockets. People who, once they found a job, stopped going around with picklocks to seek food for their children, see?

Aldo Natoli. And in this sort of lumpenproletarian magma, with a very high percentage of Southern immigrants—without jobs, people who eked out anyway they could—the Party had an enormous prestige. Actually, they saw the Party as the instrument of redemption. I remember the meetings I held in those parts, with these types, who perhaps didn't even understand everything I said, maybe also because the way I spoke was too difficult for them—and yet, the respect, the prestige . . .

Se scoppiasse la rabbia qui in borgata	If the anger of the *borgata* were to explode
Che ognuno se porta drento ar cor	The anger that is in everyone's heart
Gente bene, onesta, raffinata	You respectable, honest, elegant people
La vostra vita n'avrà nessun valor.	Your life will be worth nothing.
La giustizia, quella popolana	Justice, the justice of the poor,
Er giorno vie' che ve raggiungerà	Will reach you one of these days
La borgata allora s'arisana	The *borgata* then will be reclaimed
Col lavoro ne' la libertà	In labor and liberty.
	—Armandino Liberti

Rosario Bentivegna. The truly striking thing was how in this frightful disaster that the city was in, the fabric of society was restored, rapidly, even in these *borgate*. And the most extraordinary thing was indeed the rebirth of these people out of a state of primordial poverty. At the beginning of the '50s, things begin to change: people are aware, people ask questions, people study, people debate, people participate in these reverse strikes that were the great invention of this Roman lumpenproletariat: they built their own streets, built their own sewers, and then went and claimed payment for this work and sometimes actually got some. And in this rebirth the great builder was the Communist Party. It taught, in the first place, how to read, how to try to understand what was said, and then to discuss what was said.

3. Ceremonies

Adriana Montezemolo. I think only once did I miss the anniversary of the Fosse Ardeatine, because I was out of town—otherwise, I went each year, always. All we saw was red flags. They had every right to be there, all right, but it looked like the three hundred and thirty-five were all partisans . . .

Indeed, those two red scarves stood out amid all the black, on the first anniversary in 1945. But it is odd that so many should remember nothing but red flags—"a Communist monopoly" (Paolo De Carolis), "red flags only" (Giovanni Gigliozzi)—in a place where fights had broken out, if anything, over monarchist ones. Of course, the Communists were there. "The Party provided trucks for those who wanted to go" (Iva Manieri); on the other hand, "for many years we wouldn't go to the official ceremony; the Party organized us to go in the afternoon instead, all the workers, with our own flags" (Lina Ciavarella). "Frankly, I didn't notice a dominant Communist presence," says Paolo Emilio Taviani, many times an official speaker at the ceremony. Perhaps, in the years of the Cold War, the very existence of the red flags looked like an invasion while all others were taken for granted; perhaps, after the emotions of the postwar years, the moderates and the conservatives had taken elsewhere the struggle for memory and "left its management to the Communists, so that it seemed that it was a Communist, subversive thing" (Giovanni Gigliozzi).

One can hardly speak of a Communist monopoly when in all the commemorations, year after year, the official speakers were always only Christian Democrats. "A noble address by Dr. Francesco Diana" (commissar to the city administration of Rome); "moving oration by Prof. Nicola Signorello" (chairman of the provincial council) . . . A Christian Democrat mayor and cabinet member, Umberto Tupini, inaugurated the monument and wrote the text of the inscriptions, where his name is still prominently displayed.[13] Military orders, salutes, and bugles resonated; it all culminated in a Catholic mass. Speeches were imbued with the classical school rhetoric of references to the Risorgimento and ancient Rome; figures of martyrdom and sacrifice prevailed, the identities and the names of the killed faded into generalities, politics were reduced to patriotism and an idea of freedom that was either very vague or strictly anti-Communist. There was hardly a reference to who had killed them, aside from a generic and abstract "barbarism."

Rather than monopoly, then, we ought to speak of a divided space—the podium and the ground—within the shared space of the ceremony: a metaphor for all the tensions and balances of public space in a republic "born of Resistance" and uneasy about this birth. Below, the Left claimed its protagonist's role in the Resistance as a people's movement; above, the moderates staged their hegemony over the institutions of whose foundation that place was the symbol. One presence legitimated the other: the Center received anti-Fascist credentials from the popular presence, the Left received the sanction of democratic credibility and political legitimacy by the unitary ceremonial context. All hinged on a representation of the Resistance as a patriotic movement of the whole Italian people, and of the partisans as martyrs and victims. The image of the martyrs as "all partisans" mirrored that of the partisans as "all martyrs."

This is how the Fosse Ardeatine became a *national* monument. In order to represent the country's unity, it was necessary to suppress and deny its multiplicity and its conflicts. In the official discourse, the dead were nationalized and amalgamated as all patriots, all Italians (eleven were foreigners!), just as in reactionary gossip they were amalgamated as all Communists, all Jews, all jailbirds. The monument was included among the "Shrines of World War II," under the administration of the Ministry of Defense and the blessing of military chaplains.

The Fosse Ardeatine were turned into a monument metaphorically as well. They ought to stand for the synthesis of all the pain and horror of Nazi occupation, representing not only themselves but also all the other massacres and victims; yet, they often function instead as an isolated, exceptional place and event, a cathedral in the desert of memory.

Nicoletta Leoni. It isn't right that in Rome we should talk only of the Fosse Ardeatine. We should talk also of Forte Bravetta, we should talk of La Storta, we should talk of people killed in the streets. My grandfather had been sentenced to death, he might have died at Forte Bravetta; now, if he had died at Forte Bravetta, how would I feel when all that people talk about is the Ardeatine? But the media, if you tell them about Forte Bravetta, they don't care. Do you know why the Ardeatine are so important? Because the monument is there.

Balduina—a historically "black" (that is, neo-Fascist) neighborhood on Monte Mario. The streets bear the names of military war victims who were awarded gold medals: Ugo De Carolis, Romeo Rodriguez Pereira, Giuseppe Montezemolo, Simone Simoni, Aladino Govoni . . . They were all killed at the Fosse Ardeatine, but there is no indication of how and where they earned those medals. In a store in via De Carolis, I asked who he was: "A philosopher? No, wait: a general . . ." In via Rodriguez Pereira, two elderly ladies thought he may have been a character from *Sostiene Pereira,* a novel by Antonio Tabucchi and a movie with Marcello Mastroianni. When I told them who he was, they were genuinely moved. The name is supposed to turn the street into the signifier of the person, but it often goes the other way: the person vanishes and leaves the name to the street.

At least, in Balduina, it is clear that those are the names of war heroes of some kind. But in my own neighborhood, who is "Maurizio Giglio," an alley between via Cassia and the open fields? Who was "Manfredi Azzarita"? In the school that bears his name in the fashionable Parioli district, a student guesses—"a soldier?" Others know, because they read the faded inscription in the hall. To me, before I began this book, he was a bus terminal.

In Rome, forty-six streets bear the names of men killed at the Fosse Ardeatine. Sixteen are dedicated to military victims; not one is named for a Jew. Three quarters of these streets are in the new peripheries outside the circle road—a sort of *extra moenia* burial, like the tombs outside the gates that separated the dead from the urban space in ancient Roman times; but also a sign that those names were assigned recently, during the years of the Left administration in the late 1970s and early '80s. No fewer than twenty-five are in Spinaceto, a recent and very controversial development in the periphery; yet "never a wreath, never a bunch of flowers in the streets that commemorate the names of the martyrs. And even in Party festivals in the neighborhood, I do not recollect a single mention, a commemoration for the victims of the Fosse Ardeatine. It would have spurred us to be more aware of the meaning of our history, to lift some of the cursed dreariness that labels us as a 'bedroom community.'"[14]

The monument, designed by the architects Fiorentino, Semprini, and Aprile, and inaugurated on March 24, 1949, "ultimately is what it aims to be, a deeply agonizing place, a closed space with a glimmer of light above" (Elisabetta Agnini). "With that concrete slab looming over the graves . . . Francesco Coccia's statue [three large white male figures, with their hands tied behind their backs] "is conventional but after all it's like a folk Gospel: it must be readable"; Mirko Basaldella's gate, stylized thorns and brambles, symbols of violence and pain, "is beautiful, but it requires more attention" (Giovanni Gigliozzi). "The first time I went in there, it made me ill: I saw the names of so many comrades, friends . . . But I always drew a sense of vitality, of strength from it. I no longer get a sense of sorrow: it moves me, it thrills me. And I find that it's a wonderful idea, it's a great monument. The unknowns, the unknown graves, too. It moves me deeply" (Maria Michetti). There is a sense of austerity, conveyed by the Jewish presence, and by the military management.

Vanda Perretta. I've always taken my German friends to the Fosse Ardeatine; and it was very tough, because this was always, how shall I say, a test of our friendship: taking them to the Fosse Ardeatine, showing them [Roberto Rossellini's] *The Open City*—a film that was forbidden in Germany until the day before yesterday, as it were. And I must admit that seeing that the Fosse Ardeatine are kept by the military—that is, they haven't been turned into a tourist shrine; no souvenir stands, no holy images—thank God for the military: it means few photographs, no fooling around; the atmosphere is somewhat stark, it's bare.

"I remember I had the impression of a deep . . . a sense of heaviness. There was one slab, that commemorated a fifteen year old boy, that weighed especially on me. And I felt it over of me" (Rosa Castra). A custodian says: "When you're under there, you feel crushed, you feel small, very small, crushed under this great big stone. Actually they changed it a little, they gave it more of a curve, like a lens, to ease this effect a little. They died for the same cause, in the same moment, in the same condition, they also have the same grave. The effect is stronger perhaps because they're in a closed space, amid four walls, with a lid on top. To see them, in that space, when your eye goes around . . . it gives you a sense of how many they are."

"A mother, I remember, who had a grave next to my father's. She'd take a little chair, she'd sit, and she'd just look at her son" (Bruno Frasca). The speakers, on the ceremonial stage, are all men; the mourners, on the ground, are mostly women. The power of the place derives also from the fact that it is a contested space: a monument for the public cult of martyrs and heroes; and a graveyard for personal and family mourning. "We never say 'the Fosse Ardeatine'; we just say: 'I went to take some flowers to daddy'" (Giuseppina Ferola). Ever since the "riot" at Santa Maria degli Angeli, the public appropriation of the dead threatens to become an expropriation: "the horror of these official ceremonies and this military stuff, the present arms, the tombs, the army chaplains and these bombastic speakers . . ." (Claudio Fano); "There was something artificial to it, of canopies and stuff; it made me angry, and I told mom, 'No, I'm not coming to listen to those clowns; I'll just stay here with my father and I'll speak to them [the dead], I'll learn from them'" (Rosetta Stame).

For these reasons, not even this is the final burial for all: "Some took the bodies away, the graves were left but the bodies were taken into the family tombs. My folks, instead, were always opposed to this, because they think it makes sense: this is a place where memory is kept, it is a warning, it has a meaning" (Elisabetta Agnini). In the form she signed on joining the victims' families' association (ANFIM), Romolo Gigliozzi's wife Laura wrote: "I wish him be placed in the site of his sacrifice." During the Priebke trial, however, her daughter insisted on taking her father away and reburying him next to his wife in the city cemetery of Prima Porta. She wished both to express her dissent from the trial and to bring together the family so violently torn apart: "They were never together . . . they didn't have much time together, so it was my wish and my brother's, before we die, to bring them back together. Then I was told, look, it's a national museum, you'll never get permission" (Liana Gigliozzi).

Giuseppina Ferola. You never get a chance to be by yourself there. I can't tell the visitors or the other relatives: leave me be alone now. And now I no longer go on March 24. Because one time I talked back to a *carabiniere:* they wanted us to wait outside until the president [of the Republic] went in. And I don't think it's right. Why should I wait for the president? Let him come some other day in the year, too! Because it makes no sense to remember them once a year, and then act the opposite from what they would have wanted.

In 1963, the president of the families' association, Leonardo Azzarita, remarked that "The often disturbing rhetoric of official celebrations can no longer compensate or counteract . . . the forgetfulness of the majority." In the age of Center-Left governments, from the mid-1960s on, the Resistance was no longer considered a subversive memory. It belonged to everybody now; uncritically and ceremonially depicted as a unitary patriotic movement, the Resistance, writes Claudio Pavone, had been turned into a pillar of the status quo.[15] There are no more party banners or alternative commemorations at the Fosse Ardeatine; the ceremonies mean less and less. The distance between the official ritual and the intact grief of the families becomes more and more intolerable.

Giovanni Gigliozzi. They had these big stages, all the members of Parliament came, the city councilmen, the mayor's cabinet, they held the ceremony, the official speech, but I could feel that they couldn't care less about what was going on, they just talked business among themselves. This disturbed me very much, and so I tried to dry up the ceremony. But I thought they would make it more serious, not that they would just do away with it . . .

The city, perhaps, does not forget. But it delegates to the injured parties—the families, the Jewish community—the task of remembering for all. The nationalization of the 1950s and early '60s is replaced by a "privatization"[16] that reduces the collective historical event to a matter that concerns only those directly affected. Only the protest after the verdict that sanctioned Priebke's release in 1996—another "riot" in front of another closed door—managed for a time to make it all come alive again.

4. A Farewell to Arms:
Resistance and Silences

Rosario Bentivegna. Two years ago, I was invited to speak at a high school in Civitavecchia. This girl got up, and she was very smart and knowledgeable and spoke very well, she must have been thirteen, and she said: "Until today, I was for the partisans; now that I heard you speak I no longer am, because you were like the Fascists: you, too, killed." They don't understand that we were shooting at each other, they have this idea of the partisan as a martyr, not a combatant.

In October 1945, Edoardo D'Onofrio opened the first conference of Rome's Communist Party. He spoke of the need to counter the "reactionary character" foisted upon Rome by the ruling class; of the unity of anti-Fascist forces; of the policy toward the middle class, the young, women; of the struggle against hunger, cold, the cost of living. Only at the beginning of his speech did he mention "the Roman martyrs who fought to keep Rome from being a center of reaction": "Rome was worthy of its anti-Fascist martyrs, of our martyrs and of those of all the other parties and of the population as a whole." He never uttered the word "partisan."[17] This was not without reason. The Resistance and the war were over; the country needed to look ahead.

Marisa Musu. I went through this, how shall I call it, this interlude of armed activity; but already on June 6, 7, or 10, I was holding women's meetings in the *borgate,* in the popular neighborhoods. I immediately got rid, not of the gun, but of the mental habit of the [armed fighter], because I was immediately swept into the incredible work of a Communist Party that grew in Rome in the *borgate,* in the popular neighborhoods, extraordinary women, and all that—I had to deal with the fact that they wanted a lower price of bread, they wanted a job for their son, they wanted a drinking fountain in the *borgata.* Life was so full of things that I soon forgot the armed struggle. Actually, I think I gave up the gun eight or ten months later. First of all, because there were still Fascists around; and then, because I felt naked without my gun. After that, the gun ended up in a drawer, too.

"I've done so many things in my life, and they identify me only with one" (Rosario Bentivegna); "But afterwards in our life we did so many other things" (Maria Teresa Regard). The former *gappisti* do not change their mind about the justness of the action in via Rasella ("Were I to find myself, a young man of twenty-five, in the same situation, I think I would do it again: Rome was dominated and tortured" writes Giulio Cortini), but do not dwell on it ("I think Salinari never really spoke about it, aside from his unchanged persuasion on the action, which he never doubted," his colleague Achille Tartaro says). The identity of the likes of Carlo Salinari and Antonello Trombadori, military commanders of the central GAP, is founded on other things: teaching and writing about Italian literature for the former, art criticism for the latter. Valentino Gerratana is known as the curator of the critical edition of Gramsci's prison notebooks rather than as a former *gappista;* Mario Leporatti taught humanities and became a high school principal. Mario Fiorentini earned a *liceo scientifico* diploma as a self-taught external candidate, went on to a degree in mathematics, taught school ("I came from an experience of social involvement, and I followed this line: I would always speak for the ones in the last rows"), earned a university chair, and became a world famous mathematician ("in two different fields: homological methods in commutative algebra and projective and hyperspatial geometry").

Pasquale Balsamo worked as a journalist for the Communist paper, *l'Unità,* then for the radio and the Automobile Club. Marisa Musu traveled as a journalist and activist to China, Czechoslovakia, Mozambique, and Palestine;[18] Franco Calamandrei and Maria Teresa Regard, also journalists and writers, were news correspondents from England and from Vietnam, China, Tibet, and Cambodia: "I was in Vietnam in '54; we were in the jungle with them; Franco was the only one who went with them all the way to Diem Bien Phu. And then, when Hanoi was liberated, we marched on Hanoi on their jeeps. The liberation of Hanoi is one of the most wonderful sights I've ever seen: the red flags in the wind, and the homecoming of the soldiers who had fought in the North. At last this city was being returned to its citizens."

So, via Rasella is far from the first thing on their minds. But they are constantly forced to deal with it by attacks, slurs, threats, controversies, accusations. "Unfortunately I had to talk about it all the time, as I was targeted by threats, articles, news stories," says Carla Capponi: "If you look up the collection of *Il Borghese* [a Right-wing magazine] for those years, there's a picture of me at a Party conference, eating a sandwich; and it says, 'Here she is, eating her sandwich while three hundred and twenty . . . ', or, 'The murderous blood-dripping hands and the gold medal . . . '"

Rosario Bentivegna. I have to talk about it because they target me in the first person. I was a witness at the Kappler trial, it came out in the papers that I'd been one of those who participated in the action in via Rasella, and upon this the other side has tried to create the image of the monster. The manipulation against the partisans targeted me especially as a symbol; it even had quite an impact on my career. There's this lady who calls me up once in a while and insults me: "Murderer, you're going to pay . . ." Sometimes they're kind of screwballs; but I also got envelopes with bullets inside . . . But there were people who attacked me and then, through dialogue, understood how things stood. And there are countless people, in Rome and out of Rome, also complete unknowns, who seek me out to give me support.

The party chooses no longer to emphasize the partisan armed struggle, and this increases the former *gappisti*'s sense of isolation. In the Cold War years, the Communist Party needed to legitimize itself in the new democratic order, and it strove to do so by stressing its role in a Resistance conventionally represented as a near-unanimous movement of the Italian people—a representation also functional to those Catholic and moderate forces that wished to shelve the memory of their compromises with Fascism. On the other hand, this over-emphasized popular consensus and mobilization became the narrative foundation for one of the most advanced and democratic constitutions in the West, inspired by an idea of participant citizenship and ample representation.[19] As the revolutionary identity of the Left was played down in favor of a more reassuring image, the memory of violence became an embarrassment. The Resistance, martyred rather than fighting, is better represented through the Fosse Ardeatine than through via Rasella.

Marisa Musu. The Left, actually, embalmed the Resistance—very pretty, we were all very good . . . And this is why it never spoke out on via Rasella; because it was an action in which there was a tragic element, and it forced you to face huge problems, the problems of reprisal, the problem of how much the Resistance cost in so many ways, the fact that partisans were also, quote, mean and bad, too, unquote—that is, they were not, but it had to be explained.

On the one hand, then, the Resistance was seen as martyrdom; on the other, the partisans were often imagined as gunmen, as in the idea of having Balsamo shoot Kappler in retaliation for Togliatti. "They though we were crazy. And I'll tell you something I never said before: I remember that some comrades came to my house, it was early '45, and asked me, 'Listen, you who know how to use a gun, we need a gun, you ought to do for us what you did once as a partisan, you ought to steal a gun.' I say, 'You're out of your minds, these are no times for guns.' They were comrades, but see what they thought of us? They thought we were killers" (Carla Capponi).

The Party defended the *gappisti,* gave them jobs in its press and organization, obtained medals and rewards for them. Yet, it all leaves the impression of something done perfunctorily, defensively: "The Party's official stand was always very clear. The one thing it didn't do, and which I think ought to have been done, was that it did not denounce the lies and falsities that kept surfacing all the time.

That is, they did tell the truth; but they did not denounce the lies" (Rosario Bentivegna). This attitude, however, was not caused only by uncertainties on via Rasella or by the wish to present a pacified image of the Resistance; it was also the effect of a grave underestimation of the power and diffusion of the anti-partisan propaganda and mythology.

In 1997, the Right-wing response to the Priebke trial hinged on two charges: the claim that the attack in via Rasella was aimed at Bandiera Rossa or other, non-Communist, forces in the Resistance; and the civilian casualties caused by the bomb (the picture of little Piero Zuccheretti's body torn to pieces on the pavement was one of the most powerful icons in this campaign).[20] On the one hand, the past silence on the very existence of Bandiera Rossa did not help clarify things. On the other, the civilian casualties had been a known fact at least since the Kappler trial at the end of the 1940s, but they had been ignored and forgotten. Even such a painstaking and accurate chronicle as Robert Katz's early book on the Fosse Ardeatine, *Death in Rome* (1965) makes no mention of Piero Zuccheretti; in his 1983 autobiography, Rosario Bentivegna wrote that "there is no indication in the official sources we consulted that there were civilian casualties in via Rasella."[21]

"I never knew a thing about it; when I found out, I wrote it," says Bentivegna. This, however, made the omission even worse, a sign less of personal prevarication than of a more pervasive erasure of memory. It is hard to tell whether this was due to feelings of guilt or to the sense that Zuccheretti's death was irrelevant, and to say which would be worse. "We never thought about it anymore, because it had all been canceled out" (Pasquale Balsamo). Carla Capponi recalls "a small item" in a newspaper where it said "that a boy named Zuccheretti was dead"; but she added that they had thought he had been killed by German fire. Actually, the death notice in *Il Messaggero* (March 26, 1994) stated that the boy's death was caused by "the blind violence of subversive provocateurs."[22]

And so, when all this is revived as Right-wing propaganda, at a time when the Left undergoes a serious crisis of identity, silences become metaphors for much larger evasions and censorships.

Luciano Pizzoli. Robert Katz's *Death in Rome* was almost like gospel to me. And I'll tell you that I had to drop this myth like all others, because it isn't true either. Even in this text, I must revise all that I had to revise in my life: because the things that must be said are not said. When I was a Communist believer I thought that the truth was revolutionary; they taught me that as a child, the truth is revolutionary, Gramsci says so, Marx says so . . . So when I began to realize that half truths were being told— and by half truth I mean the thing unsaid—I began to think that things weren't right.

Unfortunately, I must say that this lack of clarity is what made me rethink all my positions toward the Party that, after all, brought me up.

After the fact, it's easy to say that Piero Zuccheretti ought to have been acknowledged and claimed as another of the many direct and indirect victims of the war and the German occupation ("four thousand Zuccherettis were buried under the ruins of San Lorenzo," Pasquale Balsamo observes); that anti-Fascist Italy ought to have dedicated plaques and streets to his memory. But this would have meant acknowledging—indeed proclaiming—that the Resistance was a war, and as such it also included its unwanted consequences, even its errors and injustices. This would have required a different political context, another type of hegemony. At the height of the Cold War, with divisions in the anti-Fascist front, the Resistance under attack, the discriminations against Communists and the trials against partisans, such a thing was probably unthinkable.

5. Memory on the Right

Emanuele Moriconi: In Italy, the cultural heritage we have is mostly on one side; there is only one vision. That of the winners, of the Left.

Portelli. You say the winners, that is, the Left. Was the Left ever in power, in Italy?

Moriconi. After the twenty years [of Fascism], the Left-wing government took power.

"It is the very concept of revisionism that is a mistake, French-type revisionism," says Gianfranco Fini, secretary of Alleanza Nazionale, "that is, assuming we find a missing piece [of information] that we didn't have before, what are the consequences? That the good guys are no longer good and the bad guys become good. Because you know better than I do that the whole process of historic revisionism is not based on a will to find out whether in some fold of, say, the civil war, we have all the information we need; but, rather, its task is to be able to say—all right, the executioners were victims, and I won't say viceversa, but almost, I mean."

"Because in the end history books are always written by history's winners . . ." (Giovanni Di Ruscio). Actually, after 1946 the Communists were never part of Italy's government (only in 1996–2001, after they had renounced Communism, were the Left Democrats part of a government coalition); and the history written from a Resistance point of view has generated but little commonsense outside their own range, in the media or in the school system; they have received mainly perfunctory attention even from the political forces that claimed the Resistance as their origin. There is, instead, a vast body of Right-wing literature on the "civil war" in general and on specific episodes, especially via Rasella. These narratives have a widespread circulation in an area of opinion that has long been relegated to the margins of political and cultural life and has drawn from this isolation identity and pride: "There is nothing worse and at the same time more unifying than to feel discriminated in one's own country. It was a sort of *samizdat* culture. Elsewhere I used a very strong image: I said, we felt at times like blacks in South Africa before the abolition of apartheid" (Gianfranco Fini).

The fact that it drew its energies from isolation, representing itself as the silenced underground bearer of shocking truths hidden by official history, helped keep Right-wing history in a ghetto partly of its own making. The Right could have developed important themes overlooked by the Left: popular consensus to Fascism, the notion of the years from 1943 to 1945 as "civil war," the very fact of partisan violence. But it took liberal or Left historians like Renzo De Felice or Claudio Pavone to articulate these themes credibly, on the basis of research—and not from the Right. Rather than doing historical research—that is, rather than dealing problematically with the past—the "*samizdat* culture" chose to bask in a rhetoric of sensationalist revelations of "truths" and "lies": "The terrible truths no one ever dared say about Italy's civil war," reads the cover of the eighteenth edition of Giorgio Pisanò's Right-wing classic, *Sangue chiama sangue* ("Blood for Blood"). Pierangelo Maurizio's pamphlet on via Rasella is called *Fifty years of lies;* the proceedings of a meeting in solidarity to Erich Priebke are titled *History, Justice and Truth Face to Face.* [23]

However, in spite of their rhetoric of truth, these texts are not be evaluated on the referential plane.[24] Their function is less an argumentative or referential than an emotional one: the venting of a sense of frustration and victimization. It does not matter, then, if they tell mutually contradictory stories (it may be averred, alternatively, that the Communist secretary Palmiro Togliatti ordered the action in via Rasella, and is therefore to be blamed for it; [25] or that he condemned it, thus confirming the irresponsibility of he perpetrators); or that these narratives are known to be inventions, lies, or errors. What makes them consistent, ultimately, is that they all lead to one conclusion: the Communist plot.

The sense of persecution and the image of the Communist conspiracy confers on these narratives a paranoid tightness. If eleven of the killed are still unidentified, this cannot be because their names were not found, but because they have been "censored by German and Italian 'reason of State.'" [26] There is no need or attempt to prove it: the mere fact that something is not known proves that there is some dark secret underneath.

The theory of the Communist conspiracy culminates in the belief that via Rasella was intended to cause the extermination of Bandiera Rossa (or, interchangeably, the Partito d'Azione, or the military front), but it has infinite variants.

For instance, the GAP's military commander, Antonello Trombadori, who was at Regina Coeli on the day of the massacre, was saved by the jail's socialist doctor, Alfredo Monaco, who hid him in the infirmary; Mario Spataro, however, suggests that it is "likely" that his name was dropped off the list handed to the Nazis by the Italian police because he was under "special protection" of the Fascist police. As in most of these narratives, surmise accretes into certainty: two pages later, Trombadori's exclusion becomes proof that the whole list was drafted by "secret Communist structures." In other words, Trombadori was saved because the Communists had infiltrated the police. How do we know that the Communists had infiltrated the police? Obviously, because Trombadori was saved.[27]

The power of this memory lies in the fact that its sensationalist tone, the indignant basking in a self-inflicted marginality reflects feelings that are widely shared by their addressees: anti-intellectualism, the petit-bourgeois sense of distrust and impotence, the frustrated wish for some form of emotional compensation. By presenting as shocking revelations the clichés which their addressees already know or believe—consensus to Fascism, the Communist plot, other Italians as turncoats—these narratives turn conformist banality into daring transgression, passivity into heroism, the silent majority into a suppressed minority. Perhaps this submerged and pervasive discourse on origins is embedded in the nation's subconscious, emerging at a time when the founding consciousness seems to dissolve.

In 1997, the highly esteemed conservative journalist Indro Montanelli wrote a letter of solidarity to Erich Priebke: "As an old soldier," he writes, "I am perfectly aware that you could only do what you did [. . .] Remember that also among us Italians are men who think right, who see right, and who are not afraid to say it even when those who think and see wrongly run rampant in the streets."[28]

"In the '50s, when [Bentivegna] was awarded his gold medal, the Communists were running rampant in the streets of Italy and those who felt horror at their ways, their thinking, their very existence, had no voice."[29] Actually, in the 1950s, Italy was consistently governed by Center and Center-Right coalitions dominated by the Christian Democrats; but these fantasies born of a need to feel like discriminated against and solitary heroes increasingly became commonsense: during his successful 1994 electoral campaign, Silvio Berlusconi consistently claimed that Italy had endured "fifty years of Marxist hegemony," and the Left, once again, mistakenly believed that such a brazen lie did not need clarification and response. As the anti-Fascist paradigm collapses under the onslaught of the new conservative Right and the ideological and moral crisis ensuing the fall of the Communist regimes in Eastern Europe, the tenets of Right-wing memory re-emerge with two complementary faces: on the one hand, as the vision of yesterday's losers; on the other, as the discourse of today's winners, the common sense of the new majority. In a self-defeating bid for "reconciliation," the institutions, even those still controlled by progressive or liberal forces, delegate to the Right the concepts of country, honor, faith, death, and sacrifice: the Fascist republic's "boys from Salò" had *values,* the partisans only *ideologies.* The real heroes of this new narrative are the ones in the middle, the ones who did nothing, the prototypes of a citizenry no longer participant (as projected in the post-war Constitution, now discredited and under attack) but, as the new buzz word has it, governable.

The Right did not only speak and write, it also acted. "It was a New Year's Eve; someone threw a Molotov cocktail into the house. Fortunately, I was in the yard, and it didn't go off. Afterwards, I got a phone call—and I told them, 'My son, it's New Year's Eve, if you need to insult me please call again tomorrow'" (Giovanni Gigliozzi, president of ANFIM). At the Fosse Ardeatine, "someone blew up a gate, they hanged puppets across the street several times, drew swastikas . . . it makes no sense, they're afraid of the dead. They say, 'It's a fringe'; but where does this fringe come from? They must have received these myths from some place . . ." (Nicoletta Leoni).

Between late January and early February 1996, Rome was covered with posters demanding freedom for Priebke. A plaque and a wreath commemorating the men of the Bozen regiment were conspicuously put in place in via Rasella (and later removed by the authorities). The ANFIM office was broken into, smeared with swastikas, hammer-and-sickles, and death threats. A bomb was planted near the offices of the partisans' association. In August, swastikas are painted on plaques and stones commemorating anti-Fascist martyrs at Ostia, La Storta, and Ostiense. Two puppets representing Rosario Bentivegna and Carla Capponi were hanged in front of the Fosse Ardeatine.[30] "And when the Priebke trial began they stunk up the whole neighborhood where Sasà [Bentivegna] lives, with posters with his picture—'Wanted, the murderer of the Fosse Ardeatine'. They found out that I live here, so they stuck them here, too, but the city removed them" (Pasquale Balsamo). Riccardo Mancini, a former prisoner in via Tasso and a witness for the prosecution in the Priebke trial, receives death threats over the phone, and so do a number of the victims' relatives who are involved in the case: "I was always in fear; I got phone calls at home, and at the office— 'Look out, watch out for your daughter; how old is she?'" (Angelo Pignotti).

The Right seems to have been obsessed with this memory, as if the massacre demonstrated its foreignness to the wounded city (in spite of its wide electoral support). Indeed, in 1993, when the Gianfranco Fini, secretary of the yet-un-reformed neo-Fascist party, Movimento Sociale Italiano, came close to winning the mayoral election, the legitimacy of the Right had to be verified at the Fosse Ardeatine.

Gianfranco Fini. It was a red-hot race, really, as you know. And a lot of times, on TV, it was: "How can you be the mayor? If you become mayor, what do you do on the anniversary [of the Ardeatine]?" I always replied, "If I become mayor, I am responsible, because it is morally and politically right to do so, in the name of the whole city." And since I deeply believed in this, after the election was over – I went."

To some of the victims' relatives, the neo-Fascist leader's visit was a long-overdue act of atonement; to others, an insult. "If he has the conscience to go, he's welcome, why not?" (Giuseppina Ferola). "The day after I heard on the radio that Fini'd been there, I went to see whether he'd left a wreath, a bunch of flowers, or something. I'd have thrown it away, if he'd been there I'd have quarreled and got myself arrested and made a public issue of it"(Orfeo Mucci). "No doubt when one makes a gesture of this kind, it is automatically a desecration. Because it's a utilitarian gesture—indeed, Fini's policy is so obvious, his acceptance into democracy, he's realized, goes through the Jews, because they're the ones that can authenticate him" (Claudio Fano). "He has that charisma, that nice, clean, polished manner—and I play the part of the hyena because I don't forgive you, I don't believe you, I don't believe what you say. And indeed I don't" (Giulia Spizzichino).

Fini's visit to the Fosse Ardeatine was also controversial within his own party, because it was a symbolic gesture that marked the official abandonment of Fascism as the party's ideology and its change of name, from Movimento Sociale Italiano to Alleanza Nazionale. "I had reached the conclusion that the time was ripe and it had to be done. I announced that I had gone to the Fosse Ardeatine at a party summit meeting. And, yes, there were a few who were somewhat embarrassed; but there was also a sincere applause. Symbolically, the [visit to the] Fosse Ardeatine anticipates [Alleanza Nazionale's] denunciation of Fascist totalitarianism, of anti-Semitism." Thus, the road that led to the acceptance of the ex-Fascists in the Center-Right coalition that won the elections in 1994 and again in a landslide in 2001, when Gianfranco Fini became Italy's vice-prime minister, began at the Fosse Ardeatine.

6. The Arch of Titus

November 1998: In the Olympic Stadium, Rome's main sports arena, the hottest game of the soccer season, between Rome's two major league teams, Roma and Lazio, is about to begin. A huge banner is hoisted over the section occupied by Lazio's fans, aimed at the opposing faction: "Auschwitz, your country—the ovens, your homes." From the other side, another banner responds: "Damn Toaff" (Rome's chief Rabbi). Commentators rush to explain that "Politics has nothing to do with it." On the same day, the ex-Fascist party, Alleanza Nazionale, garners mprevotes than any other party in the province of Rome.[31]

<hr>

Valeria Spizzichino. Yet I remember fifty years ago when we walked under the Arch of Titus [a monument in the ancient Forum]. We had been forbidden by our rabbis to walk under the Arch of Titus, because it represented the great shame, the great sorrow of the destruction of the Temple [in Jerusalem in A.D. 70], and then the great diaspora under Titus. When the state of Israel was proclaimed, we went. The chief rabbi led the way, dressed in all the vestments just as in the temple, and after him came all the rabbis and then practically all of Jewish Rome. And we stayed up until three, four A.M., dancing around the bonfires, in the Jewish quarter. I remember it perfectly, it was wonderful."

As former prime minister Giulio Andreotti said in 1964, the commemoration at the Fosse Ardeatine is "the only official ceremony in which prayers for the dead are recited jointly by the Catholic priest and the rabbi of the Jewish community." "The most moving moment in my life was when I asked Cardinal Poletti [vice-bishop of Rome]: 'Why doesn't the Pope ever come to the Fosse Ardeatine?' And John Paul II came to the Ardeatine. When I heard that he was coming, I called my friend, [Chief Rabbi] Elio Toaff, and they met for the first time. The first encounter between Jews and Catholics took place at the Ardeatine [in 1982], and they prayed together" (Giovanni Gigliozzi).

Claudio Fano. In our community, ultimately, we don't make such a distinction between [the deportation of the Jews on] October 16 [1944] and the Fosse Ardeatine, we think of it as a unified event—that uncle-so-and-so died at the Fosse Ardeatine rather than Auschwitz . . . This enormous unhealed wound is still there, and in certain classes, especially the popular classes, it is felt most of all by the younger generations.

Vittorio Pavoncello. Though the Jews were only a very small percentage of those killed [75 out of 335], yet I personally still bear a tangible sign, because at the Fosse Ardeatine my wife's grandfather and uncle lost their lives, leaving a family with no support, my wife's grandmother with a small daughter, who had done no crime, no sin, their only wrong was being Jews . . . My grandfather Vittorio, from whom I take my name, was taken to concentration camp and there killed immediately, creating eight orphans; my father in law was in concentration camp; he is seventy now and looks ninety-five because of how badly he was beaten. And another relative of my mother's lost seven relatives, the famous Di Consiglio family, and many others, with whom as years go by we meet, we talk, and we realize what the dead at the Fosse Ardeatine really were, so there is also a link of human contact with those people, and their memory, their pain, I think will resonate still for a very long time.

In the reports of the ceremonies of the 1950s and 1960s, however, it looks as though the Catholic ritual had a universal meaning while the Jewish prayer represented only a particular group. "There at the Fosse Ardeatine, for instance, there always was the Catholic priest who when March 24 comes around, says the Mass and by saying the Mass takes up a certain amount of time and all. Whereas the Jewish function is only a few minutes, you see: after you said a Kaddish, it's all over" (Amedeo Tedesco). "When the mausoleum was built, there was an attempt to create a Catholic chapel inside. And there, the rabbis of the time said that a Catholic chapel would have been against Jewish rules, so that if they wanted to they should build it outside. So it fell through, and they built it outside. While we refused to build a Jewish chapel, because such a thing makes no sense in a cemetery" (Claudio Fano). In Rome, the capital of Catholicism, the monumental icon of the Ardeatine clouds over the memory of the deportation of the Jews (in 1999, however, October 16 was proclaimed the city's "memorial day"). The first mayor of Rome after liberation paid homage to the Ardeatine and the Unknown Soldier, but not to the ghetto; Hitler Boulevard became boulevard of the Fosse Ardeatine, but until 2002 no toponym commemorated the Roman Shoah. Only in 1982, the Left-wing city administration placed a plaque in piazza della Rovere, where the Jews were held awaiting deportation. As Francesca Koch and Simona Lunadei have written, the preeminence accorded to the Ardeatine "makes it possible to isolate the Nazis and perpetuate them in memory as the only ones responsible for the city's sufferings." To commemorate the arrests of Jews made by the Italian police and the Italian spies after October 16, 1943, on the other hand, "would have appeared as an obstacle to the process of national reconciliation."[32]

The myth of the kindness of the Italian character ("Italiani brava gente," "Italians, good people") is based on a number of actual acts of solidarity. This image, however, conceals a racism that was "latent" toward Arabs or Africans as long as they didn't live in Italy, but was always very tangible and threatening toward Jews.[33] In 1960, during a revival of anti-Semitic manifestations and a campaign for the liberation of Herbert Kappler, swastikas appeared in the streets around the ghetto, and anti-Semitic calls were made to the city offices.[34] On the anniversary of the massacre, the then president of ANFIM, Leonardo Azzarita, alerted the public to these signals, though perhaps with an unfortunate choice of words, recalling "the sacrifice of our countrymen of the Jewish race."

Adriano Mordenti. I had the fortune of going to Israel in '67 during the Six-Day War, and I left behind an Italy full of friends. Until then, for the Left, the Jewish world was part of its concerns; and there was among the Jews a conviction that one could not but be a Left person. When I left for Israel, this was the situation; when I came back, I found a state of unmotivated hostility. People were beginning to say I'm not anti-Semitic, I'm anti-Zionist," which is a horrible euphemism to say "I'm an anti-Semite who is ashamed of saying it." For years, my address book kept getting thinner and thinner, every day I had to cross someone out.

Vittorio Pavoncello. I believed that the Six-Day War would throw the Jews back to the state they were in before the creation of the state of Israel, and I lived it with great apprehension, even though I could not participate very actively in the 'defense committees', the collection of food and supplies for Israel, the collection of money: I was a fourteen year old kid, and I just managed to sneak into the meetings. In the early '70s, instead, the terrorist danger hit Rome and our community, and that was when I spent many a night watching over the Temple. We made nightly rounds, we organized the defense of Jewish institutions. I went to school in the afternoon, so I could sleep in the morning and I could stay out late at night. My mother and father had their minds at ease thinking I was doing who knows what, while I was sitting in a car watching the Temple. But what really struck me was that from many sides I kept being asked, "You are a Jew: are you Italian or Israeli?"

One may well disagree agree with Israel's Palestinian policy, but it's impossible not to recognize the grave wound that was thus inflicted to Rome's democratic texture by this breach between the Jewish community and progressive forces. The Jewish community felt isolated; the Left itself was infected. On October 9, 1982, after the massacres at Sabra and Shatilah, an ultra-Left group hurled a bomb to the Temple wounding forty people and killing a two-year-old child, Stefano Taiché. The ANFIM library today bears his name.

Adriano Mordenti. The bomb at the Temple—that was even more tragic, because we were more alone than ever. You must keep in mind that a few months earlier there was a demonstration—of the unions—that marched by the synagogue and [someone] deposited a coffin under the plaque. This made a deep impression, and something broke, which was perhaps only partly healed with the great demonstration after the yellow stars, remember? And when, later, we had to carry a real coffin, we couldn't help thinking of the empty one: after all, Romans are masters at interpreting symbols. And then, the calls to the [police emergency number] 113: "Come to the synagogue, they're shooting!" And the response was, "Where is the synagogue?" "This isn't Tel Aviv, we have churches here."

"The community feels that there is a long tradition of the Jew as victim who doesn't defend himself, with only a few exceptions. It's a tradition that is broken

by the Warsaw ghetto [uprising] and then finds its epilogue in the state of Israel"
(Claudio Fano). In 1992, yellow stars were painted on the shutters of Jewish
stores in several parts of Rome. The problem was no longer only one of defense;
and a group of young Jews marched to via Domodossola, the meeting place of
the Nazi skinheads.

Vittorio Pavoncello. The business at via Domodossola came about as a consequence of
the yellow graffiti on Jewish stores. It was born out of the fact that the Nazi skinheads
were getting more and more threatening. There was a conference at the hotel Parco
dei Principi where they invited a revisionist historian, David Irving, and fortunately
he was stopped at the airport, but out there, in piazza Verdi, on a Saturday afternoon,
there was tension between the police and our demonstrators. Then there was the business of the graffiti on the walls of Boccea. I was against it, because such an action
might have caused consequences, reprisals, so I tried to mediate. Afterwards, however, I was the one who announced the action to the papers. It was a very moving
thing, because I was told that they could see in the eyes of those Nazi skinheads the
terror of seeing the Jews react. After they tore down the Nazi flag, it was carried down
to the ghetto, where a camp survivor was waiting – that whole situation was making
him ill, because it took him back to times that were not forgotten. So we picked him
up, we lifted him up in the air, we applauded him, and we gave this flag to him.

In 1997 and again in 2002, Jewish graves were desecrated in Rome's ceme-
teries. The relatives of the victims found it impossible to "forget"; the community felt that it could not afford to let its guard down. For the media, this
attitude became another pretext to represent the memory of the Fosse Ardeatine and the Priebke trial as the private business of the Jews. When the Fosse
Ardeatine was being represented as everybody's monument, in the 1950s, the
Jews were perceived as a partial, embarrassing presence; now, they seemed to be
the only ones concerned. At each turn of the Priebke trial, they were the ones
who are asked for comments: headlines read, "Priebke soon free [. . .] Toaff is
disappointed."[35]
Most Jews felt uneasy about this protagonism. When the media interviewed
him as both a victim's son and president of Rome's community, Claudio Fano
replied, "This is a problem that concerns Rome, not [only] the Jews." "I mean,
did they only kill Jews? Yes, in proportion, seventy five Jews are a mountain; but
they're still seventy-five out of three hundred and thirty-five" (Giulia
Spizzichino). This excess of visibility generated some resentment among the
other victims' families, and fed he paranoid fear of the Jewish conspiracy and
domination.[36] Thus, "Priebke is the scapegoat of Zionist persecution" (Massimo
C.); the case "was re-tried because of the Italian pro-Zionist lobbies, that are very

powerful" (Giovanni Di Ruscio). Throughout the decade, all media pressed the same question upon every victim—from the victims of terrorism to those of stone-throwings on the freeways: "Do you forgive?" The families of the Fosse Ardeatine were no exception: "My sleeve has been pulled by every journalist, and they insisted for me to make a scene—'I forgive Priebke,' or something like that" (Claudio Fano). When addressed to Jews, the question of forgiveness is especially loaded.

Claudio Fano. Look, there is such a thing as a Jewish concept of forgiveness, and it is a value for us. The concept is this: only the victim can forgive, not the relatives. Hence the value of human life. To destroy a human life means that you no longer have who can forgive you. Number two: forgiveness is the counterpart of repentance; and repentance cannot be generic, it must be heartfelt. And—now I speak for myself: no one came to me and asked me to forgive him. However, since there is this Christian concept of forgiveness, Jews are the ones who don't forgive. And why do they not forgive? Because they're God-killers.

Giulia Spizzichino. And why should I forgive him? Forgive a person who hurt another who is under the earth and can't speak to me? It's not as if my grandfather, my cousins, could come out and tell me, "How dare you forgive? Are you the one who was beaten? The bullets in the head, the climbing over my father's and my grandfather's bodies, it was me, not you. What right do you have to forgive?" I can forgive, if I ever have the strength, the pain you caused to me, to Giulia. But today I can't, and I don't think I ever will.

7. Retaliation and "Multiple Murder": The Twists and Turns of Judicial Memory

[. . .] the attack in via Rasella [. . .] is an illegitimate act of war [. . .]
—Rome Military Tribunal, July 20, 1948

[. . .] the attack perpetrated by the partisans on March 23 1944 was a legitimate act of war [. . .]
—Rome Civil Tribunal, May 26 – June 9, 1950

On July 20, 1948, a military court in Rome sentenced Herbert Kappler to life imprisonment for multiple murder perpetrated with special cruelty at the Fosse Ardeatine, and to fifteen years for the "arbitrary confiscation" of the ghetto's gold. Borante Domizlaff, Hans Clemens, Johannes Quapp, Kurt Schutz, and Karl Wiedner were acquitted "because they acted upon the orders of a superior officer." Erich Priebke and Karl Hass were officially nowhere to be found. In 1998, they would be found guilty crimes against humanity and sentenced to life imprisonment.

"One hundred relatives of the victims of the Fosse Ardeatine stood in the courtroom behind a line of *carabinieri*. When the blinding lights of the cinematographers' spotlights were turned on, and the cameras began to hum to record the images of the six defendants; when the chancellor Mario Siracusa rose to read the charges against them—it was then that a woman's voice rose shrill and menacing from the crowd and screamed to Kappler, 'I'd like to tear out those eyes that saw what was done to my father and my brother.' And gesticulating as if she were actually about to jump upon the defendant to enact her threat, the woman in black leaned across the rail and those around her barely managed to hold her back. Kappler was unable to hide his fear: he took his handkerchief to his lips, and then to his forehead, to dry drops of sweat."[37]

Giorgio Agamben writes that "perhaps the trials [from Nuremberg to Eichmann] themselves have been responsible for the confusion of the minds that has made it impossible, for decades, to conceptualize Auschwitz."[38] With all due distinction, this applies also to the Fosse Ardeatine: the hypertrophy of judicial and legal discourse—from the British and American trials of Kesselring, Kappler, Mältzer, von Mackensen (1945–1947) to the Priebke trial (1996–1998)—has made it more difficult to think historically of via Rasella and the Fosse Ardeatine.

The jurisdiction of the courts extends only to personal and legal responsibilities; it does not authorize historians to delegate to them all discourse on the past or to make an uncritical use of judicial sources.[39] The law needs certainties and must therefore clearly circumscribe the object of discourse; historical consciousness, on the other hand, calls for an ever-open contextualization: "A historian has the right to perceive a problem where a judge would find no grounds to proceed," writes Carlo Ginzburg.[40] Magistrates are expected to close cases with an unequivocal and final judgment; the judicial verdict, however, is but a chapter in a book that the historian must always keep open. Thus, the verdict that ended the Kappler trial has itself been a factor in the struggle over history and memory later on. The definition of via Rasella as an "illegitimate act of war" and the widespread belief that the court found the retaliation legitimate and condemned Kappler only for "the extra five" are examples of the traces of that verdict in institutional and public memory.

Between Soldiers

Erich Priebke says: "I had police duties, I was not a member of the military."[41] Technically, he is right: even when they performed military tasks, the SS were not part of the regular army but a voluntary party militia that acted outside of any legal sanction other than direct obedience to Hitler.[42] Thus neither he nor Kappler ought to have been judged by military courts; that they were remains, as historian Lutz Klinkhammer writes, "a mystery of Italian justice," [43] an error that imprints upon future memory a military rather than a civilian standard of judgment.

In 1948, civilian injured parties were not allowed to sue before military courts. With the families reduced to a noisy and desperate chorus at the end of the courtroom, the trial remained a question between soldiers. "As a German soldier—Kappler proclaimed—I entrust my honor to Italian soldiers and Italian judges [. . .] The judges wear on their chests the badges of honor. Thus, they know that in war orders cannot be discussed but only carried out. I am, therefore, certain that whatever the verdict may be, it will be the judgment of soldiers on a soldier." "It is best to be judged by colleagues," Priebke confirmed, half a century later. [44]

The court in the Kappler trial, however, was caught in a contradiction. On the one hand, it shared the military outlook and values, in the Cold-War climate of 1948 in which the former enemy was about to become a precious ally. On the other, it was aware that the country's conscience would not tolerate a general acquittal. Hence, a twisted compromise of a verdict that affirms and denies everything: the Resistance is illegitimate, but only up to a certain point; under certain circumstances, retaliation is permissible, but not in the case of the Fosse Ardeatine; the order was illegitimate, but Kappler might have thought it valid; Kappler thought he was carrying out a legitimate order, but went too far . . . In the end, guilt is concentrated on one defendant alone. Kappler's men were acquitted; later, his superiors Kesselring and Von Mackensen, sentenced to death by an Allied court, were released. Sentencing one culprit (and almost in good faith!) is the easiest way to absolve all the rest.[45]

Resistance, an Illegitimate War

The judicial history of via Rasella and the Fosse Ardeatine has two main chapters: one between 1948 and 1957, and one between 1996 and 1998. In both instances, military trials with the Nazis as defendants were paralleled by civilian cases in which the defendants were the partisans; always, the matter hinged on the legitimacy of the action in via Rasella.

The military court in 1948 defined via Rasella as an "illegitimate act of war." It is a formally unimpeachable definition: an international convention stipulated at The Hague in 1906 sanctions as "legitimate belligerents" only the members of the regular armed forces and those volunteers who are led by a recognizable and responsible leader, who wear a fixed sign of recognition that can be identified at a distance, and who bear arms openly. Clearly, there was no way for partisans to meet these requisites: "We certainly could not put on the white red and green band as the [police] do nowadays, or sound the bugle before the charge!" (Pasquale Balsamo). As the civil court noted two years later, the conditions of partisan warfare make these norms unrealistic; indeed, on these grounds, not only via Rasella but the Resistance as a whole would be branded as illegitimate warfare.

The military court, however, was unwilling to take these principles to their logical conclusions, declaring the Resistance illegal on the basis of an obsolete convention, inadequate to the actual involvement of civilians in modern warfare, and systematically violated by the Germans themselves.[46] Hence, another twist: the Resistance *began* "necessarily in the realm of illegality," and was still illegal in March '44; it then *became* "a legitimate belligerent organ" later, when it established a unified command (nominally under an army general). Contrary to popular belief and interested manipulation, then, via Rasella was declared illegitimate "independently of its material circumstances": not because of how it was carried out or of its consequences, but because at the time in which it was carried out all partisan actions were technically illegitimate.

On the other hand, the military court recognizes that, though illegal from the point of view of international law, via Rasella is fully recognized by the Italian state. The attack "was carried out by a military organization following general directives given by a member of the [Resistance's] military command in accordance with the committee's policy"; and, after the war, the Italian State recognized the partisan command "a legitimate organ, at least *de facto*" and "considered the partisans as its own combatants." In other words: the action was illegitimate on the international plane, but fully legitimate on the internal one; therefore, via Rasella was an illegitimate act of the legitimate Italian state, which is therefore responsible for it.

In the public controversies, as well as in later suits against the *gappisti*, however, there is no trace of this complex motivation: all that remains is the label of illegitimacy, established out of context so as to create the impression that via Rasella was a singularly and individually criminal act. On this basis, in 1949 a group of relatives of the victims of the Ardeatine sued for damages Bentivegna, Calamandrei, Capponi, Salinari, and the leaders of the Roman Resistance, Sandro Pertini (a future president of the Republic), Giorgio Amendola, and Riccardo Bauer.[47] Rather than implementing the obsolete convention of The Hague, however, the civil court applied the laws of the Italian state and reached directly opposite conclusions: "an act of war, no matter by whom it is carried out, in the interest of one's country, is not in itself, and for the individual, to be considered illicit, unless it be explicitly qualified as such by an internal law." According to the court, the absence of visible chiefs, uniforms, and weapons was justified by the conditions of guerrilla warfare; via Rasella was an act of war against an occupying enemy armed force, and "it is to be excluded that the death or wounds of citizens who happened to be near the site [e.g., Piero Zuccheretti] were intentional, and that the ensuing massacre at the Fosse Ardeatine was willed [by the partisans]." The *gappisti,* therefore, were "not culprits, but combatants"; the men killed at the Ardeatine were "not mere victims of a harmful act, but martyrs fallen for their country."[48]

In 1997, however, a Roman prosecuting judge, Maurizio Pacioni, again invoked the Hague convention and the definition of "illegitimate act of war" to start new proceedings against Pasquale Balsamo, Bentivegna, and Capponi. They were charged with *strage* ("massacre") for the death of Piero Zuccheretti and Tommaso Chiaretti (a member of Bandiera Rossa killed by the Germans in via Rasella). Pacioni was unable to bring the case to court because post-facto provisions by the Italian state exempt from sanction all actions conducted in the interest of the state during the German occupation. He therefore called for the case to be shelved on technical reasons, but he left intact the factual and moral charges: via Rasella might not be punishable, but it remained a crime[49]. More specifically, a crime of *strage:* a word which in common speech means "multiple murder" but in legal parlance refers to any "dangerous event" whose "specific intent" is "to cause the death of an undetermined number of persons." Indeed, as in all acts of war, the specific intent of via Rasella was to cause as many enemy casualties as possible; the partisans, however, were charged not with the death of the German policemen but with that of Piero Zuccheretti. The result is a perversion of legal logic, based on an undeclared gap between "dangerous act" and "specific intent": the slaughter consists subjectively in the killing of the Germans and objectively in the death of Piero Zuccheretti. Now if an event is the involuntary consequence of another event having another intention, we may speak of guilt or negligence (*colpa*), but not of specific intent (*dolo*); and, in the absence of specific intent, the charge of *strage* does not stand.

What counts, however, is not the legal reasoning but the shift in the reference of that powerful word, *strage*–"massacre," or "mass murder." The massacre no longer takes place at the Fosse Ardeatine, but in via Rasella. The legal distortion is a rhetorical masterpiece: it states that the partisans are guilty of mass slaughter, but shelving the case makes it impossible for them to defend themselves in public debate. The fact that they avoided jail apparently on a technicality amplifies the scandal: another conspiracy. The confusion is heightened by the gap between the common and the legal meaning of the word *strage:* though the case revolves around one individual death, that of Piero Zuccheretti (Chiaretti's death was quickly proved to have nothing to do with the case and was dismissed), public opinion received the impression that what was at stake was the death of the Germans. The Italian state, in other words, appeared to have charged with mass murder its own freedom fighters for attacking an armed unit of a foreign army of occupation.[50] Of course, the partisans appealed the decision, and in March, 1999 the Supreme Court once again ruled that via Rasella was a legitimate act of war, and the death of Piero Zuccheretti was accidental (the decision was later sustained by the Supreme Court). But the bitterness remains. As Pasquale Balsamo says: "I'd like to tell tomorrow's young people, if you happen to undergo another foreign occupation, close your eyes, turn aside, bear it, indeed help the invading, raiding, torturing, murdering enemy. You will earn the gratitude of all respectable, God-fearing persons."[51]

The Right of Retaliation

According to the 1948 Kappler verdict, since the partisans were both illegitimate belligerents and organs of the Italian state, Germany had a right to exact compensation from the Italian state. Under international law, this entitled the injured state (Germany) to retaliate against the civilian population of the offending one.

The occupying power, in other words, was offended by the occupied nation. Once this fascinating inversion of logic was established, the only solution ought to have been acquittal for Kappler and his men. Once again, however, the military court was reluctant to carry its findings to their logical consequences. Hence, one more twist: the court found that retaliation was legitimate only under certain circumstances, which the Fosse Ardeatine did not meet: there was no immediate danger and pressing need, the number and quality of victims was out of proportion with the provocation,[52] the human rights of the victims were violated by the manner of the execution (not by the execution itself). Also, the Germans failed to seek out the perpetrators; the "hostages" shot were not co-responsible with the perpetrators, and had not been designated as hostages beforehand. The Fosse Ardeatine, then, was not a legal reprisal but a "multiple murder." Contrary to what has become a widespread belief, then, the court found the massacre of the Ardeatine illegitimate not merely because of the five extra victims, but in toto.

Because this was not a legitimate reprisal, the extenuating circumstances of obeying a legitimate order failed: the order was visibly illegitimate, and even the military court of 1948 had no doubt that it was possible and proper to refuse an illegitimate order—unless (in another twist) one had plausible reasons to believe it to be legitimate. The court did find that because of his Nazi mentality (which thus becomes an extenuating circumstance) and "the great moral power" inherent in a Führer's order, this was the case with Herbert Kappler.

Once again, this ought to have led to his acquittal; and once again the court found a way out. Kappler, it argued, went beyond the illegitimate-but-presumed-to-be-legitimate order he had received—320 victims—because, motivated by ambition, he took the initiative of adding ten more names after he learned of the death of another soldier. Also, the negligence deriving from " his frenetic rush to carry out the operation with the utmost speed" caused the death of five extra victims.[53] He was therefore guilty in his excessive zeal in carrying out an illegitimate order which he thought legitimate.

As for the other defendants, their case was decided easily: they were taking their orders from Kappler, who was the only one in control. They could not know exactly how many victims were being executed (with one exception: the man who held the lists—that is, the missing Erich Priebke). Therefore, they were not aware of the fact that they were obeying an illegitimate order. And were all acquitted.[54]

8. A Failure of Justice

"I remember mother's pain and what she said—that's when she began to suffer badly from liver attacks that made her very ill: 'Rosetta, do you realize that they condemned Kappler merely for the extra five, otherwise he'd have gone scot free . . . '" (Rosetta Stame). Things were slightly different, but the sense of a failure of justice remained and was made keener by Kappler's escape from prison in 1976 and the revisionist climate and memory crisis of the 1990s. When Priebke was found in Argentina in 1994 and later extradited to Italy, "it's a wound that reopens" (Flavio Govoni), but to some it also appeared as the occasion to heal it.

The Priebke trial was prejudiced by the acquittal of Kappler's men in 1948. It became necessary, then, to prove that his position was different from theirs: that his role was more active and responsible, and that his character and behavior were especially worthy of blame. The lower military court (judge Agostino Quistelli presiding) set very narrow limits to the evidence that could be brought to court; yet, the prosecution managed to demonstrate Priebke's role in via Tasso, his role in the preparation of the lists of the victims, and his responsibility for the killing of the extra five. Once again, the fact that it was possible to reject the order was confirmed.[55] In the end, however, the court found that it could not apply retroactively the laws on crimes against humanity; though Priebke was guilty of multiple murder, the aggravating circumstances (cruelty, malice aforethought) and the extenuating ones (obedience, good behavior in court, old age and limited capacity to offend further, good record after the massacre) balanced in such a way that he was sentenced not to life but to fifteen years. The verdict thus fell under the statute of limitations: at the end of the trial, the court ordered Priebke's immediate release.

The reaction of the injured parties and of public opinion caused the Secretary of Justice to order Priebke to be re-arrested immediately, pending a request for extradition from Germany. The trial was later declared void (before the proceedings were over, one of the judges had predicted that Priebke would be acquitted). In the retrial, Priebke and his co-perpetrator Hass (who had emerged during the earlier trial) were found guilty of a crime against humanity; again, however, the play of extenuating circumstances determined a verdict of fifteen and ten years respectively, which again fell under the statute of limitations. Only in the appeal court will the framework of the Kappler verdict be broken at last: with a decision later confirmed by the Supreme Court, the military court of appeals denied the defendants any extenuating circumstances, and handed out a sentence to life imprisonment, to which the statute of limitations does not apply. According to the court, old age and the passing of time, far from proving Priebke's redemption, "only enhance his guilt: there is no sign in him of a change of heart, of an understanding of what he did."[56]

9. Gaeta, Celio, Bariloche

On the Circonvallazione Nomentana, just before the bridge at the end of via Lanciani, a swastika and graffiti on a wall commemorate, with the battle name he had earned for himself, an adolescent killed in a conflict with the police: "Kapplerino vive"—"Little Kappler lives."

Vittorio Gabrieli. After the liberation of Rome, I worked for a while in the Rome office of the Reuter news agency, and at the time I followed the Kappler trial, unofficially, just as an observer, and I found myself two or three meters away from this champion, from his great *Mensur,* who claimed that he had only followed war orders . . .

The *Mensur* is the scar that testifies to the German tradition of student sword duels. "It was a medieval trial that had come down to the time of my youth," Kappler explains: "The goal was not to strike the opponent, but to be able to stand still when you could no longer parry your rival's blade with your own."[57] The court described him as the "typical Nazi": as such, he presented himself and was perceived by reporters: "His usual hard mien, the pale white face that made the scar on the left cheek even more visible, the dark blue suit that made his cruel criminal face stand out . . ." Another account portrayed him "As exact as a watch, firm in every statement, implacable even to himself . . . he spoke on, leafing through his notes and the charts drawn with meticulous care during his prison years . . ."[58]

Herbert Kappler was born in Stuttgart in 1907, to a middle-class family. He joined the National Socialist Party in 1931, and the SS in 1933. "He joined the party because he saw in Hitler's political program the practical solution to the poverty that had pervaded all of Germany's labor." He says: "Under the Social Democrat government, I had two options: either the Communists or the Nazis. You know which way I went." In his police work, "he was involved in the struggle against illegal Communism and common crime, and specialized in actions against terrorism, in intelligence work, and in the organization of border police."[59] In Rome, where he was transferred in 1939, he oversaw the reorganization of Italian police: "It was this concern, and the frequent contact with Italian officers that generated within me an ever stronger love for the country that hosted me and which after a while I looked upon as my new homeland . . ."[60] After Italy's separate armistice of September 8, 1943, he participated in the rescue of Benito Mussolini from his place of detention. In May, 1945, he turned himself in to the British. After the trial, he was held in military jails at Rome's Forte Boccea and later in Gaeta.

From the penitentiary, he drafted appeals all the way to Supreme Court, which were turned down; and wrote letters, some of which were published during the Priebke trial as *Letters from Prison* (like Antonio Gramsci's). Like any prisoner who misses affection and freedom, he wrote about food, the laundry, his lawyers; there were occasional religious thoughts and references to the "faithful friendship" of "his boys" (he corresponded with Priebke at least until the mid-60s). Primarily, however, they were love letters, replete with sentimental clichés; as time went by tenderness evolved into more and more explicit intimate and erotic fantasies, which it might perhaps have been more respectful not to make public.[61]

But, unlike Gramsci's, these letters contained nothing especially lofty or deep. The court that condemned him was made up of "people unfit to judge my inner honor," who could only "defame me but not wound or hurt me." He described himself as the victim of discrimination, "of the insults, misunderstandings and humiliations" of "some financier filled with Mosaic hatred" and of the Italian people's lack of "comprehension." He mentioned the Fosse Ardeatine only once, as a normal military action: "You know very well that it gives me very much pain to have had to take part in a war measure that generated so much suffering, but I would feel the same sorrow all my life if—as a pilot—I had had to rain death on any country's cities." [62] When he held his gun barrel half an inch from his victims' heads, in other words, he was as distant from them as if he were looking down from the height of a bomber plane.

In 1972, after a correspondence of four years, he married Annelise, who immediately took up the struggle for his liberation (on her trips to Italy, she was checked in at the airport by the son of one of her husband's victims, Silvio Gigliozzi). Kappler insisted that all he did was his duty: the Fosse Ardeatine was a "horrible" action about which he said he felt morally but not legally responsible. He explained to ignorant or conniving interviewers, who didn't know enough to challenge him, that he did look for the perpetrators, and that he had carried out twenty-to-one retaliations before via Rasella. He always represented himself as a victim: "Now don't write that Kappler has a call to martyrdom," he said; "I would not feel right under a martyr's halo, I don't want to be, I don't feel I am a martyr."[63] The victim's relatives screamed when he told the court of his humanitarian concerns during the massacre, "How nice of you."

In the 1970s, the campaign for his release was renewed, in the name of Christian forgiveness, Italo-German cooperation and friendship, and anti-partisan propaganda. The military court met to consider his release; in the streets below, a new generation of the victims' families took up the struggle for memory and justice: "We were outside, the relatives outside and some of the mothers had taken along some of us who were adolescents" (Nicoletta Leoni). In February 1976, he was diagnosed with cancer and moved to the Celio military hospital in Rome; on midsummer's night he escaped, according to official versions, inside a suitcase carried by his wife.

Turbasi Roma e di dolor sospira	Rome is shaken, and in sorrow it sighs
E del Tevere suo gemono l'onde	And the waves of her Tiber moan and cry
Nella gente d'Italia vampa l'ira	In Italy's people anger flames
E la fuga di Kappler si diffonde . . .	As Kappler's escape becomes known . . .
	—Francesco Vincenti [64]

"It was an announced escape; there had been talk of Kappler's liberation for a long time already. I was very young, but I remember perfectly our demonstration at the Celio, a big big crowd, all very angry, because it was once again a perpetuation of the injustice against not only Jews but the city of Rome" (Vittorio Pavoncello).

"[My mother] was in the hospital, with a heart attack; when she heard that Kappler had escaped she nearly had another. We never really knew whether he'd escaped, or whether they'd let him escape . . ." (Bruno Frasca). "Kappler's escape was terrible. My father had accepted and rationalized certain things; but such a spectacular and shocking escape, so to speak, with very specific responsibilities . . ." (Flavio Govoni). "My mother says, here we go, Italy sold him, with our blood, they sold him with our folks' blood, because there were pacts between Italy and Germany; they sold him again, the Fosse Ardeatine once again were used to settle things in Italy . . ." (Gabriella Polli). [65]

Rosetta Stame. It was August, I remember I was at the sea . . . I see that mama is dark in the face, and I ask her, "What's the matter, mom? Are you ill? you look strange . . ." "Listen, Rosetta, I have something to tell you . . . Kappler has escaped . . ." Back then, [Francesco Cossiga] was Secretary of the Interior: we went to see Cossiga, I, my mother, Carla Capponi; I made an appeal over the radio . . . Then I went to the Ardeatine; the superintendent opened the place for me and I went inside, to the spot where they were executed, I trod the earth where they were executed; and I picked up this handful [of earth].

Nicoletta Leoni. Then in piazza delle Sette Chiese, where there is a monument to the martyrs, there was a night watch. From Portico d'Ottavia they set up a stage from which Gigliozzi and the rabbi spoke, and then a procession unfolded all the way to the Temple, and I remember that it was we grandchildren of the fallen of the Ardeatine or of the concentration camp deportees who had to carry the signs with the names of Dachau, Mauthausen, Auschwitz; we fifteen-year-olds, we grandchildren became directly involved in these events.

E vendetta vendetta vendetta	And revenge, revenge, revenge
Grideranno le Fosse Ardeatine	The Fosse Ardeatine shall cry
Attendendo di Kappler la fine	Awaiting Kappler's downfall
Maledetto quel giorno sarà.	And accursed on that day he shall be.

—Francesco Vincenti

Kappler died, free, in Germany in 1978. But the memory of his unexplained escape was still alive in 1994, when a U.S. television crew "discovered" Erich Priebke in Bariloche, Argentina;[66] "Now that he's escaped, let's make sure we don't lose this one, too" (Bruno Frasca). Born in 1913, Erich Priebke had lost both parents at the age of seven; at fourteen, he went to work in the hotel business. From 1933, he worked in a hotel in Rapallo, on the Italian Riviera; from the owner there, he writes, he learned "tolerance toward my neighbor and equality with people";[67] therefore, that same year he joined the National Socialist Party. In 1935 he was a waiter in London; in 1936, he became an interpreter and translator for the political police, which was later merged into the SS. He accompanied Göring, Goebbels, Mussolini, and Hitler on visits abroad; in 1938 he married, in 1941 he was stationed in Rome. He also played a part in Mussolini's escape and in the removal to Germany of his daughter Edda and her husband Galeazzo Ciano. After the liberation of Rome, he performed executive tasks in Brescia.

He was arrested by the Allies, escaped, was taken again, and again escaped a number of times.[68] In 1948, in Vipiteno (South Tyrol), he was baptized into the

Catholic Church. According to the judges of his first trial, this conversion "proves his total break with his Nazi precedents"[69]—as though Protestantism, of which he was a believer before, were instead perfectly compatible with the massacre; and as though the Catholic Church had never made compromises with the Nazis. Later, Priebke would thank "the Catholic Church for its help" in his escape to Argentina, where he arrived in 1948 with a Red Cross passport under an assumed name.[70]

Argentina was a favorite haven for wanted Nazis and Fascists. "The most notorious *ratline,* used by Eichmann, Barbie, and hundreds of others, was the 'Vatican' road, a chain of convents that went from upper Bavaria, through Austria and Bozen or Merano, to Genoa, Rome or Naples." High-ranking Fascists, as well as seven thousand five hundred Nazis found refuge in Argentina; a number of them concentrated in Bariloche, a resort in the Andes, where in the late 1940s the ex Nazi Ronald Richter ran a sham program for an Argentinean atom bomb. A big reunion of former Nazis celebrated Christmas in Bariloche in 1951.[71]

Priebke arrived in Bariloche in 1954. Before his arrival, he had worked as a waiter in Buenos Aires; he had exchanged letters with Kappler, was visited by former comrades and Fascists. In 1950, interviewed by an Italian journalist, he did not mention the Fosse Ardeatine.[72] In Bariloche, he worked in a hotel, opened a delicatessen ("he may have a portrait of Hitler in the back room, but he sells the best hams in town"); did volunteer work to support and manage a German school that, he said, was attended by "even Jewish" pupils (apparently, a photograph shows the swastika flag displayed over the roof of this school). He was involved in social activities, as "un buen vecino, que todos conocimos," a good neighbor we all know.[73] In his hispanicized Italian, he writes:

"In Argentina, I am a life member of the Automobile Club and an honorary member of the Argentinean-German cultural association in Bariloche, for my constant *ad honorem* activity of almost forty years on behalf of the Association and especially of the Argentinean-German school of Bariloche [. . .] As its president, I organized the cultural interchange between Bariloche and Germany [. . .] I was the organizer each year of the German national holiday, first on June 17, as a commemoration of the fallen of East Berlin in the year 1954, and afterwards the great celebration of Germanic reunion."[74]

The judges of his first Italian trial acknowledged that "he has retained an irreproachable behavior, abstaining from any criminal action [. . .] he was a quiet 81-year old retiree who belonged to an absolutely normal petit-bourgeois family." This ought to prove that he no longer had any "criminal capacity." Of course, the judges admitted, he had no opportunity to repeat the crime of the Fosse Ardeatine; but if he had had criminal tendencies, they argue, he might have committed other crimes, against private property or individuals. What the court failed to realize is that, as opposed to a common criminal, a Nazi criminal, or perhaps any war criminal, could very well be a good neighbor, a family man, a music lover, and a member of the Automobile Club.

In 1961, the Rome military tribunal shelved his case, claiming he could not be found. In fact, his whereabouts were not hard to discover; as late as 1988, the foreign ministry had received information of his presence in Bariloche but did nothing about it. Rather than recognizing this as a lack of zeal in persecuting Nazi criminals, the Right-wing press read this fact as evidence of dark secrets and conspiracies when he was finally arrested.[75] Priebke was actually convinced that his acts were no longer actionable. In 1978 and 1980, he came to Italy, met with his comrade Hass (who had been working for the Italian secret service), and went with his wife "back to the places of our past."[76]

Vera Yaria. Priebke, in July, in August of 1980, walked lightheartedly down via del Tritone, down via Rasella. I wondered who was this madman who at two P.M. walked around and sat down on the steps in via Rasella, with a little hat on, what was he looking for, with his nose in the air, stuck there on the spot of the bomb. He had a blonde lady with him; I recognized him from the pictures in the papers, and then he admitted it himself.

In March, 1994 Priebke was extradited to Italy. Both the Berlusconi administration in Italy and the Menem government in Argentina had image problems: the former was the first in post-war Europe to include an ex-Fascist party (Alleanza Nazionale), the latter needed to distance itself from the military dictatorship, especially after eighty-six people were killed by a bomb that destroyed the building of the Jewish Mutual Aid Societies in Buenos Aires. A U.S. journalist who spoke to him after his arrest found Priebke "incredibly depressed"; yet, he showed no remorse and defended his actions as absolutely normal wartime behavior.[77]

It seems that these men never understood why people are so opposed to them. They kept saying they were sorry, that it was horrible, but they hadn't the least shadow of a doubt concerning their role. "It is not a guilt someone must carry within himself, because it could not have been remedied," Priebke said in 1996.[78] His words and his arguments were exactly the same as Kappler's half a century before: time, indeed, seemed to have passed in vain. Priebke, too, thought he was a victim: "With inexplicable duplicity, evil persons insist and rage pitilessly to obtain a life sentence for me [. . .] a tenacious will that has chosen me as the symbol of a feud that must be quenched." He, too, did not recognize the tribunal: "I felt that I was not surrounded by mere operators of justice, but by political hatred, instrumentalism, meanness."[79]

During the trial, a friendly journalist noted a sign carried by the victims' relatives: "Priebke is 83; the 335 of the Fosse Ardeatine never will be!." He comments: "Hatred and resentment, fifty-two years later, are all in those lines, sprayed over the banner raised at the entrance of the Rome tribunal. And in the relatives' spitting and spite [. . .] among screams, faintings and curses [. . .]"[80] In that "terrible, narrow" courtroom, spectators had no space to breathe. "I fainted twice: we are not [treated as] human beings; we are puppets there on sufferance, who they wish so much we wouldn't be there . . ." (Rosetta Stame). The children and grandchildren of those who railed at Kappler fifty years before now railed against Priebke. "He, Erich Priebke, the last of the Nazis of that massacre, only now belatedly brought to trial, understands their anger and pain."[81] How well he understood it was shown by his expression of "complete solidarity" to the relatives of his victims: "In the war I lost two members of my family, a cousin and my wife's brother." He still did not realize that it wasn't the same.

Adriana Montezemolo. I of course throughout this last year lived very intensely all the story of the Priebke trial. I mean, it brought so many things back to memory, it was very sad, because it's not that you forget, but there's no doubt that after fifty years . . . I don't wake up at night thinking of the Ardeatine, though I do think about it, very much. But this whole business, this story of Priebke, brought it all back to life, like that . . .

Giulia Spizzichino. All the time I followed this story of Priebke, unfailingly, every night, every night, I woke up as if a hand at a given hour shook me and told me: "Well, what's the matter tonight? Aren't you thinking of us? Don't you remember us at all?" And before my eyes went by, like a, a procession—on my word of honor, all of them, all of them, I didn't miss one, until I had gone over all twenty-[nine] I couldn't go back to sleep for the anguish that swept me off.

"Meanwhile, outside, the police stops a few goons, led by the *borgata* Führer Maurizio Boccacci [leader of the Nazi skin heads], who are carrying a banner that intimates: 'No jackals, just justice, free Priebke!'" "Underneath, in viale delle Milizie, the [ultra-Left] *autonomi* are marching. We certainly expected them. They shouted 'Down with Priebke', and—on the wake of ancient, tooth-gnashing nostalgia, 'Fascists, Fascists, for you there's no tomorrow / The new partisans are coming'."[82] Once, the label "nostalgic" designated those who dreamed of bringing Fascism back; in the world turned upside down of the 1990s, the nostalgics, the ones who are out of step with history, are the anti-Fascists.

Priebke's life sentence was reduced to house arrest in consideration of his age and health. In 2001, he sued for $100,000 Rosetta Stame, the daughter of one of his victims, and Riccardo Pacifici, president of Rome's Jewish youth organization. He claimed that by calling him a torturer, they had insulted his good name. He lost the case; the final verdict was announced on October 16, 2002, the anniversary of the deportation of the Roman Jews.

10. Failure of Justice, Again

"The trial against Priebke was another infamy of the Italian partisan State; because war is war, orders are orders. Priebke was carrying out orders, the real assassin is Bentivegna" (Massimo C.). The controversy over the trial produces new grist for the mill of commonsense: "Priebke came and went in and out of Italy. Nobody ever stopped him. If they really felt so much for this thing, why wasn't it done before?" (Fabrizio Ceravolo): "After all these years, it seems to me that putting him in jail, and for life, makes no sense, because he followed his idea, and then it was so many years ago" (Francesca Silighini).

Liliana and Silvio Gigliozzi, as well a few other relatives of the victims, oppose the trial, or refuse to stand with the injured parties: "This trial," Antonio Pappagallo writes in a letter to the court, "boils down to a sterile monologue of persecution against a single person guilty of having had to obey higher orders." Anna Maria Canacci writes that "precisely because I suffered so much, out of respect for my martyred brother, I think it is our duty to forgive"; Adriana Montezemolo says that "Priebke was a young captain of no special importance, and he did his duty as a soldier; they told him to shoot, and he did."[83] The great majority, however, support the trial and participate actively, sometimes over-emotionally, often at the cost of grave sacrifice: "I had to run the house all the same; and take two or three buses every day to Rebibbia . . . you know what held me up? When I came home, people who stopped me; and they hugged me, and said, 'That coward, what are you waiting for, why don't you kill him . . . '" (Giulia Spizzichino). For the first time, the civilian injured parties – the ANFIM, the City of Rome—are allowed to stand before a military court.

"The court seems to be in a hurry [. . .] They fear that the trial on the Gestapo officer may turn into a wider judgment on the Resistance, on the right of reprisal, on the role of the Vatican . . ." Judge Quistelli cuts down the number of witnesses for the prosecution and restricts the range of their testimony: "This trial had its legs cut off from the beginning," says Elisabetta Agnini, lawyer, and niece of a victim.

"The military court," wrote the historian Enzo Collotti, "proved to be technically and culturally inadequate to judge a history of such huge import as the massacre of the Fosse Ardeatine."[84] The tribunal's lack of historical culture and awareness, however, is only a symptom of a broader void: it should have been up to others—intellectuals, politicians, the media, the schools—to sustain and articulate historical memory, and they failed to do it. The problem is not just that the court could not do this for them, but the fact that the task was arrogated to it in the first place.

"The press came to the trial totally unprepared. We [of the ANFIM] gave out hundreds of books—the press didn't know a thing" (Nicoletta Leoni). The media too, narrowed the context, theatricalized, and privatized it. They reported the first trial in detail in the current news pages, reveling in the drama of contrasts between the "icy" German and the emotional behavior of the relatives and the Jews; but they supplied little or no analysis and background in the cultural and editorial pages. They expressed proper and respectful sympathy toward the injured parties, but hardly any direct concern, as if this were not a matter that concerned us all. Indeed, the whole controversy over Fascism and anti-Fascism was increasingly represented as a feud between opposite and extreme ideological formations, while the wide and expanding gray zone between them allowed the media to pretend that it was only a matter of altruistic sentiment.

One way for the media to distance themselves from the case was to see Priebke only through the eyes of the representatives of the victims, who looked at him "as though they recognized him as different, other from them. An alien." Describing the attitude of Chief Rabbi Elio Toaff toward Priebke, the journalist Mino Fuccillo writes: "History and blood situated them, forever, in two distant universes, unable to communicate. Could they speak to each other, they would express themselves in mutually alien tongues." And yet, the Jewish essayist Stefano Della Torre objects: "If we begin to trace a separation between 'them' and 'us' as if they were two different species, as if Nazism were an 'alien' phenomenon, it would be nothing but a consolatory exorcism."[85]

Priebke and Toaff, in fact, do have a common tongue: they are both human beings, they both speak Italian. The lack of a common tongue, then, is a metaphor for a moral choice: Toaff, rightly, *will not* speak to Priebke. The media, instead, suggested a material, biological obstacle: one *cannot* speak to Priebke because he is beyond the pale of humanity and thus of language. "Toaff does not refer to Priebke as 'man', but always as 'this individual'[. . .] as though he could not discern human nature in the SS officer," Fuccillo writes).[86] This attitude may be necessary and quite understandable on the part of the victims and their representatives, but it is a cheap alibi when used by others.

If Priebke is not human, in fact, our own nature is not involved and called into question by what he did and is. Priebke, however, is neither a beast nor a machine—he is a human being, like us. As in all metaphors, it makes sense to compare him to a brute or to an inanimate thing precisely because he is not one. Riccardo Mancini, who was tortured by him in via Tasso, never spoke his name ("this being," he said in his courtroom testimony); yet, he said that "now Priebke is an old man like me."[87] To realize this is not to absolve him in the name of our common humanity but to help the humanity of which he is a member become aware of what it is capable, so that what has happened, and still can happen, shall never happen again.

Vera Simoni. He is responsible indeed; so he must be condemned. He must be condemned, to save the others, so that he can be an example also for Yugoslavia, that even after forty years, after sixty, they shall be prosecuted. Look, he must be condemned. This I say with passion, truly. Once he is condemned, I'll be the one to go and ask for a pardon, he's old, let him go back to his family and die in his family—aside from the fact that it was he who killed, tortured, he did it personally and never repented—but aside from all this, he has remained, has remained as a symbol, he is the only survivor. And then, let it be known, let humankind know, let Italy know, let France know, that they are punished.

When the punishment at first failed to arrive, the pain was intolerable. At the reading of the first verdict, which condemned Priebke but ordered his release, "the anger of the victims' relatives exploded in the courtroom. As the hours went by, the protest turned into a long siege to the military courthouse, with clashes between demonstrators and *carabinieri*."[88] Half a century and two generations after the protest at Santa Maria degli Angeli, here they were again, "rioting" against closed doors and barriers, clamoring for their right to enter, blocking the judges, the lawyers, the defendant inside.

The Jewish youth groups and Left activists rushed to the scene: "We were in close contact over the phone, waiting for the verdict. Once the verdict came, I rallied the street leaders, who spread the news and they begin to arrive" (Vittorio Pavoncello); "I called other people, the *autonomi* were there, and people we knew" (Angelo Pignotti). And the relatives came, one by one: "Someone called me, saying, 'Look, the verdict is out, it's a scandal'. I knew that my father's brother was there, and I tried to call his family because I had already heard that there was quite a scuffle" (Elisabetta Agnini). "There were people there who had lived in the first person the tragedy of the Fosse Ardeatine, the tragedy of the deportations, the tragedy of being orphaned. So great was the anger at having to suffer another injustice fifty years later, that it was absolutely impossible to bear. We barricaded inside, without water, in that infernal heat, must have been at least 110 degrees." (Vittorio Pavoncello). [89]

Nicoletta Leoni. I have three images before my eyes: Giulia Spizzichino in a corner crying desperately; my mother on the courthouse stairs screaming like a hyena; [Antonio] Margioni's son, in the toilet, is crying but since he's a man he's ashamed of being seen. And my aunt, I don't know how, she finds a chair, sits upon this chair and is stupefied . . . For them, it meant that their father was being killed [again] right then.

Angelo Pignotti. At the moment, we didn't really know what we were doing. I mean, there was this drive to . . . and finally there was this confusion, we broke through, two or three of us even managed to get inside where Priebke was, they wanted to throw him out the window, though it was impossible because it was barred. There was such a crowd, you can't imagine, all massed. Then the prosecutor came out, and he said, "It's no use you being here, what's the purpose, now?" So they parted, some went to via Tasso to cry, others to the Fosse Ardeatine.

It was late, and at the Fosse Ardeatine they found another closed gate. "The janitor had the keys, but they have cut costs, so they no longer had a night janitor" (Giovanni Gigliozzi). Finally the keys were found, the relatives went inside to cry and pray. Tullia Zevi, president of the Jewish Community, said: "They kept telling us we ought to forgive that poor old man. Instead, I am here to ask these poor victims to forgive us." "It is the triumph of justice," said Priebke's lawyer; the German historian Ernst Nolte confirmed: "Rome's tribunal has earned a great merit for its objectivity and humanity." But even for Alleanza Nazionale's Gianfranco Fini the verdict is "morally unjust and offends to civil conscience of all the Italian people." The mayor Francesco Rutelli orders that the lights be turned off at all the city's monuments, as a sign of mourning. The prime minister Romano Prodi goes to the Fosse Ardeatine: "The country is here," he says. [90] The country is also—perhaps primarily—in the besieged halls and stairs of the military tribunal.

On that August 1, 1996, a new generation picked up the task of responsibility and memory: "We were a whole line of grandchildren against those barriers. It wasn't only for grandfather; I owed it to grandma" (Nicoletta Leoni). They were twenty, thirty years old; they never met their grandfathers killed at the Fosse Ardeatine, but they grew up surrounded by the pain of their fathers, mothers, and grandmothers: "You do it out of love for the person you descend from, it's a sorrow you inherit" (Marco Sbarrini). They were the ones who stopped the new injustice, who held the line until the order came for Priebke to be rearrested. "I was grateful, grateful to those young people who rebelled; really, could I have gone and kissed their hands, I would have done it, because they were wonderful; the young men, women, who were there said: We don't accept it. Yes, they have all my gratitude" (Vera Simoni).

———◆———

Giulia Spizzichino: *It all began when I was called to [the TV program]* Combat Film.[91] *I didn't know that [under the front credits] they always showed my mother, gaunt, all dressed in black, holding a fainted woman in her arms [at the Fosse Ardeatine]. One day my cousin calls me, he says, "Do you know that every night your mother is on television, and they're asking if anyone knows these people?" I called the program, I said, "That woman is my mother." A week went by, I had forgotten all about it, and then [the host] Demetrio Volcic called me back: "Madam, I'm sending a car, would you like to come to [the studios]?" I got dressed, I went. He takes me into a big room where all the guests were; all the cameras, and me on a chair in the center. He says, "Madam, we're on the air." I was stunned, because I didn't expect it. But it was all so spontaneous, so easy; perhaps, had he told me to get ready, it wouldn't have come out so well.*

(From *Combat Film,* April 1994)

Demetrio Volcic. Ms. Giulia Spizzichino. Who is the woman we just saw?

Giulia Spizzichino. She's my mother. My mother. I had seven relatives who were killed. They had all been taken in my grandfather's house, and they were many. Seven of them were shot together: my grandfather, his sons, and his sons' sons. Three generations, in one blow. The women, with the children, including a fifteen-day-old baby, were deported to Germany, to Auschwitz, and sent to the gas chambers. None of them returned.

Volcic. How many? In just one family?

Spizzichino. In just one family, twenty-nine people.

Volcic. Madam, it was half a century ago. If you wish, you may refuse to answer. [I ask] your opinion on two things: was it wrong on our part to reopen these wounds? [. . .] and, most important—forgive me for asking this question; I ask you to forgive me: have you forgotten?

Spizzichino. No, never.

Volcic. Have you forgiven?

Spizzichino. Never. I neither forgot nor forgave. I'm sorry: never. This pain lives with me, and it will die only when I die. It's such a vivid, such a burning sorrow that I feel as if it were happening now. It's only been a few hours since I lived it. I don't talk of, of revenge; but forgive, no, I can't. My grandfather was, was an exquisite man, he was a sweet, sweet man. And my grandmother was sixty-three years old, she was a woman who was always by my grandfather's side, they never parted, never. And the fifteen-day-old baby, what harm can a fifteen-day-old baby do?

Volcic. What is the guilt . . .

Spizzichino. They were Jews.

Volcic. . . . . of these victims?

Spizzichino. They were Jews. That's all.

One day, I get a call from Argentina, and this person says, "Listen, madam, do you know that the perpetrator, Erich Priebke, lives free in Argentina?" I didn't even know who Erich Priebke was, we always spoke of Kappler. He says, "Would you like to come to Argentina, with a lawyer? Because we're having problems getting him extradited." I say, "All right." Incidentally, I am fluent in

Spanish. I arrive there, I find dozens of cameras, photographers, that meet me at the airport—a press conference, must have been a hundred radio and TV stations. It made a lot of noise: at the university, great intellectuals like Ernesto Sabato, it really made a lot of noise. And I started making the rounds of ministries, embassies, to ask for this person to be extradited. But it was tough.

When I arrived, I found that the building of the Jewish societies had been destroyed. The head of the Jewish Community told me, "Giulia, it's as though I was meeting a sister, because my sister, thirty-five, died there under that bomb." It was frightening, to see that building all, all torn down. And there I made friends with the mothers of the desaparecidos. One night I was supposed to make a speech; however, only a few minutes before I had met a mother who told me that she and her daughter had been arrested together, and they had put a hood on her daughter's head. So the daughter asked her, "Mother, I'm sick to my stomach, would you please get me a pill from inside my bag?." Not knowing anything, the mother took this pill out; she says, "Pass it to me under the hood." It was cyanide; she died in her arms. So when the moment came to speak I said: "I came here to speak of my sorrow, but I can't; I can't speak of my suffering before you." This woman, two of her sons, had been killed. Thrown off a plane with stones on their feet. And it was a very moving moment because I saw many people cry. I said, "All we have left is the hope of justice; I came here to ask for justice, and I hope you get it too."

. . . Umberto Scattoni, Dattilo Sciunnach, Fiorenzo Semini, Giovanni Senesi, Gaetano Sepe, Gerardo Sergi, Benedetto Sermoneta, Sebastiano Silvestri, Simone Simoni, Angelo Sonnino, Gabriele Sonnino, Mosè Sonnino, Pacifico Sonnino, Antonino Spunticchia, Nicola Ugo Stame, Manfredi Talamo . . .

CHAPTER 10

BORN LATER

. . . Mario Tapparelli, Cesare Tedesco, Sergio Terracina, Settimio Testa, Giulio Trentini, Eusebio Troiani, Pietro Troiani, Nino Ugolini, Antonio Ughetti, Otello Valesani, Giovanni Vercillo, Renato Villoresi, Pietro Viotti, Angelo Vivanti, Giacomo Vivanti, Gennaro Vivenzio . . .

> The category of the 'passage of time' seems to promote a peculiar legalistic mentality, whereby the matter is extinguished with the extinction of the direct perpetrators. With the passing away of the culprit, the question also passes into the realm of 'history', losing its other dimension – that of being one of the events that set the standard upon which human things are measured . . . It seems to me that the genocide is a fact before which also the not-guilty and the born after are responsible, that is, are called to interrogate themselves and to respond.
>
> —Stefano Levi Della Torre[1]

Luciano Chiolli. *So after the first Priebke trial we organized this conference and we used a photo exhibit on the Fosse Ardeatine prepared by the ANFIM. There was some kind of a tent, and we filled it with people, there was a big crowd, people from the neighborhood, witnesses, partisans; and this exhibit stayed up for a few days, and we thought it might be used as a teaching tool for the schools. And we brought in almost five hundred boys and girls, from the middle and elementary schools. Some friends and I explained the exhibit and told the history; but it occurred to us that it would have been much more meaningful in the children's minds if they could have listened to some of the witnesses.*

Ms. Ada Pignotti and Giuseppe Bolgia live in the neighborhood. We thought we could use their testimony, and I think it was a very good idea. The children were fascinated: while during the exhibition some were tired or bored, here was, instead, the narrative of these grandparents, a grandmother and a grandfather, a first-person story, Giuseppe who told about himself at thirteen, which was the age of these children, when he was hurled into adulthood, in an immense tragedy in which he loses first his mother in the air raids and then his father and he doesn't know what happened, they summon him in July to recognize a shapeless heap and he, a kid, he has to say these are my father's things, the railroad watch, an address book . . . The children were very impressed.

And most of all I must say they were impressed by Ada's tale, because Ada is a gentle, sweet woman and yet she is firm: in her memory, in her sorrow—with no resentment: hatred never alters her voice, she always has this serene, dramatically serene attitude, and this is something that always impressed me about Ada. And these children, and all the teachers, they all wept when she told of the first months of her marriage, of a marriage that was cut off so soon by the killing of her husband; the despair, the desperate search all over Rome for someone to translate those German words, the breathless agony and then the awareness of the tragedy. This, I think, was an extraordinary historical memory.

1. Movements

Portelli. I'd like you to associate freely with these words: Fosse Ardeatine.

Raffaella Ferraro. Associate? I associate with my father's memories. Because my father chanced, happened to be—his office was across from the place where they were arresting the people who later were massacred, in via Rasella. He remembers perfectly the roar, the noise. He was walking, he was stopped by a colleague, he remembers it as if it were yesterday—"Are you crazy? They're arresting everybody, they're raking in people, get away quick or they'll arrest you, too." He ran, left, and then what happened happened. He and his friends thought it was a terrible reprisal, but that the culprit who had set it off had gotten away. This is a fact, and he's been touched. Because, I mean, he was ten minutes away from death. My father doesn't speak much of all these things.

In 1968, Mario Leporatti, former military commander of Fourth GAP zone, was the principal of the Liceo Virgilio, one of Rome's most prestigious schools. As such, he was the natural target of student protest – until another former *gappista*, Marisa Musu, wrote a two-page newspaper article about him: "Students, you don't know who is Mario Leporatti." "The protest at the Virgilio was cut off, and the student movement always got along with the 'partisan principal.'"[2]

I, too, had a "partisan principal" in the 1970s, at the Facoltà di Lettere (School of Humanities) of the University of Rome: Carlo Salinari. I vaguely knew then that he had led the action in via Rasella, and it didn't seem to fit in with his institutional role and image as the antagonist to our radical unionism and the student protest. But I don't recall ever giving much thought to the matter. It all seemed so far in the past that even the protagonists had other things on their mind.

Marisa Musu. No, not with my children; I never talked about it with my children, but they are an odd generation of children, because they were born in '52, '53, so they went through '68; I think they found out I had been a partisan only when they were eighteen or so. Because after those nine months were over I never gave it another thought. I mean, I had so many other things to do—of course I talked and argued with my children: the student movement, the meetings, the collectives, and then, after I went to Vietnam, Vietnam. But that was the past, and ultimately a past that was never brought up.

At the beginning of the 1960s, the first issue of *Quaderni Piacentini,* one of the ideological and cultural organs of the New Left, announced: "No one is afraid of the Resistance anymore; it is dead, choked to death by ceremonies and official speeches," or even turned into "a prop of the existing order."[3] When the student movement exploded in 1968, the Resistance had no part in its vision and concerns. The old Left, which had its roots in the Resistance, was largely hostile to a movement it didn't understand; and the movement in turn was conditioned by the generational conflict, by its orientation toward the present, and by its internationalist vision. Writing that the protest at the Liceo Virgilio was cut off "thanks" to a partisan principal may be an unfortunate choice of words, but it may also be a symptom of a deeper lack of communication between the heritage of the Resistance and the new youth movements.

In 1968, Marisa Musu wrote, "I sense that I am witnessing an important new development, although I can hardly recognize its quality and relevance. In March, I am present at [the student confrontation with the police at] the battle of Valle Giulia[4] and I have the physical sensation—I, who have been in all the great popular demonstrations, including those in which the police fired and people died – of witnessing a revolution in the making."[5] Other former GAP members thought differently: Carlo Salinari "firmly believed that, although in the years of his youth reality had forced him to make certain radical choices, yet some of the radical demands of the students, of the movement of '68, were a basically petit-bourgeois expression of a generation of young people who have the privilege of going to the university, of being the children of a well-to-do bourgeoisie, and then it's like the springing of a rebellion which is primarily a revolution against the parents . . . (Achille Tartaro). Rosario Bentivegna wrote later that Salinari opposed "the populist and anarcho-individualistic degeneration of '68, which were to some extent the breeding ground of the murderous and counter-revolutionary practice of terrorism."[6]

On April 25, 1969, the anniversary of the insurrection and liberation of the North in 1945, students demonstrated at the official celebration of the Resistance. It was a change: the movement recognized the relevance of the Resistance and, rather than ignoring it, criticized its uses and interpretations. After a Fascist bomb killed fourteen people in a bank in Milan in December of that same year (the first of many terrorist attacks that were to follow, still largely unpunished), the movement realized that the anti-Fascist struggle was not a thing of the past, because the Fascists were still to be reckoned with. So the groups of the New Left sought some kind of relation with this history and with some of the people who represented it. In Rome, many remember Laura Garroni, one of the GAP's explosive experts, who had stayed away from politics for decades, and became active again in the 1970s in a New Left group.

Anna Cortini. Well, at some point my mother joined Avanguardia Operaia [Workers' Vanguard]. So for them she was "the partisan." They would call on her to speak at rallies, [and] she was always a shy person. She even ran in the elections, on the Democrazia Proletaria ticket, and she got a lot of votes, you remember, don't you? I remember when she would say [*in oratorical tones*]: "They've exploited us for twenty years, the Christian Democrats . . ." And everybody clapped their hands, they were all happy and excited, big applause when she came to this fatidic phrase. Mother and I wound up in the cell that did political activity at Atac [the city transport company]. Back then, it meant passing out leaflets at dawn, it meant being there at five A.M. I remember, she who was always a shy person, was sent, in the middle of the night, among these tram drivers, to give out leaflets. And I remember one of them, raging mad—he attacked us, angrily—she who never raised her voice, can you imagine her, at the crack of dawn, in the dark, with these leaflets, arguing with the union delegate, it was atrocious . . . These young people of Avanguardia Operaia loved her. She was beloved; our comrades, young people, too, would ask for her advice and things; she [was] very wise, very—down to earth. She always was a woman with a lot of common sense.

In the mid-1970s, a young man who bore the name of an uncle killed at the Fosse Ardeatine "had to expatriate to France because he was associated with the Red Brigades," a clandestine terrorist group. It's an isolated instance, but it is a token of how difficult it was to grow up in those years with that kind of heritage. A former partisan recalls: "In high school, my son was a leader in the student movement. His thesis was: 'My grandfather was shot, my father was a partisan,' he had to do more. He'd get up at four A.M. and go to a former partisans' club, Rinascita, to take karate lessons so he could fight the *carabinieri* and the police. And yet his nature was very mild; he forced himself, he broke through the barriers; he wasted ten years of his life." Franco Bartolini, former GAP member, joined Avanguardia Operaia, was arrested with his wife and son on charges of terrorism (later dismissed): "Within the—let's call it revolutionary movement, there was an original matrix, the teaching that came from the Resistance, the dream, the utopia of Communism, the true one."

A new slogan took hold in the movement: "The Resistance is red, not Christian Democrat / long live the workers' and partisans' struggle." To many activists, "militant" anti-Fascism meant physical confrontation with the Fascists. The Resistance was seen primarily as a moment in the class struggle and as an antecedent to armed struggle: Stefania Natale recalls a discussion between the Resistance historian and former partisan Claudio Pavone and the jailed members of the Red Brigades, in which the latter insistently sought "some kind of legitimization" of their actions in the precedent of the Resistance. Mario Moretti, a leader of the Red Brigades, claimed that their terrorist acts were comparable to the act of a partisan "who planted half a pound of lead in the belly of a German [. . .] who might have had a wife and five children in Bavaria."[7]

Daniele Pifano. So, this thing, the Resistance, was a true legitimization of the armed struggle that took place in the partisan struggle. In the 1970s, it's not that one legitimized the armed struggle, but anyway, aside from the fact that the armed struggle may be considered a mistake, inadequate, untimely, not corresponding to the goals, yet the spirit that was behind those comrades who acted was a spirit of liberation, a spirit of equality.

The terrorist season in Italy culminated in the 1979 kidnapping and murder of former Prime Minister Aldo Moro by the Red Brigades. It was a turning point that some failed to recognize.

Nicoletta Leoni. We heard about it in school . . . I'll admit it, I was one of those who when the news came hugged one another [to celebrate]. But you see, it wasn't about Moro as a person, it was what he stood for. Moro was a Christian Democrat and at the time we saw the Christian Democrat Party as the bosses. That's the immediate reaction; you know, at fifteen, sixteen, the Red Brigades, how they lived underground, you couldn't put a face on them, there was a fascination of sorts around them . . . Like Zorro, in a way. But then, when he was being held—"After all, what are they trying to do?" And there's always the fact that he was a man, he had a family, children . . . Then, where you look back as a grown-up, it's different . . . So many of those [who are buried]—seventeen, eighteen years old—at the Fosse Ardeatine—often I have wondered: "These kids, how did they . . . all the enthusiasm . . . perhaps they weren't even aware of what they were going up against . . ." There was a war, you were recruited—you just have to grow up. And then, at eighteen, seventeen, we all thought we could change the world; we are still of the generation [for which] the Resistance was a myth . . . in high school, for four years, every day we had the police outside the gate because we were labeled as a red school in a black neighborhood, piazza Cavour, an average of three times a week there was a bomb threat . . . [Yet] even those who were more militant than I was, the worst for them was they might be stopped by the police, arrested–but they couldn't say they'd been taken to via Tasso.

Of course, just as the Resistance may be used in the effort to legitimize terrorism, terrorism can be used to de-legitimize the Resistance—beginning with via Rasella. A Right-wing pamphlet explains that "via Rasella has set the example, the outrage of March 23, 1944 has been taken as a model by the terrorist centrals active in Eastern Europe during the cold war."[8] On the other hand, the Liberal-Socialist philosopher Norberto Bobbio labels the action at via Rasella as a terrorist act because "the choice of the means is not proportional to the end."[9]

A former GAP member takes me by the arm and leads me up via Rasella, proudly describing the action: it was a painstakingly planned attack. The only action that may be compared to it in terms of military perfection is, he says, the Red Brigades' kidnapping of Aldo Moro. "Well, yes. In fact, when Moro was kidnapped, I was quite impressed, it was a perfect action. A perfect action" (Marisa Musu). The parallel, however, is limited to the military aspect. Otherwise, the attitude of the veterans of via Rasella toward both their own experience and more recent forms of political violence demonstrates that there is no necessary connection between extreme forms of struggle and a radical or revolutionary ideology.

The former GAP members, in fact, insist that the context in which they opted for the armed struggle was exceptional and bears no analogy with the contemporary situation. The war, the authoritarian Fascist regime, the Nazi occupation justified—nay imposed—choices that are unjustified in a democratic context, however disappointing it may be. "To me, they [the armed underground groups] seemed less 'erring comrades' than a tragic misunderstanding. I hated them, because they harmed the struggle that was going on, they interrupted a democratic process"(Marisa Musu). "[In 1943] we didn't declare the war, we found ourselves in it. These ones, instead, declared the war themselves. Our violence was a response to a violence—and it wasn't the violence of the multinational corporate state, it was the violence that arrested you and you'd stay in jail for twenty years. Or get shot. Violence to respond to this violence was something else entirely; not the same thing at all" (Valentino Gerratana).

Rosario Bentivegna. The comparison to [Moro's kidnapping] offends me. It makes no sense at all: you can use a gun for self defense, or to commit an armed robbery. And yes, it's the same weapon. But it's one thing to use it in a war against a military unit, taking the risks you were taking, and it's something else to make an action like that in peacetime, against targets who are not especially on guard, and knowing you're not risking your life, either. What we had here was, at best, a bunch of fools; and in some cases a bunch of bloody murderers who used the weapon of reactionary terrorism against a democratic state.

At the top of via Rasella, as one goes down from via Quattro Fontane, on the wall at the right, a graffito reads: "1, 10, 100 via Rasella." On April 25, 1998, the Centri Sociali (alternative youth centers) celebrated the anniversary of liberation from Fascism by staging a march from Porta San Paolo to via Rasella. "We demonstrated in via Rasella when that judge tried to incriminate Bentivegna. We went there as Centri Sociali, to take a stand against this attempt to treat the Resistance as a crime. We made a connection with the liberation of our comrades from the 1970s, political prisoners, and all. It's the same with the partisan struggle: in the end, you realize that all the struggles that go beyond certain canons are considered criminal" (Daniele Pifano).

Though they often claim a link to the memory of the 1970s, the Centri Sociali—the most innovative and popular aggregation of radical youth since the 1990s—have a different attitude toward memory. They are interested in forms of sociability rather than forms of struggle, and they identify less with a political line than with a place—the occupied, self-run space, but also the city around them, in which they often must fight the Fascists for the right to exist and act. The problem is no longer the armed struggle; the problem is the kind of city they have to live in.

Duccio Ellero. In 1993, we opened the Centro Sociale [La Strada], in Garbatella. It's definitely a working class neighborhood, so it has a traditional relation with the Resistance; many of its inhabitants took part in the events of Porta San Paolo, it was raided [by the Nazis] twice. Its geographical position, which is adjacent to the Ardeatine, entailed an involvement with those events—in fact, some of those killed came more or less from that neighborhood, or had relatives in it. As the crow flies, it's less than two hundred meters from Garbatella; the people there had seen the German trucks, and then they could smell the stench, the people of Garbatella were among the first to rush to the place. It is important that our awareness predates the Priebke case; we involved the whole neighborhood on this theme; besides, a number of us were in the university, where there was a lot more going on than today. So it was in the air, and it led us, on the day of the anniversary of the Fosse Ardeatine, in '94, to be a hundred of us there. With banners, and graffiti that you can still read, we asked for justice for the Fosse.

Sibilla Drisaldi. When the Priebke trial began, there was a discussion among the Centri Sociali; there was this interest for the retrieval of memory, and some events and projects about it. Some Centri Sociali began to pay attention to those events, the Resistance, the Fosse Ardeatine. Perhaps also as a response, you may remember, when this boy was killed, they set fire to the [Centro Sociale] Corto Circuito and an immigrant boy died. In that neighborhood, the Centro is the target of aggressions both from the Fascists and from the local pushers, all the local gangsters, who are connected to the Right there. And as a response to that tragic event, the Centro Sociale decided to work on the retrieval of memory as part of anti-Fascist activity in the neighborhood.

Duccio Ellero. A year ago, on April 25 [the anniversary of liberation from Fascism, a national holiday], when there were those demonstrations of Rome's Right wing where they smeared the shrine at the Fosse Ardeatine, they smeared all the plaques at Porta San Paolo, and they took down the signboard of our center and dropped it on the monument we dedicated to all the martyrs of the liberation war. On their way back from the Ardeatine, they went by it and did it.

A student in my department says that "people are still beating each other up" over the "bad ugly story" of the Fosse Ardeatine. Daniele Pifano, an activist of the Centro Sociale Snia Viscosa, has a story about this: "They always thought of the Prenestino [the working-class neighborhood where the Centro is located] as a favorite ground for their Fascist attacks. The people here don't have a Fascist tradition, but [the Fascists] are connected to gambling dens, to petty crime, lowlife, hustlers; plus now, to soccer fans and all that . . . So one of these nights they were hanging posters about the partisan murderers, freedom for Priebke, jail the partisan murderers—in front of the schools. We would regularly clean them out, and so I was tearing one off the wall, as I should. About a dozen of them came out, they surrounded me. . ." They left him bleeding on the ground. The Centro Sociale, the neighborhood association, and the city administration responded with marches, rallies, and motions: "And then we did this nice thing in the square, a concert with the Snia dance school, a public meeting; there were some relatives of the deportees of the Fosse Ardeatine, some partisan comrades, who spoke."

Duccio Ellero. And then the whole Priebke business started. As soon as the first verdict came out, there was a great resentment in Garbatella; people came to us and said: it's disgusting, it's impossible . . . The students, the young people, were mad as hell; they said, Let's get out, let's go, let's break it up, turn the world upside down. And it's not an accident that, out of all the graffiti we made, the ones about the Fosse Ardeatine haven't been touched, they're the only ones that were not erased by the homeowners, by the merchants, the bar owners. As you come out of the Garbatella metro station, you can read on the wall, this big, in huge characters: "Down with Priebke." It's a cultural fact that stands.

2. Fragments

Portelli. If I say Fosse Ardeatine, what does it remind you of?

Emanuele D'Amore: Fosse Ardeatine? It doesn't remind me of anything.

Simone Benedetti. Practically nothing, because it's one of those things that you touch upon a little when you're in school, and then if you don't develop it on your own you forget about it.

Antonio Guidi. As for me, fortunately, it doesn't remind me of anything because I have no relatives who were involved.

A survey conducted on the occasion of the fiftieth anniversary of the Resistance shows that "the reprisal tied to the attack of via Rasella (Fosse Ardeatine)" is the one event of 1943–44 that high school students in Italy remember most: the question about it received 47.7 percent correct answers, slightly more than the execution of Benito Mussolini in Milan.[10] The statistical datum confirms my empirical impression: at the Liceo Manfredi Azzarita, named after one of those killed at the Fosse Ardeatine, about half of the students knew who he was; at the Garrone technical institute, half the class raised their hands when I asked whether they had ever heard of the Fosse Ardeatine or via Rasella.

Daniele Mezzana, who conducted the poll, is probably correct in judging that, although "there is an information gap concerning the Resistance," it could be worse. The problem, of course, as with all quantitative surveys, is what the numerical data actually mean. For instance, the wording of the question, which treats via Rasella and the Fosse Ardeatine as one event, as if one were the inevitable consequence of the other, is somewhat questionable. In addition, we are not told what is considered a "correct" answer: is it enough to have heard that the Fosse Ardeatine was a reprisal for via Rasella, or shouldn't we also inquire into what exactly young people think happened, both in via Rasella and at the Fosse Ardeatine?

Daniela Bruno. There was this attack in that street by the partisans against, I think, the SS. And the partisans, I think two of them, were in disguise, they had dressed as street sweepers and left the bomb there and went away. But beside the SS some of the dead were also—Italians, anyway. And from that Hitler decided to shoot, so to speak, they took ten Italians, for one German . . .

In young people's versions, vagueness prevails. Many have some kind of reminiscence, but hardly any have precise information. On the other hand: why should they know, why should they want to know? It's been half a century ago, ideologies are supposed to be dead, it's no longer living memory and it's not yet history—it has no significant place in the school curriculum: "Well, yes, I may remember something from middle school, from the books, because in the eighth grade we covered World War II. Now I'm in the eleventh grade, we're still studying the fifteenth century; and then, in the thirteenth grade perhaps—we don't study the nineteen hundreds, we get bored to death studying the nineteenth century, the ancient times—and then, the century we're most concerned with, the twentieth century, we hardly cover it" (Gabriele Tomassini).

Rosa Castra. You know some dates, but they are so out of the context of one's own historical reality, you know, that for you the Egyptians are next to the French Revolution, I mean, the dates may be different but as for emotional content . . . So about these Ardeatine I'll say that I'd heard of it in school, but it had never impressed me as a situation, as a real fact. I was much more affected by some documentaries I saw on TV, and some films especially; and much more than that, by the image of the statue when later on we were taken to the Fosse Ardeatine.

All the young people mention their families, school, and television as sources of their information, but I hardly ever heard a specific reference to a specific source—a school text, a family story (except in the case of direct or indirect family involvement), and far less a specific TV program. It is as though they always knew, in the form of unattached fragments floating in the air. The students in the more elite *licei* and in the downtown schools know more than those in the technical and vocational schools and of the periphery, but this is due less to educational differences (children learn of the Fosse Ardeatine, if they do, in middle school, which is the same for all) than to geographical ones. In the periphery and in vocational schools, there is a higher percentage of students whose families migrated to Rome long after the war, so they had less opportunities of absorbing the story through the environment and the urban space. And after all, the older generations do not know or understand much more than they do, and they have fewer excuses.

Historical memory, however, does not necessarily go down in linear form from generation to generation, from parents to children. Memory makes jumps or sidesteps, it skips a generation, from grandparents to grandchildren ("because of course those generations lived through the war and they have memories, they lived it on their own skin, so inevitably they will talk about it," says Pino Lo Vetere); or it moves sideways between different layers of the same generation: Francesca Pica heard about it from an older brother, Antonia Bianchi heard it from an aunt and passed it on to a younger cousin. The horizontal or lateral passage of memory implies a deeper personal involvement, because it represents a break from the de-politicized attitudes transmitted by the parents: "My aunt was great, but now she's dead. She used to explain things when I was little; but in my family it was never passed down because it's a bourgeois family, my grandfather was in the navy, a Fascist, as was the other grandfather " (Antonia Bianchi). On the other hand, the grandparents' tales relegate the events to a faraway, distant sphere; these are stories one hears less because one wants to than because the old folks insist on telling them.

Stefano Cappelli. I learned all the information on the war through my grandmother. My grandmother worked in the Duce's household; she was a seamstress, and a cook, too, and she knew both the Duce's wife and his children. But then she was also engaged to a partisan, who later was shot—I don't know, it's even in the history books.

Portelli. Do you remember his name?

Cappelli. No, I don't remember . . . I read it in the eighth grade. Actually, I don't know where he was executed, because these are stories my grandmother always talks about. He was supposed to be shot; that morning, someone changed the bullets for blanks, the partisans in collaboration with the soldiers; they shot him, and he wasn't killed. But then a German officer shot him in the head. But the name, I don't remember it. About partisans, the only information I have is this, about my grandmother's boyfriend; and then, when they all ran because the Germans made the raid; about via Ardeatina, that's all I know. I know some of her friends died but—I don't really know, but I know he was a big shot because they tried to save him . . .

As we have already seen, young people are as influenced as their elders by the clichés of the anti-partisan commonsense narrative (pro-Resistance clichés are much less common). The very few who gave me the impression of having given the matter some thought or having gathered some information about it are Right-wing adolescents: partly because the Right as a whole has been obsessed with it, and partly because in the 1990s there was a growth of youth political activism on that side. Otherwise, what prevails is a fluctuating memory on the surface of which formulas caught haphazardly out of commonsense float and drift: ten Italians for a German, the extra five, the omnipresent street-sweeper cart— "the famous cart that passed by there with the bomb inside, and they eliminated ten Germans. Ten—which they said later actually was a few more" (Pierluigi Martino); "They had blocked the street with a cart, I don't know, they closed those Germans in, then I don't know, a bomb went off . . ." (Chiara Gaudino)— and the victims' identity: "Most of them were Jews, weren't they?" (Fabio Fortino).

"Fosse Ardeatine—I don't have much of a memory . . . Yes, I did study it in school. The deportation and then the concentration camps, the ovens, *Schindler's List* . . . (Fabio Fortino); "I saw a documentary; plus, I'd heard—yes, in school, too, maybe in the eighth grade; the history teacher talked about it last year. The documentary on TV" (Enrico Bertocci). School, cinema, and television are key sources of information, but they also accentuate the confusion between the Fosse Ardeatine and the extermination camps: in school, the same moral tone is applied to the Fosse Ardeatine, Nazism, genocide; on television, young people are confused by a more casual viewing, under the sign of horror and ambiguity or just routine.

"Yes, I did follow it, but as a person who is bombarded by the media and who, willy-nilly, can't help knowing about Priebke. In the end, it's as though one went over the day's menu: Priebke again, they're still talking about that" (Francesco Bonini). If we consider that often these documentaries and films, including *Schindler's List* (or, for earlier generations, *The Open City*), are viewed in school or under school auspices, the process comes full circle.

Thus young people place at the Fosse Ardeatine generic scenes of cruelty: "There are some images in which you see [Priebke] shooting a woman and a child, they're actually seen, in a documentary" (Silvano Leoni); "A documentary: they were shooting them in the back, they were all in a row next to each other with a ditch beneath them and the Germans, and they were naked, and the Germans from behind shot them in the back—one, two, three, four" (Antonio Guidi). This confusion reinforces the persuasion that all the dead were Jews ("a massacre done by the Nazis toward the Jewish citizens—right now I don't remember the year," Emanuele Lunadei says).

Alessandro C. In the news on TV—yes, only in the news on TV, because I'd say that the Fosse Ardeatine, when I was in middle school, we hardly talked about it. It was more about the concept of war than the Fosse Ardeatine. However, practically all the casualties of the concentration camps, that the Germans I mean built especially for these, let's say, what they called them, Jews. What intrigues me most is, there were also some Italians.

Like many young people who mouth anti-Semitic slogans at soccer games, Alessandro C. has no idea what the word "Jews" means. When I ask him, what religion are they, he replies, "Catholics, of course."

The image of Priebke shooting a woman and a child suggests that images drift in not only from the extermination camps, but also from the scenes of other massacres—Vietnam, Marzabotto, Yugoslavia—in which, as Antonia Bianchi puts it, "persons of all sexes" were killed. "Many eighteen-year-olds who came [to the Fosse Ardeatine] on the twenty-fourth, and I accompanied them inside, believed that there were women, too" (Angelo Pignotti).

I don't think we need to take a horrified view of all this. Lack of memory generates a loss of sense and knowledge, but it also opens up spaces for imagination and elaboration. To the extent that the young people haven't heard about it, they have been spared the wrong narratives and clichés of anti-partisan common sense. This enables them to try to create their own narrative and interpretation out of what they know.

In this sense, perhaps the most fascinating aspect of youth memory is the weakening of the link between the Fosse Ardeatine and via Rasella. As I tried to show, the automatic connection between these two events is one source of the commonsense narrative that explains away the Fosse Ardeatine as the inevitable consequence of an irresponsible partisan action. Now, when—out of ignorance or a different perception, and often both—young people attenuate this automatic sequence of cause and effect, they can look at the Fosse Ardeatine for what they are and endow them with a renewed symbolic power.

To a large extent, of course, the loss of the connection is simply a consequence of a lack of historical information.

Federico Gherardini. I know it's a Nazi reprisal, but I don't know much more, that is I don't know exactly what is the fact to which it refers . . . I don't know what the reprisal was for; I know they took some people at random, three hundred . . . and twenty, I think, or more, and they were killed, but I don't know for what, I only know it was an act of reprisal but I don't know for what.

 Portelli. Have you ever heard of the partisan attack in via Rasella?

 Gherardini. Yes, I heard, but that's all I know.

 Portelli. But isn't there a connection with the business of the Ardeatine?

 Gherardini. I don't know, maybe—since you're asking me this question . . .

Portelli. What about the story that they posted a ban that said if the perpetrators turn themselves in we will not proceed to this reprisal? Is this a story you heard?

 Roberto Bacchiocchi. I have a vague memory . . . it may be a fantasy of mine . . . I mean, I did wonder about it sometimes . . . but I couldn't say for certain.

This missing memory enables its subjects to escape the commonsense narrative that blames the partisans for the Fosse Ardeatine: "I've never heard this one, I don't remember ever hearing anyone say that if they had turned themselves in . . ." (Tommaso Manacorda); "No, I never talked much about this—I talked more of the order, of the execution as such" (Daniele Parrotta).

Making the Fosse Ardeatine an automatic, inevitable consequence of via Rasella is, as we have seen, a way of averting the gaze, of exorcising the massacre or at least attenuating its impact, to rationalize it or explain it away. Thanks to their ignorance and distance, many young people are unable to do this, or they are not interested. Rather than focusing on the circumstances and the causes, then, they can concentrate on the event as such. Even the mistaken association of the Fosse Ardeatine with the extermination camps helps them perceive it as a senseless massacre, imagined in its naked absurdity ("the execution as such"). "I would probably be less interested in getting the facts right in terms of numbers or date; what I would like to pass on instead is the absurdity of such an act, you know? The violence with which it was carried out, the absurdity of a law of war that provides for a given number of person to be killed for each German murdered. And so there were these, this absurd number of people who were killed" (Rosa Castra). "I am more concerned—I said earlier that he was only a boy, Manfredi Azzarita—with the human sense of the situation. Because we know the facts, it is not important to know the number of persons, five more or less—the problem is not the counting error, five – the problem is: persons" (Miriam Mondati).

Matteo Zapparoli. The history, honestly, I don't remember it, I don't remember it too well, honestly. But the name makes me think—I don't know—it makes me think . . . the Fosse Ardeatine . . . I have this image, I'd say, of a big ditch were people are, are dumped—this is what I imagine, I mean—where people are dumped, what do I know, mutilated, massacred . . .

Portelli. Dumped like trash?

Zapparoli. Yes, yes, just like trash, exactly. That is, taken and thrown as if they were, I don't know, sacks of stones or, anyway, things that—you know what I'm thinking? I'm thinking of the annihilation of the value of human life, this is what I'm thinking, that is, man used as thing, as piece, how can I say, as a rag, as . . .

This generation perceives, much more closely than the one before it (but not unlike the one that lived through the war), the possibility of dying suddenly, senselessly, and before one's time. The Fosse Ardeatine are a place in which lives were cut off suddenly, savagely, where people were absurdly massacred and buried together. When asked to make associations with the words "Fosse Ardeatine," many replied "dead people " (Giulia Seller); "death; that is, it makes me think of the image of death" (Daniele Parrotta); "ruins; a parched land" (Romina Cometti); "Nazis," but also "a pyre, something like that" (Nicola Centi).

Alessia Salvatori. I remember that I was taken there; I was rather small, and I was overwhelmed by this fearful image of this sequence of, of graves, I mean. Which seemed, perhaps because I was little, infinite. And I was troubled by the idea of collective death. The concept of death itself, for a child, is a difficult one even when it's single; to see it like that, collective, endless—I remember this expanse, that had overwhelmed me. And from there, one asks: why? And then you connect it to Auschwitz, to the concept of death of the Jews, the concentration camps . . . If I were to go now I'd probably take it differently, because one may have a historical judgment, even harsher; but experiencing it as a child left me with a greater sense of pain inside.

This elaboration culminates in the experience of class trips to the Fosse Ardeatine and via Tasso. Even when the visit is carefully prepared for by the teachers, the fact that it is a break from classroom routine, together with the visual and tactile impact of the place, accentuates the emotional and symbolic mode of perception. Via Tasso "is the first contact I had, directly, with Fascism and Nazism. And it struck me because I didn't think they could reach such a cruelty" (Marzia Santilli).

Tommaso Manacorda. From that visit [to via Tasso], I remember a solitary cell on the walls of which various kinds of phrases had been carved, from the patriotic to the loving, from the sentimental to the political; and I was impressed with the idea that they were in the dark and wrote with their fingernails or the few other things they could get hold of.

Irene Sirchia. When we went [to the Fosse Ardeatine], for me it was quite a blow anyway, because I went in and I saw the burial stones and only later did I realize they were double, so it really was a blow. What shocked me was that, when I went upstairs where there are some documents, newspapers, many of my classmates were in a total couldn't-care-less mood, and some even went out for something to drink. It really was quite a blow, because I was shaken, because of course [I had heard] the stories at home and from my teacher, who is an intelligent person and was really upset when some of my classmates didn't give a damn.

Michele Manacorda. But something that really impressed me was in elementary school when we were taken to the Fosse Ardeatine. I'm afraid I can't tell you how old I was, I guess I must have been eight or nine, I was in the third or fourth grade. They took us to the Fosse Ardeatine, and the recollection is confused. It was a very peculiar mood, as only rarely can happen among children because, this I remember perfectly, I was psychologically divided between the childish enjoyment of the trip, because alas there is this, too, and instead this sense you felt of oppression, of horror consummated among those white columns, if I remember right. And then of course this, the sense of transgression in that you were feeling uninvolved, laughing in the face of such an event, this struck me. Thinking about it now, which I haven't done in years, it strikes me still. Anyway, I don't think we could have fully grasped—because after all, for a child, ten dead, a thousand dead, ten thousand dead are almost the same. I know I acquired the idea that I was going to die when my grandfather died and I was eight. It's a different idea of death, because the dead of the Fosse Ardeatine for me were, until I turned at least eleven, twelve, like the dead in a movie, not people.

Here, too, then, memory is divided within, between the spirit of play of the school trip and the impact of the place. I, too, have seen young visitors who were visibly moved, as well as class groups on a trip who came in, snapped pictures, and left showing as much emotion as if they had just visited the Coliseum. Rosetta Stame, who has often led school visits to the Fosse, recalls both lively and attentive participation, and occasional conflicts with Right-wing students. Stefania Natale, a history teacher who has often taken her students there, says that the power of the place affects them deeply on the emotional level, independent of ideological alignments.

Vanda Perretta. Two years ago I took a class, the students from a course I had taught on lyrical poetry in Germany after the genocide, after the Final Solution. Next to the book with the names, I had someone read aloud Paul Celan's "Death Fugue." An experience that left its mark on me, and on them. And there was this young girl who had brought a bunch of flowers—the women, the girls had all brought flowers—because she had a distant uncle who was one of the *carabinieri* killed at the Fosse Ardeatine. By the side of this *carabiniere* was the grave of an unknown, with no flowers on it. So the girl first laid the flowers on her uncle; then she looked to the side; then she looked at me. And then she took the flowers, left some with her uncle, and went around laying flowers on all the graves on the unknowns.

3.Epilogue: La Storta

June 4, 1988, at the Giustiniana, the North end of Rome. A commemoration is taking place before the stone with the names of fourteen prisoners killed by the SS as they withdrew from Rome on the last day of the occupation. They were shot in cold blood. There had been no partisan attack.

At the bottom of the narrow, winding path that leads to the place where the massacre was perpetrated, the official speech is delivered by the district president, Marco Daniele Clarke, of Alleanza Nazionale: ironically, the memory of these anti-Fascist "martyrs of freedom" is retold by the heirs of their enemies. Clarke and the other official speakers praise the victims who "sacrificed" their lives for a "national ideal" (one was Polish, one was British); no one mentions who killed them, how, and why, and that they did not choose to die. The word "Resistance" in uttered once, by an army general who commemorates Pietro Dodi, army officer, world-famous horseman, and member of the Resistance. Only when Carlo Castellani, a victim's son, and the Socialist partisan Riccardo Mancini gets up to speak, will the schoolchildren brought along by the nuns hear a less generic narrative about what happened.

Filadelfo Fetoni. I was coming down from this farmhouse, up above here, at the Giustinianella, carrying my parents' lunch, who were working directly opposite to where they killed them, off via Labranca. They had placed six or seven armed Germans around the place, overseeing the area, [so] that nobody should come near. He says, "Where are you going? Show me what you have in there!" I raised the lid. There was some pasta, homemade, that I was carrying down; I gave him a plateful. "But now you have to stay here and don't move." I was seventeen or so.

I saw when they took then down; they came calmly, one along the other. They made them come down from this sheepfold, it was called, where they stabled the cattle. They had kept them in there two or three days. I guess they must have been thirsty; they promised they would take them out to drink. There was a fountain down there, where the water was very cool; and they, you know, they'd been locked in this sheepfold for three days, it was hot . . .

They came down, they took them where those trees are, and then they lined them up. And as soon as they were lined up they began to shoot them with their machine guns, and they all fell. Then I saw an officer who picked one up by the hair, lifted it and finished him. To make sure they were dead. And then they left.

It'd been two days, no one knew that they were there; so I walked up that street, a country lane, and stopped a jeep with American officers. I say, "Look, they shot fourteen people—the heat, the flies, everything, they're not animals." An hour later or less, there was a truck, one of those American trucks, a Bedford, with a big sheet; they loaded them up, and took them away.

The making of this book began at the commemorative stone for these men. Therefore, these final pages are made of associations—not arbitrary, I hope, but very personal—generated by the way in which all these stories entered my life. I live directly opposite that stone; but, as one always does, I would walk or drive by it without noticing: "It's such an everyday thing, such an ordinary mental association—I mean, I come home, I see the wreath, the names . . . But by now it travels in the subconscious, really, I no longer have to pay attention to it" (Francesco Bonini). It took the Fascists to draw my attention to the monument. It was August 1994; I had just returned from a conference on Nazi massacres in Arezzo, the Right had risen to power, and the papers reported the controversy over Priebke's extradition. One morning, I saw on the stone a sign of the times: a painted black swastika.

Carlo Castellani. They left their signature. They thought they were desecrating the stone, all they did was sign their name: "We did it." It's obscene, it's horrendous. Out at Porta San Paolo, every once in a while they burn the wreaths on the plaques; they smear shit on [Teresa] Gullace's plaque . . . It's unworthy also of those who are our adversaries: messing around with the dead . . .

The Giustiniana, at the crossing between two ancient and highly historic Roman roads, via Trionfale and via Cassia, had always seemed to me (and in fact it is) a bedroom community—a place possessed of no significant identity or social life. But the day after the swastika appeared, as I shyly went to lay some flowers under the stone, I found people around it. They weren't young; they looked like artisans, mechanics, people of the periphery. They were discussing the best technical means to clean it up. And I felt that perhaps, even underneath bourgeois neighborhoods spread on top of old *borgate* and former countryside, there may still be lodes of memory.

Bruno Alfonsi. During the Germans' retreat, right at the crossroads of Cassia and Trionfale, during an air raid, the American planes, a bomb fell right in the middle of the crossroads. And it made a big hole. And there were some trucks that had come in from Viterbo, with a load of fruits, whatever, goods to sell. And the Germans, to hurry up the retreat, they loaded them up with all that was left, even human material, so to speak, they loaded it all on those trucks, with the drivers inside, and buried them. And this is the truth; at the Giustinianella, when they were digging for the sewers, they found remains of German soldiers. If you dig under there, you'll probably find some remains of human bodies, too.

It's a fascinating archeology: trucks, cannon, soldiers in arms buried under this crossing of roads heavy with history, like ancient warriors in chariots. In 1996, the whole neighborhood had to be evacuated: between via Cassia and the farm land at the end of via Maurizio Giglio (named after a man killed at the Fosse Ardeatine), the fire service unearthed a huge, unexploded bomb.

Angelo Capecci. Our house here was destroyed [on September 8, 1944], it was hit by cannon fire. The [Italian grenadiers] fired one way, the Germans fired the other, and a shell, a cannonball, burst and blew up everything, our house here was destroyed. Fortunately it was empty, because during the air raids we had all gone into hiding down to certain caves beneath Isola Farnese, near Veium, and all had repaired there, repaired to these caves.

Vanda Ravone. At La Storta, near the fork for Isola Farnese, we had our house and there were some caves, and we all slept and did everything in them. Raids every day, the

Americans, bomber planes, on the railroad and on via Cassia; there was this fog, all these fires, great black columns of smoke you could see toward Olgiata, toward La Storta, where they had set fire—as they turned back, you could hear them leave, screaming, and we huddled there, scared. There wasn't anything here, there was this fountain down in the glen, isolated, there may have been a few houses—and people had heard these shots, they'd seen this truck go down, taking these people, and these shots; they said, "They've killed," they said, "they've killed some Italians."

There were other invisible monuments on my street, which I never noticed until I began to look. The stone dedicated to the victims of La Storta is planted between two other, much less evident signs of death. About a hundred meters north, a small stone cemented to a wall just above the sidewalk bears a cross with a Polish name and a date: "Piotr Warcholzt 93.03.13": he was killed by a car as he came out of a bar where unemployed and underemployed immigrant work-ers gather. In the opposite direction, fifty meters below the stone, a few inches above the ground, I discover an American football, cut in half, tied with twine to the wire net, next to a plastic Coca-Cola bottle, also cut in the middle, with some wilted flowers in it. "That's where this boy got killed; his name was D. He died in a car accident, he was in my school, he played the guitar, we actually played with him in concert once. I go by often, and I was glad to see that the years went by and the flowers were still there, they still brought him gifts" (Francesco Bonini).

Riccardo Mancini. When the war was over, the Italian Socialist Party of Proletarian Unity—that was its name then—I worked in its office, they sent me to investigate the massacre at La Storta. I was twenty. So I came out here, and there was a farmhouse up there, the farmer's name was Virgili. His wife was there, an elderly woman. "Madam, can you tell me what happened?" "Well," she says, "I surely can. These young people, the Germans turned them over to me, and they made me put them where we kept the cows, in the shed. I gave them some milk, because they were hungry, they came from via Tasso." Here at the fourteenth kilometer of via Cassia, the truck broke down; so, they took them to this farmhouse. They didn't know what to do with them. In the morning, a German on a motorcycle came: "What must we do with these prisoners?" "Kill them." In the morning they took them out, brought them here, and shot them.

Via Cassia, from La Storta to Rome, is studded with signs of death. At the crossroads with via Braccianese, a wire crucifix is twined to the guard rail. At the end of the *borgata,* toward Rome, an elaborate marble stone, with a crossed P and X and containers for flowers, bears the pictures and names of a boy and a girl on a scroll-shaped stone: "In memory. Their friends." There used to be two more, in memory of young people killed in accidents, between there and where I live; Filadelfo Fetoni says they seemed too morbid and persuaded the families to remove them. Where via Cassia crosses the Circle Road, there stands a small rectangular pen with a rail of tree branches; inside, are vases and flowers.

Just behind the stone of the victims at La Storta is the farmhouse where the Capecci family lived; two of the sons, Mario and Alfredo, would die at Forte Bravetta and the Fosse Ardeatine. Across the street, Mario Capecci was attacked by Fascists in 1926: "He was badly hit and left in a gutter, bleeding, on the day [the Socialist member of Parliament, Giacomo] Matteotti was murdered [by Fascists] . . He was run over by the car of those criminals who were escaping after killing, stabbing Giacomo Matteotti, our comrade . . . And he had retained that faith, Socialism, he admired that man who had died like that" (Angelo Capecci).

Anciently, along via Cassia beyond the city walls, as on all main Roman roads, stood the graves of illustrious men. One of them is still visible, the burial monument of a man named Vibo Mariano, who lived and died in the second century AD; from it, the *borgata* derives its mythic name – Tomba di Nerone, Nero's Tomb. Across the street, a monument to the war dead—"To the glorious fallen of all wars"—and a wreath presented by the city, and black neo-Fascist graffiti on the sides of the fountain. Further up the road, is via Gradoli, where Aldo Moro was held prisoner by the Red Brigades. "We gave our lives," "glorious fallen" . . . The institutions of public death celebrate martyrs and heroes; they assign a meaning after the fact to these deaths—freedom, patriotism—as if to tell us that one does not die in vain, that dying is important (which is why the Roman grave must belong to a famous emperor, not an unknown). The new "monuments," however, bear the unobtrusive marks of young people ("the encounter of adolescents with the actual brevity, fragility of life," says Tommaso Manacorda) or outcasts (the Polish immigrant, the two Latin American women I saw climbing the guard rail next to a dangerous curve to leave some flowers on the site of an accident). They memorialize not public deaths, but the private grief of friends, family, and peers.

Marco Daniele Clarke. At the lower end of via Labranca, the bottom, unfortunately in a lamentable state, unfenced, barely lit, is the park of the martyrs of La Storta. There is another, bigger stone and trees, a number of trees. On each tree is a small plate with the name of one of the fallen, one of the fourteen martyrs of La Storta. The plates are new. The old ones were picked up off the ground; they had fallen off the trees, from the weather, the rains. And they were placed in a case that is kept in the district offices.

Carla Capponi. Listen, in Monterotondo [just North East of Rome] there's the story of [a partisan] who was captured, and he was shot beneath a cherry tree. Gold medal, because he was tortured. I go to commemorate him two years later, and this tree had bloomed again. And I told the mayor, don't let anyone touch it, this is a monument. He died, but the tree lives out of his blood. For a few years it was all right, it grew to be a fine tree. Then there comes a modernist mayor, who tears it all down, concrete, destroys the cherry tree and replaces it with a platform, sort of a little altar . . . Look, I was so mad—I said, "Don't ask me anymore, I'm not coming back here." While in Tuscany I saw a beautiful thing, I don't remember the name of the village; they had planted a cypress for each shot partisan, with a plate for each name. I suggested that they do the same here, too, for La Storta. They have the plate with the name on the tree; there were as many cypress trees as the dead of La Storta, and each cypress bore a name.

The trees are a symbol of life, but they are also the obstacle against which a number of adolescents crash to their death. A couple of miles south of La Storta, on the right side of the road, white chrysanthemums inside a ragged pottery vase are tied with green tape to a tree. A late evening in July, 1998 toward midnight, I saw a sad group of boys and girls laying the first flowers around another tree: it had just happened. The next day, there were notes, class pictures, the fragments of the scooter; for weeks, kids on scooters stood by the tree, watching. "He died on the tree. A driver fell asleep in his car, and hit this boy on the scooter" (Antonio Neri).

Francesco Bonini. About this business, to tell you the truth, I don't know much; I do know that here on the street [via Labranca] where I live some men, partisans I think, were shot, and the place was chosen as a last resort, or accidentally, this is the vague recollection I have of the massacre at La Storta. The only thing I remember about the place is that it was mythologized somewhat, because it was the darkest corner on the street, so "don't go there because there is the big bad wolf." There's total indifference throughout the year, and then when June 4 comes around the city workers come to clean it all up and make it nicer for the politicians on duty to go in.

On another crossroads, a few inches above the sidewalk in front of a supermarket, a bunch of flowers fills a pottery vase. "Her name was B., I hardly knew her but she was a kind of myth, this girl, because she was especially beautiful and she was famous because though she was so beautiful she was modest, very quiet, very unassuming. And this girl died in this atrocious manner, I heard many many stories, also from those who were in the car behind her, who saw her lose control, honked to try to awaken her, she ended up against a post. Sure, B.'s flowers, I looked at them often" (Michele Manacorda).

When I began to notice these signs I gained a better understanding of the symbolic function of the Fosse Ardeatine in so many young people's narratives—and it was from thinking about the Fosse Ardeatine that I gained a better understanding of the road I live on. And the adolescents' tales helped me to discern a hard essence in the partisan experience, beyond the courage, beyond the danger, beyond the ideas and the values: the constant confrontation with death.

Lucia Ottobrini. I went through a moment of—not depression, something worse, when my son died. A car going the wrong way in the Tunnel; he was on his motorbike . . . [They tried] to console me, and I began to talk, to talk, to talk . . . I remember that I must have talked for hours—and, funny, I talked about the Resistance. I don't know why I started talking about it, it was a weakness—because I thought of my son: why did you die? They killed him in the street, my son—and I ask: how can that be?

Between the war and the present generation there was a gap in the visibility of death. The children led by the hand to the Fosse Ardeatine, the children who played out there, in view of the coffins, were the last attempt of traditional culture to "domesticate" death by familiarizing it. As Philippe Ariès writes, "Until the eighteenth century, there is no image of a person in agony without at least one child in the room. To think of how carefully, today, we keep children away from death!"[11] Since the war, urban and bourgeois death has become the rule, invisible and unmentionable; there is no contact between life and death, death is unbearable, "savage," and the dead must be hidden away, especially from the children—it's none of their business, anyway. But then slowly, gradually, death did came closer and closer to them—and it was the death of peers, young people just like them, in circumstances and spaces they share ("personally, I had four . . . ," Francesco Bonini says) Nearly always it was sudden and violent: not the end of a long process, an illness; not in a hospital or at home, but in the street, at school, from accidents, from drugs, from suicide: "I don't think any of my friends died from illness" (Michele Manacorda). A rent in space and in time. And the young people had to find their own ways to "domesticate" this death, and they had to do it by themselves, with no adults to lead them by the hand. In the "city without places" and without memory, they began to mark places and memories.[12]

Raffaella Ferraro. Am I obsessed with [the death of] Marta Russo? I remember an ugly line from a lady professor from this department who said in class, "I hope it wasn't one of you." When I walk by there, it hurts me; there is this very simple identification—it could be me. I hardly ever go by where Marta Russo was killed, I stay clear of it, it's a sort of exorcism, perhaps.

Marta Russo, a law student, was killed on the main university campus by a shot fired from a window of the Law school. An assistant professor was playing with a gun and, according to the court's verdict, hit her accidentally.

Stefano Portelli. I was out there, talking, on the steps of the Humanities School. I heard no shots or anything, but the news got around, and we went, we absolutely had to go and see what was going on. Then of course I make a bit of a myth out of these things, so now I remember that the light changed on me, understand? That the sky actually went white, understand? That everyone around me was hallucinating—the image I have now is that when I heard about this the world changed—and—nothing, we couldn't just stand there and do nothing.

I don't know, but it happened an ocean of times that people died on me—people I knew, people who were doing more or less the same things I was doing—you know very well what record [my school] had, so—it happens again, it weighs you down, I don't know, each time I feel as if the world had stopped, or ought to stop, understand? I mean one finally begins to think that one of your friends may die any moment, one of the people near you—not only accidents: suicide, too! I mean—what do you know? I mean, it's so absurd, every time, that you feel that—anything is possible, understand? And when things go back to normal, you say, how can things go back to running normally again now that this person has died, understand?

A boy calls the flowers and the little plaques on the street "mausoleums," a word often used for the Fosse Ardeatine. Another young man, who helped me transcribe some of the interviews, says: "The relatives of those who were killed there speak of the Fosse Ardeatine as a place, serenely; but when we think about it, the thought hits you in the stomach, it cuts off your breath." Now that the relation with history, context, causation, and biographies has grown weaker, it seems to me that many young people see or think of the Fosse Ardeatine as a formalized and magnified expression of a mass death as unjust and absurd as the death of their peers ("*unjustly* torn from us," says a note left on the death site of Marta Russo). It is, perhaps, a de-historicized death, and therefore a powerfully symbolic one. Words and images return: "absurd," the dead thrown like garbage, and the difficulty sometimes of distinguishing the tiny plaques, the wilted flowers, the broken vases from the trash on the side of the road.

I recognized that La Storta contains the answer to many of the questions and controversies that haunt the memory of the Fosse Ardeatine. There was no "illegitimate act of war," no "cowardly partisan ambush," but the massacre took place (and stories are made up to blame the partisans here, too). A boy tells me of his contemporaries killed in road accidents, "It doesn't make sense to remember them for the only stupid thing they did in their lives": an expression of internalized guilt, but also a refusal to rationalize deaths that have no reason and no "glory" (the son of a victim of the Ardeatine said the same thing about his father: "it was a stupid death." And Vera Simoni calls "useless, stupid" his brother's death at the battle of El Alamein in World War II. Not because these loved ones were "stupid"; but because one should not die that way). I heard no adolescent try to rationalize these deaths, looking for something or someone to blame, a collective responsibility, as my generation might have done.[13] No, they died singly, one by one, and like the dead at La Storta and at the Fosse Ardeatine and in the war, they died suddenly, in the wrong place, unjustly. This is true for the "innocents" and the "victims" but also for the "martyrs" and the "heroes": even their proud and conscious dying retains an inassimilable residue of senselessness, better expressed and celebrated in the private and invisible signs of the young than in the public monuments. But then, one can also go to the Fosse Ardeatine also by oneself, alone.

Modesto De Angelis. *I felt ill at ease [in ceremonies], even though one could just be anonymous, in the crowd; I wouldn't go and stand on the stage, where they make a space for the relatives, and somebody could point me out, "He's a victim's son." Yet those empty words, those words sounded so tired. And so it happened once and I always continued that way—that I went on a spring morning, at nine, when it was just opening, and the place is empty. Now you have seen the shrine has that stone [over the graves], slightly relieved at the edge. In spring, sometimes a little bird sits there and twitters. Sometimes I went; a prayer, I spoke—softly, even though there was no one around— to those dead who I always called my boys. And if there is a regret, in all these years, is that I never was able to go one day and tell them, firmly—"Well, we made it—you made it."*

. . . Guido Volponi, Paul Wald Pesach, Schra Wald, Carlo Zaccagnini, Ilario Zambelli, Alessandro Zarfati, Raffaele Zicconi, Augusto Zironi, unknown, unknown, unknown, unknown, unknown, unknown, unknown, unknown, unknown, unknown, unknown . . .

NOTES

1 Introduction

1. Egidio Cristini, "Il massacro dei trecentoventi," recorded in Rome in 1957 by Roberto Leydi, in the CD *Avanti Popolo—6—Fischia il vento,* Istituto Ernesto de Martino—Hobby&Work, 1998. Egidio Cristini was a construction worker and an improviser in the folk poetical tradition of the *ottava rima,* the eight-line stanza also used by Renaissance poets like Ludovico Ariosto and Torquato Tasso.

2. There never was any such thing as a "Badoglio-Communist." General Pietro Badoglio was prime minister in the king's government after Mussolini's overthrow and the removal of the king and his cabinet to Brindisi, in Southern Italy; the members of the military who stayed behind and were active in the Resistance were called "badogliani." They were monarchists, conservatives and anti-Communists.

3. The Fosse Ardeatine (or Cave Ardeatine as they were then known) were abandoned caves of *pozzolana* (a "finely divided siliceous or siliceous and aluminous material that reacts chemically with slaked lime at ordinary temperature and in the presence of moisture to form a strong hardening cement," *Webster's College Dictionary*). It was used for the making of cement and concrete during the construction boom of the 1880s in Rome.

4. Carlo Galante Garrone, "Via Rasella davanti ai giudici," in *Priebke e il massacro delle Ardeatine,* Istituto Romano per la Storia d'Italia dal Fascismo alla Resistenza, supplement to *l'Unità,* August 1996.

5. Leonardo Paggi, ed., *Storia e memoria di un massacro ordinario,* Rome, Manifestolibri, 1996; Giovanni Contini, *La memoria divisa,* Milan, Rizzoli, 1996; Paolo Pezzino, *Anatomia di un massacro,* Bologne, Il Mulino, 1997.

6. The "anniversary" is March 23, commemorating the foundation of the Fasci di combattimento, from which the Fascist Party developed.

7. Vittorio Foa, "Introduzione" to Mario Avagliano, *Il partigiano Tevere. Il generale Sabato Martelli Castaldi dalle vie dell'aria alle Fosse Ardeatine,* Cava dei Tirreni, Avagliano, 1996, p. 7.

8. Claudio Pavone, *Una guerra civile. Saggio sulla moralità nella Resistenza,* Turin, Bollati Boringhieri, 1991.

9. See http://www.nerone.cc/nerone/archivio/arch19.htm. Sergio Gaggia and Paul Gwynne, "The Anniversary of the Fosse Ardeatine—24 March," March 1996. Copyright © Nerone, *The Insider's Guide to Rome.*

10. Bruce Jackson, "What People Like Us Are Saying," in Disorderly Conduct, Urbana and Chicago, University of Illinois Press, 1992, p. 243.

11. Maxine Hong Kingston, *The Woman Warrior* (1975), Vintage, New York, 1989, p. 53.

12. Washington Irving, *Diedrich Knickerbocker's A History of New York,* Putman, New York, 1963, p. 118.

2 Places and Times

1. Amos Oz, "Il Big Bang di ogni storia," *la Repubblica,* December 3, 1997, p. 40.
2. Erich Priebke, affidavit to Rome military tribunal, June 3, 1966.
3. Federica Barozzi, "I percorsi della sopravvivenza (8 settembre 1943—4 giugno 1944). Gli aiuti agli ebrei romani nella memoria di salvatori e salvati," dissertation, University of Rome "La Sapienza," Dipartimento di Studi Storici, 1995–96, p. viii.
4. Giuliano Friz, *La popolazione di Roma dal 1770 al 1900,* Archivio economico dell'unificazione italiana, s. II, vol. XIX, 1974, pp. 133–34; Italo Insolera, *Roma moderna,* Turin, Einaudi, ninth edition, 1993, pp. 63.
5. Sergio Torsello, "A Roma un giorno di primavera," *Apulia. Rassegna trimestrale della Banca Popolare Pugliese,* 4, December 1996, pp. 141–47.
6. I. Insolera, *Roma moderna,* 62.
7. Carlo Pisacane, the radical patriot killed in a failed insurrectionary expedition to Sapri, south of Salerno, in 1856. The underground partisan unit of which Bentivegna was a member during the Resistance was named after him. The 1856 insurrection in Palermo, for which Francesco Bentivegna was sentenced to death, was supposed to support the Pisacane expedition. Bentivegna's maternal great-grandfather was also executed for his part in the Palermo insurrection of 1830.
8. G. Giordano, "Condizioni topografiche e fisiche di Roma e Campagna romana," in Ministero di Agricoltura, Industria e Commercio. Direzione della Statistica Generale, *Monografia della Città di Roma e della Campagna Romana,* 1881, p. xxxi.
9. Alberto Caracciolo, *Roma capitale. Dal Risorgimento alla crisi dello Stato liberale,* Turin, Einaudi, third edition,1984, pp. 190.
10. A pamphlet for the fiftieth anniversary of the Rome Crafts Union (Nov. 17, 1996), lists forty-four crafts workers killed at the Fosse Ardeatine.
11. Ugo Pesci, *I primi anni di Roma capitale* (Florence 1907), quoted. in A. Caracciolo, *Roma capitale,* pp. 66–67.
12. Pietro Ingrao, "I nostri martiri alle Ardeatine," speech given at Terlizzi, March 24, 1968, in Antonio Lisi, *L'altro martire di Terlizzi. Gioacchino Gesmundo,* Terlizzi, Associazione Turistica Pro Loco, 1993, p. 22.
13. Rosario Bentivegna, *Achtung Banditen! Roma 1944,* Milan, Mursia, 1983, pp. 92–93.
14. A. Caracciolo, *Roma capitale,* p. 64.
15. *24 Marzo 1944. I caduti del Partito d'Azione,* Rome, 1945, "Et Ultra," p. 13.
16. Gianni [Ricci], "Azioni del Partito d'Azione," *Mercurio,* I, 4, 1944, p. 259; Francesco Motto, "Gli sfollati e i rifugiati nelle catacombe di S. Callisto durante l'occupazione nazifascista di Roma. I salesiani e la scoperta delle Fosse Ardeatine," *Ricerche Storiche Salesiane,* 24, XIII, 1 (January–June1994), pp. 77–142.
17. Ada Alessandrini, "Carlo Zaccagnini e Monsignor Pappagallo," *Mercurio,* I, 4, 1944, pp. 185–88.
18. I. Insolera, *Roma moderna,* p. 106.
19. On the Resistance in the Roman Hills, see Pino Levi Cavaglione, *Guerriglia nei Castelli Romani,* Florence, Nuova Italia, 1971.
20. Salvatore Capogrossi, *Storia di antagonismo e resistenza,* Rome, Odradek, 1997, p. 4.
21. Lidia Piccioni, *I Castelli Romani,* Bari, Laterza, 1993, p. 9.
22. *"Cencio" (Vincenzo Baldazzi) combattente per la libertà,* ed. Giovanni Ferro, Rome, Fondazione Cesira Fiori, 1985.
23. *I caduti del Partito d'Azione,* p. 20.

24. I. Insolera, *Roma moderna,* pp. 67–68.

3 Twenty Years: Fascism and Its Discontents

1. Lidia Piccioni, *San Lorenzo. Un quartiere romano durante il fascismo,* Rome, Storia e Letteratura, 1984, p. 40.
2. E. Talamo, *La casa moderna nell'opera dell'Istituto romano dei beni stabili* (1910), quoted in L. Piccioni, *San Lorenzo,* p. 19.
3. L. Piccioni, *San Lorenzo,* pp. 27–37, quoting local anti-Fascists.
4. Vincenzo Baldazzi, quoted in L. Piccioni, *San Lorenzo,* p. 31.
5. Montage of two interviews, recorded by Claudio Del Bello, October 11, 1996 and Alessandro Portelli, December 8, 1997.
6. "Aldo Eluisi. Martire delle Fosse Ardeatine," unpublished paper courtesy of his brother Bruno Eluisi; Vincenzo Baldazzi, "Prova generale della marcia su Roma," in *Il prezzo della libertà,* published by ANPI (National Partisan Association), Rome, 1958, pp. 45–46.
7. Circolo Gianni Bosio, *I Giorni Cantati,* Milan, Mazzotta, 1978, pp. 49–50.
8. Paola Bertelli, "Valle dell'inferno. Fine di un borgo operaio," *I Giorni Cantati* I, 2 (Spring 1987), pp. 16–18.
9. Maria I. Macioti, *La disgregazione di una comunità urbana. Il caso di Valle Aurelia a Roma,* Siares, Studi e Ricerche, Rome, 1988; Roberto Cipriani et al., *La comunità fittizia. Differenziazione e integrazione nella borgata romana di Valle Aurelia,* Rome, La Goliardica, 1988.
10. Italo Insolera, *Roma moderna,* Turin, Einaudi, 1993, p. 71.
11. Cesare De Simone, *Roma città prigioniera,* Milan, Mursia, 1994, p. 211.
12. De Simone, *Roma città prigioniera,* pp. 212–13; Luca Canali, *In memoria senza più odio,* Florence, Ponte alle Grazie, 1995, pp. 103–13, 152–61; Annamaria Greci, "Uno dei 335. Umberto Scattoni," *Il contemporaneo* 73, (June 1964), pp. 79–85.
13. R. Bentivegna, *Achtung Banditen!,* Milan, Mursia, 1981, pp. 48–49.
14. Maria Lea Cavarra, "Presentazione," in Enrica Filippini Lera and M. L. Cavarra, *. . . i fiori di lillà quel giorno . . ." una storia piccola,* Rome, Nuovagrafica, 1995, p. 17.
15. Carlo Lizzani, quoted in C. De Simone, *Roma città prigioniera,* p. 183.
16. Marisa Musu, *La ragazza di via Orazio,* Milan, Mursia, 1997, p. 30.
17. Giaime Pintor, *Doppio Diario,* Turin, Einaudi, 1945, letter of November 28, 1943.
18. M. Musu, *La ragazza di via Orazio,* p. 39.
19. Italo Insolera, *Roma moderna,* p. 107; Giovanni Berlinguer and Piero Della Seta, *Borgate di Roma,* Rome, Editori Riuniti, 1976, pp. 163–65.
20. Quoted in Aldo Tozzetti, *La casa e non solo. Lotte popolari a Roma dal dopoguerra ad oggi,* Rome, Editori Riuniti, 1989, pp. 8, 9.
21. Quoted in A. Tozzetti, *La casa e non solo,* p. 8.
22. *Montesacro Valmelaina 1943–1944,* ed. Antonio D'Ettorre et al., Rome, Circolo Culturale Montesacro, 1997, p. 20.
23. Anna Balzarro, "Il rastrellamento del quartiere Quadraro in Roma," in Nicola Gallerano, ed., *La resistenza fra storia e memoria,* Milan, Franco Angeli, 1999; Eitel Friedrich Möllhausen, *La carta perdente. Memorie diplomatiche. 25 luglio 1943—2 maggio 1944,* Roma, Sestante, 1948, pp. 148–49; C. De Simone, *Roma città prigioniera,* pp. 141–49.
24. Roberto Gremmo, *I partigiani di Bandiera Rossa,* Biella, Elf, 1996, p. 178. Gigliozzi is listed as a member of the Socialist underground in the form filled by his wife for the files of the victims' families association.

4 Acts of War

1. Fausto Coen, *Italiani ed ebrei: come eravamo. Le leggi razziali del 1938,* Genoa, Marietti, 1988; Susanna Nirenstein, "I cattivi ragazzi di Salò," *La Repubblica,* August 13, 1998;

Paolo Ferrari and Mimmo Franzinelli, "A scuola di razzismo. Il corso allievi ufficiali della Gnr di Fontanellato," *Italia contemporanea,* June 1998, pp. 417–44. As of July 25, 1943 the Jewish population in Italy was 40,157: Liliana Picciotto Fargion, *Il libro della memoria,* Mursia, Milan, 1991, p. 793.

2. Renzo De Felice, *Storia degli ebrei italiani sotto il fascismo,* Turin, Einaudi, 1993, p. 15.

3. R. De Felice, *Storia degli ebrei italiani durante il fascismo,* p. 15, 76.

4. Circolo Gianni Bosio, *I Giorni Cantati,* Milan, Mazzotta, 1983, p. 139.

5. Mario Avagliano, *Il partigiano Tevere. Il generale Sabato Martelli Castaldi dalle vie dell'aria alle Fosse Ardeatine,* Cava dei Tirreni, Avagliano, pp. 37–38, 125–40.

6. Otello Montanari—Antonio Zambonelli, *Gen. Dardano Fenulli (R.E. 1889—Fosse Ardeatine 1943). Biografia e Testimonianze,* Amministrazione Comunale di Reggio Emilia, 1978, p. 9–10.

7. Giorgio Rochat, "L'attentato a Graziani e la repressione italiana in Europa nel 1936–37," *Italia contemporanea,* 26, 1975, p. 33–37; Franco Bandini, *Gli italiani in Africa. Storia delle guerre coloniali (1882–1943),* Milan, Longanesi, 1971, pp. 44–45, 48.

8. Margherita Borisavjevic, letter to the National Journalism Council, April 4,1976, ANFIM archives.

9. O. Montanari—A. Zambonelli, *Gen. Dardano Fenulli,* pp. 8–9.

10. Francesca Manacorda, *L'Italia lacerata,* Rome, SEAM, 1998, p. 100; Circolo Gianni Bosio, *I giorni cantati,* p. 110.

11. When he was a prisoner in Germany after World War I, General Simoni had met the future Pope Pius XII, then the Vatican's envoy to Germany.

12. Cesare De Simone, *Venti angeli sopra Roma. I bombardamenti aerei sulla Città Eterna,* Milan, Mursia, 1993, p. 179.

13. Quoted in C. De Simone, *Venti angeli sopra Roma,* pp. 192–93.

14. C. De Simone, *Venti angeli sopra Roma,* p. 11.

15. Paolo Monelli, *Roma 1943* (1945), Turin, Einaudi, 1993, p. 68.

16. Enzo Castaldi, "La difesa di Roma," in *La difesa di Roma e i Granatieri di Sardegna nel settembre 1943,* Rome, Stato Maggiore dell'Esercito, 1993, p. 132.

17. Gen. Arnaldo Ferrara, ed., *I Carabinieri nella Resistenza e nella guerra di liberazione,* Rome, Ente Editoriale per l'Arma dei Carabinieri, 1978, pp. 9–13, 21–22.

18. C. De Simone, *Roma città prigioniera,* pp. 15–18; Maria Teresa Regard, in *Donne a Roma 1943–1944,* ed. Simona Lunadei, Comune di Roma, Ufficio Progetti Donna, 1996, pp. 44–49.

19. C. De Simone, *Roma città prigioniera,* Milan, Mursia, 1994 p. 183.

20. Vincenzo Baldazzi, "L'8 settembre a Roma," in AA. VV., *Trent'anni di storia italiana (1915—1945),* Turin, Einaudi, 1975, p. 319.

21. Luigi Franceschini, *50 anni dopo. Rievocazione dei combattimenti ingaggiati dai «Granatieri di Sardegna» alle porte di Roma l'8, il 9 e il 10 settembre 1943,* Rome, Museo Storico dei Granatieri, 1993, p. 84.

22. Luca Canali, *In memoria senza più odio,* Florence, Ponte alle Grazie, 1995, pp. 53–60.

23. Renzo De Felice, *Rosso e nero,* Milan, Baldini e Castoldi, 965; Ernesto Galli Della Loggia, *La morte della patria,* Bari, Laterza,1996; Francesco Traniello, *Sulla definizione della Resistenza come "Secondo Risorgimento,"* in Aa.Vv., *Le idee costituzionali della Resistenza,* ed. Claudia Franceschini, Sandro Guerrieri e Giancarlo Monina, Presidenza del Consiglio dei Ministri, Rome 1996, pp. 17–25.

24. R. De Felice, *Storia degli ebrei italiani,* p. 468.

25. Herbert Kappler, 1948 trial testimony, *l'Unità,* June 2, 1948.

26. R. De Felice, *Storia degli ebrei italiani,* pp. 478–79.

27. R. De Felice, *Storia degli ebrei italiani,* pp. 628–32.

28. See Kappler's testimony at the Eichmann trial in Jerusalem, quoted in R. De Felice, *Storia degli ebrei italiani,* p. 461.

29. Lorenzo D'Agostini—Roberto Forti, *Il sole è sorto a Roma,* Rome Anpi, 1965, p. 233. Celeste Di Porto is remembered as the "Black Panther" of the ghetto, the "spy of Piazza Giudia": Franco Monicelli, "Pantera Nera uccideva con un saluto," *L'Espresso,* April 17, 1960; a fictionalized account, Giuseppe Pederiali, *Stella di Piazza Giudia,* Florence, Giunti, 1995.

5 Resistances

1. At his trial, Herbert Kappler listed fourteen attacks (*L'Unità,* April 6,1948). According to Maria Teresa Regard, her husband Franco Calamandrei had listed at least forty-two armed actions before via Rasella.

2. Riccardo Neri, *Nuovo progetto storia,* vol. 3, Florence, La Nuova Italia, 1994, p. 333; A. Giardina, G. Sabbatucci, V. Vidotto, *Manuale di storia* vol.3—*L'età contemporanea,* Bari, Laterza, 1992: p. 333; italics in texts.

3. Pierangelo Maurizio, *Via Rasella, cinquant'anni di menzogne,* Rome, Maurizio Edizioni, 1996, p. 16.

4. Giovanni Contini, *La memoria divisa,* Milan, Rizzoli, 1997; A. Portelli, "The Massacre at Civitella Val di Chiana (Tuscany, June 29, 1944): Myth and Politics, Mourning and Common Sense," in *The Battle of Valle Giulia. Oral History and the Art of Dialogue,* Madison, University of Wisconsin Press, 1997, pp.129–39.

5. Enzo Piscitelli, *Storia della Resistenza romana,* Bari, Laterza, 1965, pp. 61–62.

6. Cesare De Simone, *Roma città prigioniera,* Milan, Mursia, 1994, pp. 24–26.

7. C. De Simone, *Roma città prigioniera,* pp. 79–84.

8. Interview with Franco Debenedetti, *la Repubblica,* March 8, 1996.

9. Enzo Piscitelli, *Storia della Resistenza romana,* pp.109–10.

10. The armed units of the Communist Party in the Resistance bore the name Brigate Garibaldi; their members were called *garibaldini,* like Garibaldi's followers in the Risorgimento.

11. Roberto Forti, Lorenzo D'Agostini, *Il sole è sorto a Roma,* Rome, ANPI, 1965, pp. 85–86.

12. Each prisoner was handed a lit match and told the first whose match went off would be killed. The first victim was Ferruccio Fumaroli. The game is repeated once, and then the Germans kill the other four: C. De Simone, *Roma città prigioniera,* p. 31. For a full account of the death of Silvio D'Acquisto, the myths surrounding its memory, and their function as a counternarrative to the Fosse Ardeatine, see the Italian edition of this book, *L'ordine è già stato eseguito,* Rome, Donzelli 1999, pp. 318–22.

13. C. De Simone, *Roma città prigioniera,* p. 36.

14. R. Forti e L. De Agostini, *Il sole è sorto a Roma,* pp.117–25.

15. Gianni [Ricci], "Azioni del Partito d'Azione," *Mercurio,* I, 4, 1944, p. 259.

16. Rosario Bentivegna, *Achtung Banditen! Roma 1944,* Milan, Mursia, 1983, p. 79.

17. Paolo Petrucci, *Andavano in bicicletta,* in "Avvenimenti," March 8, 1995; C. De Simone, *Roma città prigioniera,* pp. 43–45.

18. Franco Calamandrei, *La vita indivisibile. Diario 1941–1947,* Giunti, Florence 1998, pp. 155–57.

19. C. De Simone, *Roma città prigioniera,* p. 45.

20. Claudio Pavone, *Una guerra civile. Saggio sulla moralità nella Resistenza,* Milan, Boringhieri, 1991, pp. 25 ff., 38 ff.

21. Rosario Bentivegna, *Achtung Banditen!,* p. 82–83.

22. F. Calamandrei, *La vita indivisibile,* p. 21.

23. F. Calamandrei, *La vita indivisibile,* p. 234.

24. M. Musu, *La ragazza di via Orazio. Vita di una comunista irrequieta,* Milan, Mursia, 1997, p. 68.

25. Capponi must be conflating different moments. The killing of the German officer in via Veneto occurred in December 1943, while the Gesmundo and Labò were arrested in February, 1944.

26. C. De Simone, *Roma città prigioniera,* pp. 256–57.

27. M. Musu, *La ragazza di via Orazio,* p. 61.

28. M. Musu, *La ragazza di via Orazio,* p. 78.

29. Angelo Joppi, *Non ho parlato,* Rome 1949, pp. 26–27.

30. Fronte Militare di Resistenza di Roma e del suo territorio, *L'arma dei Carabinieri Reali in Roma durante l'occupazione tedesca (8 settembre 1943—4 giugno 1944),* Rome, Istituto Poligrafico dello Stato, 1946, p. 23.

31. Gabrio Lombardi, *Montezemolo e il Fronte militare clandestino di Roma,* Rome, Edizioni del Lavoro, 1947, p. 13–14.

32. G. Lombardi, *Montezemolo e il Fronte militare clandestino di Roma,* p. 52, 30–31.

33. *L'arma dei Reali Carabinieri,* p. 22.

34. G. Lombardi, *Montezemolo e il Fronte militare clandestino di Roma,* p. 34.

35. Mario Avagliano, ed., *Roma alla macchia. Personaggi e vicende della Resistenza,* Cava dei Tirreni, Avagliano, 1997, p. 69; *L'arma dei Reali Carabinieri,* p. 27.

36. Mario Avagliano, *Il partigiano Tevere. Il generale Sabato Martelli Castaldi dalle vie dell'aria alle Fosse Ardeatine,* Cava dei Tirreni, Avagliano, 1996, p. 41; Georges de Canino, "Martelli e Lordi: due amici, due eroi," in M. Avagliano, ed., *Roma alla macchia,* p. 129.

37. "La guerra dei cento fronti," in Arrigo Paladini, *Via Tasso,* Rome, Istituto Poligrafico dello Stato, 1994, p. 118; G. Lombardi, *Montezemolo e il Fronte militare clandestino,* pp.11 e 22; Filippo Caruso, *L'arma dei carabinieri in Roma,* State Printing Office, Rome, 1949, p. 13.

38. G. Lombardi, *Montezemolo e il Fronte militare clandestino,* p. 35, 43.

39. G. Lombardi, *Montezemolo e il Fronte militare clandestino,* p. 35.

40. E. Piscitelli, *Storia della Resistenza romana,* p. 260.

41. Giorgio Amendola, *Lettere a Milano,* Rome, Editori Riuniti, 1973, p. 228.

42. Otello Montanari and Antonio Zambonelli, *Gen. Dardano Fenulli (R.E. 1889—Fosse Ardeatine 1943). Biografia e Testimonianze,* Amministrazione Comunale di Reggio Emilia, 1978, p. 17, testimony of Pompilio Molinari.

43. G. Amendola, *Lettere a Milano,* p. 274; E. Piscitelli, *Storia della Resistenza romana,* pp. 258–61.

44. Felice Chilanti, "Fece applaudire i carabinieri partigiani," *Rinascita,* August 28,1965.

45. "Lotta partigiana," video and pamphlet, *Archivi di guerra,* Milan, Hobby & Work, September 1998. The most consistent purveyor of this thesis is the Fascist historian Giorgio Pisanò, *Sangue chiama sangue* (1962), CDL, Rome, 1994, p. 92. For a reply, see P. Balsamo, R. Bentivegna, C. Capponi, G. Cortini, M. Musu, "'Storici' che non sanno leggere," *Liberazione,* September 18, 1998.

46. Giulio Cortini, letter to the preliminary inquest judge Maurizio Pacioni, who in 1997 opened proceedings against Bentivegna, Balsamo, and Capponi, July 13, 1997. Cortini prepared the explosive for the action in via Rasella. He let me have this letter through his daughter, Anna Cortini.

47. Maurizio Pacioni, preliminary inquest judge, Rome Tribunal, court order of June 27, 1997; Roberto Gremmo, *I partigiani di Bandiera Rossa. Il "Movimento Comunista d'Italia" nella Resistenza Romana,* Biella, Elf, 1996.

48. Judge Pacioni concluded his inquest by admitting that the evidence for the prosecution was "mere suspicions and surmises": court order of April 16, 1998.

49. Silverio Corvisieri, *"Bandiera Rossa" nella resistenza romana,* Rome, Samonà e Savelli, 1968, p. 102.

50. R. Gremmo, *I partigiani di Bandiera Rossa,* pp. 92–93.

51. Gianni [Ricci], "Azioni del Partito d'Azione," *Mercurio,* I, 4, 1944, p. 259; Francesco Motto, "Gli sfollati e i rifugiati nelle catacombe di S. Callisto durante l'occupazione nazifascista di Roma. I salesiani e la scoperta delle Fosse Ardeatine," *Ricerche Storiche Salesiane,* 24, XIII, 1 (Januery-June 1994), p. 77–142; Lorenzo D'Agostini e Roberto Forti, *Il sole è sorto a Roma,* Roma, ANPI, 1965, p. 425.

52. A. D'Ettorre et al., eds., *Montesacro—Valmelaina 1943—1944,* Rome, Circolo Culturale Montesacro, 1997, p. 75–76.

53. E. Piscitelli, *Storia della Resistenza romana,* pp. 84–5.

54. S. Corvisieri, *"Bandiera Rossa" nella resistenza romana,* pp. 20–21.

55. Gianni Bosio, "Iniziative e correnti negli studi di storia del movimento operaio 1945–1962" (1963), *L'intellettuale rovesciato,* Milan, Jaca Book, 1998, p. 31–56.

56. Trial testimony, June 3,1948

57. Natalia Ginzburg, *Lessico famigliare,* Turin, Einaudi, 1963, p. 186. Leone Ginzburg, an important scholar and the editor of *Italia Libera,* the clandestine paper of the Partito d'Azione died under torture on February 5, 1944, after a long detention.

58. Luigi Pintor, *La signora Kirchgessner,* Turin, Bollati Boringhieri, 1998, p. 54.

59. E. Piscitelli, *Storia della Resistenza romana, p. 259.*

60. G. Amendola, *Lettere a Milano,* p. 269.

61. E. Piscitelli, *Storia della Resistenza romana,* pp. 262–63, 281; R. Forti e L. D'Agostini, *Il sole è sorto a Roma,* pp. 202–203; Maria Teresa Regard, testimony, in *Nazi! La II guerra mondiale. Il caso Priebke e le Fosse Ardeatine,* CD-Rom, Carte Segrete—*il manifesto,* Rome, 1998.

62. Franca and Giorgio Caputo, *La speranza ardente,* Rome, privately published, pp. 128–40; Marisa Gizzio, testimony in C. De Simone, *Roma città prigioniera,* pp. 77–8. Massimo Uffreduzzi, head of the Fascist youth group that opened fire on Gizzio, was sentenced to thirty years in his postwar trial, but later acquitted on appeal: the prosecution, he says, "found it unthinkable that university students, educated youth, might go and shoot to kill, or such things."

63. R. Forti e L. D'Agostini, *Il sole è sorto a Roma,* pp. 198–99.

64. C. De Simone, *Roma città prigioniera,* pp. 79–82; R. Forti—L. D'Agostini, *Il sole è sorto a Roma,* p. 203; E. Piscitelli, *Storia della Resistenza romana,* pp. 267–68.

65. *Il Tempo,* June 4,1948.

66. O. Montanari—A. Zambonelli, *Gen. Dardano Fenulli,* affidavit of Capt. cap. Ezio Bonfanti, prisoner in via Tasso; *Lettere di condannati a morte della Resistenza italiana* (1952), ed. Piero Malvezzi and Giovanni Pirelli, Turin, Einaudi, 2002, p. 193.

67. *Lettere di condannati a morte della Resistenza italiana,* p. 185.

68. "Da via Tasso alle Fosse Ardeatine," *Il Tempo,* February 2, 1945; Angelo Fumarola, *Essi non sono morti,* Rome, Magi-Spinetti, 1945, pp. 280–81.

69. *L'arma dei Reali Carabinieri in Roma,* p. 26.

70. A[ntonello] T[rombadori], "Un eroe: Giorgio Labò," *l'Unità,* October 6, 1944.

71. Curatola [Luigi Solinas], *La morte ha bussato tre volte,* Rome, De Luigi, 1944, pp. 33, 40–41. The misspelling of Priebke's name is in the text.

72. Riccardo Mancini, Felice Di Napoli, trial testimony, *Processo Priebke. Le testimonianze, il memoriale,* a cura di Cinzia Dal Maso and Simona Micheli, Rome, Mondo3, 1993, pp. 72, 90.

73. Teresa Mattei, trial testimony, *Processo Priebke,* p. 46.

74. Carlo Trabucco, *La prigionia di Roma. Diario dei 268 giorni di occupazione tedesca,* Turin, Borla, 1954 [1945], p. 207.

75. See Guglielmo Petroni, *Il mondo è una prigione,* Florence, Giunti, 1995.

76. Pietro Koch's report to General Mältzer, in R. Forti—L. D'Agostini, *Il sole è sorto a Roma,* pp. 351–53. See Peter Tompkins, *A Spy in Rome,* New York, Simon & Schuster, 1962; P.

Tompkins, "Come i partigiani operanti con l'O.S.S. contribuirono a salvare la testa di ponte di Anzio," in AA. VV. *Gli americani e la guerra di liberazione in Italia,* Rome, Presidenza del Consiglio dei Ministri, 1995, pp. 140–47.

77. C. De Simone, *Roma città prigioniera,* p. 94 segg.; E. Piscitelli, *Storia della Resistenza romana,* p. 286. The killing of Teresa Gullace is reconstructed (with some changes) in Roberto Rossellini's classic film, *The Open City.*

78. G. Amendola, *Lettere a Milano,* p. 566; R. Bentivegna, in R. Bentivegna—Carlo Mazzantini, *C'eravamo tanto odiati,* ed. Dino Messina, Milan, Baldini & Castoldi, 1997, p. 203.

79. C. De Simone, *Roma città prigioniera,* p. 103.

80. M. Musu, *La ragazza di via Orazio,* pp. 76–80.

81. R. Forti—L. D'Agostini, *Il sole è sorto a Roma,* pp. 241–47; C. De Simone, *Roma città prigioniera,* p. 127.

82. C. De Simone, *Roma città prigioniera,* pp. 130, 196; De Simone, *Donne senza nome,* Milan, Mursia, 1998 (a fictionalized reconstruction of the women's massacre at the Tesei mill).

83. Silverio Corvisieri, *"Bandiera Rossa" nella resistenza romana,* p. 165

84. R. Bentivegna, *Achtung Banditen,* pp. 230–33; a testimony of Barbarisi's daughter, Adriana Sessa, is in AA. VV., *Giustizia e verità a confronto,* Rome, Associazione Uomo e Libertà, 1997, p. 149.

85. Because of his standing as a national figure in the labor movement and the Socialist Party, Bruno Buozzi tended to attract all the attention at the memorial events.

6 Via Rasella

1. Giorgio Amendola, *Lettere a Milano,* Rome, Editori Riuniti, 1973, p. 290.

2. Quoted in Umberto Gandini, *Quelli di via Rasella,* supplement to *Alto Adige,* 1979, 1, p. 1.

3. U. Gandini, *Quelli di via Rasella,* p. 13.

4. Rosario Bentivegna, *Achtung Banditen. Roma 1944,* Milan, Mursia 1983, pp. 157–67; R. Bentivegna and Cesare De Simone, *Operazione via Rasella,* Editori Riuniti, Rome1996, pp. 19–28.

5. The poem was written soon after the action. It is quoted in Robert Katz, *Morte a Roma* (1967), Rome, Editori Riuniti, 1996, pp. 65–66n.

6. Enzo Cicchino, "Via Rasella. L'altra faccia delle Ardeatine," 1994, http://w.w.w.agora.stm.it/archivio/rasella.htm.

7. Liana Gigliozzi, quoted in Pierangelo Maurizio, *Via Rasella. Cinquant'anni di menzogne,* Rome, Maurizio, 1996, p. 22. Actually there was only one man in street sweeper's clothes.

8. P. Maurizio, *Via Rasella,* p. 23.

9. Attilio Ascarelli, *Le Fosse Ardeatine,* Rome, ANFIM, 1992, p. 123.

10. U. Gandini, *Quelli di via Rasella,* p. 16.

11. U. Gandini, *Quelli di via Rasella,* p. 16.

12. U. Gandini, *Quelli di via Rasella,* p. 17; P. Maurizio, *Via Rasella,* pp. 25–26.

13. C. De Simone, *Roma città prigioniera,* Milan, Mursia, 1994, p. 113.

14. Eugen Dollman, *Roma nazista,* Milan, Longanesi, 1949, p. 241.

15. "Evidence by SS Lt Colonel Herbert Kappler," August 4, 1945, PRO WO 310\317 (statement to the United Nations War Crimes Commission, August 4.1945. I have regularized the spelling of German names, which varies in official documents.

16. Trial testimony, in *Processo Priebke. Le testimonianze, il memoriale,* ed. by Cinzia Dal Maso and Simona Micheli, Rome, Mondo 3, 1996, p. 102.

17. P. Maurizio, *Via Rasella,* p. 26.

18. Silverio Corvisieri, *"Bandiera Rossa" nella resistenza Romana,* Rome, Samonà e Savelli, 1968, p. 112; Roberto Gremmo, *I partigiani di Bandiera Rossa. Il "Movimento Comunista d'Italia" nella Resistenza Romana,* Biella, Edizioni Elf, 1996, p. 178–80; P. Maurizio, *Via Rasella,* pp. 57–61, 71–74.

19. Franco Scotti, "L'attentato di via Rasella," *Cosmopolita,* September 23,1944; Giancarlo Perna, "L'ultimo dei Bozen: mi rifiutai di sparare alle Fosse Ardeatine," *Il Giornale,* June 16,1997. Atz's story of the sixteen men executed at the Fosse Ardeatine is a false memory.

20. Trail testimony, *Processo Priebke,* pp. 106–7.

21. Testimony at the Kappler trial, July 8,1948.

22. Herbert Kappler, trial testimony, June 3, 1948. Unless otherwise noted, all quotes from Kappler are from his testimony as reported in the trial records.

23. Hans Plack, quoted in U. Gandini, *Quelli di via Rasella.* There are two different terms in Italian for the English "comrade": the Left says *compagno* ("companion") while the Right uses the more military *camerata* ("barracks-mate"). Gigliozzi was not carrying any grenades.

24. P. Maurizio, *Via Rasella,* p. 26.

25. Aldo Zargani, *Per violino solo,* Bologna, il Mulino, 1995, p. 91.

26. Cristoph Franceschini, "Il trauma di Roma. L'attentato di via Rasella è ancora, dopo 50 anni, una ferita aperta," *Sudtirol Profil,* March 1994, pp. 8–12. In Rome, the Bozenregiment was under the command of the Fouteenth Germany Army and General Mältzer: Walter Leszl, *Priebke. Anatomia di un processo,* Rome, Editori Riuniti, 1997, p. 143.

27. Franco Calamandrei, *La vita indivisibile,* Firenze, Giunti, 1998, p. 195.

28. R. Bentivegna, *Achtung banditen,* p. 164.

29. In a later interview, Atz claimed he was asked to take part in the reprisal and refused: Giancarlo Perna, "L'ultimo dei Bozen: mi rifiutai di sparare alle Fosse Ardeatine," *Il Giornale,* 9.16, 1997.

30. Statement of August 4, 1945—PRO WO 310/137; my italics.

31. Kappler's testimony at the Military Court trial of Albert Kesselring, February 19, 1947 and at his own trial, 1948.

32. Quoted in Alessandro Portelli, "Lutto, senso comune, mito e politica," in Leonardo Paggi, ed., *Storia e memoria di un massacro ordinario,* Rome, Manifestolibri, 1996, p. 95. Only initials are used because the interview was not public at the time of publication.

33. Herman Melville, *Moby Dick,* Oxford University Press, 1988, p. 167.

34. Corrado Govoni, *La fossa carnaia ardeatina,* Rome, Movimento Comunista d'Italia, 1944, IX, p. 8.

35. A. Giardina, G. Sabbatucci, V. Vidotto, *Manuale di storia—3 . L'età contemporanea,* Laterza, 1992: p. 333.

36. Michele Battini and Paolo Pezzino, *Guerra ai civili. Occupazione tedesca e politica del massacro. Toscana 1944,* Venezia, Marsilio, 1997, pp. 223 ff.

37. Erich Priebke, statement to the United Nations War Crimes Commission, Afragola P.O.W. Camp, August 28, PRO WO 310/137; my italics.

38. *Il Messaggero,* February 1 and 9, 1944.

39. Giorgio Amendola, *Lettere a Milano,* p. 292.

40. This reconstruction is based on: M. Battini and P. Pezzino, *Guerra ai civili;* Lutz Klinkhammer, *Stragi naziste in Italia,* Rome, Donzelli, 1997; Giorgio Angelozzi Gariboldi, *Pio XII, Hitler e Mussolini,* Milan, Mursia, 1988; Walter Leszl, *Priebke. Anatomia di un processo;* M.Battini, "Il testimone inescusso del processo Priebke e l'eredità di Norimberga," in *Priebke e il massacro delle Ardeatine,* supplement to *l'Unità,* August 1996, pp. 61–78; the 1948 Kappler trial records; statements to the United Nations War Crimes Commission by Kurt Mältzer (October 1, 1946), Eberhard von Mackensen (June 27,

1946), Diedrich Beelitz (September 8, 1946), Karl Wolff (August 5,1945), Erich Priebke (August 28,1946); statement of Diedrich Beelitz, Dortmund, November 30. 1995, quoted in *Processo Priebke,* pp. 198–201.

41. "Evidence by SS Lt Herbert Kappler," United Nations War Crimes Commission, August 4, 1945.

42. Albert Kesselring, statement to the United National War Crimes Commission, September 25.1946, in M. Battini and P. Pezzino, *Guerra ai civili,* p. 443.

43. Mackensen adds that the ten-to-one ratio was decided after it was "satisfactorily established so that the SS *certainly* had in custody *more* than ten times the number of people who were to be liquidated in any case" (my italics). He concludes: "Finally, I am convinced of the following:- 1. Those who were liquidated would in any case have been liquidated by the SS, bomb plot or *not bomb plot [. . .]* 6. I did the Italian people a service by my solution and wished to spare them greater suffering than actually did fall to their lot by the liquidation which I could not avert. I believe I found a way not to have to pollute my hands with the blood of the defenceless [. . .]"

44. L. Klinkhammer, *Stragi naziste in Italia,* p. 9.

45. Albert Kesselring, testimony at the von Mackensen and Mältzer trial, November 15.1946.

46. *l'Unità,* May 6.1948. In statements to the War Crimes Commission, at the Kesselring trial and in his own trial he never mentions seeking out the perpetrators of the attack.

47. Rome Military Tribunal, verdict of July 20, 1948.

48. Carlo Trabucco, *La prigionia di Roma. Diario dei 268 giorni di occupazione tedesca,* Turin, Borla, 1954 (1945), pp. 203–4; at the Kappler trial, General Möllhausen confirmed that there were no radio announcements.

49. A document published in the official Acts of the Holy See reports that a Mr. Ferrero, an official of Rome's governor's office, called the office of His Holiness' Secretary of State at around 10:30 on March 24 to inform them of the reprisal (*Actes et documents du Saint Siège relatifs à la seconde guerre mondiale,* Rome, Libreria Editrice Vaticana, 1980, vol. 10, doc. 115). This confirms that the Vatican knew of the reprisal before it was carried out.

50. Statement of Rpt. St. fr. Erich Priebke," taken in the Afragola P.O.W. camp, August 28, 1946; PRO WO 310/137.

51. These figures are those of Kappler's statement made to the Allied authorities in August, 1945. At the trial, he juggled the numbers somewhat and was less precise overall.

52. Statement of August 28, 1946.

53. "Statement of Amonn Guenter, Male, 2nd Lieut.," 'U' POW Camp, October 13, 1945; Statement of Erich Priebke, August 28, 1946.

54. Giorgio Agamben, *Quel che resta di Auschwitz,* Milan, Bollati Boringhieri, 1998, p. 16; for a legal analysis of the Priebke trial, Walter Leszl, *Priebke. Anatomia di un processo.*

55. L. Klinkhammer, *Stragi naziste in Italia,* p. 13.

56. Gerhard Schreiber, testimony at the Priebke trial, *Processo Priebke,* pp.135 ff.; Alessandro Portelli, "Rappresentazioni del processo Priebke," in *Priebke e il massacro delle Ardeatine,* pp. 83–105.

57. Erich Priebke, statement of August 28, 1946; "Memoriale" (affidavit) to Rome's Military Tribunal, June 3, 1996, in *Processo Priebke,* p. 216; Kappler, trial testimony, 1948; Kappler, interviewed by Giuseppe Crescimbeni of the *Tempo* newspaper, in *Processo Priebke,* p. 197. In 1946, Priebke claimed that Kappler said the order came from Kesselring. Among the perpetrators, only Hans Clemens testified (on January 10, 1947), that Kappler had threatened to court martial anyone who refused to participate in the massacre ("Statement of Hans Clemens, Hauptsturmfuehrer," PROI WO 310/137. He made this statement, however, at a late date, when the "*Befehlsnotstand*" line of defense was already taking shape.

58. Priebke, statement to the Military Court of Appeals, 1998; Kappler, trial testimony, 1948.
59. *la Repubblica,* June13.1996.
60. W. Leszl, *Priebke,* p. 218.
61. Statement to the Military Court of Appeals, March 1998; W. Leszl, *Priebke,* pp. 128–30.
62. Statement to the Military Court of Appeals, March 1998.
63. Mussolini was probably informed only after the reprisal had taken place; he was furious, but even had he been in a position to do anything, it was too late: Claudio Schwarzenberg, *Kappler e le Fosse Ardeatine,* Palermo, Celebes, 1977, pp. 54–55.
64. Some of the many publications that include the text of the verdict are Attilio Ascarelli, *Le Fosse Ardeatine;* C. Schwarzenberg, *Kappler e le Fosse Ardeatine;* and Wladimiro Settimelli, *Herbert Kappler. La verità sulle Fosse Ardeatine,* supplement to *l'Unità,* April 27 and 30,1994.
65. *Italia Nuova,* July 30,1944; *Il Tempo,* August 1,1944 and June 7,1948 (the contradiction is noted in *l'Unità,* June 8, 1948.
66. Tommaso Smith, "Ignominia," *Il Paese,* March 26.1948; *Il Tempo,* March 27,1948.
67. *Il Tempo,* December 17,1996.
68. *Il Giornale,* April 7 and 10, 1996, quoted in M. Spataro, *Rappresaglia,* p. 52.
69. Quoted in the verdict of Rome's Civil Tribunal, June 9.1950.
70. Francobaldo Chiocci, "Priebke non parla, scrive," *Il Giornale,* June 4,1996.
71. Court order of April 16,1998.
72. G. Amendola, *Lettere a Milano,* pp. 293, 294.
73. *l'Unità,* June 13,1948.
74. Interview with Lietta Tornabuoni, *L'Europeo,* April 12,1964, pp. 32–42.
75. R. Bentivegna, *Achtung Banditen!,* p. 169; panel discussion, Rome, *il manifesto* bookstore, July 4,1997.
76. Quoted in Edouard Boeglin, « Une Moulhousienne, héroine de la Résistance italienne, » *L'Alsace,* Moulhouse, France, June 10,1996, p. 25.
77. F. Calamandrei, *La vita indivisibile,* p. 195.
78. Aurelio Lepre, *Via Rasella. Leggenda e realtà della Resistenza a Roma,* Laterza, Bari 1997, pp. 64–68.
79. Enzo Erra, preface to M. Spataro, *Rappresaglia,* p. viii.
80. Albert Kesselring writes that the hostility of the Italian people was such that the German army lived in a constant state of threat and assumed that all civilians were potential enemies: *Memorie di guerra,* Milan, Garzanti, 1954, p. 256.
81. In the files of London's Public Record Office, I found records of inquests over at least 145 Nazi massacres in Italy. The list did not include the worst and most notorious ones. Files for over 600 massacres upon which no action was ever taken were discovered in the cellars of the Military Tribunal during the Priebke trial: Mimmo Franzinelli, *Le stragi nascoste,* Boringhieri, Milan 2002. On Nazi massacres in southern Italy, where there was no partisan activity, see Gabriella Gribaudi, ed., *Terra bruciata,* Naples, Liguori, 2003.
82. Gianni Bisiach, *Pertini racconta,* Milan, Mondadori, 1983, p. 130.
83. G. Amendola, *Lettere a Milano,* pp. 295–96.
84. Enzo Forcella, "La storia di via Rasella. Partigiani e penne rosse," *Corriere della Sera,* March 10,1998.
85. Claudio Pavone, "Note sulla Resistenza armata, le rappresaglie naziste e alcune attuali confusioni," in *Priebke e il massacro delle Ardeatine,* pp. 39–50.
86. The passage in brackets is from Zuccheretti's interview with P. Maurizio, *Via Rasella,* p. 18.
87. Giovanni Zuccheretti still believes that is brother was sitting on top of Bentivegna's cart. According to his own legal and medical consultants, there is no evidence, and the conse-

quences would have been the same had he been, as Bentivegna claims, just turning the corner a few yards away.

88. Liana Gigliozzi, daughter of another victim of the Fosse Ardeatine and witness for the defense at the Priebke trial, also says that Priebke's lawyer, knowing she was in financial distress, told her, "I'll give you a hand, also financial, and put four hundred thousand lire [U.S. $200] in my hand. In that moment, we took them because, to tell you the truth, we didn't know how we would eat the next day."

7 The Massacre

1. Egidio Cristini, "Il massacro dei trecentoventi," in the CD *Avanti Popolo—6—Fischia il vento*—Istituto Ernesto de Martino—Hobby & Work, Rome 1998.
2. Remo Pellegrini, trial testimony, *Processo Priebke. Le testimonianze, il memoriale,* ed. Cinzia Dal Maso and Simona Micheli, Rome, Il Mondo 3, 1996, p. 31.
3. Eleonora Lavagnino, statement to the United Nations War Crimes Commission, August 31,1945; Enrica Filippini Lera e Maria Lea Cavarra, . . *i fiori di lillà quel giorno . . . ,* Rome, Nuovagrafica, 1995, p. 46; Andrea De Gasperis, quoted in Robert Katz, *Morte a Roma,* Rome, Editori Riuniti, 1996, p. 126; Giorgio Fiordelli, quoted in the periodical *Città aperta,* March1995, p. 5; Statement of Nicola D'Annibale, Rome, Sept. 9,1945, PRO WO 310/137; Riccardo Mancini, speech at the commemoration of the victims of the massacre at La Storta, June 4,1998.
4. Kappler trial verdict, in Attilio Ascarelli, *Le Fosse Ardeatine,* Rome, ANFIM, 1992, p. 128.
5. Curatola [Luigi Solinas], *La morte ha bussato tre volte,* Rome, Donatello De Luigi, 1944, p. 175.
6. The narrative comes from a speech made during the commemoration of the victims of the massacre of La Storta, June 4, 1998; a group of schoolchildren was in the audience.
7. Statement of Guenter Amonn, Second Lieutenant, 'U' POW Camp, October 13, 1945, PRO WO 310/137; Joseph Raider, quoted in Luciano Morpurgo, *Caccia all'uomo!* (1946), now in Arrigo Paladini, *Via Tasso. Museo storico della Liberazione di Rome,* Rome, Istituto Poligrafico dello Stato, 1994, p. 84. Raider was an Austrian deserter who had been taken for a spy and was detained at via Tasso.
8. *Città aperta,* March 1995, p. 5
9. "Da via Tasso alle Fosse della morte," *Il Tempo,* February 2,1945.
10. Cesare De Simone, *Roma città prigioniera,* Milan, Mursia, 1994, p. 121.
11. Karl Hass, trial testimony, in *Processo Priebke,* cit., p. 172.
12. Raider, trial testimony, *Processo Priebke,* p. 84.
13. *Il Messaggero,* June 6.1944.
14. Cardinal Nasalli Rocca, 1974, quoted in Giorgio Angelozzi Gariboldi, *Pio XII, Hitler e Mussolini,* Milan, Mursia, 1988, p. 246.
15. A. Ascarelli, *Le Fosse Ardeatine,* p. 41
16. Statement of Hpt. St. fr. Erich Priebke, Afragola POW Camp, Aug. 28, 1946.
17. "Da via Tasso alle Fosse della morte," *Il Tempo,* February 2.1945.
18. On the "myth of the good German," often associated with massacre narratives, see Nuto Revelli, *Il disperso di Marburg,* Turin, Einaudi, 1994; Alessandro Portelli, "The Massacre at Civitella Val di Chiana (Tuscany, June 29, 1944. Myth and Politics, Mourning and Common Sense," *The Battle of Valle Giulia. Oral History and the Art of Dialogue,* Madison, University of Wisconsin Press, 1997, pp. 140–60.
19. A. Ascarelli, *Le Fosse Ardeatine,* pp. 63, 66.
20. A. Ascarelli, *Le Fosse Ardeatine,* p. 65.
21. Erich Priebke, affidavit to Rome's Military Tribunal, June 3,1996, in *Processo Priebke,* p. 217.

22. Maria Stella Bové, former prisoner in via Tasso, statement of October 9, 1945. Another prisoner, Bona DePanizza, said that one of them told her that "after the killing of the civilians, he could not sleep for a long time" (Statement of Sept. 17, 1945): PRO WO 310/137.

23. Ernesto de Martino, *Morte e pianto rituale,* Turin, Boringhieri, 1975 (1958), p. 128.

24. Lia Albertelli, "La prima volta alle Fosse Ardeatine," in *Giorno di pioggia alle Fosse,* Rome, 1945, pp. 21–22.

25. The St. Callisto catacombs, Vatican territory, were a haven for hundreds of refugees and a basis for partisan priests like Don Michele Valentini and Don Ferdinando Giorgi: Francesco Motto, "Gli sfollati e i rifugiati nelle catacombe di S. Callisto durante l'occupazione nazifascista di Roma. I salesiani e la scoperta delle Fosse Ardeatine," *Ricerche storiche salesiane,* 24, XIII, 1 (January-June1994), pp. 77–142.

26. F. Motto, "Gli sfollati e i rifugiati"; [Michele Valentini], "La scoperta delle vittime trucidate dai tedeschi," *Risorgimento liberale,* June 5, 1944, appendix to Motto, and in Arrigo Paladini, *Via Tasso,* p. 79–83.

27. M. Valentini, "La scoperta delle vittime."

28. Silverio Corvisieri, *Bandiera Rossa nella Resistenza Romana,* Rome, Samonà e Savelli, 1968, p. 124.

29. Don Valentini, "La scoperta delle vittime," p. 81; Col. John R. Pollock, "Relazione sull'eccidio di via Rasella e sulla conseguente esecuzione sommaria per rappresaglia di un numero imprecisato di italiani detenuti politici," in A. Ascarelli, *Le Fosse Ardeatine,* pp. 69–71.

30. Quoted in Umberto Gandini, "Quelli di via Rasella," supplement to *Alto Adige,* 1, 1979, p. 23.

31. E. De Martino, *Morte e pianto rituale,* pp. 4–5.

32. A. Ascarelli, *Le Fosse Ardeatine,* p. 33.

33. A. Ascarelli, *Le Fosse Ardeatine,* p. 42.

34. A. Ascarelli, *Le Fosse Ardeatine,* p. 41, 48.

35. *l'Unità,* 15.6.1944.

36. A. Ascarelli, *Le Fosse Ardeatine,* p. 50.

37. F. G., "Fosse Ardeatine," *Mercurio,* 1, 1944, p. 190.

38. R. Katz, *Morte a Roma,* p. 171.

39. Giuseppe Cambareri, "Tre eroi," *Mercurio,* 1, 1944, p. 197.

40. *Il Messaggero,* June 5,1944.

41. F. G., "Fosse Ardeatine."

42. Don M. Valentini, "La scoperta delle vittime," p. 82.

43. Rosetta Stame and Sergio Volponi, trial testimony, *Processo Priebke,* pp. 77, 104.

44. Giulia Spizzichino, trial testimony, *Processo Priebke,* p. 96.

8 A Strange Grief

1. Corrado Govoni, *Aladino. Lamento per mio figlio morto,* Milan, Mondadori, 1946, p. 20. All quotes are from this edition.

2. Giovanni Contini, *La memoria divisa,* Milan, Rizzoli, 1977.

3. Corrado Govoni, *La fossa carnaia ardeatina,* Rome, Movimento Comunista d'Italia, 1944, pp. 23–24.

4. Philippe Ariès, *Storia della morte in Occidente,* Milan, Rizzoli, 1997, p. 57.

5. R. M. De Angelis, "Nelle cupe grotte ove già regnava la morte," *Il Tempo,* March 24,1945.

6. Roberto D'Agostini and Roberto Forti, *Il sole è sorto a Roma,* Roma, ANPI, 1965, p. 275.

7. Ph. Ariès, *Storia della morte in Occidente,* p. 190.

8. Giorgio Agamben, *Quel che resta di Auschwitz,* Turin, Bollati Boringhieri, 1998, p. 64.
9. G. Agamben, *Quel che resta di Auschwitz,* p. 74.
10. Ernesto de Martino, *Morte e pianto rituale,* Turin, Boringhieri, 1975, p. 77.
11. Mario Serandrei and Giuseppe De Santis, *Giorni di gloria,* 1945; parts of this film are also included in the video *Le Fosse Ardeatine,* Roma, Hobby & Work, 1998.
12. R. M. De Angelis, "Nelle cupe grotte ove già regnava la morte."
13. E. de Martino, *Morte e pianto rituale,* p. 96.
14. P. Ariès, *Storia della morte,* p. 25.
15. Panel discussion, Circolo Culturale Montesacro, Rome, May 22,1998.
16. I leave this quote anonymous because it is so intimately personal.
17. "Breve storia dell'ANFIM," in Attilio Ascarelli, *Le Fosse Ardeatine,* Rome, ANFIM, 1992, p. 97.
18. Ph. Ariès, *Storia della morte,* p. 72, 69.
19. *Il Messaggero,* May 9, 1996.
20. Giovanni Contini, *La memoria divisa,* Milano, Rizzoli, 1997; Paolo Pezzino, *Anatomia di un massacro. Controversia sopra una strage tedesca,* Bologna, Il Mulino, 1997
21. *l'Unità,* June 15,1944.
22. Until recently, a she-wolf was kept in a cage on Capitol hill, to commemorate the legend according to which the twins Romulus and Remus, abandoned in the woods, were fed by a she-wolf, and lived to become the founders of Rome.

9 Politics of Memory

1. Circolo Gianni Bosio, *I giorni cantati,* Milan, Mazzotta, 1978, p. 142.
2. Recorded December 12, 1969; see Circolo Gianni Bosio, *I giorni cantati,* pp. 16–18.
3. Silverio Corvisieri, *Il re, Togliatti e il gobbo,* Rome, Odradek, 1998, pp. 217–29.
4. Aldo Tozzetti, *La casa e non solo,* Roma, Editori Riuniti, 1989, pp.17–18.
5. Fiorenza Fiorentino, *La Roma di Charles Poletti (giugno 1944-aprile 1945)* Rome, Bonacci, pp.5, 28, 74–75.
6. "Il sacrificio dei 335 martiri in una luce di apoteosi popolare," *Momento,* March 25,1945, p. 1.
7. "Il sacrificio dei 335 martiri."
8. Gabriele Ranzato, *Il linciaggio di Carretta. Roma 1944,* Milan, Il Saggiatore, 1997, pp. 24–25, 35
9. *Il Tempo,* July 3,1945; S., *Il Re, Togliatti e il Gobbo,* pp. 267–68.
10. In the l.p. record *Roma, la borgata e la lotta per la* casa, ed. by Alessandro Portelli, Istituto Ernesto de Martino / Archivi Sonori, SdL/AS/10, 1970.
11. A. Tozzetti, *La casa e non solo,* pp. 41–42; on the woman who had an abortion after the clash with the police on March 26, 1955, see pp. 79–80.
12. Composed and sung by Armandino Liberti (1924), porter; in Circolo Bosio, *I giorni cantati,* pp. 161–63.
13. The descriptions of the ceremonies, with the texts of speeches and messages, were reported each year in pamphlets published by ANFIM. All quotes in the following paragraphs come from this source.
14. Claudia Garofalo, letter to the magazine *Avvenimenti,* October 11, 1995.
15. Claudio Pavone, "I giovani e la Resistenza. Apriamo un dibattito," *Resistenza* 7, 1968.
16. Stefano Levi Della Torre, *Mosaico. Attualità e inattualità degli ebrei,* Torino, Rosenberg & Sellier, 1994, pp. 57–9.
17. Edoardo D'Onofrio, "Relazione del segretario della Federazione comunista romana al Congresso provinciale del Pci di Roma, ottobre 1945," in *Per Roma,* ed. Giovanni Gozzini, Rome, Vangelista, 1983, pp. 63–85.

18. Marisa Musu, *La ragazza di via Orazio. Vita di una comunista irrequieta,* Milan, Mursia, 1997.

19. *Le idee costituzionali della Resistenza,* Rome, Presidenza del Consiglio dei Ministri, 1997.

20. *Il Giornale,* June 4,1996. Cesare De Simone and Rosario Bentivegna (*Operazione via Rasella,* Rome, Editori Riuniti, 1996, p. 118) suggest that the photo may be false.

21. Rosario Bentivegna, *Achtung Banditen!,* Milan, Mursia, 1983, p. 172n. Bentivegna corrected this omission in *Operazione via Rasella,* written with Cesare De Simone, pp. 29–30.

22. *Giornale d'Italia,* March 24,1994.

23. Giorgio Pisanò, *Sangue chiama sangue* (1962), Milan, C.D.L., 1994; *Storia Giustizia e verità a confronto,* Rome, Associazione Uomo e Libertà, 1997; Pierangelo Maurizio, *Via Rasella, cinquant'anni di menzogne,* Rome, Maurizio, 1996. See also Aurelio Lepre, *Via Rasella. Leggenda e realtà della Resistenza,* Bari, Laterza, 1996.

24. Rosario Bentivegna and Cesare De Simone have painstakingly discussed the errors and falsifications in the work of Pisanò and others in *Operazione via Rasella,* pp. 111–17.

25. *il Giornale,* May 8 and 9, 1996; *Il Messaggero,* September 16,1997.

26. M. Spataro, *Rappresaglia. Via Rasella e le Ardeatine alla luce del caso Priebke,* Rome, Settimo Sigillo, 1997, p. 11.

27. M. Spataro, *Rappresaglia,* p. 97, 136, 21; Marcella Monaco, testimony, in C. De Simone, *Roma città prigioniera,* p. 64.

28. *Panorama,* July 1, 1999.

29. Luciano Garibaldi, "Via Rasella: ombra comunista sulla resistenza," in *Storia, giustizia e verità a confronto,* p.133.

30. *il manifesto,* August 14,1997. The act was claimed by an ultra-Right-wing group, Fasci di azione rivoluzionaria.

31. *la Repubblica,* May 12, 1998.

32. Francesca Koch, Simona Lunadei, "Il 16 ottobre nella memoria cittadina," in Nicola Gallerano, ed., *La resistenza fra storia e memoria,* Milan, Franco Angeli, 1999.

33. Otto Klineberg et al., *Religione e pregiudizio. Analisi di contenuto dei libri cattolici di insegnamento religioso in Italia e in Spagna,* Bologna, Cappelli, 1968; Alfonso Di Nola, *Antisemitismo in Italia. 1962–1972,* Florence, Vallecchi, 1973.

34. F. Koch e S. Lunadei, "Il 16 ottobre nella memoria cittadina"; Rudolf Aschenauer, *Der Fall Herbert Kappler,* München, Damm Verlag, 1968.

35. *la Repubblica,* July 23.1997.

36. Priebke claimed that his trial was "willed by the Simon Wiesenthal center in Los Angeles"; Mario Spataro claims that its purpose is "to get hold of the huge riches confiscated by Hitler from the Jews": *Rappresaglia,* pp. 142–43.

37. *Corriere della Sera,* May 4,1948.

38. Giorgio Agamben, *Quel che resta di Auschwitz,* Milan, Bollati Boringhieri, 1998, p. 17.

39. Carlo Ginzburg, *Il giudice e lo storico. Considerazioni in margine al processo Sofri,* Turin, Einaudi, 1991; A. Portelli, "The Oral Shape of the Law: The 'April 7' Case," in *The Death of Luigi Trastulli and other Stories. Form and Meaning in Oral History,* Albany, NY State of New York University Press, 1991, pp. 241–69.

40. Carlo Ginzburg, *Il giudice e lo storico,* pp. 8–15.

41. *la Repubblica,* April 6, 1996.

42. Walter Leszl, *Priebke. Anatomia di un processo,* Rome, Editori Riuniti, 1997, pp. 72–86.

43. L. Klinkhammer, *Stragi naziste in Italia,* p. 14; W. Leszl, *Priebke.,* pp. 72–92.

44. *Il Messaggero,* July 21.1948; *la Repubblica,* May 11.1996.

45. The final verdict of Rome's Military Tribunal is reproduced in A. Ascarelli, *Le Fosse Ardeatine,* pp. 109–56 (from which I quote) and Claudio Schwarzenberg, *Kappler e le Fosse Ardeatine,* Palermo, Celebes, 1977.

46. L. Klinkhammer, *Stragi naziste in Italia,* 13); Gerhard Schreiber, "La Wehrmacht e la guerra ai partigiani in Italia 'anche contro donne e bambini,'" *Studi piacentini,* 15, 1994, pp. 97–120; Helmut Goetz, "Das Attentat im Rom und die Fosse Ardeatine (1944). Eine vorläufige Bilanz," *Innsbrücker Historische Studien,* 6, 1983, pp. 161–78).

47. Carlo Galante Garrone, "Via Rasella davanti ai giudici," in *Priebke e il massacro delle Ardeatine,* supplement to *l'Unità,* August 1996, pp. 51–60

48. Rome Civil Tribunal, verdict of June 26,1950.

49. Rome Penal Tribunal, court order of April 16.1998. Two 1944 decrees declared all illegal acts and war acts conduced by patriots against German occupation and Fascist dictatorship exempt from sanction. Yet Judge Pacione found that the Hague convention of 1906 ought to be considered part of Italian law and based his inquest on this assumption.

50. Augusto Parboni, "Nessun colpevole per la strage di via Rasella," *Il Tempo,* April 17,1998 writes that the partisans were found guilty for "killing 30 German soldiers and some civilians."

51. Pasquale Balsamo, "Da via Rasella ad Alfonsine," in *Roma alla Macchia. Personaggi e vicende della Resistenza,* ed. Mario Avagliano, Cava dei Tirreni, Avagliano, 1997, p. 100.

52. The imbalance is said to consist in part in the fact that while the German victims were privates, the reprisal included generals and colonels. The military court did not go so far as to claim that the lives of officers were more valuable than those of privates, but it said that "the damage to war operation" was thus higher.

53. Actually, if the order was not to execute 320 hostages, but ten hostages for each German casualty, Kappler might still be said to have thought he was acting legitimately. See the verdict of Rome's Military Court of Appeals in the Priebke and Hass case, April 15.1998.

54. This conclusion was reached on the basis of false testimony that Kappler himself later said he had arranged with his men: Kappler's interview with Giuseppe Crescimbeni in C. Dal Maso and S. Micheli, eds., *Processo Priebke. Le testimonianze, il memoriale,* Roma, Mondo 3, 1996, p. 197.

55. Robert Katz, *Dossier Priebke. Anatomia di un processo,* Milan, Rizzoli, 1996; C. Dal Maso and S. Micheli, eds., *Processo Priebke.*

56. "The years, in conclusion, have passed in vain for Hass and for Priebke:" verdict of the Rome Military Court of Appeals, April 15,1998.

57. Quoted in Giorgio Angelozzi Gariboldi, *Pio XII, Hitler e Mussolini,* Milan, Mursia 1988, p. 229.

58. *l'Unità,* May 29.1948; *Il Tempo,* June 2,1948.

59. Annelise Kappler, *Ti porterò a casa,* Rome, Ardini, p.198; *Corriere della Sera,* January 5,1948; *Panorama,* May 17,1998.

60. Trial testimony, May 31.1948; *Il Tempo,* June 1, 1948.

61. Herbert Kappler, *Lettere dal carcere 1948–1950,* Rome, Maurizio, 1997, pp. 73, 75, 87, 79, 131–39, 143–50.

62. H. Kappler, *Lettere dal carcere,* pp. 15, 23, 15, 45, 102. 50.

63. Interview in C. Dal Maso and S. Micheli, *Processo Priebke,* p. 197.

64. Francesco Vincenti, folk poet and singer, in Circolo Gianni Bosio, *I Giorni Cantati,* p. 179.

65. Gabriella Polli (1943), post office worker, daughter of Domenico Polli and niece of Ottavio Capozio, killed at the Fosse Ardeatine; May 18, 1998.

66. Priebke's interview was aired on *Prime Time Live,* May 5,1994. ABC's Harry Phillips and Sam Donaldson had identified the ex-Nazi Reinhard Kopps, who had been involved in the so-called "ratline" set up by the Vatican to help Nazi criminals escape to Latin America; in order to divert attention from himself, Kopps led investigators to Priebke: R. Katz, *Dossier Priebke,* pp. 18–27; on the legal aspects of extradition, see pp. 83–87.

67. Erich Priebke, affidavit to Rome's Military Tribunal, June 3.1996, in C. Dal Maso and S. Micheli, eds., *Processo Priebke*, p. 214.
68. R. Katz, *Dossier Priebke*, pp. 74–75.
69. Verdict, Rome Military Tribunal, August 1,1996.
70. *Clarín*, Buenos Aires, quoted in R. Katz, *Dossier Priebke*, p. 76. In his 1996 affidavit Priebke says he received no help from the Vatican.
71. Ronald C. Newton, *The "Nazi Menace" in Argentina, 1931–1947*, Stanford, CA., Stanford University Press, 1992, pp. 374–80.
72. *Hoy*, Bariloche, Argentina, August 22–28,1995; Ermanno Amicucci, "Un cameriere di Buenos Aires racconta la fuga di Ciano," *Tempo*, January 25–30,1950.
73. Julie K. L. Dam, "Hidden in Plain Sight," *Time*, September 4,1995; *Hoy*, August 22–28,1995; Erich Priebke, interviews by Sergio De Gregorio, *Oggi*, May 22,1996.
74. Priebke affidavit, June 3.1996, in C. Dal Maso and S. Micheli, eds., *Processo Priebke*, p. 218.
75. R. Katz, *Dossier Priebke*, p.19.
76. De Gregorio interview, *Oggi*, May 22.1996.
77. Quoted in R. Katz, *Dossier Priebke*, p. 89.
78. Statement at the pre-trial audience, April 3.1996.
79. Erich Priebke, Statement to the Military Court of Appeal, March 1998; Channel 1 News interview, January 12, 1999.
80. De Gregorio interview, *Oggi*, May 22.1996.
81. De Gregorio interview, *Oggi*, May 22.1996.
82. *Il Giornale*, June 4 and May 9, 1996.
83. Cristina Conti, letter to *Il Giornale*, July 12, 1997; Liana Gigliozzi, interviewed by Sandro Provvisionato, *Sette / Corriere della Sera*, January 16,1997; Antonio Pappagallo and Anna Maria Canacci's letters to the president of the Military Court of Appeals, January 1,1998 and no date (letters courtesy of Associazione Uomo e Libertà).
84. *il manifesto*, August 3,1996.
85. *Corriere della Sera*, May 9, 1996; *la Repubblica*, May 9, 1996; S. Levi Della Torre, *Mosaico*, p. 73.
86. I contacted Erich Priebke's lawyers about an interview for this book. They never said no, but kept postponing meetings until I finally gave up. After his first disastrous interviews with the press, his lawyers made sure he spoke only to sympathetic interviewers.
87. *l'Unità*, April 5,1996; on Priebke's "miserable senility," Igor Mann, *La Stampa*, June13 and 18,1996.
88. *la Repubblica*, August 2,1996.
89. Wladimiro Settimelli, "Memoria, lacrime e rabbia nell'aula del Tribunale," in *Priebke e il massacro delle Ardeatine*, pp. 7–38.
90. *la Repubblica, il manifesto, Il Giornale*, August 2, 1996.
91. *Combat Film* was a TV series based on footage shot by filmmakers attached to the Allied armed forces in World War II.

10. Born Later

1. Stefano Levi Della Torre, *Mosaico. Attualità e inattualità degli ebrei*, Turin, Rosenberg & Sellier, 1994, p. 56.
2. Cesare De Simone, *Roma città prigioniera*, Milan, Mursia, 1994, p. 260.
3. Editorial, *Quaderni Piacentini*, I, April1962; Paola Ghione, "La Resistenza e il '68," in Nicola Gallerano, ed., *La resistenza fra storia e memoria*, Milan, Franco Angeli, 1999; Claudio Pavone, "I giovani e la Resistenza. Apriamo un dibattito," *Resistenza*, 7, 1968.

4. Alessandro Portelli, *The Battle of Valle Giulia. Oral History and the Art of Dialogue,* Madison, University of Wisconsin Press, 1997.

5. Marisa Musu, *La ragazza di via Orazio. Vita di una comunista irrequieta,* Milan, Mursia, 1997, p. 141.

6. Rosario Bentivegna, "Via Rasella come via Fani?," *Rinascita,* February 2,1985.

7. Mario Moretti, *Brigate Rosse. Una storia italiana,* Milan, Anabasi, 1994, p. 48. His very language belies his claim: partisans never spoke so casually and cynically of killing.

8. Pierangelo Maurizio, *Via Rasella. Cinquant'anni di menzogne,* Rome, Maurizio, 1996, p. 101.

9. Giampiero Mughini, "Giustizia e libertà: il nodo è ancora qua," *L'Europeo,* October 10,1985; R. Bentivegna, "Via Rasella come via Fani?"

10. Daniele Mezzana, *La memoria storica delle Resistenza nelle nuove generazioni,* Milan, Mursia, 1997, p. 34.

11. Philippe Ariès, *Storia della morte in occidente,* Milano, Rizzoli, 1997, p. 25.

12. Franco La Cecla, "Sacralità del guard-rail," in *Mente locale. Per un'antropologia dell'abitare,* Milan, Elèuthera, 1993, pp. 115–24.

13. According to official statistics, 114,000 adolescents were hospitalized in Rome after traffic accidents in the last ten years; the dead numbered 111. A Higher Institute of Health official says that "often the remote cause [of accidents] are traumas or problems of another nature": *la Repubblica,* Rome edition, March 10,1997.

P

Index of Names

Note. Those killed at the Fosse Ardeatine are listed in **bold**; the narrators are listed in *italics*.

ACKNOWLEDGMENTS

This book was made possible by the help of many people. Marina Cau, Giuseppina Incalza, Manuela Bagnetti, Cristiana Cervelloni, Marco Morini, Alessia Guglielmi, Sara Antonelli, Lucia Antonelli, Ulrike Viccaro, Romina Cometti, Giuliano Di Cerbo, and Sara Manafra either donated their time and labor to help me transcribe tapes, or accepted substandard payment for it. The Association of the Families of the Martyrs of Italy's Liberation (ANFIM), the Rome Institute for Italian History from Fascism to the Resistance (IRSIFAR), and the Rome Center for Jewish Culture all helped me without interference. Many others (Emma Fiorentino Alatri, Luciano Chiolli, Piero De Gennaro, Massimo Taborri, and the Montesacro Culture Club) helped me find contacts and arrange interviews; Flavio Govoni granted permission to quote from the poems of his grandfather Corrado Govoni. I also wish to mention persons from the other side (Dr. Giachini, Erich Priebke's lawyer; and the leader of Alleanza Nazionale, Gianfranco Fini), who if nothing more trusted my intellectual honesty. Deborah Gershenowitz and Linda Shopes carefully edited my manuscript and suggested necessary changes and improvements; Bruce Jackson was generous with suggestions and ideas. The final form of the manuscript owes much to them all. Years of friendship and conversations with Ronald Grele and Luisa Passerini contributed greatly to my approach. Mary Marshall Clark, director of the Columbia Oral History Office, made it all possible in more than one way.

For editorial reasons, this text is significantly shorter than the original Italian version. I refer readers who are interested in Rome's modern history and Italian politics and culture (and in much more detailed background and bibliographic references) to that text or to the Spanish translation to be published by Fundo de Cultura Economica in Buenos Aires in 2003.

I am proud that none of this work was sponsored or supported in any way by any institution or business. It is a sign that some things can be done if we really want them to be.